Parmanu Politics

Parmanu Politics

Indian Political Parties and Nuclear Weapons

Dr. Sitakanta Mishra

KALPAZ

ISBN: 978-93-5128-093-4

Price: ₹ 950

First Published, 2015

Published by

Kalpaz Publications
C-30, Satyawati Nagar,
Delhi-110052
Ph. : 9212142040
E-mail: kalpaz@hotmail.com

Laser Typesetting : Bhupinder Singh, Delhi
Printed at : G. Print Process, Delhi

Cataloging in Publication Data—DK
Courtesy: D.K. Agencies (P) Ltd. <docinfo@dkagencies.com>

Mishra, Sitakanta, author.
Parmanu politics : Indian political parties and nuclear weapons / Dr. Sitakanta Mishra.
pages cm
Includes bibliographical references (pages) and index.
ISBN 9789351280934

1. Nuclear weapons—Government policy—India. 2. National security—India. 3. Political parties—India. 4. India—Politics and government—1947- 5. Nuclear disarmament—India. I. Title.

DDC 355.02170954 23

Contents

Tables

DIAGRAMS

Preface

Among the domestic variables of nuclear weapons decision-making in a parliamentary democracy, political parties constitute the most vibrant institutional element. While aggregating and articulating popular interests, they supply public representatives as policy-makers for authoritative formulations on vital issues in the pursuit of securing national interest. Within this framework, this study attempts to analyse the role of Indian political parties – especially Indian National Congress, Bharatiya Janata Party, and Communist Party of India (Marxist) – in the evolution of India's nuclear weapons policy. The phrase 'Parmanu Politics' strictly refers to the analysis of the language spoken, written and policies adopted by the above mentioned parties in India's nuclear weapons discourse. In other words, how the party system in India in general, and organisational and leadership ethos of Indian political parties in particular, has influenced India's nuclear weapons decisions is the subject matter of this study.

By the time the manuscript was complete the 16th Lok Sabha election process was on full swing. The three parties brought out their manifestos containing references to India's nuclear programme. Particularly, the BJP's manifesto while promising for an "Independent Strategic Nuclear Programme" pledged to "revise and update" India's nuclear doctrine which resurfaced the debate over the *change and continuity* of India's 'no-first-use' posture. One may argue that a revision of India's nuclear doctrine is long overdue. Western scholars view India's current doctrine as similar to the US doctrine of massive retaliation during the 1950s. Since the debate has surfaced in the political arena, one can expect that the doctrine will undergo official scrutiny sooner or later. Nevertheless, how the BJP will go about it and what shape it will culminate in is a matter of conjecture. As nuclear weapons are a sensitive issue, and for Modi as a new political leader in the national scene, the future contours of India's nuclear deterrent would largely rest on his evolving stature in the Party. How Modi's equation with other stalwarts of the Party would evolve is yet to be seen. Therefore, equating BJP's nuclear tests decision in 1998 with its urge to revise India's nuclear doctrine today would be misleading.

The study has identified four broad and overlapping trends in India's six-decade long nuclear weapons discourse. One, compared to the role of political parties, national political leadership is paramount in nuclear matters. Two, nuclear policy does not change with the change of government, but sometime changes despite the same party forming the government. Three, the stature of the Prime Minister in the party s(he) belongs to is the determining factor. Lastly, when the Prime Minister's position in the party is stable but not the national political scenario, major nuclear decisions have been arrived at mainly via the initiative of the Prime Minister. If these past trends in nuclear decision-making vis-à-vis domestic politics are any guide, the new Prime Minister Narendra Modi would first strengthen his position in the BJP while shaping the functioning of his government according to his own conceptions. Though the national political situation seems stable now with the end of the three-decade coalition era, the position of the new Prime Minister vis-à-vis the party he belongs to is yet to be consolidated. How Modi's equation with other stalwarts of the Party evolve would largely determine his nuclear weapons related decisions. However, the current debate reinforces the assumptions on the role of political parties and leaders in nuclear weapons decision-making.

Nevertheless, India's future nuclear weapons decisions will remain inexplicable largely owing to the nature of current global nuclear discourse and the regional security environment. It has been the trend since the beginning as one can find important decisions have been oral and still shrouded in mystery. However, nuclear weapons policy of India is certainly not evolved in a vacuum. India's nuclear journey, starting from 1950s when India decided to use atomic energy for peaceful purposes to the 1960s when certain sections of the public started demanding for nuclear weapons and finally during the 1990s when India unilaterally declared itself as a nuclear weapon state, is not forthright. Many variables and factors have shaped and reshaped India's nuclear weapons discourse and the political parties, among other domestic variables, are assumed to have played important roles in this study.

At the outset, India's domestic political discourse seem to be dissected by three ideological underpinnings on the basis of three sets of politico-ideological streams represented by three political parties, though there exist considerable intersection among them. The first stream is a secular, anti-imperialist and class-neutral nationalism represented by the Indian National Congress; the second stream is the pan-Indian, ethno-cultural nationalism identified with the Bhartiya Janata Party (BJP) and its brethren groups; and third stream is a secular class-oriented politics championed by the communists and socialists. Each of these three factions has its own views and stands on different aspects of India's nuclear weapons policy.

However, which political party should be given credit, and how much in shaping India's nuclear weapons policy is inconclusive. By virtue of their capacity to form government at the centre, the Congress party and the BJP has taken major nuclear weapon decisions but the CPI(M) has never found a chance to exercise such prerogative as it never formed the government, except as coalition partner. However, it can be argued that it has provided a different taste to the domestic nuclear debate thereby making the debate more democratic. The main emphasis, therefore, in the study is to compare which political party played the role in shaping India's nuclear weapons policy evolved through many topsy-turvy atmospheres during the past six-decades.

This study is primarily trying to explain the normative nuclear arming choice of India and the role of political institutions, especially the Indian political parties. Several questions the study attempts to analyse in fact are the issues around which Indian nuclear weapons debate revolves round. Firstly, if "nuclear taboo" prevails over the "nuclear myth" then why does India's case represent the reverse trend? Out of the 30 countries that have military nuclear potential and capable of launching a nuclear weapons programme on short notice, 28 are democracies. If democracies tend to display more determination on nuclear choice, then, why India followed an ambiguous nuclear policy for half a century? If the normative disposition of a country towards nuclear weapons is rooted in the identity of its society, the societal debate in turn are fostered by political parties having their root in the ideological and political inclination of the general mass. With this assumption, this study enquires the role of political parties in formulating India's nuclear weapons policy.

The introductory chapter provides a conceptual background linking national policy-making and role of political parties. It is highlighted that depending upon the maturity of the party system and their interaction within the national democratic discourse the policy outcome gets shaped and reshaped. The second chapter focuses primarily on the domestic political interface in India's nuclear weapons discourse by identifying the nuances of electoral politics. It is viewed that the answer to the question, *why did India develop its nuclear weapon capability when it did and the way it did* may lie somewhere in the politico-security spectrum. The chapter provides a brief background on the nature, structure and functioning of the three parties. The BJP and CPI(M) being carved out from their parent parties like Jana Sangh and the CPI respectively, some space is attributed to their views in this section. The third chapter describes the doctrinal aspect of India's nuclear deterrent within the context of decision-making and domestic politics.

Subsequent three chapters address the link between India's national security conception and its attitude towards nuclear weapons, especially taking into account the regional security environment. Keeping India's troublesome relations with both Pakistan and China and consequent geo-strategic environment, there was nothing terribly problematic about the importance of nuclear weapons. But how the three parties have perceived the importance of nuclear weapons for India is a matter of discussion in this section. One full chapter (Chapter Four) devoted to the Congress Party views, as it has formed the government for a long period since independence, explaining how the Party holds nuclear weapons as important, but was ambivalent for pursuing a full-fledged nuclear weapons programme. Chapter five narrates views of both BJP and CPI(M). While BJP considers nuclear weapons are "vital for national power and status", the CPI(M) thinks that India's national security is threatened not so much by China or Pakistan as by the USA, therefore posit themselves in the extreme ends.

Chapter six looks into the extra-regional powers' presence in South Asia and their perceived impact on India's nuclear weapons policy by the three parties. It is often argued that "Indian strategic policy has largely been responsive to major external events" therefore it can be assumed that its nuclear strategy must also be linked with the policies and involvement of outside powers in South Asia.

In the seventh chapter, views of the three parties on global non-proliferation regime are discussed. Both Nehru and the

Congress Party were of the view that disarmament and arms control should go hand in hand but in a phased manner. However, India's attitude towards nuclear disarmament was viewed to be altered during the 1960s, mainly after the Chinese aggression and subsequent nuclear tests explosions by it. India viewed the Chinese tests have aggravated the problem of non-proliferation. The May 1974 nuclear test continued to raise questions about India's non-proliferation position. At the same time, India continued to view the Treaty discriminatory but reiterated her intention not to produce nuclear weapons and right to develop nuclear energy for peaceful purposes.

The BJP, since its inception, stood for nuclear weapons for India and voiced against the discriminatory non-proliferation regime. In all its deliberations, the party vouched for a strong India equipped with atomic weapons. During the years, before coming to power, it supported Congress government's decision not to sign the NPT. Party was sceptical about Congress-led coalition's assurance not to sign the NPT and also about its ability to "resist the pressure for arranging regional arrangement which would amount to giving up the nuclear option". Criticising the NPT for its "double standard" in its 1992 Executive Meeting the BJP expressed it believes in the principle of sovereign equality of nations. It seems the BJP's views on NPT are in no way different from other political parties. Both the Congress and CPI(M) have expressed their opposition to India's adherence to the "Treaty at its present form" on many occasions. The CPI(M) links its arguments on non-proliferation and test-ban treaty with the issue of global nuclear disarmament. But the distinguishing factor in CPI(M)'s views is that it sees the nuclear discourse through the prism of "imperialism" and capitalism. But, interestingly, it justifies Soviet Russia's cooperation with other nuclear weapon powers in mobilising support for the nuclear non-proliferation regime. Though nuclear issues are debated on a wide spectrum and across the party line, national consensus exists for India's articulation on the non-proliferation and test ban issues.

In the concluding chapter, a comparative study is attempted on the stands taken by the three parties to evaluate the role played by them in the evolution of India's nuclear weapons policy where it stands today. The spontaneous anxiety on which the study answers at the end is, *which political party should be given credit, and how much* in shaping India's nuclear weapons policy; which leader(s) should be given how much credit. The three political parties have played their parts and deserve credit accordingly. For that matter, India's nuclear bomb seems to have many mothers. The Congress Party conceived and nurtured it, the CPI(M) questioned it, and the BJP delivered it. It would be irrational to give only the obstetrician whole credit than is due. Rightly, "all were party to the nuclear gatecrash". The political leaders have played leading roles but their preferences were filtered through the party screen they belonged to. However, India's nuclear policy cannot be explained without recognising the central role of many individuals.

In the process of completing this study I have accumulated a series of intellectual debts. Though the idea was imbibed in my mind for quite some time, inadvertently it got triggered by people I met, read or heard. I express my sincere gratitude to Professor Savita Pande without whose support and guidance this study would not have seen the light of the day.

During the initial phase, it was stupendous to gather the relevant documents, programmes, manifestos, and Parliamentary Debates of the respective parties as the study relies heavily on primary sources. However, the Library staffs of CPI(M), New Delhi, were very cooperative to locate the necessary documents and helped to get them photocopied. The staffs of the Publication Stall at the BJP office, New Delhi, were more than willing to cater to my requirements each time I visited them. The Nehru Memorial Museum Library was extremely useful to locate old documents of the Congress Party and Jana Sangh. Last but not the least, the JNU Library and the staff were very helpful in collecting relevant materials and books. The P.C. Joshi Archives in the JNU Library was helpful to locate archival literature on Left parties' policies. In the process, I have knowingly borrowed or unconsciously partaken from all that came my way relating to the subject to give the output final shape.

I express my deep gratitude to Late Air Commodore Jasjit Singh for his generous moral and intellectual support all along. I am equally thankful to Professor SD Muni whose affection and encouragement has prompted me always to look beyond the horizon. My senior colleague at Centre for Air Power Studies, Dr Manpreet Sethi has always encouraged and supported during my hardship. The loving appreciation of my hard work by Prof Abdul Nafey, Amb R Rajagopalan and Prof Chintamani Mahapatra has helped a lot to keep my morale up. I am indebted to Yeon-Jung

Ji for helping me in many ways and sharpen my ideas. Friends from JNU, especially Sanghita Mondal, Nihar Ranjan Pradhan, Duryodhan Nahak, Sweta Singh, KN Tennyson, Ram Rakkappan, and Ajaya Das kept me upbeat through the days of toil. Finally, it would not have been possible to accomplish this study had I not the strong support of my family.

November 2014

New Delhi **Sitakanta Mishra**

ACRONYMS

AEC:	Atomic Energy Commission
AIADMK:	All India Anna Dravida Munnetra Kazhagam
AICC:	All India Congress Committee
ANZUS:	Australia, New Zealand, United States Security Treaty
BARC:	Bhabha Atomic Research Centre
BJP:	Bhartiya Janata Party
BJS:	Bharatiya Jana Sangh
BSP:	Bahujan Samaj Party
C412:	Command, Control, Communications, Computing, Intelligence and Information
CANDU:	CANada Deuterium-Uranium reactor
CBMs:	Confidence Building Measures
CCS:	Cabinet Committee on Security
CD:	Conference on Disarmament
CENTO:	Central Treaty Organisation
CIRUS:	Canada India Research Utility Services
CPI:	Communist Party of India
CPI-M:	Communist Party of India (Marxist)
CTBT:	Comprehensive Test Ban Treaty
CWC:	Congress Working Committee
DCC:	Defence Committee of the Cabinet
DMK:	Dravida Munnetra Kazhagam
DRDO:	Defence Research and Development Organisation
FMCR:	Fissile Material Control Regime
FMCT:	Fissile Material Cut-off Treaty
IAEA:	International Atomic Energy Agency
INC:	Indian National Congress
JD-S:	Janata Dal-Secular
JIC:	Joint Intelligence Committee
LTTE:	Liberation Tigers of Tamil Eelam
MEA:	Ministry of External Affairs

MTCR:	Missile Technology Control Regime
NATO:	North Atlantic Treaty ORganisation
NBC:	Nuclear Biological and Chemical
NCA:	National Command Authority
NDA:	National Democratic Alliance
NFU:	No First Use
NIC:	National Identity Conception
NNWS:	Non-Nuclear Weapon States
NPT:	Nuclear Non-Proliferation Treaty
NRX:	National Research Experimental Reactor
NSAB:	National Security Advisory Board
NSC:	National Security Council
NSG:	Nuclear Suppliers Group
NWS:	Nuclear Weapons State
PLO:	Palestine Liberation Organisation
PSP:	Praja Socialist Party
PTBT:	Partial Test Ban Treaty
RJD:	Rashtriya Janata Dal
RSP:	Revolutionary Socialist Party
RSS:	Rashtriya Swayamsevak Sangh
SEATO:	South East Asian Treaty Organisation
SNEP:	Subterranean Nuclear Explosion Project
SP:	Samajwadi Party
SSP:	Samyukta Socialist Party
TIFR:	Tata Institute of Fundamental Research
UPA:	United Progressive Alliance
VHP:	Vishwa Hindu Parishad

Section-A
The Context

Nothing that man has made is bigger than the atom bomb and this bomb is not just a weapon rather "a tool for reshaping the world" (DeGroot 2005: viii). But, what prompted man to invent such a big bomb? If necessity is the mother of all inventions, was nuclear bomb a historical necessity? J. Robert Oppenheimer once marked, scientific discoveries and inventions are not only based on the dictum "whether it is useful" but also on "whether it is possible" (Oppenheimer 1953).

At the first instance, one can assume that the idea of usefulness of atomic weapons for political ends coincided with the scientific inquisitiveness on the power of atom. This coincidence streamlined the scientific community to explore the possibility of the atomie project under the patronage of political leadership. Therefore, "atomic energy had a particular presence in around representations of the state and nation reflecting its origin in the modern meeting of science and war". (Abrahm 1998: 7) Many, including the atomic physicists, hoped that the fear of atom bomb would destroy war itself. But in course of time, it has been argued that the best protection against an atom bomb is another bomb of such type (Waltz 1981). This justification made the atomic weapons policy-making open-ended. So far, two bombs have been used, many more have been piled up, currently many are in the process of replacement, and many have also been dismantled. The number of countries with such bombs is gradually increasing and many others are trying to have them as well. But the fundamental question, how nuclear policy decisions of countries are made, remains satisfactorily unanswered.

This section aims to provide the context in which political decisions on nuclear weapons in India are undertaken and evolved. Especially, it includes the political-nuclear interface, the doctrinaire aspect, and domestic political setting in which the debate over all these issues were manifested.

1

A Conceptual Construct

National policy decisions are taken not in vacuum, but the processes and reasons for specific policies are generally shrouded in mystery. Normative understanding on national policy-making would suggest that both domestic and international variables exercise important degree of influence on the policy-making process of a country. (Putnam, 1993) This study enquires only the domestic component of the policy-making process, focusing on the role of political parties in formulating India's nuclear weapons policy. In other words, what role the Indian political parties played in the evolution of India's nuclear weapons policy, to the stage, at which it is today. How the organisations and ethos of political parties and party system in India influence on India's nuclear weapons related decisions is the subject matter of subsequent chapters.

Contemporary literature on nuclear weapons discourse seem to focus mainly on their strategy, deployment, number, quality and who possess them and how. It is to understand that the policies on deployment, number, quality and possession are merely the ultimate stage in a process in which the decision may have taken long ago. (McLean 1986: xiii-xiv) But to investigate why a nation arrive at a specific policy decision, it is necessary to unravel the complex processes of policy-making and to understand the variables that condition these processes. This is possible by undertaking an enquiry of the factors and the structures—the organisations, institutions and individuals or groups—which shape or control the process. This study takes three political parties as unit of analysis in the domain of India's nuclear weapons policy-making.

At the outset, policy decision as a process is not always forthright; "it is a series of events that build towards confusion, crisis and change. The activities that lead up to specific policies are almost cacophonous in nature—some dramatic, other insignificant; some random, other patterned; some horrific, others humorous". (Gerston 2010: 73) In a democratic political set up, national policies are generally arrived after a long deliberation, sometimes severely conditioned by shifting popular sentiments. Political parties, as agents and channels of popular interest aggregation and articulation for collective goals (Matlosa and Shale 2008: 6), constitute the most vibrant domestic determinant of national nuclear weapons policies.

In addition, political parties being part of the national legislative process also shape the contours of such policies to be adhered by the concerned nation. According to Mark P. Jones, the structures and organisations of political parties and party systems in a country exercise greater degree of influence on the policy-making process in general. (Jones 2005: 2) He attributes national policy outcome to four distinct characteristics of political parties and party system that considerably condition the policy-making process.

First is the *level of political party institutionalisation*. Institutionalised party systems provide greater levels of policy consistency, and policy orientations of the parties tend to be relatively stable. (Jones 2005: 2-3) During the first two decades since Independence, India has experienced "one-party dominant system" to which Rajni Kothari calls the "Congress System", (Kothari 1964) with a highly "institutionalised" Congress Party at the helm of affairs.[1] During this period, India's nuclear policy seems to be consistent—no nuclear bomb, complete nuclear disarmament and peaceful use of nuclear technology. With the collapse of the Congress system in subsequent decades after Nehru, India experienced unstable coalitions owing to fragmentation of national political space. What way then the nuclear policy has moved with the change in party and leadership orientations is subject matter of this study.

Second, in a *highly nationalised party system*, national issues become central in legislators' career, therefore national factors help forging bonds between voters and parties. In the Indian political context, the Congress Party though nationally entrenched, nuclear weapons seem not been a career issue, especially to forge bonds with voters. On the other hand, BJP has made nuclear weapons as a major plank of its "security-first" agenda, even appealed and promised the electorate to acquire nuclear weapons if it comes to power. The Left parties seem to have taken "interventionist stance" in every debate including on nuclear weapons but without a clear-cut programme.

Third, *polarisation*, ideological or otherwise, among parties in the legislature directly influences the legislative outcome. One gets the impression that India's domestic political scenario is dissected by three ideological underpinnings. Mainly, three streams of ideology seem to have manifested in post-Independence Indian politics, though there is considerable inter-penetration as well as conflict among these three: (1) the Indian National Congress seen to operate under the banner of a secular, anti-imperialist and class-neutral nationalism; (2) the Bhartiya Janata Party (BJP) and its brethren groups represent the trend of pan-Indian, ethno-cultural nationalism; and (3) a secular class-oriented politics is championed by the communists and socialists. (Chaube, 1999) How this polarisation has influenced policy outcome, especially India's nuclear weapons policy, is a matter of debate. The analyses in subsequent chapters examine if differential ideological inclination of political parties has in any way influenced India's nuclear weapons discourse.

Fourth, a normative political understanding suggests the *presence and stability of partisan cleavages* strengthen the programmatic politics which in turn generate "higher level of policy salience". (Jones 2005: 34) Therefore, it is expected that changes of government lead to far-reaching policy changes as "competing parties are programmatically far apart". (Zohlnhofer 2009: 104) On this basis, if India's political discourse is examined, it seems India's nuclear policy has not changed outright because of the change in government, rather has changed with formation of government by the same party again. Thus, the *change and continuity* in India's nuclear weapons policy during various governments and leadership is intricately examined with the assumption that political leadership is more determining than political parties in nuclear policy-making.

Considering the above four conceptual variables, political parties and party system in India seem to show distinct characteristics at different phases of its national political evolution. This study attempts, therefore, to locate if these distinct characteristics have any bearing on the evolution of India's nuclear weapons policy. Though the political-nuclear interface is an established phenomenon, the contours of this linkage and the distinctive outcome, if any, is examined here. In the process, the subsequent sections elaborate conceptually the role of political parties in policy-making in general and their role in nuclear policymaking in particular.

The basic objective of policy-making is to arrive at right policies at appropriate moments so that national interest is best served. (Kangas 1984) In fact, *right policy at the right moment* to maximise national interest, beside other things, necessitates excellent coordination between pragmatism of *agents* involved and the efficiency of the *mechanisms* at place by which such policies are arrived at. The agents may constitute both informal and formal groups, agencies and individuals who play as platforms and mediums through which the policy-makers get the inputs and feedback on specific policies to be and are taken. Though the number of players involved in actual policy-making is very small, the *agents or agencies* that play determining role in influencing the evolution and course of national nuclear discourse are varied and diverse. (Wendt 1987: 335) They range from government officials to the general public, from media to the think tanks with different capacity. The following are some important *agents* who explicitly or implicitly influence the nuclear weapons policy-making process.

First, the executive branch, particularly the head of the government or the chief executive and the senior officials play central role in nuclear weapons policy-making. The executive not only exercise the formal power of military command, but also on practical matters oversee, direct, and look into the budget of the programme. (Lindsay 1992) Second, the executive in democratic countries is accountable to the legislature or the parliament. (Johari 1982: 489) World over, legislatures, though play minimal operational and remote doctrinal role, have considerable control over the budgets. Third, the legislature in a democratic polity is composed of groups of representatives of electorates—normally the political parties, the focus of this study—invariably shape the policy-making process. Fourth, the public and media are, in fact, the major pillars of a political system on which the decision making process rests. In open political systems, extra-governmental democratic elements and specialised non-governmental communities express their voice on nuclear weapons policies. (Fisher 1999) Fifth, behind the public domain, the scientific-bureaucratic community, by virtue of their expertise and involvement in the programme, plays vital role in the evolution of national nuclear weapons policy. (Anderson 2010) Lastly, strategic thinkers and think tanks sometimes influence policy process by their insight on various aspects of the discourse, thereby, provide back-up to the policy-makers on relevant aspects, at the same time figure out lacunas in the policies arrived at. While the media provide the medium for debate, these institutions supply the debaters. (Alexander, 2006)

Political Parties: Agents and Institutions

Among various agents that considerably determine the contours of nuclear weapons policy-making in a democracy, the political parties that constitute the domestic echelon agent. The party system on which a democratic political set up normally based on refers to "a complex social and political processes that go beyond individual leaders, societal associations, political groups and organisations to the intricate pattern of their interactions and interrelationships". (Mehra 2003: 23) The basic units of any party system are the political parties as institutions which are varied in organisation, functioning, leadership, and decision making, and do not fit into one model. (Hasan 2010: 248) Therefore, one finds considerable divergence of views and opinions on any issue basically owing to "the way they evolved, their status as the ruling or opposition party, their support bases, leadership styles and traditions, and their geographical location and spread". (Suri 2005) However, political parties as institutions "provide the crucial connection between political process and policy makers, and bring to the forefront issues affecting the interests of social groups and the public at large". (Hasan 2010: 241) How much these "institutions affect policy outcomes" is one of the classical and most important issues concerning democratic nation. (Kawanaka 2010: 1)

Essentially, this issue is largely about identifying the causality between institutions and national policies. In particular, how differences among institutions cause "variations in policy outcomes", and what role institutions play in formulating policies. (Persson and Tabellini, 2003) In a democratic political set up, political parties as political institutions affect policy outcome roughly in three ways: (1) political institutions decide, first, the players who participate in the policy making process; (2) the preference of the players; and (3) the strategy sets of the players. (Kawanaka 2010: 1) At the first instance, political parties play vital function of linking individuals to the democratic process by simplifying choices for voters—"help to make politics user-friendly for citizens". (Dalton and Wattenberg 2002: 6) The party that forms the government takes required decisions partly, based on its own ideological inclinations and organisational ethos, and partly in response to the need of the hour. The parties outside the government equally shape public opinion, pressurise the government for clarification on specific decisions arrived at. Thereby they play in managing and structuring the affairs of government by identifying with numerous key aspects of democratic process, such as: creating majority, organising the government, implementing policy objectives, organising dissent and opposition, ensuring responsibility for government actions, controlling government administration, fostering stability in the government, etc. (Dalton and Wattenberg 2002: 8) Political parties being vibrant organisations, mobilise the electorate, form the government, therefore, "their ultimate influence is on the policy outcomes of government". (Caul and Gray, 2010: 208-37)

In India, emergence and growth of political parties is related to the rise of nationalism in the country during the British rule. (Mehra 2003: 51) During subsequent decades after Independence, India has seen splintering of political parties of different ideologies and organisational ethos, sometime basing on the societal underpinnings and fractions. However, according to Zoya Hasan, most political parties lack the political capacity to take the lead in formulating and debating policies which reflect people's aspirations and needs. Although parties and party leaders do profess to stand for ideology, in reality they are flexible and not at all reluctant to give up their ideological stance or put it on the back burner, if that helps them gain a share of political power. (Hasan 2010: 251) However, three streams of ideologies as identified by Chaube—a secular, anti-imperialist and class-neutral nationalism (Indian National Congress); pan-Indian, ethno-cultural nationalism (BJP and its brethren groups); and a secular class-oriented politics (communists and socialists)—can provide the framework to examine the policy differentials in India's nuclear weapons policy conception.

To investigate the perception that nuclear policy as outcome of domestic and party politics or influenced by political leaders within the above three ideological streams, it is necessary to undertake a careful study of these parties' proceedings and pronouncements over the years. Broadly, two approaches can be adopted in this regard: first is the ideological approach according to which nuclear policy formulation may be considered a function of the political system in action or the preferences or convictions of political leaders who carry out its programme; second is the analytical approach basing on the proposition that policy rests on multiple determinants, both internal and external. (Patagundi 1987: 10) However, the perception of nuclear policy as outcome of domestic politics or party politics may help understand the origin but not suffice to explain continuation of the policy. On the other hand, the analytical approach would provide the ground to understand the continuation of policy emphasising national interest as the permanent guiding factor. But different political parties articulate national interest in different ways and forms, thereby policy continuation sometimes is not forthright. Therefore, one way to establish the pattern between political process and nuclear policy formulation is to undertake intrusive examinations of individual party functioning, ideology, pronouncements and leadership style as units of analyses in the context of one issue area (i.e. nuclear weapons) and compare them with each others'.

In this study, the three political parties (INC, BJP, CPI-M) as units of analysis are judged in the form of a question as to how far these three parties have influenced India's nuclear weapons policy making process. Here 'influence' connotes the participation in the policy-making process and their views on India's nuclear weapons posture. However, before undertaking such investigation, a brief narration on what constitutes nuclear weapons policy-making is warranted to better understand the broad contours of the issue area.

Nuclear Weapons Policy-Making Contours

The phenomenon of nuclear weapons policy-making involves a spectrum of topics spanning every stage in the evolution of debate to the actual acquiring of nuclear weapon by a state. An analysis on this respect would bring forth the "why" and "how" aspects of discourse. When one is puzzled by a happening, the source of one's puzzlement is typically a particular government action or set of actions. Then one tends to ask why such decision is taken and what rationale behind such action follows.

The Organisation Behaviour Model emphasises the distinctive logic, capacities, culture, and procedures of the large organisations like government which take such decisions. (Griffin 2007) According to this model, "acts" and "choices" are thought of instead as outputs of large organisations that functioning according to regular patterns of behaviour. (Allison and Zelikov 2004: 18-19) It highlights the aspect *from what organisational context, pressure and procedure did a particular policy emerges?* In the context of national policy-making, it necessitates an investigation on the *politics of government.* In the process, one finds such events on which decisions made are neither as unitary choice nor as organisational outputs. Rather the outcome is understood as resultant bargaining among players in the national government. The key players in government are the political parties, interest groups and individual leaders, who in essence influence the policy-making process immensely. Within this formulation, the nuclear weapons policy-making process seems nothing but solving of certain key questions based on national imperatives, debated or otherwise. They mainly constitute:

1. Is the nation to have nuclear weapons?
2. What is the plan for use of nuclear weapons?
3. What is the nation's strategy for nuclear weapons?
4. How is the force to be maintained and modernised?
5. Who has authority to order weapons to be launched and how to ensure such an order would be carried out?
6. What is its nuclear posture at the international level, what stand it should take on the non-proliferation issues at the international level?

The first five issue areas, identified by Walter B. Slocombe, signify the domestic aspects of nuclear policy-making process. (Slocombe, 2006) However, a country's need, strategy, plan of use, up keep and the decision to launch nuclear weapons are not only shaped by the domestic issues, rather influenced more or less by the external factors like regional security environment, strategies of neighbouring countries, global nuclear trend, the non-proliferation regime, etc. (Ford et al. 1977) However, the most fundamental but critical policy decision of a country's nuclear discourse is, whether it has to have nuclear weapons at all. Certainly, this decision of a nation is the outcome of the intricate interplay of group interest, leadership expositions and national ethos. Upon these considerations, a nation's attitude towards and policy on nuclear weapons is framed.

Perceptibly, no country has ever acquired nuclear weapons after a meaningful public debate. Real decisions to go for nuclear weapons have always been arrived at secretly by a close group or individuals. Even in countries like China and Pakistan where the military and political leadership closely intertwined, the basic acquisition decision has been made by the political leadership—confined to a very restricted inner core of leadership—albeit with military inputs. (Cirincione et al. 2005: Chapter 7 and 12) While countries like Germany and Japan have taken negative decision through much more public process and restrained themselves to civilian nuclear energy programmes (Ragheb 2007; Kelleher, 1968), Canada and Sweden's programme have been decided by a very small circle of civilian executive leaders and their most senior military and scientific advisors with minimal parliamentary and public/media inputs. (Robinson 2002; Arnett, 1998)

Next to the policy on "whether to acquire nuclear weapons" is the 'plan of their use'. A nation with nuclear weapons "has to make quasi-operational policies about the circumstances in which it's nuclear arsenal would be employed". (Slocombe 2006: 9) While these plans are guided by the concerned nation's national security strategy, it is the primary responsibility of the leaders to chalk out the strategy on the possible use of nuclear weapons so that they contribute to the nation's overall interests and objectives. Even where the basic objectives are defined, the operational plans need to be worked out on concrete terms clarifying what units are to do what; how orders are to be transmitted; how targets are to be identified and approved.

Once the operational plans are worked out, generally every nation takes a "declaratory position" on how it sees its nuclear weapons serve its national objectives. (Paul 2009: 117) It is seen that the declaratory positions of countries widely vary. For example, Israel known to have nuclear weapons but resolutely does not pronounce. The United States, in contrast, provides details on the structure of its nuclear force, doctrine, policy and even basic principles of targeting by various official statements. (US Department of Defence; Congressional Research Service)[2] Britain and France also provide broad outlines of their policy through various official pronouncements though are less comprehensive than the US. (Tertrais 2007) India, China and Pakistan, though overtly speak of their possession, do not go beyond revealing the broad contour of their arsenals. Russia with a more open political system now entertains public discussions about nuclear force, purpose and their place in its overall defence strategy. (Woolf 2003)

The next element of nuclear weapons policy-making is the maintenance and modernisation programme of arsenals. The issue is, if decided to acquire, how to strengthen the nuclear force, their delivery systems and other support elements. Other than the technical acquisition decisions, the aspects of subordination, custody and organisational structure in the management of nuclear weapons are equally important. (Brown 2000: 204) But the pattern of public participation in the process varies. While in case of US, and to a lesser degree with UK, the veils of secrecy have parted considerably, decisions of other states have been tightly held. (Reiss 1995) In India's case, the pattern and process seems to be lengthy and debated democratically. While specific decisions to conduct the tests and orders for scientific preparedness for the bomb are still shrouded in mystery, the shape and parameters of India's nuclear weapons policy has been a subject of open deliberation. For example, the National Security Advisory Board (NSAB), after an intensive deliberation brought out a draft nuclear doctrine that was debated for almost three years until it was finally operationalised in 2003.

The debate over the basic framework of India's nuclear weapons policy—"no-first use" but "credible minimum nuclear deterrence"—is still in vogue and various parties and leaders continue to assert their opinions to give second thoughts on the above policy. For example, a prominent BJP member and former External Affairs Minister, Jaswant Singh has called for a second look and revision of India's no-first-use doctrine. (*The Statesman*, March 15, 2011) Initiating the discussion on demand on grants for Ministry of External Affairs in Lok Sabha on March 15, 2011, Mr Singh told:

> I am of the view that the policy-framework that the NDA devised in 1998 is very greatly in need of revision because the situation that warranted the enunciation of the policy of 'no-first-use' or 'non-use against non-nuclear weapons', 'credible deterrence with minimum force', etc. has long been overtaken by events. . . . You cannot continue to sit in yesterday's policy. (*Indian Express*, March 16, 2011)

In response, the Congress-led UPA Government rejected Jaswant Singh's suggestion for a revisit of the no-first-use policy for nuclear weapons. The Congress leader and former External

Affairs Minister S. M. Krishna told the Lok Sabha that "Our policy (no-first use) remains as it exists. Government is committed to safeguarding India's security interests in consonance with our declared (nuclear) doctrine". (*IBN Live*, March 16, 2011)

Lastly and more importantly, the role of leaders, especially the political leaders or the central authority (in case of non-democratic ruled nations), who give the final order for possession and use of these arsenal, is a crucial aspect of nuclear decision-making. (Hymans 2006) The ultimate authority to give orders for development and their use generally rests with the senior political leadership. However, the central question is, should the principle of political decision-making be reinforced by technical measures that make it difficult for the weapons to be launched without receipt of some code to be transmitted to the military forces? As authority can also be delegated, the principle of succession needs to be decided. (Cimbala 2005: 20) This gives rise to another critical issue area: should the policy-making authority to launch the weapon be given only in the midst of crisis ("real time") or in perpetuity? These and other intricate issues generally involve many nuances of the linkage between systemic factors and the procedural aspects in a given polity which can be better understood within a theoretical framework of the interface between nuclear policy-making and domestic politics.

Theorising Nuclear Weapons Policy-Making

In general, nuclear weapons policy discourse is a critical blend of history, technology, and strategy. (Asaro 2000: 257) Therefore, large number of variables can be identified in the pursuit of understanding the nuances of nuclear weapons policy processes. Construction of empirical models allows one to generalise from the historical cases, technological realities and constraints, thereby one can prescribe for the current and predict on the future nuclear weapons policy prospects. But empiricism alone is not sufficient to define the causal relationship between national nuclear postures and nuclear policy-making expositions. The questions why do certain states adopt specific nuclear postures in fact denote the existence of puzzles that the contemporary world is grappling for predicting the future of international security. (Sagan 1996/97: 54) "Since wars begin in the minds of men", preparedness for war is also designed in the minds of men. For those involved in the theoretical debate over how nuclear weapons policies are arrived at, whether the study on policy orientation can be separated from the phenomenon of "domestic coalition building" (Ogilvie-White 1996: 43) is a critical issue area. Therefore, in order to understand the causes of certain strategy or attitude of a nation towards a certain phenomenon, it is pertinent to (1) trace the circumstances in which an actor or group of actors arrive(s) at such policies; and (2) study the brains or the traits/personalities behind such policies.

Before jumping into the ideological explanation on the nuclear weapons behaviour and motive of nations, it is pertinent to analyse the "theory of political decision making" as nuclear weapons policies are essentially political decisions (Cohen and Lee 1986). The decision-making approach, which Richard C. Snyder brought to the awareness of political scientists, maintain that there are those who hold formal or informal positions of power and authority frame policies for certain events. (Snyder 1962) These policy-makers can be located within a bureaucratic or administrative network or within representative groups privileged with information supply and authority to implement the policies. These persons draw on a memory of past events and frame their behaviour upon expectations about the future. They are however, subject to possible pressures arising from the society. At a given moment, these policy-makers will be made aware of a particular situation for which they will consider changing the policy or type of behaviour that has been practiced. This process is continuous: the situation occurs; information about the situation is passed to the policy-makers; possible behaviours relative to the situation are considered; a policy is made either to change behaviour or to stay with the previous behaviour; the policy is then implemented and in turn a new situation is created. (Price 1975: 418-19) This explanation provides an understanding of 'how' the policy-making process proceeds. However, theories dealing with individuals in policy-making domain are incomplete as they fail to take into account the 'circumstances' in which this behaviour occurs. (Farnham 1990: 83)

Robert J. Art identifies "two waves" in the evolution of policy-making theories. The "first wave" policy-making theorists (Roger Hilsman, Samuel Huntington, Richard Neustadt, and Warner Schilling) have applied a bureaucratic but essentially political perspective. For them, policy-making was not simply a matter of determining the policy with the greatest expected utility; rather they held that the nature of the political context influenced what a policy-maker could reasonably hope to accomplish and therefore, ought to be taken into account in his calculations. So, the concern of the first wave theorists was with the impact of the entire political context on the policy-making process. (Art 1973) The second wave theorists (Graham Allison, Morton Halperin and Richard Snyder) went a good deal further in moving the focus of interest away from the individual policy-maker and towards the political system itself. (Art 1973) The Bureaucratic Politics Model, a part of the second wave, asserts that the policy positions of individuals derived primarily from their roles, rather than from a process of "internal debate". (Snyder and Sapin, 1962) Also political decisions were seen as the result of a process driven by the interaction of bureaucratic interests, not by the decisions of individuals. (Allison 1971) During 1970s and 80s, there emerged various psychological approaches to which Barbara Farnham calls the "third wave" of theories on policy-making. These theorists (Guilford, John Steinbruner, Robert Jervis, Janice Stein, and Philip Tetlock) were essentially concerned with the influence of "cognitive factors" or "motivational phenomenon" on policy-making. Thus, their main emphasis is on the "policy-makers' mental operations". (Guilford 1979: 8)

When general policy-making theory is applied to nuclear weapons policy-making of nations, all these trends do necessarily explain the "why" and "when" of national policy parameters. Graham Allison's three models (rational-actor, orgnisational-process, and government-politics model), though specific to the decision-making process, do clearly demonstrate the influence of "actors", "factors", "choices" in policy "outputs". (Allison 1971) Barbar Kellerman of Fairleigh Dickinson University has added another three models (Small Group Model, Dominant Leader Model, and Cognitive Process) to further pin-point in the effort to understand the policy-making process. (Kellerman 1983) However, when all these models of policy-making are applied to nuclear weapons policy-making, no model can go beyond the actors-factors analysis when nuclear discourse is much more than this framework. Though national security is the standard referring point to decipher any nation's nuclear posture, many states are viewed to have opted atomic weapons merely for national prestige. It is argued that nuclear weapons posture serve important symbolic function—both shaping and reflecting a state's identity. According to this perspective, state behaviour is determined not by leaders' calculations about the national security interests or their parochial bureaucratic interests, rather by deeper "norms" and "beliefs" about what are legitimate and appropriate in international relations. (Sagan 1996: 73)

As is emphasised, only empirical investigation of the circumstances or the *setting* may not suffice to understand the WHY aspect of specific nuclear postures. Dr Conardo Varotto, the father of Argentina's once-secret uranium enrichment programme, said "the bomb is in the human heart or it isn't . . . we could have done it, but we didn't, because the bomb was not in our hearts." (Quoted in Hymans 2006: ix) Dr Varotto's basic point was that specific nuclear postures reflect the 'psychology of the leaders' to which Hymans identified as a discrete "policy-making pathway" that leads from "different national identity conceptions, through emotions towards the ultimate nuclear choice". (Hymans 2006: ix) A similar trait can be observed in Zulfikar Ali Bhutto, the former Pakistani President, who took the historical decision to fabricate atom bomb for his country in a meeting with the top Pakistani nuclear scientists in Multan, January 1972. In the historical secret meeting, Bhutto told the scientists ... "this is *a very serious political decision,* which Pakistan must make, and perhaps all Third World countries [emphasis added] must make one day ...." (Quoted in Weissman and Krosney 1983: 45)

It is hardly surprising that contemporary security studies debate is woven around the temporal interest of nations and by nature power-centric and policy oriented, mainly defined by Western scholars. (Nizamani 2001: 3) Therefore, one always confronts with questions like: Are the theoretical bases explaining the security discourse of the Western world fit for analysing issues of the non-Western world?; Is Third World a unique category which merits a separate analytical framework? To this extent, the empirical study on the policy-making process seem inadequate and an ideological-value laden study may provide appropriate framework to look into the nuances in nuclear policy-making process of the post-colonial (Third World) states. The following section considers therefore the subjectivity of the nuclear discourse by applying various contemporary approaches to international system.

There are two competing theoretical camps found attempting to uncover how states arrive at specific nuclear weapons policies. The first camp takes the "realist" view that states adopt specific nuclear weapons policies depending upon the specific security situation.[3] (Bracken 1999) Classical realism views the working of the international system is anarchical, therefore, considers nuclear weapons as "absolute weapons" and beneficial for states. (Hymans 2006a: 456) In other words, states in international anarchy need to deter potential enemies and in the age of atom "the gold standard of deterrence is nuclear". Those countries believe their interest is threatened and nuclear weapons offer the best protection, their policy-makers tend to adopt such myth. Neo-realism, the structural form of realism, traces the motive of specific nuclear policies to the balance of power and security dilemmas. (Waltz 1981; Mearsheimer 1990) According to this stream, the domestic nature of states, regimes, groups, or individuals is irrelevant to nuclear policy formulation and outcome as feeling of insecurity by the state and the their policy-makers is the major drive in the search for nuclear weapons.

But the realist framework seems too abstract to allow precise understanding of the conditions under which policy-makers adopt a specific nuclear posture instead pursuing other options. (Lavoy 2006) Therefore, the realist framework viewed insufficient to explain the timing and nature of policy shifts because it operates at a *systemic level of analysis*. (Singer 1961) It does not take into account specific political, technical, or psychological factors that condition national thinking, perception of the national leaders and their policy-making pattern. It also fails to explain, why at certain point of time a state adopt a certain posture? For example, why India tested nuclear devices in 1974 and 1998, not in 1968? And why India adopted the no-first use policy instead of the first-use policy? Similarly, why South Africa not Sweden or Saudi Arabia, why France but not Germany or Japan choose the policy they follow? In order to have a *subjective understanding* of why some countries seek certain nuclear weapons posture instead of other options, or why some countries adopt 'yes-bomb policy' while others follow a 'no-bomb policy', an alternate theoretical perspective—idealism—has been applied by many scholars.

This alternative camp—the "idealists"—emphasise "the causal power of ideas including identities, perceptions, emotions, cultures, etc.", and consider that states and their policy-makers gradually stop worrying and "learn to love the bomb". (Potter 2003) Professor Jacques Hymans of Smith College (USA) contends that the idealist paradigm can better explain the nuclear weapons discourse of states. In his understanding, the idealist approach by focusing on ideas produced by national, cultural, or individual attributes explain much about the worldviews, motives, and policy orientations of national leaders or groups (Hymans 2006b). Policy-makers are driven towards the bomb or foreclose the option to have the bomb by the idea that it is beneficial or unnecessary respectively. But this idea is not purely the result of international anarchy as is argued by the realists. The idealists admit that it is policy-makers' perceptions of the bomb's utility prompt them to adopt the policy favouring or discarding nuclear bomb. (Gompert 1998) The idealist approach focus on the psychology of national leaders emphasising the constraints of cognitive behaviour triggered by domestic or international factors. Also they posit "strategic culture as a driving force behind nuclear bomb" policies of nations. (Levoy 2006: 435)

Basically, the idealist camp has developed its analyses on three levels: the international level, the domestic level and the individual level. At the international level, idealists stress the importance of international "norms" or "normative predispositions" that guide nuclear weapons policies of states. As the way realists explain nuclear norms as "taboo" and "myth", the idealists also used the explanation but somewhat differently. In most countries, as the idealists view, the development of nuclear weapons is considered morally prohibitive, incompatible with the country's identity and international outlook. (Frey 2006: 4) These norms, or the "nuclear taboo", are major factors in preventing states to acquire nuclear weapons. (Tannenwald 2005) In some states, however, these "negative norms" for the idealists, are overridden by a positive set of norms—"nuclear myth"—causing nuclear weapons to become shield or symbol of invulnerability to perceived threats or "the regalia of major power status" that prompt a nation to acquire them. (Frey 2006: 4) Specifically, a normative understanding of the role of norms in nuclear weapons policy-making explains that democracies do not act more peacefully than authoritarian regimes on nuclear matters per se but generally take a more determined position on the bomb. (Frey 2006: 15) The idealists, however, take similar stand as like the realists when they say countries are more prone to the 'nuclear myth' with regard to the acquisition of nuclear weapons, they are more committed to the 'taboo' with regard to their use.

While some idealists focus their study on broad, global trends and ideas about the desirability of nuclear weapons by states, others stress on important societal constituencies (work at the domestic level) that are strong enough to adopt policy supporting for nuclear weapons. (Sen 2000: 16-24) Some other idealists who look into the domestic-level variables emphasise the relationship between domestic political coalitions and alternative nuclear postures. For example, Etel Solingen opines that the study of this linkage can provide additional insights into why certain nations veil their nuclear weapons programmes and defy widely-accepted international norms. (Solingen 1994) In his view, countries ruled by coalitions of social and economic groups pursuing economic liberalisation are more likely to cooperate internationally on nuclear non-proliferation than are countries ruled by inward-looking coalitions with radical fundamentalist ideologies. Finally, some other idealists emphasise the role of individuals or the "motivations of state leaders" (Hymans 2006) owing to the reason that nuclear weapons programmes are often secret and under the tight control of the top leaders. Jacques E.C. Hymans calls these political leaders as "oppositional nationalist" who see their nation as both naturally at odds with an external enemy and as naturally its equal if not its superior. (Hymans 2006: 2) In his view, the nuclear weapons policies are "revolutionary choices". The resulting decisions will primarily reflect the policy-maker's "national identity conception" (NIC), which stands for the leader's understanding of his nation's identity—his sense of what the nation naturally stands for and of how high it naturally stands in comparison to others. (Hymans 2006: 12–13)

Beyond the dyadic explanation (realist vs. idealist), two other theoretical frameworks draw attention: the neo-liberal institutionalism and the constructivist approach. The neo-liberal framework calls greater attention to international factors in domestic politics that ultimately determine national nuclear course of action. (Costanzo 2002) On the other hand, constructivist approach emphasises the role of domestic factors in international relations by saying that "international reality is socially constructed by cognitive structures". (Adler 1997: 209) The constructivists identify the impact of "norms" and how it contributes to states' nuclear forbearance. Therefore, the approach takes a middle ground between rationalist approaches and interpretive approaches. Irrespective of which sector influence to whom to what extent, it is to recognise that there exist a constant interaction between the domestic and international sphere, therefore, "domestic politics and international relations are somehow entangled" to which Robert D. Putnam calls "two level games". (Putnam 1993: 431) However, if norms or institutions are the chief factors behind national nuclear decisions, why some countries go for acquiring it while some others do not prefer them. It is seen national leaders sometimes advance "reasons of state" as justification for forming policies to acquire or renounce nuclear weapons. (Abraham 1998)

Another methodological argument is that, democratic and economically outward-looking countries generally are averse to decide for nuclear weapons when inward-looking closed political economies are prone to nuclear craze and temptation. (Solingen 1994) But these assertions are not universal. India's is a classic example. India is the largest democracy in the world, tested its second series of nuclear tests in 1998 after it adopted the liberal economic model. Therefore, theorising nuclear discourse is a "multi-factor heuristic task" as no single factor is solely accountable. (Connor-Linton 1988)

One may notice, on the basis of these and other theoretical explanations, that as many nuclear-striving states, there advanced so many justifications. Theorists have also tried to put all the variables together to put forwarded their own convictions on nuclear discourse. But neither a universal explanation of state behaviour in the realm of nuclear weapons policy-making is devised yet, nor can effectively be constructed. None of the theories alone is adequate to interpret and account the policies of nations. It is not that the strategic thinkers or the theorists are incapable of doing so, rather the statecraft involving the international, national, domestic and individual level discourse is so dynamic, it is almost impossible to narrow down to a precise cause or influence.

Also many find individual traits as the determining factor and the national psyche, character, norms and culture, in other words, the *subjective aspects* govern the policy-making process. But the policy outcomes cannot be attributed to a single factor. It is to understand that the nuclear discourse is more politics and psychology than physics and security. Scott D. Sagan, therefore, rightly asserts that "nuclear weapons like other weapons are more than tools of national security; they are political objects of considerable importance in domestic debates. . . ." (Sagan 1996-97: 55) Sagan has devised three models—the security models, the domestic politics model and the norms model— in pursuit of his search for appropriate explanations of nations' nuclear weapons policy-making behaviour.

The *security model* belongs to the realist paradigm as it explains that specific nuclear policy of a certain country has many important causes, but the forceful cause is the perceived deteriorating national security situation. Owing to the enormous destructive power of the nuclear arsenals, any state desirous of strengthening its national security would prefer to acquire a "minimum" nuclear weapons capability to balance against its rivals. Other than its deterrent utility, nuclear weapons as diplomatic and coercive tools for a state. (Sauer 2007) In pursuit of acquiring nuclear security, policy-makers may adopt two postures: (1) develop their own nuclear arsenals; and/or (2) join a balancing alliance with a nuclear power for an extended deterrence guarantee. Therefore, policy-makers' perception and response to national threats may lead them towards nuclear weapons option. Moreover, the threat from nuclear weapon state tempt a nation to acquire the same therefore, George Shultz once summarised that "proliferation begets proliferation" meaning thereby "every time one state develops nuclear weapons to balance against its rival also generate a nuclear threat to another state in the region, which then has to initiate its own nuclear weapons programme to maintain its national security." (Sagan 1996–97: 84) In the process, national nuclear policy-making is nothing but "strategic chain reactions" of states.

The security model also provides the same security justification for states those who opt to roll back nuclear weapons programme. South Africa rolled back its nuclear weapons programme in 1991 owing to the perceived radical reduction in the external threats. (Horton III 1999) In fact, the risk of a Soviet-led attack on South Africa was virtually eliminated by 1989. The security model is also used to explain nuclear restraint policies of nations. Argentina and Brazil began their nuclear weapons programme in 1970s but their joint declaration in 1990 to abandon their programmes by recognising that the two states pose no security threat to each other. (Perkovich and Choubey 2010: 14) States like Ukraine, Kazakhstan and Belarus decided to give up their inherited nuclear arsenals owing to the fact that they didn't perceive Russia as a major military threat to their security and also the increased US security guarantees to them has made their nuclear weapons unnecessary. (Kiernan 2010) Therefore, the realist explanation depends primarily on the statements of motivation by the key policy-makers "who have vested interests in explaining the choices they made would serve national interest best". (Sagan 1997: 63)

The domestic politics model, though accepts the existence of threats to national security in the international system, seen as more malleable and subject to interpretation. Hence, security threats are not the central cause of nuclear weapons policies of nations according to this model. They are considered "mere windows of opportunity through which parochial interests can jump". (Sagan 1997: 65) But the main point of reference for this model is the domestic actors consisting of the scientific community, professional military personnel and the politicians who encourage or discourage governments from pursuing the bomb. These actors, to satisfy their parochial interests and to "justify their existence" sometimes form "coalitions" that are strong enough to control the government's policy-making process, either through their direct political power or indirectly through their control of information. From this perspective, one can expect that the nuclear arming decision or a reversal decisions do not occur when external security threats are increased or diminished respectively; rather they are taken when the scientific-military-industrial complex initiate to do so or also sometimes policies are arrived at with the occurrence of major internal political changes. Sagan advocates that this model most strongly fits the Indian nuclear weapons discourse to which he terms as "unusual nature". (Sagan 1997: 68)

But Sagan's third model (norms model) suggests that nuclear policies are shaped neither purely by the bureaucratic interests, nor by security rational; rather they are conditioned by "deeper norms and shared beliefs" of a nation about what actions are legitimate and appropriate in international relations. This model emphasises the importance of roles, routines, rituals as individual and organisational interests are shaped by the social roles as much as through reasoned decisions. This highlights that nuclear weapons programmes serve symbolic functions reflecting leaders' perceptions and policies reflecting a state's identity. Therefore, Sagan calls the phenomenon as "nuclear symbolism" to which Joseph Nye Jr. termed "Nuclear Ethics". (Nye Jr. 1986) It is perceived that possession of nuclear weapons enhances international prestige and status of a state. States possessing these arms are given greater weight in international discourse; they are brought into more top level international discussions of all kinds and their views are treated with greater respect. For example, owing to the possession of nuclear arsenals, UK and France who have fallen behind Japan and Germany in economic strength are still considered great powers. Thus, according to this model, states may seek nuclear weapons: to maintain or achieve great power status; to be assured of a seat at the "head table" in international forums; to enhance their prestige within a region or grouping of states; to address a perceived inferiority in international hierarchy; and to demonstrate political independence and self-reliance to be able to resist political pressures from the nuclear superpowers. (Epistein 1977: 21–22) Whether the domestic political constituencies like political parties are influenced by these considerations especially in Indian context is examined subsequently.

However, it is also viewed that renouncing of nuclear weapons programme by a country also equally elevates its political stature and prestige. (Epistein 1977: 22) Then, why some states chose to continue with nuclear weapons irrespective of all international pressure when renouncing them promises equal pay-offs? This involves the perceptions of the policy-makers conditioned by security situation, culture, personality traits and domestic political environment, etc. Therefore, theorising nuclear weapons policy-making in absolute terms is not an easy task. Security requirements, national priorities and national objectives of nations differ widely; so also are their policies and strategies for the reason that at any certain point of time, state behaviour is conditioned by plethora of variables. "Rational" policy-makers only decide which alternative would minimise loss and maximise national gain. The policy-maker makes a "rational choice" that consists of selecting such alternatives whose consequences rank highest in the "policy-makers' payoff function". (Simon 1955) However, differences in policy-making groups or agents often result in policy shifts or alternations.

Survey of Literature

Though, there is no dearth of literature on India's nuclear arming behaviour, a comparative study on the domestic sources of nuclear policy-making, especially on the role of the major political parties, is unavailable. Only there exist stray attempts by many on the policies of individual parties. At the conceptual level, only a handful of writers have examined the role of domestic constituencies or institutions in national policy-making. The realist thinkers in India take-up many internal impetuses (e.g., domestic politics, leaders' perceptions and state's intention based on its civilisation, etc.) along with Kenneth Waltz's structural formulations, to explain India's foreign policy and national decision making than explaining systemic process in international politics. (Zakaria 1999; Gideon 1998)

Since nuclear weaponisation is a sensitive issue, role of domestic variables in shaping nuclear policy becomes more visible. A normative understanding of the role of norms in nuclear policy-making explains that democracies do not act more peacefully than authoritarian regimes on nuclear matters *per se,* but generally take a more determined position on the bomb (Frey 2006). While they might be more prone to the "nuclear myth" with regard to the acquisition of nuclear weapons, they are more committed to the "nuclear taboo" with regard to their use.[4, 5] But nuclear arming decision-making does not stand alone. There exist a causal relationship between the role of national agents and the international system. James Rosenau was one among the first scholars to call attention to this area by his taxonomy of "linkage politics". (Rosenau 1969) To him, domestic politics and international relations are often entangled; there always exist a correlation between "domestic and international conflict behaviour" and national policies are mere manifestations of this complex entanglement. But his explanation does not sort out the puzzling tangle as questions like "when", "how" and "why" states behave the way, are not been clarified.

The *domestic-international linkage* is conceptually looked into by Robert D. Putnam in his article "Diplomacy and domestic politics: the logic of two-level games" (*International Organisation,* 42(3) 1988). Putnam's generic observation is that international discourse is somehow linked to national affairs and national affairs in turn shape the nuclear behaviour of the nation. Very often this linkage politics turns into "conflict behaviour" and the final shape of a state's nuclear policy evolve and guarded by the "state strength" or structural factors. At the national level, domestic groups pursue their interests by pressurising the government to adopt favourable policies, and politicians seek power by constructing coalitions among those groups. (Putnam 1988) At the international level, national governments seek to maximise their own ability to satisfy domestic pressures while minimising the adverse consequences of foreign developments. Thus, national political leaders appear at a double-edged calculation. On the other hand, a state is not a unitary actor; it is conceptualised as a "poliarchy" composed of actors with varying preferences, who share power over policy-making and domestic politics is more influential than international factors, thus *domestic political explanations of state behaviour* are more appealing. (Milner 1997)

In the context of domestic-international interface, interests, institutions and information, all explain the *rational choice* in policy-making. But statesmen find themselves in a double-edged calculation of constraints and opportunities involved both at the domestic and international level. (Evans et al. 1993) This line of argument reveals that there exist an intrinsic relationship between regime-type and policy-making, and the bargaining that take place between them.

The reason to bring domestic politics more explicitly into the study of nuclear behaviour of a country is the existence of a relationship between domestic political coalitions and alternative nuclear postures. (Solingen 1994) Etel Solingen argues that the study of this linkage can provide additional insights into why certain nations veil their nuclear weapons programmes and defy widely-accepted international norms. To him, countries ruled by coalitions of social and economic groups pursuing economic liberalisation are more likely to cooperate internationally on nuclear nonproliferation than are countries ruled by inward-looking coalitions with radical fundamentalist ideologies.

Though Solingen's assertion bears some truth, it cannot be universal. Especially in case of India, it is just the opposite. Under Nehru's leadership though India was an inward looking economy, extended all support for global non-proliferation initiatives. In contrast, under Narsimha Rao's coalition government, known for its LPG (Liberalisation, Privatisation and Globalisation) programme in restructuring economy-making it outward-looking, India did not embrace Pakistani overture for a nuclear-free-zone rather was preparing for a test in 1995 that was caught by the US surveillance. It is the same coalition government that categorically rejected India's adherence to NPT in 1995. This peculiar Indian behaviour needs deeper introspection.

Raj Chengappa in the *Weapons of Peace* (2000) asserts that, for long, India's nuclear issue has remained confined to small, incestuous circle of strategic experts. Also much of India's true nuclear history remains oral, but the nuclear question straddle almost everything fundamental to India as a nation. A coherent authoritative official document on India's nuclear history is not available and therefore there exists considerable dissension and misperception.

(Subrahmanyam 1998) However, apart from the scientific aspect of building the bomb, there was its military dimension and more importantly the political, ideological and even economic rationale that had to be fathomed. However, the evolution of India's nuclear weapons programme has a chequered history. It has traveled from a point of nuclear aversion to the "option open" policy otherwise known as "recessed deterrence" (Singh 1998) to which many also say it as 'nuclear ambiguity'. However, this policy finally culminated in a "credible minimum deterrence" posture with a triad force structure consisting of aircraft, mobile land-based missiles and sea-based assets. (NSAB, "India's Nuclear Doctrine 1999")

Literature on the evolution of Indian political system vis-à-vis its nuclear policy is non-existent. One can find the enormous growth in organisational and functional aspects of political parties in the post-Independence period and how they have emerged as stable entities in the national security discourse. In an article "Parties under Pressure" (2005), K.C. Suri narrates how the gradual increase in the importance of nuclear weapons in the national security discourse is co-terminous with the gradual consolidation of party politics in the country. In the same tone, William Walker in an article "Viewpoint: India's Nuclear Labyrinth" in *The Nonproliferation Review* (1996), asserts that India's *body politik* remains deeply attached to the nuclear discourse and its domestic political and psychological dependence on nuclear weapons has tended to increase. The reason, as advanced by Todd S. Sechser, being the domestic political incentives that played critical roles each time in their evolution. To that extent, A.N. Ram in the *Riding the Nuclear Tiger* (1999) points out that India's 1998 tests were a direct consequence of a series of domestic factors, including the ruling BJP's desire to ward off hardliners, heighten its future re-election prospects, bolster its position among coalition government allies, and be seen as a "promise-keeping" party. He asserts that the 1998 nuclear tests were a "reactionary departure" from a well-conceived and tested policy which balanced commitment to independence and peace and this longstanding chauvinist goal of the Hindu Right has hijacked India's nuclear policy.

By applying the *domestic politics model of proliferation*, Weixing Hu in an article "New Delhi's Nuclear Bomb: A Systemic Analysis" in the *World Affairs* (2000) identifies the parochial interests of political forces in a domestic power struggle where he explains that when the international level bargaining on India's nuclear status failed, the domestic discussion was doomed to produce strong resistance against the international non-proliferation regime. This defiant national sentiment probably paved the way for the BJP's nuclear decision in 1998.

Beyond these conceptual and theoretical arguments, analysis of the general *national sentiment* towards the bomb and the *attitude and motivation* of individual political parties, their ideology, personality of political leaders and their motivation towards nuclear issue would be more revealing. Timothy D. Hoyt in a paper "Shades of Realism: The Impact of Personality, Ideology, and Systemic Pressures on Indian Foreign Policy" (2003) examines the role of ideas, individuals, organisations and institutions within the state and consequent structural pressures to explain state behaviour. But an objective evaluation entails that there is an element of "circularity" and "ad hoc-ism" to which Ashok Kapur in the book *India's Nuclear Option: Atomic Diplomacy and Decision Making* (1976) says the "scientific and political czarism" premised on the attitudinal factors of the politico-bureaucratic community. His study directs attention to a need to investigate the interaction between politicians and scientists and other advisors in and outside the government. Perhaps keeping this aspect in mind, Praful Bidwai and Achin Vanaik in the book *South Asia on a Shot Fuse* (1999) says, the crucial explanations for India going nuclear must be sought on the domestic terrain of Indian politics. But, the real difference between different political parties on nuclear policy is not defined in these studies. Only in the *BJP and the Evolution of Hindu Nationalism: From Periphery to Centre* (1999) by Partha S. Ghosh distinguishes BJP's nuclear track-record with the Congress where he says it is "moreover form than substance". But, the study does not bring this comparison with the left parties.

How the domestic politics influenced BJP's decision is attempted by Kanti Bajpai in a paper titled "The BJP, Domestic Politics in India, and the Bomb" (2006). In judging the contours of domestic politics vis-à-vis nuclear policy-making, he asks the question: if the BJP had not come to power in March 1998, would the test have happened anyway? And in his analysis, the answer is "probably not". In the same line of argument, Sumit Sarkar in his article "The BJP Bomb and Aspects of Nationalism" (1998) refutes the BJP's official explanation on the test as a response to the growing threat to national security, saying that relation with both China and Pakistan that time was improving. Even he refutes the electoral imperatives that prompted BJP to go for the test; rather he locates the cause of the test in the BJP's organisational and ideological spectrum.

However, the left fraction of India's political discourse represents no single monolithic party (Suri 2005) and equally their pronouncements have been inconsistent and contradictory. The book *Conduct of India's Foreign Policy* (1996) by K. D. Mathur and P. M. Kamath brings out this aspect highlighting how these parties are against military pacts, but not with communist countries; they favour disarmament, but advocate Communist military strength; they demand banning of nuclear weapons, but approve building of the China's nuclear arsenal; they oppose manufacture of nuclear weapons in India, sometimes on shady grounds. The volume fails to answer to what extent they influence the Government's nuclear and foreign policy? In fact, the foreign policies of the Marxist Party CPI(M) are similar to the CPI except that they want complete recasting of foreign policy to suit China's objectives. They think that India's security is threatened not so much by China or Pakistan as by the United States. {CPI(M)}, *Political-Organisational Report of the Central Committee 1968*; Banerjee 1966)

The Communist Party of India (Marxist) publication *Against Nuclear Jingoism* (1998), a collection of views from statements from *People's Democracy,* where leaders like Harkishan Singh Surjeet, N. Ram, Prakash Karat and Sitaram Yechury have linked the nuclear test with Hindutva agenda and warned the nuclear weaponisation pursuit is a disastrous course and branded it as Jingoism that the BJP-led government followed.

The above studies though touch and highlight different aspects of nuclear-political interface, left many gaps unattended. The fundamental question, to what extent the political parties have comparatively contributed in the evolution of India's nuclear weapons discourse remains unanswered. Whether the party or the leadership of the party has a major role in the process?

Questions and Assumptions

This study is primarily trying to explain the normative nuclear arming choice of India and the role of political institutions, especially Indian political parties, in the process. This study attempts to address, several questions in fact; the issues around which Indian nuclear weapons debate revolves round. Firstly, if norms of "nuclear taboo" prevail over the norms of "nuclear myth" then why does India's case represent the reverse trend? It is seen, out of the 30 states that have military nuclear potential and capable of launching a nuclear weapons programme on short notice, 28 are democracies. If democracies tend to display more determination on nuclear choice, then, why India followed an ambiguous nuclear policy for half a century? If the normative disposition of a country towards nuclear weapons is rooted in the identity of its society, the societal debate in turn are fostered by political parties having their root in the ideological and political inclination of the general mass.

It is seen that the three political parties have taken different stands at different times on the issue of nuclear weapons. Why is this so? Is it only because their respective ideological inclinations prompted them to do so? As viable institutions, their party ideology remains constant, but why is it that at different situations these parties take different positions on the same issue? Or is it only their electoral strategy that changes from election to election, in turn their stand on different national issues? The party leadership is an important factor, which determines the behaviour of a party in many ways. But domestic political circumstances (electoral politics) and the presence of weak governments do not often allow national political leaders to make concessions on sensitive issues like nuclear weapons. Even strong party leaders do not always take hard decisions.

At times, domestic environment gets linked with the global environment and thereby domestic political discourse accordingly gets shaped. Political parties, as stakeholders in domestic environment, effectively respond to the external stimuli. But do they compromise their ideological inclinations while responding to the external stimuli? How far the three political parties have responded while taking stands on India's nuclear programme? Is India's nuclear doctrine, in any way, an outcome of BJP's response to the external stimuli? Are the responses of the Left parties, who urge India to give up nuclear weapons, also linked to the developments in the external environment? Was India's ambiguous nuclear posture in any way deliberate? Why only the BJP, not Congress and Left parties, took the nuclear test decision after 24 years of the first underground test in 1974?

These and many other research questions are discussed in the study with the broad assumptions that (1) national political leadership is more a determining factor than the political parties in India's nuclear weapons decision making; and (2) India's nuclear policy does not change with the change in government. Sometimes it changes despite the same party forms the government again. The fundamental questions on which the study rests are: Do political parties and domestic politics account for India's nuclear weapons decision-making? If yes, in what way, and to what extent?

As the three political parties in India have sustained opinion on the nuclear discourse, the study looks into policies and deliberations of the Indian National Congress, the Communist Party of India (Marxist) and the Bhartiya Janata Party. The Aam Admi Party (AAP), a recent phenomenon in Indian politics, though reportedly linking its mobilisation strategy with the anti-nuclear movement in Tamil Nadu, has yet to form its stand on India's nuclear weapons policy.

Thus, the scope of the study is confined to the systemic national nuclear debate, nature of these party organisations and ideologies, nature of their leadership, and electoral strategies in the context of India's nuclear weapons policy. It identifies the linkage of all these with the matrix of *national identity conception,* leaders' identity types, emotional patterns and opposing effects of normative nuclear pre-disposition. The study also looks into whether the three parties have followed different policies at different situations. A comparative study is undertaken, taking into account the three parties' nuclear weapons policy vis-à-vis their position in the domestic politics; broadly, it examines to what extent they have influenced India's nuclear weapons policy during her evolution to the stage, where it stands today. The subsequent chapter specifically provides a base to the entire study by looking into India's political system, nature of domestic politics, relative electoral position of various political parties, and their interest in nuclear weapons discourse, in other words, the *domestic linkage of India's nuclear weapons discourse.*

Notes

1. Dominant party system which rest primarily upon the capacity of a single leader, who enjoys wide public appeal, is without a dominant competition within the party or without.
2. The US Department of Defence brings out all important policy formulations like the Nuclear Posture Review, Nuclear Weapon Systems

Sustainment Programs, etc. Also the Congressional Research Service, a think tank that provides reports to members of Congress on a variety of topics relevant to current political events including information on nuclear arsenals.

3. The main expectations of realism or, more accurately, neo-realism are: (1) the recurrence of balances of power in the world political system; (2) the tendency of states to balance, that is, to strengthen, themselves in the face of foreign threats; and (3) the inclination of states to imitate one another and to become socialised to the international system. Realists say that states usually balance against the most serious military threats to their security; rarely do they bandwagon, that is, accommodate or appease those making threats. States can try to balance "internally" by relying on their own military capabilities or "externally" by relying on the military capabilities of allies. Defence planners generally prefer internal balancing, because it leaves less to chance and less to the will of others; however, this strategy requires levels of national determination and resources that are beyond the reach of many countries.
4. Common belief is that nuclear weapons protect a country by deterring potential aggressors from attacking. By threatening massive retaliation, the argument goes nuclear weapons prevent an attacker from starting a war.
5. One of the key calculations of the non-nuclear state springs from the taboo, which is an unwritten international prohibition since the Hiroshima and Nagasaki attacks that nuclear weapons should not be used, especially against non-nuclear states. Non-nuclear initiators thus believe that the nuclear defender is self-deterred through the operation of the taboo in addition to other possible restraints. The presence of taboo can be inferred from the fact that there exists no international law or treaty that explicitly bans the use of nuclear weapons, and yet nuclear states have refrained from making use of their advantage in armed confrontations vis-à-vis nonnuclear states, even when such attacks would have made military sense.

2

The Political-Nuclear Interface

The remark, nuclear weapon has an "awesome appearance on the political scene" (Walcolmson 1985: ix) captures the essence of the chapter that follows written purely in the Indian context. The contour of nuclear decision-making in general and India's in particular, has many facets. Only the domestic political aspect of it is the focus of this section. It is viewed that the answer to the question, *why did India develop its nuclear weapon capability when it did and the way it did* may lie somewhere in the politico-security spectrum. But, it is stupendous to demarcate the contours of politics from security in the context of nuclear weapons decision-making as politics always impinges upon security strategy and vice versa in a democracy. In the Indian context, the issue seems more complicated and the linkage not convincingly established. It is equally difficult to quantify the political pressure on India's nuclear weapons decision-making. Therefore, the link either remains a given or something worth exploring.

The System

To comprehend the domestic political scenario vis-à-vis the nuclear weapons discourse of India, one need to have a basic understanding on the structure and evolution of the Indian domestic-political fabric, thereby the nuances of domestic politics. For nearly two decades, Indian political scenario was dominated by the Congress Party. In 1967, non-Congress government led by temporary coalition arrangements among splintering parties tried for an alternative, though for short periods until BJP emerged as a right-wing national party. In the mean time, many regional parties emerged who started asserting their presence in the national security and foreign policy debate. India's nuclear weaponisation programme has evolved in such a politico-ideological background.

The political system of India is parliamentary democracy—a kind of democratic polity, wherein the supreme power rests in the body of people's representative called Parliament. It is a system in which Parliament enjoys a place of primacy and pre-eminence in governance of the country. (Kashyap 1987: 4) The Parliament consists of the executive i.e., the President and the legislature comprising two houses (Rajya Sabha and Lok Sabha). (Tripathi 2002) The maximum strength of the upper house (Rajya Sabha) is not more than 250 members; the maximum strength of the lower house (Lok Sabha) is 552.[1] Under the constitution of India, the head of the executive is the President, but act only on the "aid and advice" of the Council of Ministers with the Prime Minister at the head.[2] However, the relationship between the Executive and Legislature is one that is most intimate. Also the judiciary in India is an authority that coordinates with the legislature and the executive.

Effective checks and balances operate among the three branches of the government for which no organ transgress its assigned sphere. Rajni Kothari, while profiling Indian political system as "distinct" and "complex", argues that it should not be assessed by any supposedly universal (or Western) criterion (Kothari 1970). Also the functioning and nature of Indian state is matter of debate. The constitution of India though establishes a democratic state with a modern institutional framework, critics view it as centralised in nature, bureaucratic in form and capitalist in context. (Kashyap 1995; Lizphart 1996)

Moreover, periodic elections are held and a "functioning democracy" (Kohli 2001: 4) is firmly at place since independence. In spite of the existence of basic civil liberties, India's democracy has been "democracy from above" (Mitra 2003): for most of its existence, it has been more of a gift from the elite to the masses than something the masses have secured for themselves. "A tremendous concentration of power in the hands of a few and consequent elite-dominated political mobilisation are the undeniable features of Indian democracy". (Jayal 2007: 137)

The plethora of political parties and their role in national life is another crucial aspect of Indian political system. But any explanation on Indian political parties based only on the "interest group approach" (parties as discrete organisational entities apart from governmental institutions) may fail to grasp the systemic relationships of dominant and dissident structures in the articulation of which government and party are inextricably intertwined. Therefore, one needs to examine the party system in India not so much in the fashion of the interest aggregation theory but "as part of an interacting process of governmental penetration and performance at various levels". (Palmer 1971: 208) Therefore, Rajni Kothari says, "it is a party system with a difference oriented towards building and authoritative structure of political affiliations downward to the base, assimilating new and divergent interests upward to the centre, and weaving all these into a framework of organisation that was originally designed as an oppositional movement Indian politics...". (Kothari 1970: 154) In the same line, Paul Brass says, "party politics in India displays numerous paradoxical features, which reveal the blending of Western and modern forms of bureaucratic organisation and participatory politics with indigenous practices and institutions". (Brass 1990: 64)

With the process of the national political consolidation after three centuries of colonial domination, the Indian party system and political parties have been institutionalised to a high degree (Bhambhri 1999). The political ferment in the first few years of independence generated a highly conducive climate for the formation of political parties. And when the general elections came in 1951-52, there were a large number of political parties. "The total number of parties," according to the Election Commission of India, "went up to as many as 178, excluding the 14 recognised all-India parties...." (Election Commission of India 1955: 189) Although difficult to determine the exact number of parties formed in this country, it is believed that there were over 200 parties between the year 1947 and 1974. (Kothari 1970: 11) By 1997, the number of parties registered with the Election Commission rose to 291. The variation in their origin and organisation, size and strength and beliefs and behaviours are so wide and distinct that many are called parties only by courtesy. There was no standard method of classification of parties although smaller parties are often referred to as single issue parties, personality parties, election parties, local parties or minority parties for convenience. However, Indian political parties are generally divided as national and regional parties considering their area and capacity of operation though at many time, it is found that regional parties effectively influence national discourse.

The categorisation of political parties into national and state parties is too broad to reveal their real characteristics, essential

List of Political Parties in India

National Political Parties

1. Bahujan Samaj Party (BSP, led by Mayawati)
2. Bharatiya Janata Party (BJP led by Rajnath Singh)
3. Communist Party of India (CPI, led by A.B. Bardhan)
4. Communist Party of India (Marxist) (CPI(M), led by Prakash Karat)
5. Indian National Congress (INC, led by Sonia Gandhi)
6. Nationalist Congress Party (NCP, led by Sharad Pawar)

State Political Parties

1. Aam Admi Party (AAP)
2. All India Forward Bloc (West Bengal)
3. All India Anna Dravida Munnetra Kazhagam (AIADMK, "All India Anna Federation for Progress of Dravidians") (Tamil Nadu, Puducherry)
4. All India Trinamool Congress (Meghalaya, West Bengal)
5. Arunachal Congress (Arunachal Pradesh)
6. Asom Gana Parishad ("Assam People's Federation") (Assam)
7. Biju Janata Dal (Orissa)
8. Communist Party of India (Marxist-Leninist) Liberation (Bihar)
9. Dravida Munnetra Kazhagam (DMK, "Federation for Progress of Dravidians") (Tamil Nadu, Puducherry)
10. Federal Party of Manipur (Manipur)
11. Indian Federal Democratic Party (Kerala)
12. Indian National Lok Dal ("Indian National People's Party") (Haryana)
13. Indian Union Muslim League (Kerala, registered as 'Muslim League Kerala State Committee')
14. Indigenous Nationalist Party of Twipra (Tripura)
15. Jammu and Kashmir National Conference (Jammu and Kashmir)
16. Jammu and Kashmir National Panthers Party (Jammu and Kashmir)
17. Jammu and Kashmir Peoples' Democratic Party (Jammu and Kashmir)
18. Janata Dal (Secular) ("Peoples' Party (Secular)") (Karnataka, Kerala)
19. Janata Dal (United) ("Peoples' Party (United)") (Bihar, Jharkhand, Nagaland)
20. Janathipathiya Samrakshana Samithy ("Association for Defence of Democracy") (Kerala)

21. Jharkhand Mukti Morcha (JMM) ("Jharkhand Liberation Front") (Jharkhand, Orissa)
22. Kerala Congress (Kerala)
23. Kerala Congress (Mani) (Kerala)
24. Lok Jan Shakti Party (Bihar)
25. Maharashtrawadi Gomantak Party (Goa)
26. Manipur People's Party (Manipur)
27. Marumalarchi Dravida Munnetra Kazhagam (Tamil Nadu)
28. Meghalaya Democratic Party (Meghalaya)
29. Mizo National Front (Mizoram)
30. Mizoram People's Conference (Mizoram)
31. Nagaland People's Front (Nagaland)
32. Pattali Makkal Katchi (Tamil Nadu, Puducherry)
33. Rashtriya Janata Dal ("National People's Party") (Bihar, Jharkhand)
34. Rashtriya Lok Dal ("National People's Party") (Uttar Pradesh)
35. Revolutionary Socialist Party (West Bengal)
36. Samajwadi Party ("Socialist Party") (Madhya Pradesh, Uttar Pradesh, Uttarakhand)
37. Shiromani Akali Dal (Party of Akal - Authority for the Political matters of Sikhs) (Punjab)
38. Shiv Sena ("Army of Shivaji") (Maharashtra)
39. Sikkim Democratic Front (Sikkim)
40. Telangana Rashtra Samithi ("Telengana National Association") (Andhra Pradesh)
41. Telugu Desam Party ("Telugu Nation Party") (Andhra Pradesh)
42. United Democratic Party (Meghalaya)
43. United Goans Democratic Party (Goa)
44. Uttarakhand Kranti Dal ("Uttarakhand Revolution Party") (Uttarakhand)
45. Zoram Nationalist Party (Mizoram)

Other Parties Represented in the Lok Sabha

1. All India Majlis-e-Ittehadul Muslimen
2. Bharatiya Navshakti Party
3. Janata Dal (Secular) (Surendra Mohan faction)
4. Loktantrik Jan Samta Party
5. National Loktantrik Party
6. Republican Party of India (Athavale)
7. Sikkim Democratic Front

Other Parties Represented in the Rajya Sabha

1. Swatantra Bharat Paksh

Table. 2.1 Splintering of Parties in India—National Elections 1951-2014

Year	*Parties with Seats*	*Parties Contesting*	*Vote Share (%) of Largest Party*
1951	22	53	45
1957	12	15	47.8
1962	20	27	44.7
1967	20	25	40.7
1971	24	53	43.7
1977	18	34	41.4
1980	18	36	42.7
1984	17	33	48.1
1989	24	113	39.5
1991	24	145	36.4
1996	28	209	20.3
1998	42	176	25.6
1999	38	169	23.8
2004	38	230	26.5
2009	---	364	28.55
2014	34	466	31

Source: Compiled from "Election Results-Full Statistical Reports", *Election Commission of India,* UR: http://eci.nic.in/eci_main/StatisticalReports/ElectionStatistics.asp.

difference among them and most importantly the proportion of their presence in the national political discourse. Vertically, they can be divided into four groups—the major, the medium, the minor, and the sub-minor upon the basis of their size and strength. (Markandan 1990: 783) Also horizontally, they can be divided on the basis of the ideology criterion. (Kumar 1986: 21, 44) Ideology, however, is not strictly adopted by every party. Therefore, it is prudent to consider their scope, extent, objectives and means adopted for achieving their objectives to distinguish them from other similar groups. On the basis of their objectives, S. N. Sadashivan has divided political parties in India into fourteen groups: the Social-Democratic groups, the Socialist group, the Marxian group and the Religious-Centric group, the Secessionist

(Autonomy) group, the Princely group, the Feudal group, the Linguist group, the Social Justice (denominational) group, the Liberal group, the legionary (Extremist) group, the regionalist group, the Tribal group and the anarchist group. (Sadashivan 1977: 22)

In pre-independence India, political parties were organised by a group of enlightened men, who wanted to improve Indian society or rouse political consciousness against the British rule. They were neither contenders for power nor had they taken shape in accordance with the demands of society. They were not the creations of a social will, but they had striven to create a social will. (Brass 2001) They were originated to educate and mobilise society for political action against the government. But, in the post-independence era, the political scenario of India gradually changed and accordingly the functioning and organisation of political parties has also been changed. Objective of political parties in the pre-independence period was not to contend for power, rather for freedom. (Suda 1966) In the post-independence period, the objective of political parties obviously has been to come to power and offer as alternative to the electorate to form government through the tactics of mobilisation. (Ralhan 1998) However, Indian political parties "maintain the tradition of subordinating constitutional paramountcy and restraints to sheer expediency and defiance of authority and disobedience to law" as a means to realise their ends. (Sadashivan 1977: 25)

In such a structure, based on their ideological and organisational ethos, different political parties take different stands on different issues and proportionately influence the national decision making process. Even the electoral compulsions and political process sometime influence national decisions more than anything else. Important issue like the nuclear weapons is no exception. The party that forms the government frames national nuclear policy, more or less, on the basis of its own ideological leanings, its perception of national interest and national security. Other parties outside the government also take positions on government policies by aggregating and articulating the opinion of the electorate. In multi-party systems, this becomes more complicated; moreover, in India, the national debate on nuclear issues sometimes seem more complex, may be owing to different decisions by different parties on the same issue depending upon the nature of the situation they perceive.

Currently, there are six national parties and more than three dozens of state parties in India (*Election Commission of India* 2004) who (sometimes) participate in the national nuclear policy debate. But for the purpose of this study and, in general, three major national parties are found consistently influencing India's attitude towards nuclear issues by virtue of their grip over power and influence on the electorate. They are: the Indian National Congress (INC), the Bharatiya Janata Party (BJP) and the Communist Party of India-Marxist (CPI-M). The following section looks into the evolution, organisation, and functioning of these parties as a prelude to the intended discussion on their stand on nuclear issues.

Indian National Congress (INC)

The birth of Indian National Congress in 1885 was not as a political party with well-defined ideology, but as a pressure group to mediate between Indian people and the British administration—petitioning the British government for political and administrative reforms. (Masselos 2005) Gradually, it became the instrument of Indian freedom struggle and a mass movement. By the time of independence, it was a mass-based organisation though controlled by middle class and business community. Nevertheless, it was amalgamating all strata and ideology, entrenched every corner of the country. (Borgohain 1982: 60-61) After independence, Mahatma Gandhi proposed for the dissolution of INC and to convert it into Lok Sevak Sangh to rid of the unhealthy competition of power. (Ghose 1991: 375) But, Sardar Patel took a diametrically opposed stand and wanted to purge the Congress of other political groups and sought to make a cohesive and disciplined political party. By amending its constitution in 1948, he transformed its all-embracing character to a close-knit political party of disciplined cadre with single ideology. (Hirose 1994: 76) Congress in its new role as a government party then combined the functions of continuing the political movement and of a political party of a nascent state embarking on liberal democratic political order. (Rudolph and Rudolph 2008: 15-39)

However, the Congress was a grand coalition with great historic antecedents, representing the Indian nation in most of its essentials. (Tripathy 1986: 13) From 1947 until it broke-down in 1967, the Party was at the centre of Indian politics spanning four distinct phases in its post-independence development. The first phase (1947-67) was the period of the 'Congress system'; the second phase (1967-77) was characterised by the decline and disintegration of the Congress system and the consolidation of power by a small oligarchy; the third phase (1978-84) witnessed the development of a new system because of the domination of Indira Gandhi and the party became Indira Congress or Congress (I) (Baxter 1993: 105); the last and current phase (from 1985 on) under Sonia Gandhi's leadership the party seems to have regained its status.[3]

The Indian National Congress is formally a mass party with "a dues-paying membership divided into two categories of primary and active members". (Brass 1994: 69) It has an elaborate, hierarchical organisational structure extending from local to district to state to all-India committees culminating at the top in a Working Committee, and the Executive Committee with an elected President as its head. The objective of the INC, according to its constitution, "is the well-being and advancement of the people and establishment in India, by peaceful and constitutional means, of a socialist state based on Parliamentary Democracy in which there is equality of opportunity, and of political, economic, social rights, which aims at world peace and fellowship" (Article I, *Constitution of Indian National Congress*). Since the beginning, the support base of the party remained much broader. But, a survey conducted by D. L. Sheth on Indian electorate in 1975 emphasises the aggressive character of the party, while concluding certain segments of population (the middle-aged and old-voters and less of the young, higher proportion of illiterates than highly educated voters, and more rural than urban supporters) lend their support disproportionately. Its occupational and caste-base is highly diversified with slightly greater supports from middle caste groups and Muslims. Though, its economic base is very broad based, slightly less support it receives from the higher income groups. (Sheth 1975) But, more recent study shows the mass-base of the party is rejuvenating with Sonia Gandhi, who cherishes the Gandhi family values and Rahul Gandhi who has embarked on mobilising the young generation. (Sood 2010)

Ideologically, the party is considered as centrist, committed to democracy, minority rights, secularism, a centralised form of federalism and mixed economy. (Hasan 2002: 9) The Party proclaims to have adhered to the ideology of "nationalism, secularism, democracy and socialism". (*Congress Sandesh*, Sonia Gandhi, Opening Remarks, AICC, April 6 1998) It also proclaims to operate under the banner of a secular, anti-imperialist and class-neutral nationalism. In its 1989 Election Manifesto, the Party had promised "power to the people" through Panchayati Raj and Nagarpalika. (*Congress Manifesto* 1989) From the very inception, the Congress Party has stood for a free, democratic, just and secular India. This mystification of Congress ideology goes back in Indian history to Mahatma Gandhi. From around 1920 to 1947, Gandhi was the leading figure in Indian political scene through the ideological direction that he provided to Congress. But his ideology did not live past him. Even his brightest follower, whom he liked most, did not follow his ideology. Nehru's dreams of modern India had nothing Gandhian about them. After Nehru, there was a brief interlude when Lal Bahadur Shastri in his position as the sole fountainhead of Congress ideology proclaimed "Jai Jawan, Jai Kissan".[4] Soon after, Indira Gandhi's vision of socialism was a departure from Gandhi, Nehru and Lal Bahadur Shastri. (Chawla 2004) Less than a decade after Indira Gandhi's death, it is the same Congress initiated economic reforms and demolished licence-permit-quota-raj, built assiduously by Indira Gandhi and Nehru. Its socialistic visions have gradually been driven towards capitalist orientations. The party now is the champion of economic reforms, liberalisation and globalisation. Therefore, the party has evolved through ideological contradictions and probably that is its greatest strength to swim across the changing situations. (Chawla 2004)

In terms of its role and position in the domestic politics, the Congress Party is the longest serving party that has formed government more times than any other political party in the national politics. Out of the 13 Prime Ministers of India, seven belong to the Congress Party alone.[5] However, its march from the early Independence period to the present form is not without thorns. The Party has suffered repeatedly from factional conflicts. (Bandhu 2003: 268) The Party organisation in the 1950s and 60s was highly factionalised, internally competitive, though within the paramount Congress ideology. (Singh 1981) However, Nehru remained in complete mastery of policy and politics of the Party. (Nair 2000: 53) When Nehru was Prime Minister, the equation between him and the Congress Party Presidents was both cordial and conflicting. J. B. Kripalini, Pattabhi Sitaramayya, Purusottam Das Tondon, U.N. Dhebar and N. Sanjiva Reddy were the Party Presidents who have great admiration for Nehru and his leadership. Also for two years (1953-54), Nehru himself was the Party President. On the other hand, when P.D. Tondon got elected as Party President in 1951 defeating Nehru's candidate Acharya Kripalini, Nehru had refused to join the Working Committee of Tondon. When five sessions of AICC failed to resolve this crisis, Tondon had to quit his office to make way for Nehru's candidate. (Sanghvi 2006: 38) However, he "never tried to combine the two posts, the Party chief and the office of the Prime Minister. There was no need for him to do that because of his stature". (Sanghvi 2006: 37)

The issue of who would be supreme—the Party President or the Prime Minister---was raised once by Acharya Kripalini, who suggested that the Prime Minister must submit to the party as he is the member of the party and owed the position to the Party. But Nehru disagreed by saying that the Prime Minister is responsible to the Lok Sabha and thus to the sovereigners–voters, therefore cannot subordinate his position to the party president. (Sanghvi 2006: 37) During Nehru's leadership, the Prime Minister played important role in determining the agenda of the Congress Working Committee, which is normally prepared by the Party President and the General Secretary. (Borgohain 1982: 23) Though different persons held office of the party during Nehru, every decision on policies was taken at Nehru's behest by the party, mainly for two reasons: (1) dominating personality of Nehru as Prime Minister; and (2) also as a person. (Sanghvi 2006: 38)

After Nehru, Indira Gandhi emerged as the influential leader of the party, which came to be called as Congress (R) for "Requisitioned"—referring to a requisitioned party meeting summoned by Mrs Gandhi during the split—but later meaning "Ruling Congress". (Brass 1994: 72) After a second split in 1977, the Congress of Mrs Gandhi became known as Indira Congress or Congress (I). Gradually, the party came to be controlled by personal retainers of the Nehru family. After Indira Gandhi, the party was led by Rajiv Gandhi, and for a short interregnum after him the leadership was with personalities outside Nehru family. After the assassination of Rajiv Gandhi in May 21, 1991 and with Sonia Gandhi's refusal to assume leadership, the party was directed by a group of Rajiv's closest followers. P.V. Narasimha Rao was the second Congress leader and Prime Minister (first was Lal Bahadur Shastri) not from the Nehru family and known to have taken many important decisions on the nuclear policy.

To strengthen the leadership and the organisation of the party, Mr Rao sought organisational elections, which were held in April 1992 and he was elected himself as the president of the party. The Congress, though formally known as a mass party, became a cadre-based party in the 1970s and 1980s with prominent popular leader at its head. (Brass 1994: 73) But, the party organisation at the local level was dominated by regional demagogues, who maintained strong local structures of powers, for example, Arjun Singh from Madhya Pradesh and Sharad Pawer from Maharashtra, et al., Deveraj urs, Tarkeshwari Sinha, Jankiballabh Patnaik, Ahmed Patel, Abdul Rehman Antulay, Kamalapati Tripathi, H N Bahuguna, K.Kamaraj, Marri Chenna Reddy, Anjaiah T, B P Chaliha, Shivcharan Mathur, Chiman Bhai Patel, Sitaram Kesari, Karpuri Thakur, Karunakaran and G K Moopanar. Pratap Singh Khairon Bhajan Lal. Subsequently, though the Congress remained a pre-eminent party, the system can no longer be considered as "one-party dominant" system. However, its pre-eminence is indicated by the still considerable interval between its popular vote and seat shares—even in 1989 and 1991—and that of the next largest party, which was 22 per cent in 1989 and 17 per cent in 1991 for vote shares and 10 and 22 per cent, respectively, for seat shares. (*Statistical Report on General Elections, 1991 to the Tenth Lok Sabha*, 1992) In the 2004 general election, the party has secured 27 per cent (145) of the total seats and 26.7 per cent of the total vote polled, and in 2009 election 28.55 per cent. (*Election Commission of India 2009*)

Since the last few decades, coalition making has been an imperative of Indian politics which has singularly influenced the functioning of every political party including the Congress Party. (Singh and Saxena 2008) Since 1967, the Congress Party has resorted to coalition building, sometimes even with ideologically incompatible parties, sometimes with difficult, assertive and potentially unruly regional allies and supporters. This, in fact, constrained many times its decision making choices. During 1991, Narasimha Rao was heading a coalition which known to have taken many important nuclear policy decisions. (Arnett 1998: 23) Since 2004, the Congress Party led coalition headed by Manmohan Singh successfully concluded the Indo-US nuclear deal though its left allies withdrew support. The political process in the country has seen many ripples over the debate on India-US relations and the Congress-led UPA government's decisions. Therefore, though Congress Party remains prominent, the political system of India is no longer considered a one-party dominant system. (Jain 1994: 163)

Bharatiya Janata Party (BJP)

The BJP is the reincarnation of the Jana Sangh, the Hindu nationalist party founded in 1951 by Shyama Prasad Mukherjee. Between 1989 and 1992, it emerged as the "most dynamic political force in the Indian party system". (Brass 1994: 87) Formally launched as an independent political organisation in February 1980, after split of the Janata Party on the RSS issue, most of the members of the erstwhile Jana Sangh, along with a few others, left the Janata Party to form the BJP. Therefore, it is viewed that the party has "continuity with the Jana Sangh in its discipline and well knit organisational set up and in its linkage". (Khan 1997: 246)

As far as party ideology is concerned, the BJP believes in "Gandhian socialism".[6] The party says that its socialism is inspired not only by Gandhi and Jayprakash Narayan but also by Deendayal Upadhyaya, who stood for "integral humanism", "Hindutva or Cultural Nationalism".[7,8] While laying emphasis on the Hindu idiom in its election manifestos, the BJP stands for "justice for all and appeasement of none" (BJP, *Vision Document 2004*). The Party favours smaller and stronger states, uniform civil code and desires to abolish Article 370. It strives for national power based upon an explicit appeal to Hindu nationalism. The basic idea it emphasises that "India is a Hindu country and that Hindus have a right to be proud of their history and culture and to draw the central symbols of national identity from them". (Brass 1994: 87) The BJP and its allied organisations like the Vishwa Hindu Parishad (VHP) have been seen to focus their appeal to Hindu identity around the creation of a new cult of *Ram* centred upon the drive to build a temple to *Ram* in Ayodhya. Though Hindu religious beliefs and symbols serve the BJP as a focus for creating a national identity, the party's goals, as it proclaims, are secular: *to transform India into a modern, industrial, military power with a united nation and a disciplined workforce.* (Saha 2004: 141) The BJP, while in power at the Centre, could not pursue ideological tenets such as Ayodhya or the Civil Code, may be to "different political affiliations", as told by its ideologue Vinay Katiyar to *Pioneer*, and may be also to ensure that its allies continue their support. (*Pioneer* 27 June 2004)

The BJP is viewed as one of the few parties in India to have a popular-based governing structure, but in reality its "organisation is weaker" and "lacks a cadre-based structure" that can penetrate below the district level to project its influence. (Adeney and Sáez 2005: 71) It has also been blamed for public spats between different factions of the party. The topmost leader in the Party is supposed to be the Party President who, according to its constitution, remains for a three-year term. There are several Vice-Presidents, General-Secretaries, Treasurers and Secretaries. The National Executive of the party consists of an undetermined number of senior party leaders from across the nation. It is the highest decision-making body in the party. At the state level, a similar structure is in place, with every state unit being led by the respective Presidents, who officially serves a three-year term. (Article VII: Organisational Structure, *BJP Constitution*, www.bjp.org) The rank-and-file leadership of BJP largely derives from the cadre of the Rashtriya Swayamsevak Sangh (RSS), which has millions of affiliates. It also maintains close links to other Sangh Parivar organisations, such as Vishwa Hindu Parishad and Swadeshi Jagran Manch. (Noorani 2000: Introduction)

Though the support base of the BJP is essentially the same as that of the erstwhile Jana Sangh, it has been increased subsequently over the years. Mostly, it is a party of the urban-educated Hindu middle class—professionals, small businessmen and white-collar workers. (Jayapalan 2001: 540) In 1967, when it won 36 seats in Lok Sabha with about eight per cent of the popular vote thereby emerging as the first national alternative to the Congress, the Jana Sangh has made the Congress (I) as well as the communists nervous. (Graham 1987) Therefore, they have allied in one form or the other to isolate it in Indian politics. In 1977 with 98 of its men in Parliament under the Janata banner, it received only three cabinet positions. In 1984, the BJP only secured two Lok Sabha seats but polled 7.4 per cent of the national votes, ahead of the Janata's 6.7 per cent votes. But the Party polled 12.58 per cent of votes in 1989. In 1991 Lok Sabha elections, the BJP emerged as major party by nearly doubling its national vote share from 12 per cent last time to 22 per cent. (Rana 2006: 382) It came second after Congress I winning 119 seats. In the Lok Sabha elections 1999, BJP secured 23.75 per cent of the vote polled and bagged 182 seats. In 2004, the Party secured 138 seats (25 per cent) and 22.2 per cent of the total vote polled. In 2009 general election, the Party won 116 seats (22 seats lesser than 2004) and 22.16 per cent of the total votes. (*India Election Affairs* 2009) It indicates that the Party has become vital political force, which strives to foster *integral nationalism*.

BJP's chief objective is to build "India as a modern, progressive and enlightened nation" drawing inspiration from India's ancient Hindu culture and values. (*Manifesto: Lok Sabha Election 2009*) The key ideologue of the party, Deendayal Upadhyaya, who authored the *Integral Humanism*, laid down the foundations for this view. According to him, the very source of meaning in Indian society is the concept of "national identity". The BJP perceives that demonstrable military power was an essential component of its drive to create a great India. (Kundu 2004: 10) Nuclear weapons, therefore, are viewed by the party as currency-of-power without which India would never be taken seriously on the world stage. Probably this was the reason why BJP advocated for the nuclear tests as overt display of nuclear weapons is essential to ensure national security.

Another important aim of the party is to achieve full territorial and political integration of Jammu & Kashmir with India. Therefore, it advocates for strong national defence, small government and free-market economic policies, but *Hindutva* and Integral Humanism have been its core philosophy and identity. The "BJP and its supporters feel India must remain vigilant against threats from Pakistan, the People's Republic of China, and elsewhere such as Bangladesh and even the LTTE in Sri Lanka". (Pandey, Internet source) As per the party's constitution, the objectives of the party is "to build up India as a strong and prosperous nation, which is modern, progressive and enlightened in outlook and which proudly draws inspiration from India's ancient culture and values and thus is able to emerge as a great world power playing an effective role in the comity of Nations for the establishment of world peace and a just international order." (Article II: Objective, *Constitutioin and Rules Bharatiya Janata Party*) The Party aims at establishing a democratic state which guarantees to all citizens irrespective of caste, creed or sex, political, social and economic justice, equality of opportunity and liberty of faith and expression. However, the core agenda of the BJP is inspired by Hindu nationalism.[9]

Communist Party of India (Marxist)

The CPI(M) is an offshoot of the leftist movement in the country. Since the 1930s, the Left movement in India has been broadly divided into two streams—Socialist and Communist. After independence, these two broad streams have split into several political parties. But, the post-independence history of splits and mergers culminated in the division of the Communist movement into two main political parties in 1964: the CPI(M) has support base in West Bengal, Tripura (for a decade only), Kerala; the Communist Party of India or CPI has base in Kerala, West Bengal and Bihar. While the CPI is considered as right faction, the CPI(M) is known as the left faction of the Communist movement in India. But it claims to be the legitimate communist party of India.

In respect to party structure, policies and management, the CPI(M) is no different to other political parties with its organisation in most of the states. It has 19 State Committees and seven

State Organising Committees. But the party's bastions have only been Kerala, West Bengal and Tripura. The General Secretary is the top leader and an 87-member Central Committee is the highest policy making body of the Party. But the day-to-day running of the party is reviewed, managed and crucial decisions taken are by the apex politburo.[10]

As far as the ideology of the CPI(M) is concerned, it proclaims to inherit the progressive, anti-imperialist and revolutionary traditions of the Indian people. The Party proclaims to have "modified its pro-Chinese stance and sought direct the communist movement in accordance with the political and historical realities existing in India". (Malik et al. 1998: 123) Under the leadership of Jyoti Basu and E.M.S. Namboodiripad, the Party adopted an independent course for Indian communists, maintaining distance from both the Chinese and Soviet Communist parties. The Party has sought to independently apply Marxism-Leninism to Indian conditions and to work out the strategy and tactics for a people's democratic revolution, which can transform the lives of the Indian people. ("About Us", *CPI(M) official website*) Initially, the party favoured the tactic of united front from bellow and alliance with peasants and workers to defeat the Congress which it regarded as part of bourgeoisie. The constitution of the party reads that it is the "revolutionary vanguard of the working class of India. Its aim is socialism and communism through the establishment of the dictatorship of the proletariat. In all its activities, the party is guided by the philosophy and principle of Marxism-Leninism which shows to the toiling masses the correct way to the ending of exploitation .... The Party keeps high the banner of proletarian internationalism." (Article II, *Constitution and the Rules under Constitution*, CPI(M))

The support base of the party is the middle and lower classes. The working class, agricultural labour, poor peasants and employees concentrated mainly in West Bengal, Kerala and Tripura are its bases. Regarding the electoral performance of the party, and its position among parties, it is the third group in the Parliament. Since its formation in 1964, the CPI(M) has gradually increased its popular votes polled in the elections. In the last few elections, contesting on an average 15 per cent of the total seats, the CPI(M) has been getting around 6 per cent of the votes. In the 2004 elections to the Lok Sabha, it won 44 seats adding 11 more to its earlier tally of 33 in the 1999 elections. (*Elections*, Communist Party of India (Marxist)) According to the official website of the Party, the membership of the Party, which was 118,683 at the time of its formation, has grown to 10, 17, 444 in 2008. ("About Us", *CPI(M) official website*) The Party's official website proclaims that the significance of this development "lies not only in projecting the growing strength of the Left and its increasing relevance but also the vantage position that it has acquired in Indian politics". (CPI(M), *An Introduction*, www.cpim.org) The Party *Programme* claims that "the Communist movement has played a progressive role in Indian politics since inception. With its mass base, popular appeal and its alternative policies to the bourgeois-landlord regime, the Communist movement is a significant force in the country's political and social life". (*CPI(M) Programme*, www.cpimkerala.org)

Electoral Positions of the Parties

Arguably, India possesses the most complex political party system in the world (Bell 2000). "Combining a first-past-the-post, single-member district system with intense regional differences, and serious religious divides, India finds itself stuck with a plethora of political parties". (Bell 2000: *Internet Source*) In the 1996 Lok Sabha elections, no fewer than 209 political parties participated (Election Commission of India, *Statistical Report on General Elections 1996*); some parties competed nationally but most of the parties contested only on a regional or local basis. With this variety in political voices with world's second largest population, India's achievement of coalition government is equally miraculous. However, two overlapping trends can be marked in Indian political scene. One, since Independence till 1967, the Congress party had dominated the Indian political scene to such an extent that India was often described as a "one party dominant system". (Pye 2004: 44-59) Two, since the late 1960s, "minority parties in Parliament have often been majority parties in state legislatures and, single political parties have generally failed to win a parliamentary majority, particularly since 1989". ("Country Studies Program", *Internet source: www.mongabay.com*) As a result, parliament is often run by coalitions of political parties.

In the 1962 Lok Sabha elections, the Congress Party continued its impressive 20-year run, winning 74 per cent of the seats in the Lok Sabha with 45 per cent of the popular vote. No other opposition party won more than six per cent of the seats in the Lok Sabha that year. However, the 1967 elections brought an end to Congress dominance in national politics. (Morris-Jones 1967) But the party managed to sweep victory in 1971, gaining 44 per cent of the vote, and 68 per cent of the seats in the Lok Sabha. (Heginbotham 1971: 1133) For the first time in Indian politics, the opposition was united and prepared to challenge Congress dominance. The Janata Party, a coalition formed by a variety of anti-Congress forces, ran their campaign against the internal emergency government of Indira Gandhi, and won support of the electorate, winning 55 per cent of the seats in the Lok Sabha (compared to Congress's 28 per cent) with 41 per cent of the popular vote. However, after Indira Gandhi, Rajiv Gandhi took office as prime minister and solidified the Party's control of the legislature in 1985, winning 76 per cent of the seats in the Lok Sabha partly owing to the sympathy for the assassination of his mother. (Nikolenyi 2009)

By 1989, the Congress seemed to have lost direction and lacked any coherent strategy to advance. It could win only 197 seats in the Lok Sabha. Owing to the lack of any clear majority, a government was formed by a coalition of the Janata Dal, the BJP, and the two Communist parties. However, owing to internal conflicts and a lack of cohesion in the coalition, Congress party returned to power in 1991. It won 46 per cent of the seats in the Lok Sabha, with 37 per cent of the vote, and was able to manage a coalition. The 1991 elections also saw the rise of BJP. (Nikolenyi 2009) It gained 22 per cent of the seats in the 1991 Lok Sabha elections emerged as the main opposition to the Congress government. As Narasimha Rao, the Congress Prime Minister, suffered corruption charges, public support for the BJP grew. In 1996, BJP won 30 per cent of the seats in the Lok Sabha, compared to Congress's 26 per cent, despite receiving a smaller percentage of the popular vote. However, as the BJP was unable to devise a coalition, a government was formed by the United Front (communist and leftist parties) and Congress, with H.D. Deve Gowda as prime minister. In 1998, the collapse of this coalition necessitated a fresh election. This time, BJP had learned to devise pre-poll alliances. The result was a victory for the BJP, which won 180 seats (short of majority) but was able to gather 264 representatives to support a vote of confidence. (Karat 2004) The Congress won only 141 seats, and became the main opposition party. In 1999, another set of elections occurred, due to the collapse of the ruling coalition. Voters once again supported the BJP, giving it 34 per cent of the seats in the Lok Sabha and 24 per cent of the popular vote. Congress, while amassing a greater share of the popular vote, was only able to secure 21 per cent of the seats, and saw the BJP once again form a coalition.

While the past 40 years of Indian politics has been the story of the Congress Party, the rise of Hindu nationalist party in the early 1990s has provided the electorate at best another alternative to the Congress. Other parties and groups more or less have been catalysts or determining factors in the coalition formation. It is already mentioned, the CPI(M), after the split from the CPI in 1964, is successfully contesting every Lok Sabha election and has been supported well in Kerala, West Bengal, and Tripura. It has grown stronger than the CPI, and now obtaining around 4-7 per cent of the seats in the Lok Sabha. (Karat 2004)

Within this electoral-political framework, India's nuclear policy has evolved. As discussed in the previous chapter, the nuclear governance and decision making necessitates the political guardians to decide if their nation needs to acquire nuclear weapons and also the modalities of their up-keep and use. The "logic of political survival" is often linked with and as a determining factor in a nation's nuclear discourse. Domestic constituencies like political leaders, political parties and domestic politics are normally the governing factors in a democratic set up. The decision-maker has to balance between the political survival of the group he belongs to and national nuclear ambitions. Therefore, it is pertinent to enquire if there is any threat to the incumbent governments' survival when India's nuclear decisions were taken. Before investigating this linkage, it is also pertinent to have a cursory look at the nomenclature of India's current nuclear weapons policy.

The Interface

In the view of lack of archive material owing to the oral decision making tradition, tracing the exact contours of political-nuclear interface in India is difficult. Perhaps for the fear of security leaks and danger of foreign agents getting access to secret records, hard documentary evidences were not maintained. Therefore, nuclear policy decisions of India, says Ashok Kapur, were almost "a kind of tacit agreement" (Kapur 1976: 21). However, he views that India's nuclear policy "represents a political response" and the "domestic factors, including moral and political norms", have been more significant in determining India's nuclear policy. Further, he says that the "tensions between domestic interests have made this policy appear ambivalent and ambiguous. . . . India's domestic imperative . . . policymaking processes and institutions also have affected its nuclear history: Indian political leaders and the leading scientists have consciously excluded the military from nuclear decision making, again for internal reasons."

To outline the role the domestic constituencies play in shaping India's nuclear decision-making, one need to look into the Indian political fabric and the functioning of the constitutional set up. Many scholars argue that, the most important factor which influences India's decision on nuclear weapons is the domestic politics, especially the political parties and their leaders. But the *political-nuclear interface* is not forthright in a multi-party democracy like India. (Jha 2002) Moreover, the issue of nuclear decision-making is far more complicated in a parliamentary system where the supremacy of parliament and the prerogative of the executive to take initiative are integrated into the system (Paranjpe 1997: vii). Thus, the executive privilege on the one hand and the ability of the Parliament to influence the policy formulation (Sen 2007: 45) on the other is the crux of the debate when the role of political parties in formulation of nuclear policy is in question. In other words, it is to trace how successive Prime Ministers or political leaders have shaped national nuclear discourse and how other stakeholders such as different political parties and members have used the legislature to influence the same.

At one level, one finds the nuclear issue purely as a domestic concern related to the problem of development of a Third World state striving to achieve scientific and technological aspects of modernisation. (Sabato and Ramesh 1980: 37) At another level, one can find the security or strategic implications of nuclear policy both on the regional and global discourse. (Chand 1993: Chapter 3) But the intriguing aspect is how these decisions are arrived at through the twists and turns between the executive and legislature. Generally, best decisions are taken by striking a balance between the executive privilege and popular control through the legislature. (Milner 1997: 119) If John Lock's idea on government—legislature is incapable of handling foreign policy issues and the executive should be given open-ended right on these matters in the interest of public good (Locke 1821)—is any guide, most of nuclear weapons decisions have so far seem to have been solely taken by the executive covertly. However, stakeholders in the legislature (the opposition political parties and leaders) have always raised the issue thereby influencing course of policy in many ways. The debate that arises out of the issue provides sufficient fodder for domestic politics. But politics has intrinsic relation with ideology (Schwarzmantel 2008) that forms a prism through which alternative policy suggestions evolve. Also nuclear issues attract wider audience (Eiser et al. 1995), therefore, every political faction form their opinion and try to acquire a foothold in the discourse. India's body *politik* is no exceptions to these thumb rules.

A cursory look at the evolution of India's nuclear debate brings home the impression that nuclear weapons though debated in the political and scientific circle in the early days, was never preferred as immediate option. Views in favour of nuclear weapons programme started to emerge in the political-strategic circle vigorously only after the 1962 Chinese invasion and subsequent nuclear tests by China. (Subrahmanyam 1998: 26-27) Within the Congress Party, some leaders started to question government's policy of non-weaponisation. For example, K.C. Pant, then a young leader, advocated for nuclear weapons at the 69th Annual Session of AICC at Durgapur, 1965. There are numerous instances of Parliamentary debates over India's nuclear options. But, there was no unanimity among the political parties and leaders over the issue, at least up to 1970. (Nanda 1971: 38-41)

Differences amongst various political parties and leaders (discussed in detail subsequently) over the issue of the necessity of nuclear weapon for India can clearly be demarcated. Debates over this issue in the Parliament in the post-1962 period, though could not decide whether India need nuclear weapons, mark increasing concern over the security implications of a nuclear China. The table below is based on a survey conducted by Ashis Nandy, an Indian political-psychologist, on the attitudes of Indian elite on nuclear arms, conducted in 1972, much before the right-wing BJP's emergence. His findings show that the Congress which dominated the decision-making apparatus for long and the small regional parties, from which it had sometimes tended to draw support, were not in favour of India acquiring nuclear bomb.

The survey also shows differential attitudes of Indian elite to the bomb up to 1972 which marks a consensus against India acquiring the bomb. Therefore, Nandy predicted that this attitude "would not show any dramatic change over time or as a result of changes in the structure of power in the country". (Nandy 1972: 1533) To

Table 2.2. Attitudes of Different Types of Elite to Nuclear Armament (1972)

Party Type	*Attitudes to Nuclear Arms*				
	Strongly Agree	*Agree*	*Undecided*	*Disagree*	*Total*
Congress	11.8	11.8	5.9	70.6	100.0
Rightists	11.1	66.7	0.0	22.6	100.0
Communists	0.0	45.5	0.0	54.6	100.1
Socialists	8.3	33.3	0.0	58.3	99.9
Regional Parties	10.0	20.0	0.0	70.0	100.0
Independents	2.7	44.6	2.7	50.0	100.0

Source: Ashis Nandy, "The Bomb, the NPT and Indian Elites", *EPW*, August 1972, p.1535.

him, the possible reasons for the edge which the anti-bomb position enjoyed could be due to following factors:

1. It is possible that the earlier policy of non-alignment and the associated aversion to Super Power rivalry was dominant in the elite sectors, particularly amongst those who could be said to constitute the Establishment.
2. It is also possible that the more intense nationalist temper that has come to dominate the political idiom (generated by wars, processes of modern isation and industrial-urban growth which have led to new awareness of the nation as a depository of secular allegiance, and increasing political influence, and increasing political influence of the less universalist professional politicians) has not yet made that deep inroads into the belief-value system of the critical elite sectors.
3. It is possible that almost all elite viewed that of India become a world power it first need to become an economic power. Therefore, it should not spend resources on the bomb.

This does not mean that there was no opinion in favour of the bomb among the political elite. Nandy points out many reasons behind a small group of elite who had strongly favoured the bomb. He says, first the feeling that India's security is threatened by certain powers who could be checked only with the help of nuclear weapons. Second is the fear that there is no scope for dialogue with the powers which constitute this threat. (Nandy

1972: 1535) It is obvious that Nandy could not have visualised a drastic transformation in the political structure by the emergence of a different political group (BJP), who could change the long-held nuclear belief system in the country.

According to another survey on public opinion conducted four years before the 1998 nuclear tests by David Cortright and Amitabh Mattoo shows that the number of proponents of nuclear weapons for India was more than the opponents; meanwhile, the number of supporter of official policy of "keeping the open option" was double the proponents of nuclear weapons. (Cortright and Mattoo 1994) The survey reveals that, there is marginal difference between those who supports nuclear weapons and those who oppose among the Congress affiliated people. But the gap is much more in case of both the BJP and CPI/CPM.

In fact, by late-1980s, with the revelation of Pakistan's clandestine nuclear programme and especially after the disintegration of Soviet Russia, nuclear debate in India got intensified. Critical discussions in India in January 1991 started to emerge on the merits and demerits of going nuclear and costs associated with such decision. The discourse at the time was in fact motivated by accounts of Pakistan already possessing nuclear stockpile. A.Q. Khan's admission to Kuldip Nayar at the height of the Brasstacks crisis played a critical role in shaping Indian perceptions of the regional security environment, post-1987. A seminar, entitled

Table 2.3 Political Affiliation of Political Elite with Different Nuclear Views.

	All	*Supporters of Official Policy*	*Nuclear Advocates*	*Nuclear Opponents*
Base (in actual numbers)	992	563	326	83
	(Figure below are percentages)			
Cong. (I)	25	26	25	21
BJP	13	11	18	5
CPI/CPM	4	4	2	7

Source: Cortright and Mattoo, *A Study of India's Nuclear Choices*, Nov-Dec 1994 p. 22.

"Nuclear Pakistan and Indian Response," was sponsored by IDSA and included commentary from K Subrahmanyam, Gen. Sundarji, Jaswant Singh, Gen. Vohra and Praful Bidwai. Many members within the Congress party started to rethink India's nuclear options. Even Prime Minister Narasimha Rao was known to have prepared nuclear test that was exposed by US surveillance. (Muralidharan and Cherian 1998)

It is evident that the impact of the nuclear factor on domestic politics and vice-versa is substantial, irrespective of the orientation of nuclear debate in the body *politik*. On the one hand, nuclear weapons and related issues have been a constant feature of electoral politics as all parties have included them in their election manifestos. On the other hand, nuclear weapon issues and policy options have been discussed vigorously in the legislature, shaping the legislative articulation on the subject. Lastly, at the individual level, the relative position of the Prime Minister in the party he belonged to has markedly conditioned the national nuclear weapons decisions. Subsequent chapters dwell upon these aspects in detail locating the pattern of nuclear decision making in India.

Notes

1. Indian Parliament, Internet Source, URL: http://www.parliamentofindia.nic.in/
2. President of India is the constitutional head of Executive of the Union. Real executive power vests in a Council of Ministers with the Prime Minister as head. Article 74(1) of the Constitution provides that there shall be a Council of Ministers headed by the Prime Minister to aid and advise the President who shall, in exercise of his functions, act in accordance with such advice. The Council of Ministers is collectively responsible to the Lok Sabha, the House of the People. *The Constitution of India,* Ministry of Law and Justice, Government of India, 2005.
3. This period of one-party dominance has been referred to as the Congress "system" in Indian politics. Rajni Kothari, "The Congress 'System' in India", 1964, University of California Press.
4. *Jai Jawan Jai Kisan* was a slogan given to India by the then Prime Minister of India Lal Bahadur Shastri in 1965. It means 'hail the soldier and hail the farmer'. Soon after Shastri became Prime Minister, India was attacked by Pakistan. At the same time there was scarcity of foodgrains in the country. Shastri gave this slogan to enthuse the soldiers to defend India and simultaneously cheering farmers

to do their best to increase the production of food grains to reduce dependence on import.

5. Jawaharlal Nehru (1947-64); Gulzarilal Nanda (May-June1964, January 1966); Lal Bahadur Shastri (1964-66); Indira Gandhi (1966-77, 1980-1984); Rajiv Gandhi (1984-89); P.V. Narasimha Rao (1991-1996); Manmohan Singh (2004-14).
6. In its *Vision Document 2004*, in line with what Mahatma Gandhi had said, the BJP believes India cannot rise to her full potential without the revitalisation of rural India. Its vision of an ideal Indian village is one that has the following attributes: (a) self-reliant society and dynamic economy; (b) modern infrastructure and basic amenities; (c) full employment to all able-bodied persons; (d) free of social and economic exploitation; (e) harmonious, cooperative and caring environment; (f) Antyodaya or concern for development of the last man; (g) effective functioning of Panchayat bodies; and (h) a vibrant cultural life that displays both modernity and pride in Indian traditions.
7. "Integral Humanism", the guiding philosophy of the BJP, was first presented by Pandit Deendayal Upadhyaya in the form of four lectures delivered in Bombay between April 22 and 25, 1965. This advocates the simultaneous and integrated programme of the body, mind and intellect and soul of each human being. His philosophy is a synthesis of the material and the spiritual, the individual and the collective.
8. "Hindutva or Cultural Nationalism" presents the BJP's conception of Indian nationhood, as explained in the following set of articles. It must be noted that Hindutva is a nationalist, and not a religious or theocratic, concept.
9. Hindu nationalism is collectively referred to the expressions of social and political thought, based on the native spiritual and cultural traditions of India and Nepal. Scholars like Girilal Jain argue that the term 'Hindu nationalism' which refers to the concept of 'Hindu Rashtra' is a simplistic translation and is better described by the term Hindu polity. (Girilal Jain, *The Hindu Phenomenon*, 1994)
10. CPI(M) Official Website, URL: http://cpim.org/content/leadership

3

Doctrine, Decision-Making and Domestic Politics

By the time, India emerged as a modern sovereign nation, the nuclear era had already dawned on international politics. Owing to this, the "nuclear factor" in India's national thinking is a natural corollary of global nuclear trend. It is widely believed that India's initial motivation to tame the atom came not from a nuclear threat of a declared enemy, but from the then prevailing socio-economic conditions in the country, India was initially concerned more with socio-economic aspect of nuclear technology rather than its strategic utility. After independence, while initiating to reap the benefits of civilian use of new technology, India resorted to "no weapon" policy advocating comprehensive disarmament based on age-old cultural values. Accordingly, her foreign policy goal was set to spearhead new era following distinctive foreign policy based on the Nehruvian principle of "global influence without military power." (Wilcox 1972: 9; Hilali 2001) But, the strategic dimension of nuclear technology drew India's attention at a certain point of time owing to factors (discussed in the subsequent chapters) that prompted her leaders finally to acquire the bomb.

After the first nuclear test [Pokhran] in 1974, India followed an "ambiguous" nuclear policy. This ambiguity referred to the condition wherein the nuclear weapons option was kept open, but in a state of "animated suspension".[1] This ambiguous posture is the offshoot of India's demonstrated ability to make nuclear weapons, but self-imposed denial policy. This peculiar approach constituted: (1) maintaining large strategic establishment to produce fissile materials; (2) design nuclear weaponry; (3) develop various delivery systems simultaneously and (4) continuing to refrain from any public decision to create and deploy nuclear arsenal. This means, developing some components of an arsenal while desisting from creating the complete arsenal. According to Ashley Tellis, this was the logical derivation of "India's calculated assessment that 'preserving the option' would provide deterrence advantages without imposing any of the costs and risks associated with actually deploying nuclear weaponry". (Tellis 2001: 13) However, George Perkovich is of the opinon that though there was some "intentions" to go for the bomb even during Nehru's leadership, enough technical capability was not mastered for such an ambition. (Perkovich 1999: 20)

India's Nuclear Doctrine

One year after the Pokhran-II nuclear tests, the National Security Advisory Board (NSAB) released draft report (August 1999) and called for "a doctrine of credible minimum nuclear deterrence" under which nuclear weapons would be used for "retaliation" only. (*Report of NSAB on Indian Nuclear Doctrine*, August 17, 1999) It is a short document (four pages), divided into eight chapters with parenthetical indication of the number of paragraphs in each chapter: Preamble (6); Objectives (7); Nuclear Forces (2); Credibility and Survivability (3); Command and Control (6); Security and Safety (3); Research and Development (2); Disarmament and Arms Control (5). This document outlines the "broad principles for development, deployment and employment of India's nuclear forces". Details of India's policy and strategy concerning force structures, deployment and employment of nuclear forces flow from this framework. The broad principles of the doctrine are:

1. India's nuclear weapons are meant to deter nuclear weapons threat. Unlike other nuclear weapon states, India's nuclear weapons are not meant to deter the use and threat of use of conventional weapons, chemical weapons, biological weapons or generalised formulation of protecting national interests any time anywhere. The doctrine requires that the nuclear policy should seek to deter, rather than fight a war with nuclear weapons. India will not resort to the use or threat of use of nuclear weapons against states which do not possess nuclear weapons, or are not aligned with nuclear weapons powers.
2. The doctrine rests on the principle of "No First Use" (NFU) even against nuclear threat or use. It commits Indian nuclear

policy to one of retaliation only. Para 2.4 of the draft paper express it in the following terms: "The fundamental purpose of Indian nuclear weapons is to deter the use and threat of use of nuclear weapons by any State or entity against India and its forces. India will not be the first to initiate a nuclear strike, but will respond with punitive retaliation should deterrence fail."

3. India's nuclear force structure include "triad of aircraft, mobile land-based missiles and sea-based assets" is no way less robust than any other nations', which would be "fully employable in the shortest possible time." Also a "robust command and control system" and "effective intelligence and early warning capabilities" including space-based assets are prescribed to manage the force.
4. As a defensive doctrine of no-first-use and limiting the use of nuclear weapons for retaliation only, India's draft doctrine is in total harmony with the UN Charter. Article 51 of the Charter under Chapter VII clearly endorses "the inherent right of individual or collective self-defence if an armed attack occurs against a Member of the United States.
5. The doctrine emphasises that global, verifiable and non-discriminatory nuclear disarmament is India's national security objective. The draft doctrine makes it clear that India will not follow the disastrous route of the first tier nuclear weapon states who built up tens of thousands of nuclear weapons in a mindless arms race. It only possesses a second strike capability, which would be used to inflict unacceptable damage to the aggressor.

It seems that India's nuclear doctrine is no less sophisticated in comparison to any other advanced nuclear weapons state. Experts view India's nuclear force structure very robust and similar to that of the USA. (Kapur 2010: 22; Liebl 2009) A subjective analysis would indicate that the principle of 'minimum deterrence' is relative and vague. If any of her neighbours goes for enhancing nuclear arsenal, India has to redefine "minimum" deterrent capability to maintain the minimum. Despite being critically debated over the years, India's nuclear doctrine of 1999 has not changed substantively since the operationalisation announcement in January 2003. However, the BJP 2014 election manifesto has promised for an "independent strategic nuclear programme" updating and making it "relevant to challenges of current times." (BJP *Election Manifesto 2014*: 39) If BJP keeps its promise, after undertaking a review of the geo-strategic situation around India, the party may set the process for reconsidering India's Draft Nuclear Doctrine.

Objectively, the Doctrine in its current form is viewed similar to the US doctrine of massive retaliation during 1950s and contradictory to the Indian objective of minimum deterrence. (Joeck 2013: 115) Francesco Calogero says, "If this becomes the basis of nuclear-weapon policy of India, it will impede progress towards the achievement of a nuclear-weapon-free world" as the doctrine itself fixes this ultimate goal (Calogero 1999). To Achin Vanaik, the provision of triad structure is completely contradictory to its projected objective of eventual elimination of nuclear weapon from the world. (Vanaik 2006) However, Rajesh Rajagopalan views that India's doctrine is based on "existential deterrence"—simply the existence of powerful forces capable of inflicting punishment, denying success, imposing costs,—which is by nature more optimistic, stable and relatively harmless than "deterrence by threat of punishment." (Rajagopalan 2005) It is to introspect how adequate or relevant is India's current nuclear use policy specifically when South Asian nuclear threshold is remarkably lowered by introduction of TNWs and miniaturisation of nuclear warhead by Pakistan. Michael Krepon views "deterrence stability is far from assured on the Subcontinent and is likely to deteriorate . . ." (Krepon and Thompson 2013: 11) and more importantly when subconventional violence poses greater threat to deterrence stability. (Perkovich in Krepon and Thompson 2013: 31)

Command and Control

A viable nuclear command and control system helps in preventing accidental or unauthorised use of the strategic forces. Therefore, Command and control of nuclear weapons may said to comprise two fundamental but conflicting aspects: positive and negative control. "Positive control concerns the authorisation of nuclear operations. On the other hand, negative control seeks to prevent "accidental or unauthorised use of nuclear weapons including possible theft by sub-state actors." (Gregory 1996: 3–4) When India's nuclear weapons are meant for defensive purposes and deterrence only, the credibility about the capability of her nuclear force (including the political will to exercise the nuclear option when necessary) needs to be assured. So, an effective command and control system is an important ingredient of her nuclear policy. Components of the command and control of nuclear weapons includes: manufacture, custody, manning and operation, military command, planning the strategy for using nuclear weapons (their number, type, and deployment and the controlling agencies, methods and targets of their employment). This also includes the political decision to use or not to use nuclear weapons (Osgood 1962: 21).

Therefore, a nuclear command and control system is designed to support national nuclear strategy but surprisingly, the military has been all along excluded from anything to do with the subject of nuclear weapons development. Even the country did not have any clear-cut strategic perceptions for use during their development or at the time of conduct of nuclear tests in 1998 (Pahwa 2002: 2). However, "Indian Nuclear Doctrine" prepared by the NSAB in 1999 and being operationalised in 2003 mentions the following on India's command and control:

1. Nuclear weapons shall be tightly controlled and released for use at the highest political level. The authority to release them for use resides in the person of the Prime Minister of India, or the successor(s) designated.
2. An effective and survivable command and control system with requisite flexibility and responsiveness shall be in place. An integrated operational plan, or a series of sequential plans, predicated on strategic objectives and a targeting policy shall form part of the system.
3. For effective employment, the unity of command and control of nuclear forces, including dual capable delivery systems shall be ensured.
4. The survivability of the nuclear arsenal and effective command, control, communications, computing, intelligence and information (C 412) systems shall be assured.
5. The Indian defence forces shall be in a position to execute operations in an NBC environment with minimal degradation.
6. Space-based and other assets shall be created to provide early warning, communication and damage/detonation assessment.

Three distinctive characteristics can be discernible on the Indian nuclear command and control: (1) absolute civilian-political control; (2) short reaction time and complex hierarchical structure; and (3) two main objectives- (a) to support the command function, and (b) the survivability in a nuclear environment. In Indian political set up, the Prime Minister is the chief executive even though the President is the Supreme Commander of the armed forces. The apex body responsible for all matters impinging on India's security is the Cabinet Committee on Security (CCS) headed by the PM. The CCS, constituted by Prime Minister Inder Gujral in 1997, is the modern day avatar of the erstwhile Defence Committee of the Cabinet (DCC) that failed to survive the 1962 Himalayan debacle. (Singh 2007) Members of the CCS that is headed by the Prime Minister, include the Defence Minister, the Home Minister, the Finance Minister and the Minister for External Affairs. Other members of the Council of Ministers, the Armed Forces-Chiefs of Staff and the Secretaries of concerned ministries may be invited to attend the deliberations whenever their advice is considered necessary. (Tellis 2001:428-67)

Parallel to the CCS and with almost the same membership is the National Security Council (NSC). This too is headed by the Prime Minister. The NSC is assisted by the Strategic Policy Group (SPG) and the National Security Advisory Board (NSAB). Secretariat support to the NSC is provided by the Joint Intelligence Committee (JIC). The Prime Minister, as the head of the Cabinet, exercises ultimate control over all nuclear weapons. In the Indian context,

Fig. 1.

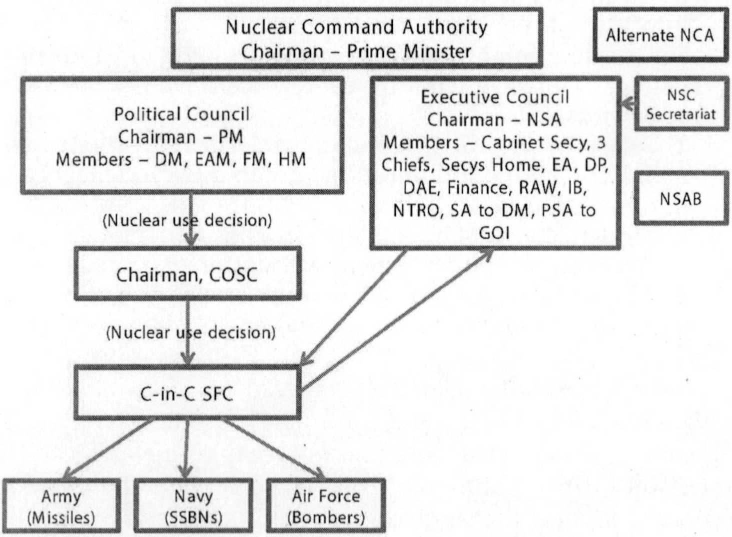

Structure of Indian Nuclear Command and Control.

Source: Manpreet Sethi, *Nuclear Strategy*, New Delhi: KW Publishers, 2010, p. 166.

the Prime Minister and the CCS is designated as the National Command Authority (NCA).

The NCA is advised by the National Security Council (NSC) and supported by the Strategy Programme Staff (SPS) constituting representatives from the three defence services, science, and technology establishments and other experts from related domains, including the Ministry of External Affairs. The Strategic Armament Safety Authority (SASA) that functions directly under the NCA is responsible for all matters relating to the safety and security of India's nuclear and delivery assets at all locations. In terms of preparedness, efficiency of response systems in possible escalatory scenarios, and surprise attack scenarios, regular drills are conducted. Specialised units have also been deployed for operation in a nuclearised environment. (Saran 2013)

The principle of civilian control over the employment of Indian nuclear forces is inviolable. However, if situation warrants the decision-making process and control may pass into the hands of professional military men. This could be by design or by default. It is necessary to have a clear line of succession in case political leadership is decapitated by a nuclear strike or the Prime Minister is unavailable for some reason so that decision-making is not stymied at a crucial juncture. (Kanwal 2001: 165) Similarly, in certain circumstances, pre-delegation of authority is necessary. For example, if the entire civilian leadership is eliminated in a multi-warhead first strike (an improbable but not an impossible event), nuclear decision-making would come to a standstill unless the authority to approve a retaliatory strike had been pre-delegated to military commanders.

Whatever may be the nuances of the draft doctrine, the stage that India's nuclear weapons discourse has reached is marked with many twists and turns. The period from 1947 through 1974, during which Indian scientists developed the technical means to produce nuclear weapons within a polity that had moral doubts and competing priorities (Nanda 1972). Also, from 1975 through 1995 during which India surprised herself, the US and much of the world by not conducting follow-up nuclear tests and not building a nuclear arsenal. Many explanations have been advanced on India's nuclear behaviour. Assuming that security concerns singularly determine state interests in acquiring nuclear weapons, the prevalent literature posits that if insecurities are removed, unproliferation should occur. But India's nuclear programme challenges these assumptions.

According to Perkovich, India's nuclear weapon capabilities have assumed deeply rooted domestic importance, independent of the security consideration. (Perkovich 1999: 20) He says, "the process of building nuclear weapon capabilities has created interests, bureaucratic actors, beliefs, perspectives and expectations within the state and society". This view suggests that, "proliferation qualitatively changes the state that engages in it, altering the array of interests that must be addressed before unproliferation can occur". (Perkovich 1999: 20; Bhusan and Katyal 2002: 129) In case of India, as a democracy, these changes and their effects are particularly important. Interestingly he argues that, "democracy in India"—and perhaps in other states—makes "unproliferation even less likely". In support of this assumption, he points out that, seven of the eight declared and undeclared nuclear weapon states are democracies and the hope of stopping further spread of nuclear weapons over time may depend on these states' willingness to pursue nuclear disarmament, or unproliferation. It is interesting therefore to investigate the pattern of India's nuclear weapons decision-making.

Institutional Framework of Decision-Making

As pointed earlier, owing to the oral nature of nuclear decision-making, not much hard evidence can be traced on the nature, causes and factors that lead to the decisions by political leaders to acquire the bombs. In addition, Indian nuclear policy-making is viewed to be "highly personalised and concentrated in a handful of political leaders and scientists. (Perkovich 2002: 9) While many of these activities have been secret, the issue of whether to build, test, and deploy nuclear arsenals in general has been debated openly and longer than in any other nation. The decision regarding when and where to test, what kind of weapon to be built, have never been opaque whereas the debate over India's capability has featured unusual attention.

Unlike the Parliamentary Standing Committee on Defence, the Cabinet Committee on Security, and the National Security Council no other structure was available these days, before to discuss and decide on India's nuclear weapons programme. The Defence Committee of the Cabinet (DCC), the oldest forum, failed to survive the 1962 Himalayan debacle. Constitutionally, the President of India as Head of the State serves as Supreme Commander of the armed forces. (*The Constitution of India*, Part V, §53(2)) However, "the preponderance of power resides with the Prime Minister" who is elected by his peers in the Lok Sabha. (Sukla 1989: v) The Prime Minister has, by tradition, always held the position of cabinet minister responsible for science and technology, which includes the Departments of Atomic Energy and Space. (Rao 2008: 244) Therefore, in the Prime Minister's capacity as Minister of the Department of Atomic Energy, s(he) works closely with the department's senior scientist, who serves as Chairman of the AEC. In turn, "successive chairmen have exerted extraordinary influence over India's nuclear activities and policies". (Perkovich 2002: 9)

Indeed, there are no arrangements within India's institutional structure to provide independent scientifically expert checks and balances on the nuclear and defence establishments. Within the government, a Cabinet Committee on Political Affairs formed has the highest decision-making group and only in 1998, the government decided to create the National Security Council which assumed important role in this area. (Anand 2001) This body thus represents the most important bureaucracies involved in Indian nuclear policy. However, successive Prime Ministers have formulated policies without consulting the Cabinet Committee many times. The parliament has little formal power to affect nuclear policy beyond its role in questioning the government, the ministers and overseeing financial accounts. (Perkovich 2002: 10)

In contrast to the other country's programmes, one of the distinct features of Indian nuclear discourse is, that it is an extension of civilian nuclear enterprise. All other nuclear weapon powers have started nuclear programme with a military purpose and their civilian programme started much later. But, India started her nuclear journey with noble purpose but the imperative of nuclear weapons was felt later. The time when India felt the necessity of nuclear weapons, the international community was already apprehensive of the spread and the non-proliferation regime was superimposed. Therefore, India's nuclear weapons decisions were taken with utmost secrecy, without being openly debated. Either the decisions were taken exclusively by the head of the government (the Prime Minister) or in consultation with his close aids. Therefore, the core of the Indian nuclear policy mechanism is small and represents highly personalisation and elitist. (Sharma 2005: 167) It has been a prerogative of the leader and/or the political party in power to decide the policy.

However, an objective study on the timings of India's nuclear decisions reveals that they have been taken most of the time during political crises or the time when the stability of the government was at stake. But the justification advanced for such decisions by the incumbent government is simply the "deteriorating national security situation". (*Suo Motu Statement* by Prime Minister Atal Bihari Vajpayee, May 27, 1998) For example, it was Prime Minister Lal Bahadur Shastri who initiated the Indian nuclear-explosives programme in 1965. But, a series of events put a brake on that programme. These included the passing away of Lal Bahadur Shastri, Homi J. Bhabha's death in Europe in a mysterious plane crash, and the political instability triggered by an initially weak government under Prime Minister Indira Gandhi when India eventually conducted a nuclear detonation in 1974. (Chellaney 1998) Same was the situation when the NDA government lead by BJP took the decision to test in 1998. Does this mean the domestic political situation has a bearing on India's nuclear weapons decisions? Can one say that this domestic political bickering has been manifested in such phasal nuclear weapons decisions? This points to the linkage of Indian domestic politics with her nuclear weapons decisions, discussed in the subsequent section.

Domestic Politics and Nuclear Weapons Decisions

As nuclear discourse has wider audience, politics often tend to acquire a foothold in the discourse. Also, nuclear discourse revolves round state behaviour; and state behaviour, beside other factors, is shaped and guided mostly by the political leaders in democracy. But, leaders sometime target nuclear issues to mobilise their political agenda, to that extent, sometimes for their political survival. (Koopmans and Duyvendak, May 1995) In a democracy, political parties develop attitudes and principles towards nuclear discourse and consequently formulate policies commensurate with their ideology. (David and Hands 1990) Sometimes, various parties conflict on the issue having divided perceptions and policy options. In this respect, India's case is no exception. George Perkovich asserts that contrary to the assumptions of the realist theory the motivations for India's acquisition of nuclear bomb was based more on the domestic politics than external security needs. "The process of building nuclear weapon capabilities has created interests, bureaucratic actors, beliefs, perspectives, and expectations within the state and society". Further he asserts that "domestic factors including moral and political norms have been more significant in determining India's nuclear policy . . . . Often, tensions between domestic interests have made this policy appear ambivalent and ambiguous." (Perkovich 2002: 6)

As far as the process of India's nuclear policy making is concerned, Perkovich is of the opinion that "it has been highly personalised and concentrated in a handful of political leaders and scientists. While many of the state activities have been secret, the issue of whether to build, test, and deploy nuclear arsenal has been debated more openly and longer than in any other nation" (Perkovich 2002: 9). His observation holds some truth as one can easily perceive by judging the power of the Parliament to affect nuclear policy. Beyond its roles of questioning government ministers and overseeing financial accounts, it virtually enjoys no control. Also the military establishment plays minimal role in Indian nuclear policy. (Bhonsle and Gupta 2007: 28; Perkovich 2002: 10) Since the emergence of coalition era in Indian politics, nuclear issues have been more or less the peg of politics. Except for once in 2008, nuclear policy of the country has never been a factor in testing the survival of the incumbent government. But, different political parties seem to have utilised, some way or the other, the debate over the nuclear programme for political mileage. For example, many argue that Indira Gandhi tested a nuclear device in 1974 only for "political currency" and same is the case with BJP in 1998 when it conducted four tests. (Kapoor 2009: 2) Even before coming to power, the BJP has promised in its election manifestos to conduct nuclear tests and develop nuclear weapons for India once it comes to power.

The political-nuclear interface in India, though gradually became intensive, especially after the 1960s, was inherent in her polity since Independence. India's attitude towards nuclear weapons was marked by the perception of political/scientific stalwarts like Mahatma Gandhi, Jawaharlal Nehru, Homi J. Bhabha, et al, "New Delhi's initial aversion to nuclear weapons" was an offshoot of the Gandhian idea of non-violence. (Ghose 2007: 982) But, the instinct to exploit nuclear technology for peaceful purposes was equally marked by Nehru's modern temperament and "Bhabha's scientific inquisitiveness" which led to the setting up the Tata Institute of Fundamental Research (TIFR) in 1945 which groomed an entire generation of Indian scientists and the Atomic Energy Commission (AEC) in 1945. (Deshmukh 2003)

After independence, under the leadership of the Indian National Congress the main task of the statesmen was to bring development eradicating poverty. The idea to exploit atomic energy for this objective perhaps had never been contended "across the national political spectrum". (Raja Mohan 2002) But in 1955, when the Left party was in the opposition and the Sino-Soviet collaboration in the nuclear field was announced, no record is available as to why the offer of the USSR for a same kind of agreement with India was not accepted. If non-alignment was the guiding principle of India's international engagement, why just after one year India signed an agreement with Canada to supply a National Research Experimental Reactor (NRX)? It is mentioned that the Canadian offer largely was a fruit of the friendship between Bhabha and W.B. Lewis, the leader of the Canadian design team, as well as between Nehru's and the Canadian Premier Lester Pearson. (Menon 2000: 71)

Meanwhile, voices were raised in the media that "weapons option should not be entirely foreclosed and perhaps this may have prompted Bhabha to declare before the Parliamentary Consultative Committee on atomic affairs in December 1959 that India had progressed to a stage where if political directive was received, a bomb could be made without external assistance." (Menon 2000: 71) In 1961, the Zerilina reactor went critical, and Nehru announced that although India could make the bomb in two years, it choose not to do so. (Albright and Hibbs 1992: 27) Rear Admiral Raja Menon (Retd.) says the strength of "Indian nuclear research was far ahead of China but seems quite incredible that the country did not explode a nuclear device earlier." (Menon 2000: 71)

One perennial theme of India's nuclear and foreign policy is, until there is a true global consensus and movement towards comprehensive nuclear disarmament India would maintain its weapons option. (Bidwai and Vanaik 1997: 49) In the wake of Chinese nuclear tests in 1964, the domestic pressure on the Shastri Government to give up the policy of nuclear abstinence and initiate weapons programme was immense. By January 1965, India had already announced two out of the three negatives which went by the name of strategic policy: no to the bomb, no to a nuclear umbrella, no to NPT that followed. At the Durgapur session of the Congress (1965), the Prime Minister Lal Bahadur Shastri faced heavy pressure from some party members to give up the "no nuclear bomb now" policy. (Quoted in Subrahmanyam 1998: 27) However, categorically said "India would not embark on a nuclear programme now", implying that policy could change. (Subrahmanyam 1998: 27) In September 1965, India Pakistan went to a full-scale war and during this time a hundred Congress MPs (Member of Parliament) signed a statement saying that India should make a nuclear bomb to avoid the increasing Sino-Pak collusion. (Kapur 1976: 195) It is believed that this was the time when Shastri sanctioned the proposal put forward by Dr Bhabha on investigating a "Subterranean Nuclear Explosion Project" (SNEP). (Malhotra 2004; Kapur 1976: 165)

Thus, Shastri was led to take into account the pro-bomb lobby in the nuclear debate by declaring that India had the capability to make weapons, even though she did not wish to exercise, and by ordering the activation of India's nuclear option by preparing for a SNEP. (Mattoo 1999: 17) In December 1964, at a press conference in London, Shastri revealed India's efforts to obtain a nuclear guarantee from the nuclear weapons states. (Noorani 1967: 490–92) According to K. Subrahmanyam, "in the wake of China's nuclear threat—Lal Bahadur Shastri was believed to have requested the British Prime Minister, Harold Wilson, for an extended deterrence by Britain on his visit to that country during December 1964 but there was no favourable British response". (Subrahmanyam 1998: 27) Given the limited information in the public domain, reason for India's quest for a nuclear guarantee is hard to discern what exactly the Indian leadership had in mind when it sought to acquire such guarantee from the great powers.

Successive developments in South Asia, like the Bangladesh Liberation War (1971) viewed to have influenced India's nuclear discourse. The lessons of the war are unforgettable for India. India won her strategic goals under coercion from the two nuclear powers— US and China-—and with the support of USSR. (Dixit 2002: 213) The presence of *USS Enterprise*, the US nuclear-powered aircraft carrier in Indian Ocean during the war brought home the impression that India should go nuclear. (Dixit 2002: 213) Perhaps, US pressure during the war mingled with Pakistan's post-war plan to carry forward its nuclear weapon programme (for not to face any humiliation by India) prompted Indira Gandhi to give green signal to the nuclear programme. It is not only the external factors that prompted her to go for the test. Ashok Kapur says that "the final decision [to test] was taken in the context of

Mrs Gandhi's domestic troubles." (Kapur 1976: 165) Further he says that, Mrs Gandhi had not consulted any of her high ranking aids. India's then Defence Minister Jagjivan Ram, the second most powerful member of the cabinet was informed on May 8, 1974 about the scheduled test (just ten days before the test) but he was not consulted for the decision. India's then Foreign Minister, Swaran Singh was informed only two days before the detonation, thus indicating that the Ministry of External Affairs was totally bypassed. (Kapur 1976: 165)

Another important phase in India's nuclear policy ranges from 1979 to 1998, where India maintained strategic restraints and propagated for nuclear weapon free world. In 1982, India put forward a Programme of Action on Disarmament which called for freeze on the production of fissile material and on the production of nuclear weapons or delivery systems. (Sethi 1999: 397) The most forceful plea by India for a sincere and time bound effort towards nuclear disarmament was made by Rajiv Gandhi at the UN in 1988, where he called upon the international community "to urgently negotiate a binding commitment to an action plan for ushering in a non-violent world free of nuclear weapons". The action plan he advanced was a three stage programme for the elimination of nuclear weapons starting from 1988 to 2010. (*Action Plan for Ushering in a Nuclear Weapon Free World and Non-violent World Order,* 1988 in Sethi 2010: Appendix 2151-56)

When Rajiv Gandhi was convinced that the world community had unanimously rejected his Action Plan, he had no choice but to give green signal to attain nuclear weapon capability. (Subrahmanyam 1998) As a result, by 1990, India is reported to have fully developed nuclear weapons programme. Following Rajiv Gandhi's footsteps, the successor governments—Narasimha Rao and I.K. Gujral—had seriously considered nuclear tests but refrained from that owing to US pressure and their assessment of the political and economic costs of such tests. The "unconditional and indefinite extension" of NPT in 1995 fundamentally altered India's attitude towards CTBT. (Raja Mohan 2004: 14) By December 1995, India was ready to conduct the test by neutralising all international pressures. But, US began to notice the Indian preparations and started putting pressure to hold back.

Undoubtedly, influence of domestic variables like the ideology of the party in power, the perception of the leader, public opinion and bureaucratic-scientific community lobby play their role in shaping the nuclear discourse. International politics and therefore security considerations cannot only be attributed to what happened in May 1998. Rather the timing of the test is related to domestic political developments. (Ram 1999: 58) To deconstruct the BJP's decision to conduct the nuclear tests in May 1998, it is necessary to pay attention to two major factors: (1) The political and strategic culture of BJP which emphasises the importance of "keeping promises" and which is obsessed with national power and prestige; and (2) the political survival of the BJP-led coalition and Vajpayee's ability to sustain the government after a narrowly won election. (Bajpai 2009: 17)

According to Kanti P. Bajpai, "India had been on the edge of nuclear testing for a long time". (Bajpai 2009: 35) Successive governments had considered testing—more importantly in 1982, 1995 and 1996. Indeed, in 1996, Vajpayee himself had given Indian scientists permission to test. (Chengappa 2000: 35) In the end, though for a variety of reasons, each Prime Minister had drawn back, including Vajpayee. But Vajpayee took another course. The prevailing domestic political environment and "the political and strategic culture of the BJP impelled the party to face the issue of whether or not it should conduct a test once it was in power. Therefore, this factor is viewed as a structural driver of the test." (Bajpai 2009: 17)

Over the years, the BJP seems to have convinced itself and sought to convince others in comparison with other parties, that it only carries through policies right for the country. This assertion is matched by its proclamation that "it is the only principled and nationalist party—that works hard to sell both to its own members and the public." In effect, the party propagated an image of itself as a political force that is above the petty, tactical, cut-and-thrust of everyday politics. (Mishra 1998: 3) The BJP proclaimed that in conducting the tests it was only doing what the other parties knew was right for the country but did not have the courage to do because of the international repercussions of testing. (Mishra 1998: 3) It also argued that the earlier PMs did not test owing to the fear of US sanctions and they had "underestimated India's potential" and "nobody among them had a correct sense of history or vision and mission of this great country of 1,000 million people." (Mishra 1998: 3) After the tests, a Vajpayee aide explained that "the vulnerability of the NDA government in the early days in power and the PM's desire to keep his promises were important considerations in the decisions to test...it was also to say that he had kept his word on something he had been advocating India should do for the past thirty years." (Quoted in Chengappa 2000: 50) Beyond the political culture of the BJP, there is its strategic culture. Related to the theme of "sacrifice" and cost in domestic politics, there was the BJP's obsession with a strategic culture of "national power" and "status" and in this "strategic imagery" nuclear weapons are a vital component. (Cohen 2005: 280-81)

Within this politico-strategic environment, there was nothing terribly problematic about the importance of nuclear weapons. It is true that the Congress Party, among others, also holds nuclear weapons to be important, but remained always in an ambivalent attitude towards a full-fledged nuclear weapons programme. (Basrur 2001) For the Congress leaders, nuclear weapons have at best been perceived as a "regrettable necessary and a terrible weapon fits only for defence and constitutes only one element of national security". (Chengappa 2000: 52) With the BJP, nuclear weapons are seen as "vital for national power and status". Brajesh Mishra, Vajpayee's National Security Advisor, said in an interview, "I have always felt that you cannot in today's world be counted for something without going nuclear." (Quoted in Swaminathan 2003) In BJP's strategic thinking, it was not necessary for a state to wait for economic and technological power before developing military power rather the reverse is true: national power comes primarily from military strength, with economic and technological power coming in the wake of military power. (Swaminathan 2003) Thus soon after the test, a Vajpayee aide argued Narasimha Rao's policy of "nothing but economy" was modified to read "security first and the rest will follow." (Quoted in Perkovich 1999: 442)

It seems that the strategy of subversion of the established order is an assertion of power–pure and simple, even if one seeks to assimilate and accommodate in that order, was the guiding force of BJP's conception of powerful-India. According to Kanti Bajpai, an important aspect of the decision to test could be the political survival of the BJP leader A.B. Vajpayee. "If the political and strategic culture of the BJP made it almost certain that the party, at some point in power would authorise nuclear testing and the building of an overt nuclear weapons programme, Vajpayee's own political survival was the reason why he tested when he did." (Bajpai 2009: 39)

Nuclear Deal and the Domestic Political Scenario

It was apprehended by many that the "Indo-US nuclear deal could be casualty of India's fractured domestic politics". (Kumar and Jones 2007) There was growing apprehension for sometime in the political-scientific circles that the nuclear accord may "unravel". (Kumara and Jones 2007) It was also seen how the political wrangling over the deal bitterly fractured India's domestic politics leading to withdrawal of support by the Left parties from the UPA government. Whether the nuclear deal has exposed the splits in desired domestic consensus over nuclear issues or the political bickering and ideological underpinnings unnecessarily complicated the process of Indo-US nuclear agreement, is a matter of introspection.

However, India's political scene was on the boil during mid-2008 when CPI(M) declared its withdrawal of support to the Manmohan Singh government [CPI(M) Central Committee 2009: 5] and at the same time the Samajwadi Party, a regional party, offered support to the minority government. Though the India-US nuclear deal is not directly about India's nuclear weapons programme, certain provisions therein implicitly linked to the nuclear weapons issue. The opposition BJP, though supported UPA government's policy of forging a strategic partnership with the United States, viewed the nuclear deal as "a trap", more discriminatory than treaties like NPT and CTBT. However, the BJP was virtually divided on the entire issue. A section of the Party, ideologically closer to the Rashtriya Swayamsevak Sangh (RSS), virulently opposed the deal as "capitulation of the country's sovereignty and national interests". Equally, the other faction within the BJP grudgingly finds itself in broad affinity with the UPA government's policy. (Bhatt 2007) The main reason "why BJP opposes the deal" is over a provision in the treaty that threatens to demand the return of all equipments and fuel supplied by the US if India tests any nuclear weapons. (Bharatiya Janata Party 2008)

The Left parties, in the meanwhile, threatened not only to withdraw support to the UPA government if it goes ahead with the deal, but threatened to vote against the government in a no-confidence motion in the Parliament. However, in the Left ranks, there were quite a lot of confusion. While one of the Left constituents, the Revolutionary Socialist Party (RSP), withdrew its representatives from the 15-member nuclear panel, Forward Bloc (another Left party) threatened to follow, if the CPI(M) and CPI vacillated over their opposition to the deal. (Biswas 2008) Finally, the Left not just withdrew support, but launched nation-wide agitation against the Government's decision to sign the deal. The Left voiced opposition to the deal on two major issues: (1) nuclear sovereignty—independence and unhindered development of India's civilian (and military) nuclear programmes, and (2) the pro-US foreign policy thrust provided by the deal. (*Left Stand on the Nuclear Deal* 2008) To address the opposing views of the Left parties and the Congress, the UPA-Left Coordination Committee was formed for compromise formula but could not help. When Prime Minister Manmohan Singh went ahead for negotiation with the Nuclear Suppliers Group (NSG) for waiver of restrictions imposed on India and subsequently the Hyde Act, the CPI(M) withdrew its support from the coalition. (*People's Democracy*, XXXII (27), July 13, 2009)

Surprisingly, arch rivals such as the Samajwadi Party and Bahujan Samaj Party (BSP) as well as the Rashtriya Janata Dal (RJD) and Janata Dal-Secular (JD-S) vied with each other to support the Congress-led UPA government, which needed just nine more MPs to get the 272 figure needed to sustain the government. The SP and BSP, which fought elections against the Congress in Uttar Pradesh and elsewhere, came to pledge their support to the UPA to "strengthen secular forces" and to keep the BJP out. Mayawati and 'Trinamul Congress' (with 21 MPs) announced their unconditional outside support to the UPA government with the purpose of weakening communal forces in the country and keeping the BJP-led NDA away from power. The Janata Dal-Secular (JD-S) leader H.D. Kumaraswamy also announced his unconditional support for the UPA. (*Hindustan Times*, May 19, 2009)

The political activism that followed developments in the nuclear deal has certainly underlined the bickering of coalition politics. Many viewed the political gimmicks followed as 'coalition of convenience" or "politics of opportunism" when Amar Singh extended his party's support to Manmohan Singh government. (Puri 2008) Manvendra Singh, (son of Jaswant singh), an MP from Barmer in the Lok Sabha, even went up to the extent of saying:

> The Indo-US nuclear agreement is a political deal masquerading as a technology treaty. The essence of the deal is politics, with technology and the energy, it is supposed to bring simply a smokescreen. Power, to light up India, is not the driving

> force behind the deal. It is politics and to be charitable to its prime proponents, of a global scale. The aim is to redraw the global politico-strategic framework under the guise of providing technology, energy, and power. But like all power that is not earned, produced, there is a cost. And it is this cost that gets the goal of most Indians. (Singh 2008)

Most important question that emerged out of the row over the deal is, "if coalition politics is good for our democracy". Politics, of course, makes strange bedfellows, but when national security is in question and especially when nuclear issues are involved, political oneness and maturity is desperately warranted. In the past, many coalition governments, both at the centre and the states, have collapsed due to the inherent weakness of coalition set up. That too, in the Indian context, coalitions are nothing but the coming together of a few unscrupulous and shameless political parties for their own gain. (Venkatesan 2008) For example, Sharad Pawar, who walked out of Congress, opposing the *'videsi'* Sonia Gandhi, did not mind today to become a political ally of the Congress. Jayalalitha (AIADMK) and Karunanidhi (DMK) have swung from one ideological spectrum to the other (i.e., BJP and Congress) for sometime now. Left parties, which oppose the Congress in states such as Kerala and West Bengal, did not mind supporting the same party at the Centre. How this kind of coalition tussle would evolve in the future is a matter of speculation. Nevertheless, nuclear issues have their strong presence in domestic political alignments from time to time.

Note

1. The capacity and option to make nuclear weapons was neither exercised nor foreclosed. Strategic thinkers like Air Commodore Jasjit Singh termed this state of India's nuclear policy as "Recessed Deterrence".

Section-B
The National Security Factor

In the suo motu statement, Prime Minister Vajpayee in the Parliament on May 27, 1998 justified the nuclear tests as an outcome of the "deteriorating regional security environment", particularly: (1) for the growing cooperation between China and Pakistan on nuclear weapons and missile development; (2) the continuing proliferation of nuclear weapons and delivery systems; and (3) the lack of progress on global nuclear disarmament. (suo motu statement by Prime Minister Atal Bihari Vajpayee, May 27, 1998) In his words, "A country of 100 crore cannot be left to the mercy of others . . . nuclear weaponisaiton is in self defence. Our enemies should know that we have nuclear weapons so that they will not attack us." (Hindustan Times, May 30, 1998: 1) In his letter to various heads of state clarifying India's compulsions Vajpayee wrote:

> *We have an overt nuclear weapon state on our borders, a state, which committed armed aggression against India in 1962. Although our relations with that country have improved in the last decade or so, an atmosphere of distrust persists mainly due to the unresolved border problem. . . To add to the distrust, that country has helped another neighbour of ours to become a covert nuclear weapon state. At the hand of this bitter neighbour we have suffered three aggressions in the last 50 years. (Text of the letter reprinted in The Hindu, May 14, 1998)*

In contrast, six decade ago (on 24 July, 1957), Nehru had declared that "India will in no event use atomic energy for destructive purposes. . . . I am confident that this would be the policy of all future governments." (Kapur 1976: 99) However, the years passed between the Nehru era till the end of the Cold War were not smooth. Year by year India seems to have learned and felt the politico-strategic importance of nuclear deter-

rent. Since then, political scenario of the country has undergone many changes. New Parties have emerged. Many coalition governments have been formed. Many critical national decisions were taken. In the same manner, the regional and global security environment has undergone manifold changes. However, the critical years since independence till India declares herself a nuclear weapons state in 1998, the issue of nuclear weapons vis-à-vis national and regional security has always been in the mainstream and the focus of analyses of the first two chapters in this section.

The third chapter of this section looks into the three parties' perspectives on other nuclear weapon countries outside the region (extra-regional powers) and whether they are a factor in India's nuclear weapon strategy.

Along with narration on Congress Party's early views on national security vis-a-vis nuclear weapons, the views of the parent organisations of BJP and CPI(M)—the Jan Sangh and CPI—are given space for better understanding the root of the debate of respective parties.

4

Regional Security Factor: Congress Views

What constitutes South Asia today was actually the British India. Therefore, considerable overlapping of culture, ethnicity, language, tribe, religion, etc., can be seen among all the eight constituting nations of this region. (Kumar 2005) India's national security discourse is intrinsically linked to the South Asian geo-strategic landscape which is India-centric.

After Independence, the INC had practical monopoly over national politics and had had the sole responsibility to shape and manage national security affairs. Even before 1947, the INC was active to visualise India's defence structure intact. For example, the Nehru Report (1928) of the INC had asked to transfer the control of the army to the proposed new national government. It had frankly admitted the truth of the principle that self-government for India would be very difficult to achieve without an effective Indian Army, but, it had declared that: "We do not accept the constitutional principle that without an Indian or Dominion Army India cannot obtain Dominion status. . . ." (CWC, *All Parties Conference* (Lucknow) 1928) Therefore, the day the hope for India's independence started to condense, the mainstream political group, i.e., the Congress Party had visualised a strong India to effectively guard against any threat to her national sovereignty. On nuclear issues, the Congress Party was determined from the very beginning. In its 54th Session in Meerut in 1946, the Party was alarmed at the trends of international developments and at the appearance of the atomic bomb as new weapon of war, and expressed the Congress ideal of international justice and peace. (AICC, *Congress Sessions At a Glance* 1946)

Soon after independence, Prime Minister Nehru expressed his belief that morality and self-interest inspire and direct Indian security and foreign policy (Power 1964: 257). Perhaps, this is partly because of the nature of prevalent international politics and partly because of Nehru's own ideological inclination. The trend in international politics in the post-World War II period left few options for a newly independent country like India to direct its national and international discourse. The predominant element in the international environment was the US-USSR rivalry. For Indian practitioners, however, two other Cold Wars—between former Soviet Russia and China and between America and China—created opportunity for Indian diplomacy to manoeuvre. There were cracks in the Sino-Soviet relations rooted in nationalist rivalry and the mistrust between Stalin and Mao that went back to 1927. The Indian leadership under Nehru presumed that they were bound to create a schism between the two that could be exploited to India's advantage. The three Cold Wars at the international plane (America-Soviet, Sino-Soviet and Sino-American), one at the regional level (Indo-US) and one hot-cold war relationship also at the regional level (Indo-Pak) meant that the international and regional structures were fragmented and multi-polar. (Basrur 2008: 1–4) In this context, India had to arrange its affairs and a peaceful (no war) environment was deemed necessary to exploit the space available in the pursuit to build India strong.

Also the geopolitical environment in South Asia, its linkage with the world politics had a bearing on Nehru's ideas and policies. (Kapur 2003: 144) According to Ashok Kapur, the subcontinent was multi-polar from the 1950s to the 1980s and beyond. (Kapur 2003: 146) He highlights three central alignments during the Cold War: Sino-Pakistan, US-Pakistan and India-USSR. So, the sub-continental multi-polarity revolved around a structure of fine relationship. Two alignments (Sino-Indian, Indo-Pak) were negative relationships or that of strategic conflict (either because of war, and expectation of war or fundamental differences of strategic interests) and three other alignments (mentioned above) were positive. All these factors prompted Nehru to devise a course of action, popularly known as "Nehru Model", comprising a foreign policy strategy guided by non-alignment, an economic policy guided by socialistic principles and a defence policy basing on five principle of 'peaceful coexistence' or Panchsheel. (Narayanan 1997)

In the post-Independence period, the Congress Party had maintained its "umbrella character" by comprising members from various strata and ideology. (Kurien 2008) According to Paranjoy Guha Thakurta and Shankar Raghuraman, the Congress was "the only political party that not only represented all sections . . . was unique among political parties in that it afforded an opportunity to all sections to put forward their claims and points of view. . . ." (Thakurta and Raghuraman 2007) But except a few members close to Nehru, all others were hardly involved in security and foreign policy matters. According to Paul F. Power, normally in security and foreign policy matters, Nehru had sought and received advice from an inner circle comprising Lord Louis Mountbatten, Girja Shankar Bajpai, K.M. Panikkar, Maulana Abul Kalam Azad, Sarvepalli Radhakrishnan, V.K. Krishna Menon, Mrs. Vijaya Lakshmi Pandit, and his daughter Indira Gandhi who has held high posts in the Congress. (Power 1964: 260) However, Nehru was the master of his own thoughts on international and security affairs and to a significant extent, directly responsible for the formulation and conduct of Indian foreign and security policy. (Power 1964: 260) It is viewed, therefore, that the decision making system during the Nehru period was "starkly ad-hoc in nature and designed primarily to suit the personality of Prime Minister Nehru"—who preferred to deal with these matters personally—even Krishna Menon seldom took stand on any point or even made contribution when the Prime Minister was in the chair (Parasnis 2002). Especially after Independence, Nehru became both President of the Party and the Prime Minister, therefore, there was good deal of harmony and coordination between the party and the governmental policies. (Borgohain 1982: 100)

India's approach towards national security can be seen, therefore, as personification of Nehru, instead of the Congress Party. Neville Maxwell, to that extent, viewed that "Nehru's policies were India's and vice-versa". (Maxwell 1974: 633) There was, in fact, no difference of opinion between the President of the Congress Party and the Prime Minister. Many view that during the 1950s, Nehru articulated a highly moralistic brand of politics that emphasised comprehensive economic development and, towards that goal, the harnessing of atomic energy for peaceful purposes. (Ganguly 1983: 30) According to Ashley Tellis, India's approach towards nuclear power under the leadership of Nehru was "Janus-faced". (Tellis 2001: 10) Not only in nuclear matters but also his views on overall defence structure were indicative of his temperament.

For example, soon after Independence the first Commander-in-Chief of the Indian armed forces, General Sir Robert Lockhart, presented the paper outlining a plan for the growth of Indian Army to Prime Minister Nehru. Nehru's reply was: "We don't need a defence plan. Our policy is non-violence. We foresee no military threats. You can scrap the army. The police are good enough to meet our security needs". (Quoted in Noorani 2006) On September 16, 1947, he directed that the army's then strength of 2, 80,000 be brought down to 1, 50,000. Even in fiscal 1950–51, when the Chinese threat had begun to loom large, 50,000 army personnel were sent home as per his original plan to disband the armed forces. It was only after the 1947–48 war in Jammu & Kashmir, he realised the armed forces are essential ingredient of any sovereign nation.

Soon after Independence, Nehru separated the Army, Navy, and Air Force from a unified command and abolished the post of commander-in-chief of the armed forces, thus bringing down the status of the seniormost military chief. During the 1947–48 war with Pakistan in Kashmir, Nehru known to have interfered with purely military decisions at will, which delayed the war and changed the ultimate outcome in Pakistan's favour. (Parasnis 2002) According to R.V. Parasnis, in the post-Independence period, national decision-making was mainly "designed and carried out on Prime Minister Nehru's will and perceptions. Neither the Congress Party nor any individual ever challenged his decisions". (Parasnis 2002)

However, the Jana Sangh's allegation was that "there were widespread discontent in the public mind regarding the Nehru government's Pakistan policy which in effect was only an extension of Congress's Muslim appeasement policy. Dr Shyama Prasad Mookerji's resignation from Nehru Cabinet was viewed as outcome of this issue. (*Bharatiya Jana Sangh Party Documents* 1973: "Foreword") As far as the nuclear power issue is concerned, it seems there was a consensus among all political fractions that it would alleviate the country from endemic poverty. And the ideals of freedom struggle—non-violence, peaceful resolution of conflict—were so pervasive that there was absolute consensus in India for opposing and condemning the use of nuclear weapons. "...Ideologically, the country as a whole was against the use of nuclear weapons anywhere and against any people". (Birla Institute of Scientific Research 1982: 89) Therefore, even if threats from neighbouring states were visualised, neither any political party nor any leader had a different view from Nehru's.

During the introduction of Scientific Policy Resolution in Lok Sabha on March 4, 1958, Nehru categorically mentioned "the scientific temper and the application of technology must be made consistent with responsible internationalism and reconciled with the highest ideals of age". (*Lok Sabha Debates*, quoted in Alam 1988: 12) Nehru's understanding of the potentialities of nuclear energy also was result of his long association with the subject. He had studied physics at Cambridge, read science in the spare moments and was fascinated by the theory that almost everything could be made radioactive. It was solely his enthusiasm to reap the fruits of nuclear science and technology that within 12 days of getting freedom, a meeting of the Atomic Energy Research Board was held. (*Nuclear India* 1977: 3) It vindicates that Nehru's ideas on nuclear issues was guided by his own scientific temperament mixed with ideals of the age. His scientific temper got shaped by his close association with Homi Bhabha. It is his personal interest and ideas that prompted him to give full freedom and autonomy to Bhabha establish research facilities on which India's nuclear programme is standing upon today. (Narain 1990: 3) It is his own views on war and peace nurtured during the freedom struggle shaped his idea about nuclear weapons as well.

Even though the regional security situation was not in favour of India, building of nuclear weapons to guarantee national security was not attempted during the immediate Independence period. In the views of Ashley Tellis, "while the history of the Indian nuclear programme predates the country's independence in 1947, the strategic environment India faced for most of her independent life did not demand that any clear-cut decisions be made regarding its nuclear status". (Tellis 2001: 10) Rather the entire attention was to stabilise the political and economic situation of the country. Though communal violence in the post-Independence period was rampant, no member of the Congress Party was ever demanded nuclear weapons. Rather there was uncompromising opposition to nuclear weapons and to nuclear weaponry *per se* was considered as instruments of "high politics". (Tellis 2001: 10)

On the other hand, the horror of Hiroshima and Nagasaki was alive in the minds of the people; there was consensus against nuclear weapons. Nehru's consciousness of the power of scientific knowledge and its impersonal and amoral character led him to the realisation that highest ideals of humanism and scientific spirit had to function together to which he called 'scientific humanism' (Patnaik 1990). Referring to the new challenges posed by a mighty revolution in the technology of war as well as peace and demanding new answers, Nehru once said:

> On the one hand, the nuclear bomb and the destruction of Nagasaki and Hiroshima illustrates the horrendous revolution that has taken place in military technology and on the other, the application of nuclear energy to peaceful and constructive purpose has opened up limitless possibilities for human development, prosperity and overabundance. This major challenge confronts our times with a choice between co-destruction and co-prosperity and makes it imperative for the world to outlaw war, particularly nuclear war. (Quoted in Karanjia 1966: 65)

It seems that India's post-Independence attitude towards nuclear weapons and consequent national policy was major reflection of Nehru's own ideals and choice, and the Congress Party as a whole seems to have played minimal role. Mainly two regional issues involving two of India's neighbours characterised India's security concerns during those days: the India-Pakistan and Sino-Indian border dispute. But in none of these issues the relevance of nuclear weapons was highlighted, particularly not within the Congress Party. For instance, Nehru had the firm belief and conviction that all bilateral irritants between neighbouring countries can amicably be solved through diplomacy. This view of Nehru was corollary to his foreign policy ideas which based on "global influence without military power". (Hilali 2001: 749)

With regard to China, it became apparent to Nehru after 1954 that Chinese transgression was not confined to Tibet, but were into territories which India considered to be legally her (MEA, *White Paper I*). Border patrols sent into the hills to ascertain the situation and found Chinese troops occupying localities on the 'Indian' side of the Tibetan border in Ladakh, Uttar Pradesh and Assam and in some instances border incidents led to casualties. Initially, India took a tolerant view as these transgressions were made by local Chinese frontier forces with mistaken ideas about the precise alignment of the Indo-Tibetan boundary and without the support and knowledge of the Chinese Central Government. According to *MEA White Paper*, with the intention of not to disturb the general friendship between China and India, Nehru decided to withhold knowledge of the transgressions from the Indian public and took the matter up directly with Zou En Lai and the Central Government of China. The correspondence between the two leaders during the years 1954–60, published as series of White Papers in 1959-60, when it was no longer possible to conceal the seriousness of the dispute. Therefore, till the end of 1960, nuclear weapons in the context of Sino-Indian border dispute had never been raised, rather the Congress Party under the leadership of Nehru, adhering to the principles of Panchsheel and Asian Solidarity, was convinced that minor irritants in the Sino-Indian relations would be amicably solved. In 1948 at Jaipur, the Indian National Congress declared that "closer bonds of fellowship and cooperative efforts" among Asian states would be fostered in the future (Rajkumar 1952: 9)

As far as threat from and Pakistan is concerned, there available no evidence of such linkage. Though, Nehru was clear about Pakistan's tactic to woo USA to get military aid against India, he only decried the American move as an export of militarism and Cold War to the subcontinent, threatening the peace and stability of the region. (Appadorai and Rajan 1985: 229) USA military aid to Pakistan was officially conveyed to Nehru in late February 1954 with an assurance from Dwight Eisenhower that USA would strive to prevent Pakistan's diversion of US military assistance against harming India. President Eisenhower offered military aid to India as well. But Nehru informed USA that the problem was not American motive, rather the effects of its action internationally and within India and Pakistan. While Nehru sought to cut back on people-to-people contact between USA and India, he sent strong message to Pakistan. (Kux 2002: 111) He conveyed to Pakistan Prime Minister Mohammed Ali Bogra that "if vast armies are built up in Pakistan with the aid of American money ... all of our problems will have to be seen in a new light." (Gopal 1979: 184)

Nehru amplified his concerns in a letter to his Chief Ministers by saying that US aid would change the balance of power in the region and exacerbate threats against India whether the US wants that or not (*Jawaharlal Nehru: Letters to Chief Ministers* 1986, cited in Kux 1992: 109). But how far and whether this issue played any role in shaping India's nuclear programme is unclear. Even in 1956, when Pakistan established an Atomic Energy Commission, the event was perceived as its enthusiasm for atomic energy and its interest in capitalising the international cooperation offered through the Atom for Peace initiative. On these bases, Perkovich argues that "Pakistan did not play an important role in India's nuclear policy making in the years from 1948 to 1963. Pakistan posed no nuclear threat." (Perkovich 2002: 47)

According to Stephen P. Cohen, "from its inception, India going nuclear seemed to be less a technical question than a political one". (Cohen 2005: 159) Probably the lack of movement in the direction of overt nuclearisation stemmed from the perception that despite strategic challenges it faced, the security environment India confronted for most of the post-Independence period had in general been benign. According to B.M. Jain, the Nehruvian legacy of suspicion about militarised power politics and its attendant distaste of nuclear weaponry as the currency of global power interacted with the older Gandhian moral synthesis, which emphasised "community" over "state" and "service" over "coercion", that manifested in India's ambiguous nuclear poster in later days. (Jain 1994: 53–77)

Beside the issue of colonial exploitation, the dangers flowing from the arms race were never far from Nehru's mind. (Damodaran 1990: 473) He talked length, both in Parliament and in Congress sessions on the dangers inherent in the nuclear race. In June 1957, the AICC considered the nuclear danger urgent enough to justify a Special Resolution. The resolution viewed with "distress and alarms the continuance of nuclear and thermo-nuclear test explosions in spite of their proven danger to present and future generations of mankind . . . ." (AICC *Resolution* 1957) Nehru was then in the vanguard of movements for stopping nuclear weapons testing in the atmosphere and for an international convention banning the use of nuclear weapons. (Jaipal 1990: 429)

However, there is considerable divergence of opinion on Nehru's decisions on India's nuclear weapons policy. While many argue that Nehru was unequivocal about India not opting for nuclear weapons, many others, like George Perkovich, take a different stand on the issue. Perkovich, though not clear if Nehru's decisions had any linkage with regional security imperatives, asserts that both Nehru and Bhabha were full cognisance of India's future strategic needs and therefore formulated such policy under the level of "peaceful purposes" which generated multiple options for future. Even another Indian scholar, Bharat Karnad, is of the same opinion when he says, Nehru "clearly signaled his intention to have Bhabha's programme develop the atom bomb to make the country 'self-reliant' in security as well." (Karnad 2002: 182)

According to Perkovich, "at the level of intention, Nehru did not rule out military use" of India's nuclear know-how. Rather, Nehru recognised the military potential of the new project on which India was embarking under his and Bhabha's leadership. Further he says: "Contrary to . . . conventional understanding, the founders of India's nuclear establishment recongnised and welcomed from the beginning the options in military dimension gave to India, notwithstanding Nehru's genuine hope that India could retain a purely peaceful mission. They did this in 1948, before the Communist takeover of China, before any major external military threat to India was posited." (Perkovich 2002: 20) In justification, Perkovich emphasises the deliberate "stringent secrecy" maintained in the initial stages of India's nuclear programme. He cites the debate in the Constituent Assembly after Nehru introduced the Atomic Energy Act in 1948 to create an Atomic Energy Commission and the legal framework for action. The Act called for research and development of atomic energy in *complete secrecy* and established "state ownership of all relevant raw materials".

The debate on the *secrecy* aspect of India's nuclear programme, as Perkovich says, "Revealed the essential ambiguity of the incipient nuclear programme and provides useful evidence for evaluating the common claim that India's nuclear programme began with no intention to develop nuclear weapons capabilities". (Perkovich 2002: 18) The Act was criticised on the basis that the secrecy provision are much beyond the legislation governing the US and British Atomic Energy Commissions. Dr Sitaramayya, a chemist, feared that monopoly and secrecy would inevitably corrupt the enterprise in India, as elsewhere, and cause "the preparations of war, more than peace". (Abraham 1995: 34) S.V. Krishnamurthy Rao, criticising the Act, asked why India should impose greater secrecy than the US and the UK which were unlike India also building nuclear weapons. (*Constituent Assembly of India, Legislative Debates* 1948: 3323) In response, Nehru argued that the case for secrecy in India derived from the need to protect Indian materials and prospective know-how from being exploited by the industrialised countries in a colonial manner. (*Constituent Assembly of India, Legislative Debates* 1948: 3315)

Rao further questioned that whether India had "wherewithal for all this secrecy and research" and positing that the Indian bill did not allow for the oversight and checking and balancing mechanisms contained even in the US Atomic Energy Act.

Repeating his question Rao said, "May I know if secrecy is insisted upon even for research for peaceful purposes?" In response, Nehru said "Not theoretical research. Secrecy comes in when you think in terms of the production or use of atomic energy. That is the central effort to produce atomic energy." Further Rao asked: "In the Bill passed in the UK secrecy is restricted only for defence purposes". Nehru, in reply, said: "I do not know how you are to distinguish between the two." (*Constituent Assembly of India, Legislative Debates* 1948: 3328) This reply is implicit of the fact that rhetorical distinctions between military and peaceful atomic projects could not obscure the reality that development and application of atomic know-how and technology is essentially dual-purpose.

Nehru's implicit acknowledgment of the dual nature of India's nuclear programme was further amplified by Professor Shibban Lal Saksena. Evocatively criticising the naïveté of the argument of Rao, Prof Saksena said:

> Science is power, both for good and for evil. . . . If we have not got the knowledge and the ability to use this power, there is no virtue in our saying that we shall not use it for destructive purposes. . . . We all know that atomic energy is today the most important scientific discovery. Unless we spend upon it lavishly . . . we shall not be making the best use of our talents and materials. . . . Until we have the capacity to use atomic energy for destructive warfare it will have no meaning for us to say that we shall not use atomic energy for destructive purposes. (*Constituent Assembly of India, Legislative Debates* 1948: 3332-33)

Nehru, without challenging Prof Saksena's portrayal, acknowledged that the nuclear project in India, as in the US and UK, was potential source of military as well as economic power. He said:

> Somehow, we cannot help associating atomic energy with war. That is the present context of our lives. . . . The point I should like the House to consider is this, that if we are to remain abreast in the world as a nation which keeps ahead of things, we must develop this atomic energy quite apart from war . . . we must develop it for the purpose of using it for peaceful purposes. . . . *Of course, if we are compelled as a nation to use it for other purposes, possibly no pious sentiments of any of us will stop the nation from using it that way.* But I do hope that our outlook in regard to this atomic energy is going to be a peaceful one . . . (*Constituent Assembly of India, Legislative Debates* 1948: 3333-34)

Whether Nehru in reality had visualised India's future strategic requirements and maintained therefore the secrecy or whether his ideals of peaceful coexistence and morality ruled over his quest for India's future technological growth, is still a matter of debate. However, "from 1948 through 1963, nuclear policy barely figured in Indian politics". Perkovich strongly believes that "while Bhabha and his colleagues, with Nehru's backing, were steadily developing India's nuclear weapons potential, the polity knew practically nothing about it". (Perkovich 2002: 40) When faint signs of challenge to the Congress Party appeared after the 1957 Lok Sabha election with surprising gains by the Communist Party of India (CPI), the issues of concern were the rising taxes, poverty, unemployment and corruption. Even none of the India's major English language daily newspapers devoted any attention to the possibility of an Indian nuclear weapons programme. (Bhatia 1979: 115)

Even if Nehru's approach was idealistic, it didn't last long. Subsequent political leadership took divergent stands on the nuclear issue. The regional security imperatives of subsequent decades played its part in drawing attention of the political leaders towards nuclear weapons. Members within the Congress Party started to take divergent opinions, justifying the perceived threats to the nation, more specifically after the 1962 Sino-Indian border war. However, the Congress Party and the Parliament endorsed Prime Minister Nehru's decision against manufacturing a bomb. (Hilali 2001: 739) But a study by Leonard Beaton and John Madox on the issues states that during that time the high priority given to the atomic energy programme for complete self-sufficiency in all related techniques suggest that "Nehru, advised by Bhabha, had decided to give the country an option to produce nuclear device by 1963 in case this should be politically or militarily necessary". (Beaton and Madox 1962: 141) If this perception holds any truth, by 1964-65, Bhabha and his team definitely had moved India to the point where they could seriously consider becoming a nuclear weapons state, as Bhabha known to have claimed in February 1965 that India could go nuclear within eighteen months. (Abraham 1998: 126) Therefore, "politics, economics and morality, rather than technology", as viewed by Cohen, "were the uppermost issues when the first major public debate over nuclear weapons took place in the wake of the Chinese explosion". (Cohen 2005: 159)

But, the China-threat as a drive for Indian leaders' decision to seek nuclear weapons is discarded by George Perkovich. Even he denies the international security consideration has anything to do with India's nuclear decision-making during 1948 to 1963, though Bhabha was consciously developing nuclear weapons capabilities prior to the emergence of a Chinese nuclear threat. (Perkovich 2002: 59) Rather, to Perkovich, "the main motivations for India's initial plans to acquire the means to produce nuclear explosives had more to do with Bhabha's and Nehru's beliefs that nuclear technology offered India a shortcut to modernity and major power status" and thereby it can transcend its recent colonial past.

Post-Nehru Nuclear Decisions

The Chinese aggression in 1962 brought the Congress leadership into question. The domestic pressure was mounting and in early 1964, India announced a five-year defence plan which amounted to five per cent of national income. Though, US agreed to provide military aid but denied F-104 fighter aircraft that was given to Pakistan. In April 1964, India and Canada concluded an agreement for the heavy water moderated CANDU reactor after India agreed for non-diversion of the technology and fuel provided by Canada to the non-civilian programme, and would only be used for "peaceful purposes". However, according to Ashok Kapur, while approving Bhabha's memo describing the deal reached with Canada, Nehru wrote in the margin that "apart from building power stations and developing electricity, there is always a built-in advantage of defence use if the need should arise". (Kapur 2003: 193–94)

After Chinese aggression, though Nehru was under tremendous pressure, no overt contention against his decisions was raised. After Nehru's death (27 May 1964), Congress Party was led by the staunch Gandhian, Lal Bahadur Shastri. He, as a Congress Party leader, maintained "a life of truth in politics". (Srivastava 1995) But in contrast to Nehru, Shastri seemed to have succumbed to pressure from the Party members. One reason for selecting Shastri, instead of Morarji Desai, as successor of Nehru could be the State level political leaders' intention of a weaker Union government after living through the accretion of centralised Prime Ministerial power during the Nehru era. (Frankel 1978: 242) Shastri's ascendance to Prime Ministership was coincided with the entering of the first spent fuel from the CIRUS reactor to the plutonium reprocessing plant at Trombay. Another important event that greatly shaped India's nuclear future is the Chinese first nuclear test on October 16,1964. The pressure for India to respond was mounting rapidly.

Here, the first hypothesis—*national political leadership, not political party, is the determining factor in India's nuclear weapons decision making*—can be examined. In case of Nehru, nuclear decisions were seem to be based purely on his own understanding and vision of India and the Congress Party never dissented to his decisions. Lal Bahadur Shastri assumed Prime Ministership with the idea that he is inheriting an unambiguously peaceful nuclear programme. (Perkovich 2002: 63) He was a leader with all integrity, but the decision for the SNEPP that he took is viewed contradictory to his Gandhian ideals. How and why a man of his age and conviction could change his moral values altogether is a mystery. It must be the situation and the influence of the people around him that compelled him to take such a decision. It is assumed that the reason could be the pressure from the Party members and the popular pressure generated after the Chinese tests. If that is true, the assertion that only the political leadership, not the political parties, a major determinant is not confirmed. The following sections amplify this contention.

Debate after Chinese Nuclear Tests

When the Chinese nuclear test began to stir an Indian debate, Shastri was attending a Conference of Non-aligned Nations in Cairo, where he urged leaders of other states to "persuade China to desist from developing nuclear weapons". He said, "India's nuclear establishment is under firm orders not to make a single experiment, not to perfect a single device. . . ." (Mirchandani 1968: 25) As was expected, the opposition parties missed no opportunity to emphasise the increased danger from China after it tested the bomb. In small numbers, Congress Party members too began to join those who demanded a change in government policy.

The general body of the All India Congress Committee went into a secret session on November 8, 1964 at Guntur, Andhra Pradesh, as result of a demand by restive Congressmen on the nuclear weapons option. (Noorani 1967: 495) The majority of speakers in the meeting wanted Government to show greater awareness of the "new situation" created by the Chinese blast. Bibhuti Mishra, General Secretary of the Congress Parliamentary Party strongly pleaded (on November 7, 1964) that India should make the atom bomb. He said:

> If we do not decide today to make the bomb, events will force us after some time to do so. If suddenly China attacks us, we will have to seek the help of the USA or Russia. This should not

be. We must have our own bomb. (*NTI India Profile*, "Nuclear Chronology")

Mr Mishra wanted a national referendum to be held on this issue. In his opinion, unless India strengthens itself, she could not command respect and prestige. Even his opinion was supported by several other members of the Congress. Bhagwat Jha Azad, another member of the Congress Parliamentary Party's Executive Committee, moved an amendment to the official resolution in which he asked Government to reserve the right, in the event of the threat to India's independence, to use nuclear weapons for national defence. (*Lok Sabha Debates*, November 23, 1964, col. 1280) P.V. Narasimha Rao, the then Andhra Pradesh Law Minister, pleaded for efforts to render ineffective the political and military advantages which China might accrue by the possession of atom bomb. He suggested to actively collaborate with other atomic powers. (*Lok Sabha Debates*, November 23 1964, col. 1280) However, after an intensive debate of two-hours, the resolution of the committee endorsed "no-bomb" policy but asked Government to "re-double" its efforts for the development of the peaceful uses of atomic energy. Speaking on the occasion, Prime Minister Shastri told "we will try to eliminate the threat and terror of nuclear weapons rather than enter into competition with other countries to make or produce atom bombs here". (*Lok Sabha Debates*, 23 November 1964, col. 1280)

In the Parliament, Shastri was firm on his stand. He told a Congress Party member in reply to a question in the Rajya Sabha on November 17, a month after Chinese nuclear blast, that the government favoured a discussion by the UN of the situation created by the Chinese explosion (Ganguly 1999: 151). On November 24, 1964, the Lok Sabha held its first debate on the implications regarding Chinese nuclear explosion. Bhagwat Jha Azad called upon the Minister for External Affairs to ask if the government's use of nuclear power for the defence of the country is a crime. (Chakma 2005: 192) But Defence Minister V.K. Krishna Menon made a strong plea against India going nuclear by saying that "possession of nuclear devices is a danger to India for if China takes it into her head to drop a bomb on us in order to create panic, then she can easily tell the world that we dropped it on them, just as Pakistan does things to us and then says that we attacked them" (Quoted in Rusch 1969: 756–7).

On October 27, 1964, the Executive Committee of the Congress Party discussed Government's nuclear policy in a closed door meeting. Members in the meeting known to have expressed unanimous view that India must maintain lead over China in nuclear science and technology. (Rangaswami 1964) The view was, India at present may not go in for a nuclear weapons programme, but it should be technologically prepared to produce the bomb in a short notice, if necessary. However, the draft resolution prepared by Foreign Minister Swaran Singh approved the government's policy not to manufacture atomic bombs. In the AICC (7–9 Nov) meetings Shastri kept on emphaising the priority of rallying on international community, particularly the US and Soviet Union, to address the danger of nuclear proliferation. The interesting thing happened in the gathering is that a petition demanding India to acquire "an independent nuclear deterrent to protect herself against any possible threat from China", signed by one hundred members was presented. (Rangaswami 1964) But Prime Minister Shastri and his supporters didn't budge. Instead, on November 27, 1964, in reply to Jan Sangh-led opposition move in the Lok Sabha in the form of a motion to persuade the Government to change its policy, Shastri said: "The cult of the bomb is a danger to world peace and we reject it categorically". However, he had no objection to atomic energy being used for peaceful purposes.

The 69th Annual Session of the Indian National Congress, held in Durgapur in January 1965, was a landmark event where the bomb issue was vigorously debated. The pressure from the Congress Party members on the Prime Minister was tremendous. K.C. Pant, then a young Congress leader, vociferously argued for India acquiring nuclear weapons. (Opinion by Pant 1998: 59–62) Speaking on a resolution, Shastri argued that India had consistently demanded a ban on atomic weapons since the first blast occurred at Hiroshima and Nagasaki and it would be improper if India now departed from its stand, because China had developed nuclear weapon. He categorically said: "How can we go against the principle we have been working for so long?" (Mirchandani 1968: 35) However, he went on to declare that "our policy is not to manufacture the atom bombs *at present*". By the phrase "at present" he probably meant that he is not sure about the distant future and future governments. This is in complete contrast to Nehru's pronouncement that "Indian leaders, present and future, will not decide to manufacture nuclear weapons".

Towards the end of 1964, the Congress Party was completely divided on the nuclear bomb issue. For example, while Finance Minister Morarji Desai supported Shastri's views, Minister of Communications Jagjivan Ram had demanded, in a speech at a public meeting at Bikramganj (Bihar), India to develop nuclear weapons to safeguard her freedom, though later he changed his stand. The Defence Minister Y.B. Chavan asserted that the bomb would not significantly increase China's military strength pointing out that the short-term threat remained Chinese conventional forces. (Mirchandani 1968: 26) The opposition was seizing on the Chinese test to challenge the overall leadership of the Shastri government. The debate over India and nuclear weapons intensified and the new Prime Minister faced serious challenge to establish his authority within the Congress Party. Threat to his leadership was from within the Party itself as members had already lost confidence in Shastri's leadership owing to his inability to solve the food crisis. (Perkovich 1999: 69) Even before the Chinese test, in September, the opposition had generated enough support to compel a no-confidence debate against the government in the Lok Sabha.

To remain in power, Prime Minister Shastri had to address the food crisis and security situation created by the Chinese nuclear test. In July 1964, Shastri accentuated the shift in power by forming the Prime Minister's Secretariat to strengthen his weak hand against rivals in the Congress party. (Frankel 1978: 251) With the domestic crisis over the food shortage in the background, the debate on nuclear weapon continued to mount. The pressure within the government for acquiring nuclear weapons was building up. An intensive six-hour discussion took place in a Cabinet meeting, where Swaran Singh (Minister for External Affairs) S.K. Patil (Minister of Railways) and Bhabha discussed on nuclear weapons programme. Only two ministers, Y.B. Chavan (Defence Minister) and C. Subramaniam (Food and Agriculture Minister), had opposed India going nuclear. It is believed that in this meeting "discussions had gone far enough for Shastri to authorise Bhabha to come up with estimate of what was involved in India's attempting an underground explosion". (Rochlin 1964: 2)

As a matter of fact, the domestic nuclear debate was occurring against the backdrop of "a fast deteriorating economic situation. While explaining his anti-bomb policy to party colleagues in the Cabinet meeting, Prime Minister Shastri focused on the economic and moral-political costs. He argued that the production of a single atom bomb would cost Rs 400 to 500 million, not the Rs 100 million as Bhabha claimed for fifty atomic bombs. Therefore, bomb building would divert scarce resource from developmental projects. (Rangaswamy 1964: 1) The other justification Shastri advanced was that "the possession of nuclear weapons would be directly opposed to the policy of peace and non-violence" nurtured by Gandhi and Nehru. (Rangaswamy 1964: 1)

Another extensive debate over India's foreign policy and nuclear weapons policy took place during November 23-24, 1964 in the Lok Sabha. Three alternative motions on nuclear policy were proffered in the debate:

(1) Call for immediate production of an atom bomb;
(2) Call for embarking on "nuclear-based defence installations in the country"; and
(3) A general reorient of foreign policy in the light of Chinese bomb.

According to Perkovich, the parliamentarians were lacking the expertise and sophistication to conduct systematic analysis and debate of the nuclear issue. (Perkovich 1999: 76) However, the government stand, as Defence Minister Y.B. Chavan said, was to rely on the balance of power dynamics—India could be protected by the balance of power dynamics among the nuclear weapon states. He said, "If such a war [nuclear] breaks out, we have friends to support us". (*Times of India*, November 21, 1964) But, this sanguine outlook had faded during the debate in Lok Sabha. No parliamentarian argued for India to passively rest its security on the belief that US or the Soviet Union or both would intercede decisively if China threatened or actually used nuclear weapons against India. In the Lok Sabha, there were two voices. First, as Bhagwat Jha Azad of the Congress Party argued, Chinese intimidation required India to be prepared to "go all out to use nuclear power for the defence of the country". Nath Pai also lambasted the notion of turning to the US for security assistance, who refused to supply F-104 fighters to India. Harish Chandra Mathur of the Congress party argued that India should do whatever was necessary to stand up to China. He said, "There is no other morality; our moral duty is the security of this country, dignity of this country, the honour of this country and the safety of this country. Everything else will have to be subjugated to that". (*Lok Sabha Debates*, November 1964, Col. 1280)

Second, there were many members within the Congress who viewed China's nuclear arsenal do not target India. R.K. Khadilkar, a Congress MP from Khed proclaimed that:

> China with its conventional arms is not capable of invading this country. Let us take a realistic view of the situation. . . . This bomb is not directed towards India. . . . It is directed at the world powers, the super powers. . . . It is directed against the nuclear monopoly of the western powers and not towards India. . . . Let this House realise that our conflict with China is a very limited conflict. It is not going to lead to war. (*Lok Sabha Debates* November 24, 1964: col. 1478-79)

Khadilkar's assertion triggered uproar in the House. Some viewed him speaking on behalf of the Chinese government; others said he was speaking for American lobby, but his speech emboldened several others. V.B. Gandhi noted that China has been cautious in handling the Quemoy and Matsu disputes. "Also take our own experience of aggression against our borders. China has desisted from pressing its advantage. That only shows that China is not as rash as it is make to appear". (*Lok Sabha Debates* November 24, 1964: col. 1521) Likewise, Ali Mirza pointed out that, historically nuclear weapons had provided little usable power: "What gain has any country in the world got from the atom bomb? Has it helped France in Vietnam or Algiers? Has it helped Great Britain in Suez or Cyprus? Has it helped the USA anywhere in this wide world? This is only a terror. China said that it is a paper tiger. This is not the correct approach." (*Lok Sabha Debates*, November 24, 1964: col. 1532-33) According to U.M. Trivedi, "In Asia there are two giants; one of them is India and the other is China. If one giant grows and the other remains a dwarf, certainly the dwarf will be killed, and there will be no time for the dwarf to arm himself". (*Lok Sabha Debates* November 24, 1964: 1512) Further, he maintained that the theory today in the world is 'each nation unto itself'.

Beside the China issue, the division was on the cost factor of the programme. Those who argued against bomb programme cited the higher cost figures; those who argued for the bomb programme cited Bhabha's calculations. Supporters of nuclear weapons programme, following the security-first logic of realism, rejected the notion that defence interests could be traced off for other concerns. Nath Pai, rebutting Masani, directly said: "Shri Masani talks of the price. I want to be free; so I must pay the price". (*Lok*

Sabha Debates, November 23, 1964, col. 1300) While moderating the conflicting and unresolved tussle over the nuclear issue, Mark Anthony said: "I am aware of the fact that with almost a thousand crores of defence expenditure that has contributed largely to the run-away inflation to the astronomical rise in food prices . . . " He viewed that China may aim to "stampede" India into excessive defence spending in order to prompt internal crisis. Therefore, he concluded that, India should not enter the race for producing the atomic or a hydrogen bomb. But, he suggested for a middle path, an alternative— "India must pursue from today, from tomorrow, the development of nuclear technology and know-how." (*Lok Sabha Debates*, November 23, 1964, col. 1315) Most of the leaders preferred a middle ground and supported the idea to speed up the development of technology and know-how that would enable them later to decide to make weapons. Indira Gandhi, the then Minister of Information and Broadcasting, said in an interview on French television at Paris on October 22, 1964 that "India is in a position to produce the bomb within 18 months. But, I think we should not deviate from our stand and should use atomic energy for peaceful purposes only." (Quoted in Mirchandani 1968: 30) Even Finance Minister Morarji Desai viewed manufacturing nuclear bomb by India as "suicidal" (Bose 1985: 1595).

This intensive debate and consequent division in the Congress party and counter-attacks by the opposition seem to have made Sahastri's leadership vulnerable. Speaking over thirty minutes in Hindi, he first disabused his critics having the notion that moral considerations alone determined his government's resistance to building nuclear weapons. After such intensive debate Shastri seemed aware that domestically derived inhibitions could not justify an absolute rejection of nuclear weapons. He might have felt the necessity of politically and strategically robust policy. Presumably, he declared the *non-weapon policy is subject to change.* In response to members on both sides of the House, he explained that Government's decision not to produce the atom bomb was not based on moral considerations rather, it is based on practical and realistic considerations, especially keeping in mind its impact on the economy. By clarifying government stand on nuclear weapons not permanent, he said:

> I cannot say that the present policy is deep-rooted, that it cannot be set aside, that it can never be changed. . . An individual may have a certain static policy . . . but in the political field

> we cannot do so. Here situations alter, changes take place, and we have to mould our policies accordingly. (Quoted in Mirchandani 1968: 34)

In fact, the domestic debate over the exercise of nuclear weapons option intensified with the first Chinese test in October 1964 and it became more intensive after China's successive tests. On May 14, 1965, China conducted its second nuclear test. Even after China's first test, Shastri had reportedly said that Government would adhere to its "declared policy" in spite of China goes for another test and he do "not favour emulating the Chinese example". (Kapur 2001: 133–37; Bhatia 109) But, by the time China tested its second device, the mood within the Congress Party had shifted towards keeping India's option open. And the expectation of the Congress members and pressure from other parties was enormous challenge for Shastri to establish himself as strong leader, especially in the context of the vacuum created with the demise of a stalwart like Nehru. That was, therefore, the testing time for his leadership.

Probably, with an aim to prove his integrity, Shastri tried both to cherish Nehruvian idealism while decided pragmatically not to be rigid on nuclear issues. This is clearly evident when he said that he is *not considering to embark on nuclear weapons production "for the time being" and the "policy may change if warranted"* (emphasis added). And that was in fact the turning point or a departure from India's post-Independence defence policy. But, one may argue that the new policy was the outcome of the intensive debate and pressure generated both within the Congress and in the Parliament. The Prime Minister had to succumb to the pressure, but very tactfully he could balance his idealism with the demands of national security imperatives. (Basrur: 2)

Therefore, unlike Nehru, nuclear weapons decisions by Prime Minister Shastri were more influenced by the Congress Party and party politics. Equally strong was the pressure from the opposition party and more specifically, by the environment emerged out of Chinese nuclear tests. Though Shastri's assertion that India has the capability to develop nuclear weapon within a time frame, if warranted was viewed at some quarters as overestimation of India's technical preparedness, the consequent debate highlighted the effects of domestic political dynamics on national decision-making process. For example, as quoted by Perkovich, an Arms Control and Disarmament Agency memorandum opined that "Shastri's government is much more subject to the political pressures of the day than its predecessor under Nehru. To stay in power, it must reach out for support and be on the popular side of national issues to a much greater extent than the Nehru government". (Quoted by Perkovich 2003: 496) However, his decision though a crucial change in policy was only a half turn. After reminding the House that India could produce a nuclear bomb within "two or three years" if necessary, Shastri reaffirmed the commitment of India's nuclear establishment to peaceful work only. He said:

> . . . as far as we can progress and improve upon nuclear devices, we should do so, as far as development is possible, we should resort to it so that we can reap its peaceful benefits and we can use it for the development of our nation. . . . Just assume that we have to use big tunnels and we have to clear huge areas, we have to wipe out mountains for development parks, and in this context if it is required to use nuclear devices for the good of the country as well as for the good of the world, so then our AEC is pursuing these same objectives. (*Lok Sabha Debates*, November 27, 1964, translated by Pravin Kumar)

Congress Views on Indo-Pakistan War 1965

In the wake of conflict with Pakistan in September 1965, the "make-the-bomb" demand acquired a new ferocity. Adding this, China's menacing posture during the war with Pakistan gave impetus to those who vouched for the bomb. An increasing number of Congress Party members began to speak their thoughts out freely and publicly. A day earlier the ceasefire with Pakistan (September 22, 1965), about 100 Members of Parliament belonging to all parties addressed a letter to the Prime Minister urging an immediate decision to develop nuclear weapons. (Chakma 2005) The MPs pointed India's "bitter experience" on account of the denial of aid by Western Powers during the conflict. They pleaded that "India's survival as a nation and as a democracy, both the face of the collusion between China and Pakistan, casts a clear and imperative duty on the government to take an immediate decision to develop our nuclear weapons". (Chakma 2005)

Even Congress Party members at the regional level expressed support of India going for nuclear bomb. Five days after the ceasefire, the Speaker of the Madhya Pradesh State Assembly, K.L. Dube strongly expressed support. (Mirchandani 1968: 39) On 2nd October, 1965 the former Chief Minister of Madhya Pradesh

D.P. Mishra said in an interview at Bhopal that he was in favour of India making the atom bomb. (Mirchandani 1968: 39) He added by saying that "let us not forget that our Prime Minister has never said that India would not go in for the atom bomb under any circumstances. He has merely said that at present the Government of India's policy is not to make it. We should not forget the two words '*at present*' contained in his statement". Mehr Chand Khanna, a member of the Central Council of Ministers, demanded at a public meeting in New Delhi that India must make the atom bomb. He told "we do not want to attack anybody with atomic weapons but we must have them for our own defence against those who have such weapons". (Quoted in Mirchandani 1968: 40)

Six weeks after the end of Indo-Pakistan conflict, 43 members of the Lok Sabha jointly tabled a question in which they asked the Prime Minister whether "after the recent Sino-Pakistan hostile overtures, government had lately reviewed the earlier decision not to go in for production of the atom bomb". (Mirchandani 1968: 40) Prime Minister Shastri replied by saying that "despite the continued threat of aggression from China which has developed nuclear weapons, government have continued to adhere to the decision not to go in for nuclear weapons but to work for their elimination instead." But that was the time, as is believed and reported in *New York Times* (November 30, 1965), Shastri had given go-ahead for the work up to a point about three months from an explosion.

If this report is to be believed, Shastri's decision was undoubtedly the outcome of the domestic political pressure emerging out of the regional security situation and the apprehension on his political and leadership integrity. As Perkovich points out, Shastri's hold on power had been tentative from the beginning. The severe food and price crisis further undermined his colleagues' confidence that his leadership would help them retain their positions at the polls. According to *Times of India* report, during early January 1965 in the annual session of the Congress Party "the most ruthless criticism of the government" was witnessed (cited in Frankel 2005: 265). As already the embarrassing defeat at the hands of Chinese in 1962 had cast an aura of incompetence and airiness around Congress's conduct of security policy, a similar passivity in the face of the Chinese tests seemed to have tarnished the Party's image further. Perkovich asserts that "with so much else going wrong, Shastri and his colleagues could not afford to appear as weak defenders of India's national pride and strength.

Thus, his no-bomb position could not rally a majority even within the Congress Party. To maintain his leadership he had to shift". (Perkovich 2002: 85) Therefore, one may view that Shastri's policy shift from October to late-November 1964 is mainly accounted for the nuclear politics within the Congress Party.

Post-Shastri Congress and Nuclear Weapons Decisions

Prime Minister Lal Bahadur Shastri died at a moment when he was starting to gain popularity and control over the Congress Party. His sudden demise at Tashkent on January 11, 1966 brought Indira Gandhi to the leadership of the Congress Party. For Mrs Gandhi, the domestic, economic and regional security situation was not much different than Shastri time. Answering the question in the Lok Sabha on March 1st, 1966, whether government would consider nuclear umbrella from other powers as an alternative to manufacture nuclear weapons, Mrs Gandhi said, "the government's policy on this matter has been clear and it remains the same". (Quoted in Mirchandani 1968: 43) She further said:

> We are anxious not to do anything which will precipitate the crisis and lead to the development of nuclear weapons in many more countries. The policy of restraint which we have adopted must, therefore, continue. This is not because we believe that certain big powers should have a monopoly of these destructive weapons, but because we are generally anxious to see total nuclear disarmament. (Quoted in Mirchandani 1968: 43)

Similarly, in the Rajya Sabha, replying to the question how government proposed to safeguard the nation's security in view of reports that Pakistan planned to test an atom bomb in 1968, Mrs Gandhi said, Pakistan is not in a position to make a bomb, although she could conceivably get one from somewhere. She categorically mentioned that "if we make one, Pakistan will definitely get a bomb from somewhere or the other. . . . We are anxious not to do anything which will precipitate the crisis." (Mirchandani 1968: 43) By that time, discussions on the nuclear issue had become regular agenda in all meetings of the Congress Party. When the Congress Party met in the beginning of May 1966, its General Secretary K.C. Pant, among others, known to have said that he did not wish to hustle government into manufacturing the atom bomb, but he wanted the country to advance technologically to a position; where if need arose it could manufacture one quickly.

China's Third Nuclear Test

On May 9, 1966, China exploded its third bomb and claimed that it contained "thermo-nuclear material", indicating that it had set-off her first hydrogen bomb. As was expected, the news of China's test broke a storm in the Parliament next day. A leading member of the Praja Socialist Party H.V. Kamath called upon the Minister of External Affairs to make a statement on a "matter of urgent public importance". (Mirchandani 1968: 44) The Congress members seemed to vie with opposition critics in deriding what they characterised as adherence to a moralistic stand. (Mirchandani 1968: 44) On the occasion, External Affairs Minister Swaran Singh said:

> We had made a careful assessment of the situation in consultation with our Service Chiefs and atomic energy experts even when the first nuclear device was exploded by China. . . .the mere fact that China has carried out its third nuclear explosion does not vitiate the earlier conclusion, though at the same time, the policy is kept under constant review.
>
> . . . In the meantime, in the matter of peaceful development of atomic energy, we are pushing ahead and giving it top priority. The world recognises that we are one of the countries which are capable of becoming an atomic power in a reasonably short time. . . . Finally, I would assure the House that the defence of our territorial integrity will be the paramount consideration guiding our policy in this field. (Quoted in Mirchandani 1968: 45-46)

Prime Minister Indira Gandhi, intervening in the discussion, said, "I do not think our policy is at all a negative one. . . . We are building up our atomic power. Of course, we are using it for peaceful purposes, but in the meantime we are increasing our know-how and other competence. I fail to understand myself how our production of one bomb or two bombs will help us. The belief that China can attack any country with nuclear weapons with impunity, I think, is a misconceived one." (Quoted in Mirchandani 1968: 46) The above statements by two Congress Party stalwarts denote a subtle change in government's nuclear policy. While some MPs viewed this policy a continuation of the Shastri's earlier statement, the media interpreted it as a definite shift.[1] A day after the Lok Sabha discussion (May 10, 1966), in the meeting of the Executive Committee of the Congress Party in Parliament, the bomb issue was discussed for ninety minutes. Against the demands of various members for manufacturing nuclear weapons, Prime Minister Gandhi gave no promise to reconsider government's nuclear weapons policy. On May 21, 1966, the AICC held a three-day session at Bombay. But the meeting discussed domestic issues only in spite of opposition party's demand for a change in government's nuclear stand. (Varma et al. 1968: 364)

However, the Secretary of the Congress Parliamentary Party, K.C. Pant, urged government at a public meeting to give up its policy of "nuclear celibacy" and make the country technologically prepared for making the bomb. (Mirchandani 1968: 48) K.C. Pant claimed that China's prestige and status had risen after its entry into the Nuclear Club and criticised the government for not making the bomb even under unfavourable circumstances. Equally, there were supporter of the no-bomb stand within the Congress Party. Indira Gandhi's rival for the Prime Ministership Morarji Desai, the then Deputy Prime Minister, was a staunch supporter of government's policy. On August 21, 1966, while inaugurating the Hiroshima Day Exhibition in New Delhi, he told "we must not be tempted, bullied or frightened into giving up that most sacred principle". (Quoted in Mirchandani 1968: 49) His stand didn't change even after China conducted its fifth nuclear test. He emphasised rather strengthening India's conventional forces to help win any war with China.

Congress Views on China's Subsequent Nuclear Tests

The debate *whether India should-might-will-can go nuclear* continued with China's subsequent nuclear tests. On October 27, 1966, China tested a live nuclear bomb mounted on a guided missile. This sparked fresh waves of reaction in India, mostly along the party lines. While the debate as usual became very intensive, the government didn't budge from its no-bomb stand. On December 28, 1966, China conducted its fifth test, (the third test in the same year). But, this time the debate had settled down with the government's no-bomb policy and even the public and media seemed used to it. Indian press did not treat China's latest test as an extraordinary piece of news. (Mirchandani 1968: 52) Even the Congress Party's election manifesto of 1967 made passing reference to the Chinese aggression of 1962, but did not touch at all nuclear explosion by China.

China's first hydrogen bomb test took place three months after the Fourth General Election to Lok Sabha following which Indira Gandhi formed the government with 54.84 per cent of the total seat with 40. 78 per cent of the total vote polled. (*Election*

Commission of India, 1967: 75) At the domestic level, though China's hydrogen bomb issue did not create much upheaval unlike the earlier times, it certainly created fresh waves of disquiet. (Mirchandani 1968: 58) Also the international impression of Sino-Indian balance of power seemed to have smashed. (Mirchandani 1968: 57) However, the demand for an Indian deterrent or for India accepting a super-power nuclear umbrella was alive and as usual, was raised along party lines. In response to the 60-members demand for a motion in the Parliament, External Minister Affairs, on behalf of the government, rejected the plea for India going nuclear. (*The Guardian*, October 29, 1964) Also there was apprehension on the Sino-Pak collaboration on the nuclear field. Questions were raised along the party lines what India's response would be if such situation arises. Expecting these issues in the Parliament, Swaran Singh gave a long deliberation. (*Statement by Sardar Swaran Singh*, "Documents", Patil 1969: 60-61)

In his statement, Swaran Singh said that China's hydrogen bomb explosion has caused "grave concern". However, nuclear policy of China and its impact on India's security has been under study and "all practicable ways and means of ensuring our security are constantly under examination". (Quoted in Rochlin 1964: 2) He also rejected the Swatantra Party's opinion to go to the super-powers for nuclear umbrella. In reply, he said, "We should try to stand on our own legs rather than mortgage our freedom and independence to any country, however strong it may be". On the issue of Sino-Pakistan cooperation, he said, "we have no information that Pakistan is planning to manufacture the atom bomb". Their nuclear know-how is very elementary now and they would take many more years to have a bomb, if they take a decision any time". However, the China-threat to national security was looming large. When India was preparing for its Independence Day in 1967, the hoax news on China's plan to fire its first medium-range ballistic missile with a nuclear warhead into the Indian Ocean across Indian territory raised public concern. (Noorani 1967) In reply to the agitated House, Swaran Singh acknowledged that the government is aware about China's production of medium-range ballistic missile and also revealed that China may "fairly soon" acquire short-range ballistic missile. (Noorani 1967) Responding to the assertions of the Swatantra Party and Jan Sangh's allegation that "India always depend on the mercy of God", he suggested not to be panicky and "umbrellas do not help, especially when the rain is sharp . . . we must think of how best we can protect ourselves." (Noorani 1967: 498)

Dual Trends

By the time Indira Gandhi took over the Congress Party leadership, the debate over India going nuclear had become a recurring feature of domestic politics. The debate started to come to the front during Shastri era and got manifested, though lately, during Indira's Prime Ministership. But two apparent trends that marked the nuclear weapons policy of India which continued till the late-1990s. First, building India's nuclear "bomb did not entail a specific decision in time but rather a continuous accretion of scientific and technical capability and political momentum, stymied occasionally by countervailing political, moral and economic considerations". (Perkovich 2002: 146) Second, owing to perceived political cost and consequent hesitation for taking a straightforward nuclear weapons decision both by Shastri and Indira Gandhi, India's nuclear weapons policy became *ambiguous*. Shastri and Mrs Gandhi both seem to have avoided "the liabilities of either embracing nuclear weapons or rejecting the option completely". (Perkovich 2002: 124)

Therefore, it can be argued that, while the Congress Party initially was responsible for laying down a viable atomic technology infrastructure, it is equally responsible at later stage for making India's nuclear weapons policy ambiguous. This policy of the Party might be a manifestation of the pressure from its own members and from other political parties also like Jan Sangh for building the bomb. This ambiguous policy became more pronounced, firstly, during Dr Sarabhai's avowal for non-weaponisation. Secondly, with the non-proliferation regime mounting pressure on India not to embark on nuclear weapons programme this ambiguity continued for almost two decades until BJP led-coalition government decided to conduct the second series of tests in 1998.

The China Factor During 1970s

India's nuclear debate got reinvigorated with China's first launch of satellite in April 1970 as the event made clear China's ballistic missile capability to launch nuclear warheads at distant targets. (Chakma 2005) The event elicited alarm in Indian political circle. In a meeting organised by the Indian Parliamentary and Scientific Committee on May 9-10, 1970, eminent scientists, academicians and politicians urged in Delhi the government to revise its policy and produce nuclear weapons immediately (Hazelhurst 1970). Especially, the pressure was from the left-wing of the Congress Party. (Perkovich 2002: 152)

During this time, according to Perkovich, "three camps" were clearly visible in India's nuclear weapons debate. (Perkovich 1999: 156) While one camp argued against nuclear weapons, the second proposed a crash programme to build a small nuclear arsenal to be delivered by aircraft and in time, by ballistic missile. The third camp favoured a steadier, less provocative long-term arsenal with attendant command, control and warning infrastructure. But Congress government's policy on opting for nuclear weapons was as usual basing upon the socio-economic issues and peaceful use. At the Third Conference of the Heads of State and Government of the Non-aligned countries at Lusaka on September 8-10, 1970, Mrs Gandhi highlighted the tremendous potential of the peaceful uses of nuclear energy, including peaceful nuclear explosions, for the developing world. (*Foreign Affairs Reports* (New Delhi) September-October, 1970: 85)

However, according to K. Subrahmanyam, "There could be no question that the basic motives that triggered off the Indian nuclear test in 1974 were the China factor (and US nuclear intimidation)". (Subrahmanyam 1998: 32) If one examines China's activities on the nuclear front during the late sixties and early seventies, Subrahmanyam's assertion seems to hold truth. By that time, there was sufficient evidence regarding China devoting substantial resources to the development of both nuclear warheads and missile delivery systems.[2] Were all the Chinese preparations meant for India?

By that time, the view among the strategic community was that China's professed purpose in going nuclear is to "oppose the nuclear blackmail and threats by US imperialism and its collaborators and to oppose US-Soviet collusion for maintaining nuclear monopoly". Even in a communiqué issued after the third nuclear explosion the Chinese Government said: China's sole purpose in developing nuclear weapons is defence and her ultimate aim is to eliminate the nuclear weapons. . . . at no time and in no circumstances will China be the first to use nuclear weapons." Also, within the Indian intellectual circles, there was a view that if an aggressive nuclear threat is aimed against India, there would certainly be a counter threat from the major nuclear powers. (Mirchandani 1968: 93)

Irrespective of all solemn declarations by China, India was definitely apprehensive of China. The major question was, will the United States risk a nuclear attack on its own cities and use nuclear weapons against China to discharge moral obligation to defend India? At that stage India had the Canada-India reactor and a stockpile of weapon-grade plutonium was being built up. With this plutonium, BARC had designed the Purnima reactor and this enabled the scientists to gather data necessary to design a nuclear explosive device. Since, there was commitment that the Canada-India reactor would not be used for purposes other than peaceful, finally Mrs Gandhi gave the go-ahead to the scientists sometime in October 1972 for a "peaceful nuclear explosion" but no record is available to explain her decision. (Subrahmanyam 1998: 30)

To decipher the motives of Indira Gandhi's decisions, particularly on security and nuclear matters, one needs to examine the relationship among the following factors as identified by Ashok Kapur: (1) Indira Gandhi's motivation, political interests and compulsions; (2) assessments by the Indian bureaucracy of external and internal security threats and the budgetary, military and intelligence requirements; and (3) motivations and policies of external powers that impinged upon India's security concerns. (Kapur 1976: 49)

To appraise Indira Gandhi's nuclear decisions, one needs to see first Mrs Gandhi as an actor in the theatre of Indian politics. During the initial stage of her Prime Ministership, her compulsion was to create a string of favourable effects and temporary success to strengthen her position. (Chakma 2005) The slogan *Garibi Hatao* helped her to win the election with absolute majority. According to Ashok Kapur, "Her January 1966 decision to cancel the nuclear test project may be attributed to inexperience to the pressure of other priorities (i.e., staying in power). Her decision in February 1968 not to sign the NPT reflects fear of Cabinet disapproval and the nature of bureaucratic advice. It seems, during the whole of the late-1960s, neither she understood nor cared for nuclear affairs. Yet, she was making the case against the NPT on grounds of principle and national interest." (Kapur 1976: 49) Also Kapur views Mrs Gandhi's 1974 Pokhran test decision "was a product of scientific advice, a diplomatic demonstration to the major powers in India's environment, a popular gesture and a method to disarm India's bomb lobby". But, it is because of this bureaucratic advice, external pressure and her unfamiliarity with the discourse, she failed to pursue the test to its logical conclusion. (Kapur 1976: 52) Therefore, it seems, Mrs Gandhi's compulsion was not to formulate policies but to engage in *ad hoc* policy actions primarily to promote her ascendancy in Indian politics and to take advantage of the immediate situation.

The run up to the 1974 Pokhran-I tests was marked by many regional security problems which the Congress Party had to cope-with. Remarkable among them was the 1971 Bangladesh crisis. Also external powers, especially the USA, former USSR and China played their part influencing the South Asian security environment (discussed in greater detail in the subsequent chapter). But, there are differing views on whether the Bangladesh crisis and consequent involvement of the major powers especially USA by sending the *USS Enterprise* to Bay of Bengal was a factor in Congress Government (Mrs Gandhi's) decision to go for the nuclear test. The common argument is that the security threat arising out of the Sino-US rapproachment and the US presence in the Indian Ocean during the crisis was a determining factor in Mrs Gandhi's decision for the 1974 tests to which George Perkovich vehemently discounts. Perkovich asserts that "the decisive factors that led to the detonation of a nuclear device in 1974 were the Atomic Energy Commission's determination to prove its mettle and Indira Gandhi's sense that India would gain confidence in itself as a nation and her as a leader.

According to Perkovich, the final decision to conduct the test was the result of an *ad hoc*, intuitive process that lacked rigorous security analysis". (Perkovich 2002: 161) He views that, the Pakistani nuclear capability was incipient at that time, and the war indicated that "China did not seek militarily to threaten India's security or challenge its preeminence in the subcontinent" or even no indication is there that China played any direct role in assisting Pakistan in the crisis. (Perkovich 2002: 165) What then prompted the Congress Government led by Mrs Gandhi to decide for the test? According to a survey, even 46 per cent of the members of Congress party were in favour of going nuclear, while 49 per cent were against it, the rest were undecided. (Nanda 1971: 39)

An investigation into the geo-political scenario of the country and the region vis-à-vis the Congress Party's position reveals that there occurred many major developments in and around the subcontinent. India's win in the 1971 war also enhanced Indira Gandhi's popularity and credibility. (Masani 1975: 229) Congress

Party gained absolute majority in the fifth general election in 1972. It won more than 70 per cent of overall seats in the state legislative assemblies and the Party's vote rose to 47 per cent from the previous level of 42 per cent in 1962 election. But internally or organisationally, the Congress Party under Mrs Gandhi was falling into disorder owing to disassociation of the former Communists from the more traditional Nehruvian Congress members that widened the cleft in party organisation, ideology and cohesion. (Frankel 1979: 479-83)

However, during early 1972, the nuclear policy resurfaced in the domestic debate. On March 17, 1972, in the Lok Sabha the government was asked whether the war with Pakistan in 1971 "brought out the necessity for India to have more modern weapons" and if so "whether government propose to embark upon the manufacture of nuclear bombs". Defence Minister Jagjivan Ram said, modernisation of army is undergoing and nuclear energy is meant only for peaceful purposes and possession of nuclear weapons is not a substitute for any other military preparedness. (*Lok Sabha Debates*, March 17, 1972) In the AICC meeting at New Delhi on June 1-2, 1972, the Party adopted the resolution saying "People all the world over were convinced that atomic weapons should neither be produced nor used. The only way to save the world from the catastrophe of another world war was acceptance of co-existence." The Party endorsing Prime Minister's initiative in holding talks with Pakistan in the quest for durable peace in the subcontinent, the then Foreign Minister and Congress leader S. Swaran Singh said "it is our earnest hope that the . . . two neighbours—Pakistan and China, would also move in the direction in which there may be good neighbourly relations. . . ." (*AICC Proceedings*, New Delhi, 1–2 June 1972, Zaidi 1984 (vol. 23): 162–63, 168)

Pressure continued to build within the Parliament for a more robust nuclear posture and during the debate over the defence ministry budget all parties, except the two communist parties, called for developing nuclear weapons. This debate resurfaced in the Parliament in November 1972. Answering to a pointed question on the "progress . . . in feasibility study and other preparations for the experimental nuclear explosions for peaceful purposes", Mrs Gandhi said "the Atomic Energy Commission is constantly reviewing the progress in the technology of underground nuclear explosions both from the theoretical and experimental angles and also taking into account their potential economic benefits and possible environmental hazards" (*Lok Sabha Debates*, November 3rd, 1972: Col. 49).

The above statement by Gandhi makes clear that the possibility to prepare for an underground test was already taken by that time. Perkovich, by citing many factual evidences about the timing of the decision for underground test, asserts that the decision was taken prior to the war with Pakistan and the US deployment of the *Enterprise*. (Perkovich 2002: 171–72) He cites Jagjivan Ram saying the decision was taken three years before the test, placing it somewhere in 1971 but his interview with Homi Sethna reveals a different picture—Mrs Gandhi seem to have "authorised fabrication of a device for peaceful nuclear explosion on September 7th, 1972". However, according to Perkovich, "it may be conjectured that support in principle for developing a nuclear explosive device was solidified by late 1971, that concentrated work on building the vital components began in spring 1972 and that formal prime ministerial approval to make final preparations for PNE occurred in September 1972" (Perkovich 2002: 172). But the decision or the preparation was never recorded or made public as one can deduce from the Rajya Sabha debate on November 15, 1973 when Gandhi was asked in writing "whether any final decision has been taken to conduct experiments to develop nuclear blast technology ... whether any time schedule has been set for the purpose", to which Mrs Gandhi replied almost negative by saying that such decision would be taken "only after satisfactory answers to all these problems [theoretical and experimental questions; economic questions; environmental and ecological effects are available". (*Parliamentary Debates*, Rajya Sabha, November 15, 1973: cols. 138–39)

Contrast to Perkovich's argument, for K. Subrahmanyam, "there could be no question that the basic factors that triggered off the Indian nuclear test in 1974 were the China factor and US nuclear intimidation" (Subrahmanyam 1998: 32). In an interview to the *Indian Foreign Affairs Journal* in 2006 Brajesh Mishra reveals how China was positive towards India before and during the war (Mishra 2006). According to him, towards the end of August 1971, after the Indo-Soviet Friendship Treaty, he proposed Mrs Gandhi to engage China before the war begins and also to convince China how India value it even after having the treaty with Soviet Union. Brajesh Mishra was sent to China when the war was on. During his conversation with the Director of Chinese Foreign Office, Mishra asked about China's reaction regarding the war. The director revealed that the Americans had been pushing China to take some action on the border against India. But, he assured Mishra saying "Mr Chargé d' affaires need not worry, China will act in accordance with international law". (Mishra 2006) And true to his assurances China did not do anything to that extent. Even in the AICC Gujarat meeting on October 9–10, 1972, Party President Shankar Dayal Sharma said, "we are continuing our endeavours to normalise relation with China on the basis of mutual respect for sovereignty, territorial integrity and non-interference in each others' internal affairs." (*AICC Opening Remarks by the Congress President,* Zaidi 1984 [Vol. (22): 225]

The issue of China as a factor in India's 1974 nuclear tests is an open-ended debate. But from Brajesh Mishra's account, it seems there was considerable concern on China's behaviour vis-à-vis the 1971 war, at least at the official level. Probably, that is why Mrs Gandhi was convinced to Brajesh Mishra's proposal to engage China. But, how far China factored in her decision for the nuclear test in 1974 is still shrouded in mystery. It is not clear, whether regional security imperatives were behind the decision for the nuclear test in 1974, but generally it is viewed that the decision was based partly "on intuition, bureaucratic and technological momentum, and the personal, enigmatic calculations of the politically beleaguered prime minister under the influence of trusted nuclear scientists". (Perkovich 2002: 178)

Most of the Indian and foreign scholars view political considerations moved Mrs Gandhi to decide for the nuclear test. It is true that the political situation of the country was worsening in 1974, even though Congress Party won narrowly in Uttar Pradesh state election in February 1974. In January 1974, Morarji Desai, Mrs Gandhi's rival, erupted in rioting and announced his "fast unto death" to compel her to dissolve the Gujarat state legislative assembly. (Frankel 1979: 526-27) Equally in Bihar, J.P. Narayan was protesting in demand of "an allround devolution, political, economic, social, educational, moral and cultural". (Frankel 1979: 532) Also political turmoil spread across the nation when 1.7 million railway workers called for a strike that began on May 8th and Narayan was reportedly coordinating with the activity. According to the Congress Party report, the Right and the Left appeared to be attacking all government policies. ("Resolution of Political Situation", *AIC Resolution, Congress Marches Ahead-10* 1974: 16) Definitely the political situation of the country was precarious.

The scientific community, who were involved in the test preparations, especially Rajaramanna and P.K. Iyengar, is of the opinion that the PNE was simply done, when the scientists were ready. (Ramanna 1991: 89) The July 1974 session of the CWC at New Delhi, where a resolution was adopted by the Party hailing "the achievement of Indian scientists in carrying out successfully the underground nuclear experiment for peaceful purposes. . . ." The AICC, congratulating the scientists and the Prime Minister for this achievement, welcomed "the clear statement of the Government of India reaffirming their intention of using nuclear technology for peaceful purposes and not for manufacturing nuclear weapons." (*CWC Resolution on Nuclear Explosion*, July 1974, New Delhi, Zaidi 1984: 219) The Congress Working Committee rejoiced for the fact that "this notable and important experiment has been based on indigenous effort, and that in the process, India has not violated any of its international obligations".

If the decision was purely a scientific imperative, Mrs Gandhi could have taken the confidence of the cabinet, at least of her close aides, for such an important event. Important members of her cabinet like the Defence Minister Jagjivan Ram, the Minister of External Affairs Swaran Singh, etc., were informed a few days before the explosion. This may have done to maintain secrecy, but it shows that the reasons for the 1974 nuclear test decision lies not only in the domestic politics and regional security considerations but the decision-making style of an individual 'decision-maker'. Indira Gandhi's decisions on future test proposals made by the scientific community clearly mark this aspect. For example, by 1982, BARC and DRDO, under the leadership of Ramanna and V.S. Arunachalam respectively, produced a design for a device that would weigh between 170 and 200 kilograms and in early 1983 they made their case for another nuclear explosion to Prime Minister Gandhi. (*NTI*, "Nuclear Chronology") During their meeting, Ramanna and Arunachalam tried to convince Mrs Gandhi whether India should or should not acquire the bomb before Pakistan does so. As the scientists wished, she tentatively approved the request. But within twenty-four hours, she reversed her decision and conveyed the scientists to hold on. Even during the early years of her second tenure as Prime Minister, she was in favour of not forswear further nuclear explosion. (*NTI*, "Nuclear Chronology") However, no information is available regarding what factor(s) actually changed her mind.

In the context of regional or national security, India perceived a number of threats, especially emanating from Pakistan during this period. First, by this time it was clear that Pakistan is nuclear capable. A.Q. Khan himself was boasting of leading his country ahead of India in nuclear matters. (Sreedhar 1987: 57) Second, there were reports on Sino-Pakistan nuclear collaboration. Thirdly, there was fear of Pakistani support to Sikh insurgency in Punjab. At best, Mrs Gandhi, in her second term, reversed Morarji Desai's nuclear aversion policy by not foreclosing the possibility of further nuclear explosion. But throughout 1982, she downplayed the nuclear issues. For example, during her meeting with US President Reagan, she categorically denied any intention to conduct a test, instead told him that the test rumour was generated by the BJP. (*Delhi Domestic News Service* 1982) In an interview in January 1982, Mrs Gandhi, while replying to whether India would follow suit if Pakistan developed nuclear weapons, said, "The threat is one of conventional arms and not of nuclear weapons. I am very much against war of any kind and especially, nuclear war. But I don't think I can give a categorical answer and bind the Indian government to any position." (*Statement on Foreign Policy* 1982: 25–26)

Also Prime Minister Gandhi vehemently rejected the US intelligence reports on Indian intention for launching air strikes against Pakistan's uranium enrichment plant at Kahuta and the reprocessing facility at PINSTECH in Rawalpindi which was planned in March 1982 according to the report. Neither did she authorise for such an attack, nor permit to conduct the second nuclear explosion despite technical readiness. One factor could be the domestic political situation that demanded more attention as in State Assembly election that year the Congress party had faced major defeat in Andhra Pradesh and Karnataka. (*India Today*, January 31 1983: 18) Second, Mrs Gandhi's curiosity for nuclear explosion might have waned owing to international pressure after 1974 tests. Third, since Pakistan did have nuclear arsenals by that time, she might have thought that it is not prudent to conduct a test that would create a chain reaction from Islamabad, further deteriorating regional and national security. Until July that year, Mrs Gandhi was categorical that "India had no intention of embarking on the nuclear weapons programme". (*India News* 1983: 1)

Overall, during this period, Mrs Gandhi and the Congress Party's nuclear policy was based on "a less risky strategy of bide time, avoid provocations, pursue diplomacy and keep the nuclear powder dry while downplaying explicit interest in nuclear weaponry". (Perkovich 2002: 254) Of course, there were number of deliberations in the parliament on the issue of Pakistan's nuclear programme and the Sino-Pakistan nexus and India's response thereof. On March 30, 1984, Narasimha Rao addressed the concerns on Congress government's policy on the issue of Sino-Pakistan collaboration in the nuclear field by saying that "the government kept constant watch on all developments affecting India's security". On the question of whether India should "continue with the policy of using nuclear energy for peaceful purposes when Pakistan is preparing an atom bomb" with Chinese help, Rao cited a statement by the Prime Minister in the Lok Sabha on March 28 that "Government is vigilant in the matter. Indian scientists are keeping abreast of all aspects of research and development concerned with modern and relevant technologies". (*Lok Sabha Debates*, Mar 30 1984: Col. 398) In an earlier deliberation (March 23, 1984), parliamentarians pressed to know what steps the government is taking on the assumption that Pakistan did have nuclear capability. In response, Defence Minister Venkatraman replied that "you need not match the tank with the tank and this and that". (*Lok Sabha Debates*, March 23, 1984, Col. 402)

Indira Gandhi's Second Term

During Indira Gandhi's second term as Prime Minister, the 'nuclear-Pakistan' factor was not enough to budge Congress Party's ambiguous nuclear weapons policy. However, this doesn't mean that Indira Gandhi, and the Congress Party was callous about Pakistan. While addressing a gathering of Indian Army Commanders on October 11, 1984, Mrs Gandhi told that "Pakistan's nuclear programme has brought about a qualitative change in our security environment". (Oberdorfer 1984) On October 16, 1984, Mrs Gandhi ordered to seal the Indo-Pak border. (Oberdorfer 1984) But, it is unclear why she became more calculative this time even though the security situation was warranting some action in the nuclear front before and more importantly, when the scientific community was prepared and in favour of such an act. But, Mrs Gandhi refused a meeting with concerned scientists subsequently on this issue. (Perkovich 2002: 244)

The probable reasons for Mrs Gandhi's attitude towards the nuclear issues may be: (1) the negative consequences of 1974 tests; (2) her own abhorrence of nuclear weapons; (3) absence of a Pakistani nuclear provocation in the form of test explosion in response to India's 1974 test, which might have gave an impression that India is better off holding its nuclear fire. (Perkovich 1999: 244) Her aids—P.N. Haksar, P.C. Alexander, Krishnaswamy Rao Sahib—have also brought her the probable repercussions resulting out of another test explosion; and (4) the fear of assumed attacks on each other's nuclear facilities vindicated that even without nuclear bombs a rudimentary deterrence is in operation. Probably owing to these reasons, there emerged a buffer between the decision-maker and the 'strategic enclave' (scientists and other votaries of nuclear weapons). The people around Mrs Gandhi might have persuaded her that nuclear weapons would not provide usable solutions to imminent problems as they are not usable and India's well-being require other priorities. This also shows Mrs Gandhi's "chariness towards the nuclear scientists and the military, as well as the increased role of professionals, broad-gauged advisors in the Prime Minister's office. . . ." (Perkovich 2002: 259)

According to General Sundarji, this led to a situation between the mid-seventies and the mid-eighties, where "India's nuclear decision-making appears to have enjoyed something between a drugged sleep and a deep post-prandial siesta". (Sunderji 1993: xiv) Further, he asserts that India did not have "a coherent nuclear weapons policy and worse still", she [Indira Gandhi] did not have "an institutionalised system for analysing and throwing up policy options in this regard". (Sunderji 1993: xv) Most importantly, one tragic domestic event that altered India's nuclear trajectory was the Golden Temple calamity and consequent assassination of Mrs Gandhi by her Sikh bodyguards. The Sikh uprising and *Operation Blue Star* deepened the Indian polity's preoccupation with the challenge of internal order and drove the national leadership attention out from the nuclear issue. (Kapur 2009: 79) One can speculate, in which way India's quest for nuclear weapons could turn had Indira Gandhi remained alive.

Post-Indira Nuclear Policy

Rajiv Gandhi took over the leadership of the Congress Party at a time, when the regional nuclear order was getting shaped; especially, Pakistan was nearing the capacity to produce nuclear weapons. This had increased the pressure on Congress government to develop strategies and capabilities for maintaining military supremacy over Pakistan. And, for that matter, each new Prime Minister, inspite of his inclination, felt compelled to reconsider the subject *de novo*. (Karnad 2002: 268) If one analyses Rajiv Gandhi's approach towards nuclear discourse, it seems, though he did not address the calls to develop and deploy weapons, he did also not restrain the 'strategic enclave' from maturing its scientific-technical capability. (Perkovich 2002: 261)

The Congress Party won 49 per cent of the vote (415 out of total 542 Lok Sabha seats) in the election held in December 1984, just two months after Indira Gandhi's assassination. (*Election Commission of India 1986*) According to the Statistical Report 1985, while the BJP managed to get 7.7 per cent (only 2 seats) of the total vote cast, the two Communist parties won 28 seats in combine. Though, Congress was in a better position from electoral point of view, the internal law and order situation was demanding more attention as the Punjab crisis, the post-assassination violence of Hindus against Sikhs and the insurgencies in Assam and northeast were alive. Therefore, initially, nuclear issues were put to the back. But during Rajiv's leadership, India's nuclear weapons policy seem to have been influenced more by his personal ideals—"skepticism about the value of nuclear weapons" mixed with "traditional Prime Ministerial ambivalence." (Perkovich 2002: 263, 287)

Rajiv Gandhi, as a political leader, was averse to the traditional ways of Indian bureaucracy and politics; he had little interest in hearing the views of others who may not agree with him. (Deshmukh 2004) Also, the shadow of Indira Gandhi was all pervasive on the bureaucracy and the stalwarts of the Atomic Energy Commission. Initially, they treated Rajiv as the son of Indira Gandhi, not as a formidable figure in his own right which resented him more than anything else. He had a "push-button attitude" on matters of decision making (Perkovich 2002: 261–62) At the beginning, he was inclined towards nuclear disarmament, and was totally against nuclear weapons (*Rajiv Gandhi: Selected Speeches and Writings* 1987: 5). Perhaps, his peg of idealism prompted him to project India's image as a leader of the nuclear disarmament, but interestingly he did nothing to stop the scientists and engineers from refining India's nuclear weapons capabilities.

On the issue of regional security vis-à-vis India's nuclear weapons programme, Rajiv Gandhi initially didn't "see a situation arising . . . [to] start . . . making the bomb." Rather he told that "just the fact that Pakistan made a bomb would not make us change our policy". (Quoted in Joeck 1990: 86) In a broadcast to the nation, two weeks after Indira Gandhi's assassination, Rajiv Gandhi expressed that the first requisite for nation building is peace; "peace with our neighbours and peace in the world". (*Rajiv Gandhi: Selected Speeches and Writings* 1987: 5) He told in the same broadcast that "Indira Gandhi reminded us that the most important single challenge before the world today is the threat of nuclear war. We shall continue her relentless crusade against the arms race." However, developments in the neighbourhood seem renewed the pressure from members within the Congress on Rajiv Gandhi. By early March 1985, Pakistan's clandestine nuclear programme was revealed; A.Q. Khan himself provocatively told that Pakistan can carry out an "atomic explosion in a very short time, if required, without conducting any test." (Namboodiri 1985)

By May 1985, members of Parliament demanded a more robust response to Pakistan's nuclear programme. For example, the H.M. Patel, former Janata government finance minister, urged India to go nuclear. (Reddy 1985) On the one hand, Rajiv government having absolute parliamentary majority could withstand opposition pressure. On the other hand, in order to assure his constituents that USA would help constrain the Pakistani threat, he tried to push the Regan administration during his visit to the United States in June 1985. He also communicated his concerns to Pakistan directly through an interview with Mushahid Hussain, Editor of the *Muslim*, where he said "a nuclear arms race in the subcontinent would only subject both our peoples to the worst possible fate on earth". (Quoted in Sengupta 1985: 116) But, this does not mean that he was not aware of his ranks in the Congress Party. Being aware of the possible discontent and pressure from the Party members, as was happened during Shastri's Prime Ministership especially after the Chinese nuclear test in 1964, he sounded a hard line. In the AICC meeting on May 1985, Rajiv Gandhi said "We feel that they [Pakistan] are developing a nuclear weapon . . . [and] We are looking into various aspects of this question to see what action we should take." (Reddy 1985)

It seems, Rajiv Gandhi meant to do something on the nuclear front and at the same time was careful not trigger a nuclear competition. He judged India's identity and interests not to lie in building, testing or deploying nuclear weapons and India should not be alarmist or at loggerheads with Pakistn. This stand was clarified by the then defence minister, Narasimha Rao, in the AICC meeting.

(Reddy 1985) Rajiv Gandhi in his interview with the *Good Morning America* television programme on June 4th 1985 said that "we do not have a nuclear weapon . . . We exploded an experimental device in 1974 and we have not carried on any more work on that line at all. We have not exploded any more devices. We have no stockpile. We do not have a nuclear weapon". (Quoted in Perkovich 2002: 267) He also rejected the news of preemptive strike on Pakistan's nuclear installations. But later he said, he would really "re-think India's policies" if Pakistan develops nuclear weapons. (Perkovich 2002: 267) The same *Good Morning America* reported on July11, 1985 about Pakistan's successful test of nuclear triggering package for a nuclear weapon. (Spector 1990: 332) The Indian media and the opposition in the Parliament reacted strongly and a consequent demand to spell out counter-measures by the government was mounted upon the Prime Minister.

Initiatives during Rajiv Gandhi

Harsh realities following the regional nuclear developments had bearing on Rajiv Gandhi's nuclear decisions during the last phase of his Prime Ministerhip. Initially, it seems, he had no intention for nuclear weaponisation and operation doctrine for India. But to nutralise domestic discontents, he constituted a small secret inter-disciplinary committee that included two Chief Ministers, Karunakaran and Saikia, Arun Singh, Pratap Kaul, Cabinet Secretary, Dr Ramanna, the Chairman of AEC, Charman of the Chief of Staff Committee General Vaidya, Director of R&AW, Girish Saxena, Director of Intelligence Bureau, Barari, Dr Bimal Jalan, Chief Economic Adviser, Khandelwal, Chairman, Joint Intelligence Committee and K. Subrahmaniyam. (Subrahmaniyam 1998: 39) After the last meeting of this group on November 5th, 1985, Admiral Tahliani constituted a task force consisting of Lt. Gen Sunderji, K.K. Nayyar, Air Marshal John Greene, Chidambaram and APJ Abdul Kalam which produced a report saying that India could have a balanced deterrent programme within ten years, at a cost of Rs. 7,000 crore. (Subrahmaniyam 1998: 41)

As mentioned earlier, though Rajiv welcomed the committee's effort, but had no intention to move for manufacturing nuclear arsenals. (Perkovich 2002: 275) This is amply clear from an interview during his trip to Japan in November 1985. In the interview he said, "We lived with Chinese weapon for long. But our relation with Pakistan is more turbulent. . . . We have managed without" the bomb and "we would like not to develop a weapon and we are not developing a weapon". (*Hindustan Times*, Nov 29, 1985) Rather to demystify Pakistan's speculation of Indian attack on Kahuta, Rajiv Gandhi initiated Confidence Building Measures (CBMs) on a non-attack of each other's nuclear facilities agreement during President Zia's visit to New Delhi in December 1985. But A.Q. Khan's interview by Kuldip Nayar in January 28, 1986 where Dr Khan proclaimed that Pakistan has enriched uranium to weapon grade and could test a bomb through laboratory simulation as a surprise. When Nayar narrated Dr Khan the comments of Dr Ramanna that Pakistan "don't have anything . . . No bomb, no men, no rationale", Khan screamed at and said "Tell them we have it. . . . [We] don't have to test in the ground any more. We can test in the lab. Let me assure you, we have tested". (Quoted in Levi and Scott-Clark 2007: 151)

The publication of Khan's interview in the *Observer* on March 1, 1987 escalated the domestic nuclear debate. In late February, in Rajya Sabha, the opposition and the Congress (I) members demanded a review of defence policy in the light of Pakistan's nuclear programme. (*Delhi Domestic News Service* 1987) Also General Sunderji briefed the Prime Minister on the necessity of going nuclear. Though Rajiv Gandhi was very firm not to exercise the weapons option, he didn't foreclose the option for doing that. (Deshmukh 1994: 62) At the same time, he did not discount 'Pakistan-threat'; but had his own conception of how to deal with Islamabad. In his conception, he wanted Pakistan to know that if India is attacked with nukes, it can blow Pakistan off the map. (Perkovich 2002: 283) But Rajiv was neither in favour of adhering to a launch-on-warning doctrine nor to a Cold War type command and control system.

If one examines his later pronouncements and the views of the members of Congress Party, it may sound that Rajiv though proclaimed India not require nuclear bomb, at times assured for a more robust line. For example, he once mentioned that "we intend meeting President Zia's threat. We will give an adequate response." (Diaz 1987: 1) Also on April 27, 1987, defence minister K.C. Pant told the Lok Sabha that "the emerging nuclear threat to us from Pakistan is forcing us to review our options . . . I assure the House that our response will be adequate to our perception of the threat". (*Reuters* 1987) Above two statements by Congress leaders show that both Rajiv Gandhi and the Congress were compelled to reconsider nuclear weapons option but what concrete or overt step was taken is unknown. May be, subsequent tumultuous domestic atmosphere might have diverted the attention of Rajiv Gandhi from developing a clear-cut nuclear policy. Issues like the defeat of Congress in the Haryana state election, revelation of Bofors issue, resignation of defence minister V.P. Singh and his campaign against Rajiv were the main distracters. Other regional issue like Sri Lanka's request for military help to fight the LTTE may have diverted attention.

Apparently, during the Congress government led by Rajiv Gandhi, the Indo-Pak rivalry and domestic politics had affected India's nuclear decision-making more than the China-factor. During this period, China made positive overtures towards India but in the later stage, some Indian initiatives, such as, the convert of North East Frontier Agency (a part of which is claimed by China) into a full-fledged state—Arunachal Pradesh seem to have annoyed Beijing. In protest to Indian action, China reportedly deployed troops and stockpiled nuclear weapons in Tibet, to which China refuted. (Elkin and Ritezel 1986) Another issue during the spring of 1987, just after Brasstacks that seems to have alarmed China, is the launching of the Chequerboard exercise in the Indian sector of the northeastern Himalayan region. (*India Today* 1988) But during the same time, Rajiv, while addressing the Army Commanders, declared that India wanted to settle the boundary question with China through peaceful negotiation and Chinese officials too conveyed that they had no hostile intentions. (*Delhi Domestic News Service* 1987; Hoffman 1989: 231) Despite pulling back troops by both sides and subsequent eight rounds of bilateral talks on the border issue with China, the domestic nuclear debate never waned. The single issue of China's deployment of nuclear weapons in Tibet flared arguments in favour of India acquiring nukes. However, the flare-up with China did little to change the Congress government's nuclear policy.

Admixture of Realism and Idealism

Rajiv Gandhi while not restricting the scientific community to upgrade nuclear know-how did not recede from his lofty idealism in nuclear weapons matters. In his deliberations on "A World Free of Nuclear Weapons" at the UN General Assembly on June 9, 1988, he proposed for a binding commitment by nations to eliminate nuclear weapons in a planned, phased manner by the year 2010 at the latest. (*An Action Plan* 1988) (This aspect is dealt with more details in the subsequent chapter), but his initiative went to deaf ears. In December 1987, he visited both China and Pakistan. During the 4th SAARC Summit in Pakistan, he raised optimism on the prospect of Indo-Pak friendship and cooperation. (Jabeen et al 2010: 133) His visit to China was a breakthrough in the history of Sino-Indian relations and there emphasised peace, tranquility and solving of border dispute through consultations. (Acharya 2005)

On the other hand, probably fascinated by technology, Rajiv Gandhi didn't restrict the scientific community to advance technological capacity to build and deliver nuclear weapons. During his Prime Ministership, research reactor Dhruva was commissioned which provided India the source of weapons-grade plutonium. (Joshi 1998) He also managed to keep away the military establishment from nuclear policy, sometimes keeping them busy for providing suggestions, which he decided not to take action, sometimes completely isolating them from any policy matters; thereby, managed to reconcile idealism and realism in India's nuclear weapons discourse and could preside "over a decaying political system in a more complicated world". (Perkovich 2002: 292)

Post-Rajiv Debate

By the time Rajiv Gandhi finished his first term, the ambiguous nature of India's nuclear weapons policy was started to settle. On the one hand, the Prime Minister sometime approved the preparation of ready-to-assemble devices (to prepare militarily deliverable nuclear weapons), the number of such devices to possess and movement of weapon component within the country. (Perkovich 2002: 294) This gave a sense to the scientific community that they are authorised to advance nuclear explosive capabilities as long as they did not actually assemble or test. On the other hand, there was no weapon programme as such, yet the devices were made that could be turned into nuclear weapons if India was attacked. (Perkovich 2002: 295) May be out of frustration for the rejection of his proposal at the international level, Rajiv Gandhi gave go-ahead signal to the scientists.

Subsequently, the domestic, regional and international situation started to experience wide alterations. At the domestic level, the Congress Party's hold over electorate started to weaken. In the 1989 elections, it suffered a major setback. With the support of Indian communists and the Bharatiya Janata Party, V.P. Singh and his Janata Dal formed the government. Congress led by Gandhi became the Opposition. In 1991 fresh elections were announced and during the election, except the BJP, no other political party raised the nuclear weapons issue significantly. (Perkovich 2002: 304) In the final results of the elections held in May and June, the Congress (I) Party won 226 of the 543 seats in the Lok Sabha and formed a minority government under Prime Minister Narasimh Rao. (*Election Watch* 1991)

Narasimha Rao's Leadership

When Soviet Russia withdrew forces from Afghanistan, US involvement in Pakistan started to decline and the idea of India-Russia-China strategic triangle started to emerge. (Rahm 2001) Within this background, Narasimha Rao assumed the Congress Party leadership, and with his economist Finance Minister Dr Manmohan Singh, implemented the economic liberalisation policy. During this period (mid-1980s), Sino-Indian relations started to improve, reducing thereby, the salience of nuclear weapons debate. Also Rao traveled to Beijing during September 6–9, 1993, where the two governments agreed to reduce troops and respect the cease-fire lines along the disputed border. (Sidhu and Yuan 1999) That time, India's nuclear weapons policy remained static and ambiguous. But on the Indo-Pak front, relations between them turned acrimonious and both countries started nuclear sabers with rhetoric and display of their arsenals.

By this time, the regional security situation particularly the nuclear order was clearly visible for three important developments: (1) refusal by President Bush to certify in October 1990 that Pakistan did not possess nuclear explosive capability and the invocation of Pressler Amendment; (2) Pakistan-China nuclear technology cooperation; and (3) Pakistan's intention to bring in the five nuclear weapon powers into the Indo-Pakistan nuclear issue. Though not sidelining the regional nuclear reality, Rao emphasised economic development as India's greatest strategic imperative. For him, "if we cannot make ... our economic sinews ... strong, India would have no political clout ... no one is going to take it seriously". (Rao 1995: 181) For Prime Minister Rao "the debate on nuclear and missile policies could distract and divert India from its major objective". (Perkovich 2002: 347)

In pursuit of putting India on the 'emerging power' trajectory, Rao emphasised the necessity of India's engagement with the

USA. He made a visit to US on May 17, 1991, and discussed nuclear issues in private meeting with President Clinton who continued to pursue the policy of "cap, rollback and eliminate" India's nuclear and missile programmes. (Haass and Rose 1997) Rao reportedly gave Clinton the assurance of non-deployment of ballistic missiles in the near term. (Bobb 1994: 47) In the meantime, when India was occupied with the US, Pakistan didn't want the bilateral nuclear issue to be subsided. On August 23, 1991, Nawaz Sharif, the then opposition leader, proclaimed that Pakistan possesses atomic bomb (*Dawn* May 24, 1994) which, as usual, found its way to Indian domestic politics, on the verge of state elections. But not to be diverted from the political-military agenda, Rao advised the party members in the Congress Parliamentary Party meeting, not to worry, instead he asked to concentrate on the election preparation in their respective constituencies. (Gupta 1994: 46) Towards the end of 1994 and during early 1995, domestic politics took nuclear policy off the government's agenda owing to the state elections and consequently one sees Congress Party's defeat in Andhra Pradesh, Karnataka, Gujarat and Maharashtra. It is viewed that the political instability since 1991 till 1995 affected India's nuclear weapons decisions in many ways and the Congress Party attention on nuclear issues.

K. Subrahmanyam, in a commentary in *Strategic Analysis* said, though the credit for ordering to assemble nuclear weapon goes to Rajiv Gandhi, the credit for restarting the development programme of the weapon, after Morarji Desai halted it, belongs to Indira Gandhi. But, it was Narasimha Rao who is really responsible for operationalising the programme. (Subrahmanyam 2004: 595) During Rao's Prime Ministership, India was under considerable pressure from the US to roll back her nuclear programme. But, according to Subrahmaniyam, Rao had kept Vajpayee informed of the progress in the nuclear programme when Rao left office. This fact is evident from Vajpayee's eulogy to Narasimha Rao acknowledging the latter as the true "architect" of Shakti nuclear tests of May 11, 1998. (Raja Mohan 2004)

Two important developments in the nuclear domain seem to have inflicted sufficient impact on Congress Party's nuclear decision-making during Narasimha Rao period: first, the indefinite extension of NPT and the pressure to adhere to CTBT; second, China's nuclear test on May 15, 1995, just four days after the extension of the NPT. Other allied issues, such as China's shipment of thirty M-11 missiles to Pakistan, the passage of Brown Amendment that authorised release of withheld military equipment to Pakistan, China's missile test towards Taiwan, were perceived as "deterioration of nuclear environment" in the nehighbourhood (Subrahmanyam 1998:50). These developments seem to have exacerbated the domestic debate over the Congress government's capability to drive India's nuclear weapons policy forward. Presumably, influenced by these considerations, Prime Minister Rao decided to conduct the test towards the end of 1995 and gave go ahead to Dr APJ Abdul Kalam and Chidambaram during the summer that year to start preparatory works. (Subrahmanyam 1998: 51; Perkovich 2002: 365)

With election looming, what could have prompted Rao to take such a decision? According to Perkovich, "a detailed threat analyses of how developing nuclear weapons would affect these threats" did not appear. Rao had considerable experience in foreign affairs, but displayed little interest in details of nuclear policy. He innately disliked the notion of nuclear deterrence and tended to think of nuclear policy in moral terms." (Perkovich 2002: 365) Even he "did not have a nuclear deterrence strategy. He didn't think about when it will be used, against whom". He didn't think these things were usable, and he was not planning to use them. Perkovich further identifies the possible political implications of such decision by the Prime Minister which, he might have thought, would increase his options. First, he could silence the strategic community by holding out the prospects of tests; second, he could outflank the BJP by testing if they mobilise popular sentiment on the nuclear issue; third, if it is proved that India cannot afford the consequences of the test, he could take the excuse that he had been prepared for the test, but for the best interest of the nation maintained restraint. Unfortunately, US satellite detected activities in the Pokhran test site and Rao had to postpone the test for the enormous pressure by US.

The eleventh Lok Sabha elections occurred in stages between April 27 and May 30, 1996. The main contest was between the Congress Party and BJP. On the nuclear issue, the Congress Party downplayed, without clarifying whether and under what conditions India should conduct nuclear tests or exercise its nuclear option. It mainly focused on its objections to the CTBT and reiterated that India's nuclear programme is peaceful. (*Hindustan Times*, April 29 1996) Rao's failure to conduct the test and the Congress

Party loss in the election marked the starting of a new phase in India's nuclear history.

Notes

1. Both the Indian and international media viewed it as a shift of policy. *The Hindustan Times* detected that this is "a somewhat vague indication of a possible shift in the Government's nuclear policy". *The Patriot* reported it as "a clear shift in official thinking on nuclear policy". According to *The Washington Post* "as pressures on the Indian Government to 'go nuclear' mounted further observers today, sensed a change of India's earlier refusal to exploit her resources to respond to Communist China's nuclear testing".
2. US Defence Secretary Robert McNamara told in a conference of United Press editors on September 18 1967 that "there is evidence that the Chinese are devoting very substantial resources to the development of both nuclear warheads and missile delivery systems". *Congressional Quarterly* 1967: 2013.

5

Regional Security Factor: Views of CPI(M) and BJP

Views of CPI(M)

As parent organisation, from which the CPI(M) was carved out, the Communist Party of India (CPI) was the first and the largest single opposition to the Congress in the parliament. During the pre-independence period the CPI had "extra-territorial sources of political and economic guidance.[1] When power was transferred to the Congress Party, it left the CPI weak and unpopular and tried to remove antagonism aroused during the war years by giving tactical support to Nehru Government". (Nizami 1971: 2) The role of CPI in Indian politics has been best summed up by UN Dhebar in the following words:

> Of the Opposition parties, the most noisy is the Communist Party. Having traded for a long time in the old wares of slogan-mongering, demonstrations, obstructions and vituperations, it now seeks to woo a section of the Congressmen who, it thinks, are simple enough to fall a victim to its manoeuvres. It talks of increase in production in its way. It talks of Panchsheel, but is red to wink at China over border. (Dhebar 1962: 34)

The party itself was in a dilemma since the Chinese aggression against India in 1962. (Banerjee 1967: 83-88) This issue culminated in a rift and division of the party and emergence of the left fraction—CPI (Marxist)—in 1964. This fraction is inspired by China and had always criticised the Congress Government ever since it started functioning. They regard the government as conservative and reactionary, but there have been agreements between them and the Congress in matters of foreign policy, because of its friendly relations with socialist countries. Surprisingly, the party "flatly refuse to accept that China committed an act of aggression in defiance of international law apart from a breach of faith with Nehru who was its closest ally". (Nizami 1971: 19) The CPI(M), emerged as an independent political entity in 1964, thinks that India's national security is threatened not so much by China or Pakistan as by the USA (Banerjee 1966). It favoured a pact of mutual friendship between India, Pakistan and Sri Lanka; to that extent it even suggested that India should take the initiative in the matter, and that as the most preliminary and at the same time essential step, India should send an ambassador to Peking (Beijing). (Banerjee 1966: 87) On the Kashmir issue, the CPI(M) is convinced that merely "shuffling the pack" in the State can be dangerous. It suggested that the government should now try to win the confidence of political parties and the people in order to find a solution to the problem. (Banerjee 1966)

If one looks into the history of Communist Party's views on nuclear issues, in the post-Independence period, the CPI extended support to Nehru's initiative regarding the standstill agreement, calling a halt to the hydrogen bomb tests as the first step towards total banning of weapons of mass destruction. The Central Committee of the CPI welcomed and extended support to the proposals made in Parliament on April 2nd, 1954 in this regard. (*Resolution of the Central Committee*, April 1954: 18–19) Speaking in the Lok Sabha on the manufacture of nuclear weapons, Hiren Mukerjee said: "Nuclear weapons are doing a lot of damage, corrupting generations yet unborn, God knows, what kind of physical and psychological infirmities. ... All the weapons of the world can be defeated by one weapon which has got the strength of the spirit behind us." (*Lok Sabha Debates*, November 27, 1964: col. 2279–82) The CPI stands also for general and complete disarmament but "does not rule out the possibility of making atom bomb if India felt threatened by any outside power". (Ghosh 1962: 94)

Reacting to China's explosion of hydrogen bomb, Ramamurthi of CPI(M) said that it was open to any country to manufacture own nuclear weapons if felt threatened, particularly when the nuclear powers had not refrained from making nuclear bomb and stockpiling such weapons. China, he said, felt threatened; India certainly had the right to manufacture atom bombs if it so desired. (*The Statesman*, May 12, 1966) On China's nuclear test, the (CPI(M)) along with CPI, agreed with the government's non-nuclear policy, though the motivations of the Communists and the government were different. While supporting the government's nonaligned and non-nuclear policy, the CPI reacted quite differently to the Chinese bomb than did the Congress party. Their primary concern was imperialists' offer of a nuclear umbrella. The lead article in the CPI pro-Moscow weekly *The New Age* read: "The U.S. imperialists are again peddling their "nuclear umbrella" . . . The Chinese nuclear test is their "excuse" for reiterating the oft-rejected offer. The change in leadership of the Soviet government is also sought to be used by them, to make their filthy goods more attractive. On guard against the new conspiracy of the imperialists! On guard against the sinister campaigns already launched by the right reactionary forces in the country". (*The New Age* October 25, 1964: 1) In the Lok Sabha, the CPI(M) did not support the government, though their public policies were the same. Rather than viewing the Chinese bomb as a threat and demand national policy response, they saw it as an opportunity to condemn the twin evils of Chinese and US imperialism. (*The New Age* October 25 1964: 1)

The CPI(M) responded to the Chinese test very different from that of their former comrades. Jyoti Basu said that he "could not blame China for going in for atomic bombs". (Quoted in Mirchandani 1968: 53) Citing Chinese assurances that they would never be the first to use the bomb, he dismissed the suggestion that China's nuclear capability posed a new threat to India. The CPI(M) also said that it stood for an independent foreign policy based on opposition to imperialism, a policy based on opposition to nuclear war and imperialist wars, and peaceful settlement of India's dispute with socialist China and with Pakistan. But, its manifestos made no reference to nuclear explosion by China. It held a session three weeks after the Chinese explosion and passed a resolution urging the government to take the initiative in breaking the deadlock in the border dispute with China, but made no comment on the latest development in China. (Mirchandani 1968: 27)

In regard to China and Pakistan, the CPI(M)) advocated peaceful settlement of all disputes. Despite the continued hostile attitude of China, the Party viewed that it is in the interest of the Indian people and the country as a whole to explore all avenues for a peaceful settlement with China either directly or through the good offices of friendly neutral powers and propose no-war pact to China. (*Resolution of the National Council of the CPI*, Feb 5–12, 1963:

26–27) With regard to Kashmir, the Party demanded a lasting accord with Pakistan on the basis of making the existing ceasefire line as international boundary with mutually agreed adjustments. The CPI(M) called on people to demand the government to take necessary initiative to settle disputes with China and Pakistan and re-establish normal friendly relations with neighbouring countries. (*The Statesman,* September 21, 1965) Mostly, its attitude towards the Indo-Pakistan conflict was determined by the stand of China (i.e., whole-hearted support of Pakistan and did not consider her aggressor) on the issue (Nizami 1971: 157-58). The CPI(M) felt that India and Pakistan could not afford to live as enemies and that good neighbourly relations between them alone could lead to the progress of the two countries; therefore, the party welcomed the Tashkent Summit. (*Peoples Democracy* January 2, 1966)

After the nuclear test by India in 1974, the CPI(M) congratulated the scientists saying that "it is gratifying to note that this success is achieved by our scientists without depending upon foreign collaboration or being tied down to foreign know how" (*People's Democracy,* May 26 1974: 2). Further, the Party expressed that it has "always upheld the right of our country and every other country to develop its own nuclear capacity . . . ." The party also defended the government for not signing the NPT. However, it held that India "should not go for atomic weapons, but use nuclear energy for peaceful purposes and for immediate economic and social uplift of hundreds of millions of our people". (*People's Democracy,* May 26, 1974: 2)

The 1998 nuclear tests by the BJP took the Indian Left, both the CPI and CPI(M), completely by surprise. This is because, says Achin Vanaik, "the Indian Left has never categorically opposed the Indian bomb—they supported the posture of ambiguity and considered it to be stable. . . . The Indian Left were among the most "sincere" of those committed to ambiguity in the country. That is to say, "they were among those most determined not to go forward towards exercising the nuclear option". (Vanaik 1998: 55) This stand of the party is clearly amplified in the *Election Manifesto 1999* of CPI(M) where it listed six actions in regard to "National Security". (*Election Manifesto, 13th Lok Sabha* 1999: 11) They are:

1. Halting nuclear weaponisation; revert to nuclear policy of developing India's independent technological potential while not signing any international treaty which is discriminatory.

2. Not signing CTBT; work for universal nuclear disarmament and commitment by the nuclear weapon states for denuclearisation within a time frame.
3. Giving moratorium on testing parliamentary sanction and opening talks with Pakistan for a denuclearised South Asian environment.
4. Cancellation of the Indo-US military cooperation agreement which links up India with the US global strategy.
5. Removal of nuclear weapons from the US military base in Diego Garcia in the Indian Ocean.
6. Create a national security apparatus which will work within the framework of the parliamentary democratic system.

The CPI(M)'s this stand was reasserted before the Shakti tests in 1998. Reacting to BJP's position on exercising the nuclear option, the Polity Bureau member Prakash Karat told *Frontline* that his Party opposed the BJP's position on exercising the nuclear option. The CPI(M), he said, remains firmly committed to the concept of universal nuclear disarmament. "The acquisition of nuclear weapons", Karat said, "would trigger an arms race in South Asia". He also said that the party was in favour of retaining the "nuclear option" but this did not mean that his party supported weaponisation. He was in favour of continuing the Agni missile programme instead of freezing it under US pressure. (*Frontline*, 11–24 Apr 1998) The party mentioned about this in its programme at the Special Conference at Thiruvananthapuram in October 2000 that:

> The decision of the BJP-led government to go in for nuclear weaponisation after the tests in Pokhran in May, 1998 marked a dangerous new phase in India's external and nuclear policies. It has created the situation for a nuclear arms race in the subcontinent with Pakistan responding to India's nuclear tests. The jingoistic nuclear policy has undermined the long-standing policy of non-alignment and peace. It has made India more vulnerable to imperialist pressures headed by US imperialism. (CPI(M), *Programme*, 2000: Sec. 4.5)

Also during the 16th Congress of the Party, it is asserted that "India has become more vulnerable to imperialist pressures and the BJP government seems now ready to capitulate on India's long-standing position of not signing discriminatory treaties like the CTBT and the NPT." (*Political Organisational Report*, CPIM, Oct 5–11 1998: 76) The Party also approved the idea of holding broad based conventions involving intellectuals and other eminent citizens to mobilise public opinion against nuclear weaponisation and the jingoism of the BJP. The CPI(M) called for (a) not going in for weaponisation and deployment of nuclear weapons; (b) India should continue to oppose discriminatory treaties and not sign the CTBT. (*Political Organisational Report*, CPIM, Oct 5–11 1998: 77) The Party leader Jyoti Basu in a lecture said, "the revival of the nuclear arms race in the Indian subcontinent and the five super-powers' failure to chalk out a timetable for the elimination of atomic and hydrogen bombs make us afraid for the future". (Basu 1998: 10) Criticising the BJP, Sitaram Yechury said:

> The pseudo-nationalist jingoism that was sought to be whipped up with Pokhran-II was projected as an assertion of India's pride. In the wake of the international and domestic outcry at such undisguised jingoism and the imposition of sanctions, this BJP-led government has led India into a course of deceitful compromises made behind the back of Parliament and the people." (Yechury 1999: 10)

The CPI(M) stand on India's nuclear weapons policy is clearly discernible from various statements by the Polit Bureau. One such example is the Press Statement of the Polit Bureau on 21 July, 2005 which mentioned that, "the CPI(M) has opposed the nuclear weaponisation agenda of the BJP-led government. It does not subscribe to the views emanating from those who advocate nuclear weaponisation as a path for India's "great power" status. The CPI(M) and the Left parties have argued constantly for India to have an "independent nuclear policy." (Polit Bureau, *Press Statemement*, 21 July 2005) In its 16th Lok Sabha Election Manifesto, the party expressed "continued dialogue with Pakistan to resolve all outstanding issues" (p. 18).

Right Wing Views: Pre-BJP Era

The political group that vehemently argued on the importance of nuclear weapons for India since the early days is the Bharatiya Jana Sangh (BJS), which became Bharatiya Janata Party (BJP) in December 1980. But owing to its weak numerical strength in the legislature throughout its initial existence, it remained "on the margins of Indian polity" (Chandra 1998). In 1952, it won only three seats in the Lok Sabha with 3.06 per cent of the national vote. In 1957, the Jana Sangh won four seats with 5.97 per cent of the total votes. Subsequently, it absorbed a large part of the political base of the Hindu Mahasabha and the RRP, the total score of the three parties being five MPs with 7.17 per cent of the votes. The high watermark of the Jana Sangh, before it became the BJP, was reached in 1967 when it won 35 seats with 9.35 per cent of the popular vote, with the Hindu Mahasabha and the RRP having disappeared as political forces. But in 1971 the number came down when it got 22 seats in the Lok Sabha and 7.4 per cent of the votes. (Jaffrelot 1998: 40)

Perhaps, owing to this low electoral strength Jana Sangh's influence on government's policy formulations, especially on national security and nuclear matters was not very effective. It was only known as a political group that favours India acquiring nuclear weapons. On numerous occasions, the Jana Sangh has strongly raised and pressed for nuclear arsenal "for reasons rooted in its ideology, in its grandiose conception of India as a great power that has been denied for too long, and in its shaky political position". (Menon 1998) For Jana Sangh, nuclear weapons are an article of faith, part of the essential identity of a powerful, awe-inspiring, militarist "Hindu India" that can boast of its "manliness" and "virility" and thus prove to the world the superiority of "Hindu civilisation." (Bidwai and Vanaik 1998)

In the regional security context, if one enquires about the policies of Jana Sangh, the causes that gave birth to this political group on October 21, 1951 come to the front. One factor that contributed directly to the birth of the Jana Sangh was the exodus of Hindus from East Bengal during middle of January 1950. (Jhangiani 1967: 5) In the words of Deendayal Upadhaya, the Jana Sangh "was not a disgruntled, dissident, or discredited group of Congressmen who formed the nucleus of the party" rather "it was felt that the ruling party had failed to harness the enthusiasm created by freedom to the task of realisation of the great potentialities of the country". (*United Asia*, January 1962: 28) Stalwarts like Shyamaprasad Mookerjee, Neogy, Tondon and Dr Mathai felt that the Congress party has been drifted from nationalist *Bharatiya* sentiment; therefore, the necessity arose for a separate party. (Jhangiani 1967: 10)

Based on its conviction for building Indian political atmosphere on *Bharatiya* ideology, Jana Sangh believed in *Akhand Bharat* (undivided India), implying that India and Pakistan can ultimately become one. (Jhangiani 1967: 46) The Jana Sangh was vehement in its denunciation of Pakistan. During the Eighth Annual Session, its President Pitamberdas accused the Congress government of pursuing the policy of appeasement at the expense of India's vital interests and cited the transfer of Berubari to Pakistan without taking the people and Parliament into confidence. (Jhangiani 1967: 47) In his view, "Pakistan has taken the maximum advantage of India's nonbelligerent attitude". Therefore, in the Seventh Annual Session of the Jana Sangh at Nagpur in January 1960, it was suggested that the Government of India should adopt a "firm and realistic policy . . . to put a stop to Pakistan's aggressiveness and create confidence in the people of this country". (Jhangiani 1967: 47) Resolution No. 3 of the 11th Annual Session of the Sangh says that "it has been the considered view of the BJS that Pakistan by its very genesis and nature is destined to treat India as its enemy No. 1, so long as it exists." (Annual Session of BJS, *Resolutions*, 28–30 December 1963)

Deva Prasad Ghosh in his presidential address at the BJS Pratinidhi Sabha at Jaipur Session in April 1956 told "it is the considered opinion of the Jana Sangh that Pakistan has no *locus standi* in Kashmir. She is an aggressor and should be treated as such. . . . Jana Sangh will make efforts to get Pakistan declared aggressor by UNO and will take all possible steps for the liberation of Pak-held Kashmir." (Ghosh 1956)

The Jana Sangh was equally critical regarding China. The Sangh accused the Government of India, as it did not help Tibet in 1950 when China occupied it. On the Chinese aggression in 1962, the Party viewed that it did not come as a sudden surprise (Jhangiani 1967: 61–62). The Party was rather conscious of Chinese designs and had all along been warning the government of the imminent danger. Therefore, it viewed "the problem of China is India's own creation and same is the case with Pakistan". (Kishore 1969: 100) When Zou En-lai came to New Delhi for talks, Jana Sangh organised a mass demonstration criticising the government for its "masterly inactivity" in respect of China's "cartographic invasion" and urged the government to remain firm. Also it demanded the government for a basic change in policy towards China. (Poplai 1962: 55) It suggested India to follow the foreign policy guided by "enlightened self-interest", meaning thereby "the de-recognition of China . . . liberation of Tibet, joint military pact with Pakistan and direct association with the Western Bloc." (Gupta 1964: 40) Both Pakistan and China, according to the Party are India's "natural enemies" therefore, advocated for a policy of "reciprocity"—hitting back—following the same attitude what China and Pakistan have towards India, "hence the importance of defence". (Kishore 1969: 32)

Evidently, the Jana Sangh was the foremost and outspoken proponent of India acquiring nuclear weapons. It also found support from some sections in the Congress Party and from some sections of the public opinion, but neither the rightist Swatantra Party nor the pro-Moscow or pro-Peking wings of the communist fractions in India supported Jana Sangh's views that time (Kapur 1976: 182). Ashok Kapur views "Jana Sangh's advocacy of nuclear deterrent for India is consistent with its general policy of urging a reorientation in India's defence thinking". (Kapur 1976: 182) The main premise of party's such advocacy was that "Pakistan and China are India's natural enemies". (Kishore 1969: 32)

The Jana Sangh was advocating nuclearisation since 1951 when the Congress government led by Nehru was emphasising "neighbourly and friendly relations" with China. This was 13 years before China went nuclear. The Sangh accused the Congress government of misleading the public regarding Sino-Indian relations during late-1950s when the government knew in 1956 about Chinese territorial intrusions into the Aksai Chin area in Ladakh. (Jhangiani 1967: 59) In 1962, before the Chinese test, the Sangh stated in its election manifesto that India should develop an atomic bomb. (*The Nuclear Weapon Archive* 2001) The Jana Sangh's formal support for the development of nuclear weapons was confirmed in a resolution passed in the Patna Session of the Sangh's General Working Committee on 4th December, 1964, where it stated that "the Working Committee, therefore, considers it imperative that an all out effort be made to build up an independent nuclear deterrent ... and urges the government of India to revise its stand accordingly". (Patil 1969: 79)

In the same resolution, the Jana Sangh vehemently criticised the Congress government policy in dealing with the issue of Chinese threat vis-à-vis Indian nuclear deterrent. In the Party's opinion, "India was fighting an undeclared war with China for last two years. The fact has been known for quite some time that China was feverishly active trying to detonate nuclear device of its own. The serious implications which China's success would have in regard to this Sino-Indian involvement, and the psychological impact and atomic bang by Peking would have on other Asian countries . . . ." (Patil 1969: 79) But it criticised by saying that "the Government in its smug ostrich like complacency" not only refused to do anything of the kind but it further kept on confusing and misinforming public opinion by raising an economic bogey to silence the popular demand for own atom bomb. (Patil 1969: 79) While questioning the utility of Government's policy of asking China to stop testing, the Sangh also welcomed President Lyndon B. Johnson's offer of a security guarantee for non-nuclear weapons states, but nonetheless emphasised India's need to have an independent atomic capability. (Kishore 1969: 132–34)

On February 26, 1966, just before his death, Savarkar, the premier ideologue of *Hindutva*, had called on the Indian government to "immediately equip India with nuclear weapons and missiles." (Quoted in Sarkar 1998: 1726) For him, that was the logical extension of the slogan he had proclaimed way back in 1942: "Hinduise the nation and militarise Hinduism." (Sarkar 1998: 1726) After emerging as the second largest opposition party in the parliament in the 1967 general election, Jana Sangh stated in a formal resolution that: "Communist China has developed nuclear warheads and missiles [while] the government of India is still harping on the Tashkent spirit and is not prepared to develop its own nuclear deterrent. It is pledged to increase the strength of all three wings of the armed forces, development of independent nuclear deterrent and top priority to development of defence industries." (Ralhan 1998: 83)

The BJS charged the government with confusing and "misinforming the public" by raising an "economic bogey" to silence the growing popular demand for India to build its own atom bomb. (Bhatia 1979: 76; Patil 1969: 79) *The Organiser*, Jana Sangh's weekly mouthpiece, sarcastically noted that "contrary to expert opinion that a 10 kiloton bomb would cost Rs 17.5 lakh [$350,000], Comrade Menon has put the cost at Rs 12 crore [$25.2 million] and the PM has put it at Rs 40–50 crore [$84–105 million]." (Rosen 1967: 23–24) Yet, according to the Jan Sangh, "no price is too high to pay, where the country's defence is involved". In their policy statement, the BJS lashed out at the government's "pseudo-pacifist inhibitions" and its "air of superior international morality". In a less caustic tone, the Jana Sangh charged that India was losing ground in the competition with China for the leadership of new nations of the world. It noted that, of all the non-aligned nations, only India seemed to regard it as a breach of international morality. However, the Jana Sangh trusted neither the Communists' neo-imperialism nor that of the Americans. They also downgraded the feasibility of obtaining a reliable nuclear guarantee from the two great powers to protect India from nuclear blackmail. (Couper 1969)

The Jana Sangh appealed to the nationalist desires of Indians to be regarded as a world power—not a world moral power, but a world atomic power. During its winter session (November 23–25, 1964), the Lok Sabha held a debate on international affairs, which erupted into a nuclear weapons row. The debate centered on interpretations of China's motivations and how India should respond. The Jana Sangh took the lead in advocating the Realist approach for India to develop nuclear weapons to negotiate with the international community from a position of strength, regardless of the cost (*Lok Sabha Debates*, November 23 1964, col. 1280). In the *Resolution* passed by the Bharatiya Karya Samiti of the BJS (4–6 Dec 1964), it deeply regretted for,

> . . . the Government's failure to realise the seriousness of the threat posed to India's security by China's entry into the nuclear club. The lackadaisical manner in which the Government of India has been dealing with this matter is evidenced by the fact that an issue of so vital importance has not even been referred to the Central Cabinet for its considered opinion. (BJS, *Resolution*, 4–6 Dec 1964)

According to Bachhraj Vyas, former President of the BJS, the nuclear explosion by China not only "upset the balance of power" in Afro-Asian countries, but it also posed a serious threat to India's integrity. (*Hindustan Times*, November 11, 1964) In his view, in response to the collusion between Pakistan and China, India should fully arm herself and give up the posture of renunciation of nuclear arms (*Times of India*, April 6, 1965). Also the Party launched a nation-wide campaign to press the government to manufacture nuclear weapons. (*Hindustan Times*, October 20, 1964) At the first meeting which was observed as National Solidarity Day (October 20, 1964), Atal Bihari Vajpayee said that the atomic explosion by China aggravated the dangers to South East Asian countries. Welcoming President Johnson's initiative to help non-atomic powers, he advocated for India developing her independent nuclear deterrent. (*Indian Express*, October 20, 1964) The Working Committee of the Jana Sangh said that the Government of India's present policy of nuclear abnegation could well prove "suicidal" in view of China's unconcealed expansionist ambition. (*The Statesman*, 7th December, 1964)

Prime Minister Shastri's proposal at the Cairo NAM Conference to send a mission of non-aligned countries to China to stop testing A-bombs was unacceptable to the Jana Sangh. (*Organiser*, 9 November, 1964: 4) Also Shastri's tentative shift of nuclear policy by saying that "I cannot say that the present policy is deep rooted, that cannot be set aside, that it can never be changed" could not satisfy Jana Sangh either. (Perkovich 1999: 81) It felt that it is not sufficient to say that India is capable of manufacturing nuclear bomb. The "claim that we have the capability of manufacturing nuclear bomb will carry conviction only when we have at least an A-bomb or our own." (*Organiser*, November 9, 1964: 4) Bachhraj Vyas in his presidential address at the 12th Plenary Session of the BJS said that there is no alternative for India, but to go for the manufacture of atomic bomb; BJS is not prepared to embrace death at the hands of Chinese invaders. To put a check on the vicious attitude of "war-mongering and vile-threatening" of China, India has to make the bomb. (*BJS Resolution*, 24 January, 1965; Ralhan 1998: 154–58) On the other hand, the party was of the view that an US nuclear umbrella would be a much more effective deterrent against China than a single bomb or two of our own. (*Organiser*, November 9, 1964)

The Jana Sangh vehemently attacked the Congress government for failure to manufacture a nuclear device for its own. (*Organiser*, October 26, 1964: 3) On November 24, 1964, the Jana Sangh moved a substantive motion in which it regretted the government had failed to appreciate the serious threat to India's security due to China's successful entry into the nuclear club. On November 27, 1964, the Jana Sangh introduced yet another motion in the Lok Sabha calling for the manufacture of nuclear weapons but Shastri managed to win a voice vote against the resolution on the ground of economic, moral and political costs. After two years and four days after the third Chinese nuclear test, the Jana Sangh president Balraj Madhok, demanded for India an independent nuclear deterrent. (Chaulia 2002: 215–234)

During the 1967 national election, nuclear policy stood small and only loud call for building nuclear weapons came from the Jana Sangh. Its representation in the Lok Sabha rose from 14 to 35 seats. (Frankel 1979: 356) In its election manifesto, the Sangh demanded a change in the country's defence and foreign policies in view of the "continued aggression by Communist China and Pakistan and their future designs". The manifesto listed seven steps as essential for increasing the nation's defence potential. The fifth point in the list was manufacturing of nuclear weapons and missiles. Balraj Madhok subsequently told that he wanted India to develop her nuclear deterrent for the simple fact that "China is India's enemy. It has developed its own defence potential. I cannot condemn China for this. It has every right to do so. I would insist on my government and people that they should also take up a nuclear programme and develop those very weapons which China has and Pakistan has." (Quoted in Mirchandani 1968: 53) Criticising government's response to the Chinese Hydrogen bomb in June 1967, the Jana Sangh member V.M. Chordia said "our policy in these matters always seems to be to depend on God. But remember, God only helps those who help themselves. The government must change its policy to suit new situations". (Mirchandani 1968: 59–60)

The Sangh renewed its pressure on the government in April 1970 when China for the first time launched a long-range rocket carrying a satellite into orbit. After four years when Indira Gandhi's government conducted nuclear tests, the Central Working Committee of the Jana Sangh issued a resolution on June 2nd, 1974 declaring May 18 as a "red letter day in Indian History" and saluted the Indian scientists, who had "placed India on the nuclear map of the world" (Mirchandani 1968: 65). The nuclear explosion was described by L.K. Advani, the then President of the Jana Sangh, as "one of most heartening bits of news in recent years". (Quoted by Weinraub 1974) But after Indira Gandhi's first term, when the non-communist opposition parties—Jana Sangh, the Congress (O), the Socialist Party and Bharatiya Lok Dal—decided to fight against Mrs Gandhi's Congress under the banner of Janata Party lead by Morarji Desai, in the March 1977 general election, the nuclear policy did not figure in the campaign. (Pillai 1977: 37) Even after Janata Dal formed government with the leadership of Desai who staunchly disavowed, nuclear weapons for India, and more importantly, when China carried its twenty-second nuclear test out in late September 1977, the "Jana Sangh took a detached view". (Mirchandani 1968: 66) The Jana Sangh members in the Janata Dal government cabinet did not dissent from Moraji Desai's line.

Interestingly, the Jana Sangh, which was advocating for India developing nuclear weapons all along and criticised vehemently Congress government's policies, remained silent during Morarji's Prime Ministership. It is a matter of debate, if BJS did not dissent from the Janata Party policies on nuclear weapons owing to the fact that Atal Bihari Vajpayee became the External Affairs Minister and L.K. Advani the Minister of Information and Broadcasting in Morarji's cabinet. Vajpayee's presence in the Desai cabinet might have compelled BJS to shift its traditional nuclear advocacy. (Ghosh 1999: 329)

Views of Bharatiya Janata Party

Inheriting the legacy of BJS, the BJP considers itself as a party of "law and order". (Upadhyaya 1979: 28) However, the initial aim of the Party, as said by the then BJP president L.K. Advani, was to "influence policy decisions by becoming a force to reckon with in parliament. According to the Party's former General Secretary K.L. Sharma, "it is a party with a difference". (Quoted in Noorani 1991: 7) In the same tone, A.B. Bajpayee said in an interview that the BJP is different from the BJS "in many ways". (Noorani 1991: 7) But, the party's "position on nuclear deterrence was identical to that of the BJS". (Ghosh 1999: 339)

Before attempting to enquire BJP's stand on regional security situation and India's nuclear policy, it is pertinent to elaborate the regional security situation during the time when the Party emerged in the national political scene. First, BJP emerged in Indian political scenario in the backdrop of Soviet intervention in Afghanistan. Though the Party supported the Indo-Soviet ties, disapproved the presence of Soviet forces in Afghanistan and called for India to follow an independent foreign policy. (Zaid 1980: 650) Second, during the Cold War, Pakistan became a "frontline state" of the US; financial-military assistance was pumped into it, which helped Islamabad maintain parity with India's military might. Third, with end of Cold War and disintegration of Soviet Union, the strategic environment around India and the world at large changed. Factors like, loosening of traditional alliance with Moscow, uneasy relationship with US, China's strategic encirclement of India through military alliance with Pakistan and Myanmar and fear of marginalisation in the post-Cold War era, all seem to have forced India to rethink its approach to national security. (Mallik 1998: 193) Fourth, by the time BJP emerged as a national political party in India's political horizon, Pakistan's clandestine nuclear programme was fully revealed. During the 1980s, BJP ideologues, therefore, used to talk about the need for a "Hindu bomb", as opposed to the "Islamic bomb". (Cherian 1998) But gradually, this ideological justification was shifted to "national security" as a factor, and it was emphasised that the acquisition of nuclear weapons is an urgent necessity to protect India's security interests. (Cherian 1998)

How far this situation had impinged upon BJP's nuclear decision making has been a matter of debate. Article II of the BJP's Constitution says that "the Party pledged to build up India as a strong and prosperous nation, which is modern, progressive and enlightened in outlook and which proudly draws inspiration from India's ancient culture and values and thus is able to emerge as a great world power playing an effective role in the comity of Nations for the establishment of world peace and a just international order". (Article II: Objective, *Constitutioin and Rules of Bharatiya Janata Party*) The BJP has always attached highest importance to national security and the necessity of nuclear weapons in national security strategy.

When in May 1985, the Parliament debated the Pakistani nuclear programme, the BJP resumed its usual call for building atom bomb. On July 11, 1985 when ABC's *Good Morning America* reported Pakistan's successful test of nuclear triggering package for nuclear weapons, BJP reacted sharply. (Spector 1990: 332) It declared that India could no longer afford a "policy of drift and escapism". In July 21, 1985, a National Executive Resolution of the Party declared that "reports from Pakistan indicate that the threat of a Pakistani nuclear bomb is real" and an immediate response to this, is necessary. The BJP, therefore, called upon government to take immediate steps to develop India's "own nuclear bomb". (Zaid 1980: 431-32; *The Times of India*, July 22, 1985) Even before A.Q. Khan's interview with Kuldip Nayar was public, the BJP president L.K. Advani said in late January 1987 that "India must produce the nuclear bomb as there is no alternative". (*The Times of India*, January 20, 1987: 16) This was the time when Rajiv Gandhi government was dealing with Reagan administration persuading to restrict Pakistan. On the other side, Congress government was occupied with the domestic problems, and more importantly with the LTTE issue. However, concern about Pakistan's nuclear programme was alive in BJP's agenda. In December 1987, Vajpayee again urged India to make nuclear weapons. (*News India*, December 11, 1987)

The 1989 election manifesto of BJP pleaded for "optimum defence preparedness including production of nuclear bombs and delivery systems". (Ghosh 1999: 341) Also this aspect was repeated during the 1991 election. During the 1996 election campaign, the party's main plank was national security. It said "Pakistan was carrying on a proxy war which should not be fought with kid gloves". The party promised that if it comes to power it would ensure the end of such a proxy war with an "adequate response". (*The Hindu*, 8 January, 1996) On the nuclear question, the party rehashed its old strategy of "keeping the option open".

In its 1998 Election Manifesto, the BJP enumerated that:

> The internal and external security environment has deteriorated sharply in the last decade. The previous Governments have been found wanting in their efforts and determination to face these threats and are responsible for this. Since 1991, the country's defence budget has been declining in real terms. . . .Successive weak and irresolute Governments have imperiled national security. (*BJP Election Manifesto, 1998*)

After coming to power in 1998, the BJP went for the Pokhran II tests in a hurry, defying its earlier words that it would seek the advice of the National Security Council on the nuclear issue and will go for a comprehensive review of the security situation. (*BJP Election Manifesto, 1998*) But the Party succeeded in conducting tests where other parties were either hesitant or situations did not permit them to do so. The official explanation extended in defence of the tests was "deteriorating regional security environment". In an interview with the *India Today*, the then Prime Minister Atal Bihari Vajpayee while answering the question why did he decide to conduct the tests in May 1998 said "We conducted the series of nuclear tests in keeping with our commitment made to the people of India during the election. . . . The decision to carry out these tests was guided by the paramount importance we attach to national security". (Chawla 1998)

In the same interview, replying to the question, what was the compulsion to carry out the test and what was the new reality the government discovered that prompted it to test at that point of time, Prime Minister Vajpayee said:

> Important measures ... are guided by long-term imperatives based on a sound appraisal of regional and global security realities. It is important for us and the world to know that by con-

> ducting the latest tests, India has responded to a stark regional and global reality that has evolved over the past 50 years.
>
> We live in a world where India is surrounded by nuclear weaponry. No responsible government can formulate a security policy for the country on abstract principles, disregarding ground realities. . . . the greatest meaning of the tests is that they have given India Shakti, they have given India strength, they have given India self-confidence.... India has never played politics with national security. . . . (Chawla 1998)

Also, in the aftermath of the 1998 tests, defence minister George Fernandes stated China a "bigger potential threat" than Pakistan and described how his country was being "encircled" by Chinese military activities through alliance building with Pakistan and Myanmar and the deployment of Chinese nuclear missiles in Tibet. (Lague 1998: 13) Though, the security rationale has been pronounced more often, considerable ambiguity and consequent heated debate over the issue can be perceived both in India and outside. It was revealed that the only step taken by Vajpayee in his 13-day Prime Ministership in 1996 was a green signal to the DRDO and DAE to begin preparation for a nuclear test. (Chengappa 2000: 411-13) K. Subrahmaniyam described "the testing by the BJP-led NDA government was a continuation of the policy of the P.V. Narasimha Rao government, which in turn flowed from Rajiv Gandhi's decision to develop nuclear weapons . . . . What was started by Rajiv Gandhi government was fulfilled by the Vajpayee government when it tested nuclear weapons". (Quoted by Chand 2008) This fact is also amplified when Vajpayee acknowledged while paying tribute to Narasimha Rao that the "real architect" of 1998 tests was Rao himself. (*The Tribune,* December 29, 2004) Mr Vajpayee said at a literary meeting at Gwalior that while Rao was demitting office in May 1996, he had handed him a "piece of paper that contained brief information about preparations for nuclear explosion at Pokhran (and) suggested continuing with these preparations, as neighbours (China and Pakistan) already possessed nuclear weapons". (Malhotra 2004)

Subrahmanyam also opined that the then National Security Adviser Brajesh Mishra was the prime driver behind Vajpayee government's decision to conduct nuclear tests. When Pakistan tested *Ghauri* missile on 6 April, 1998, Mr Mishra called him (Subrahmanyam) and asked, "What should India do?" Subrahmayam suggested to ask A.P.J. Abdul Kalam, the then chief of DRDO, to do a missile test to counter Pakistan. (Chand 2008) However, Brajesh Mishra says the decision to exercise the N-option was entirely "security driven" and provoked by "a nuclear neighbour to the west of us and another to the north, both working in tandem". (*India Today*, May 25, 1998) Also the first official explanation for the tests was presented in a letter to the US President Bill Clinton, where Vajpayee explicitly cited the China factor. (*The New York Times*, May 13, 1998) On the other hand, Achin Vanaik views that the security explanation was a convenient way of "selling to a general public" though the fact that India-China relations have steadily improved over the last 15 years to the private dismay of Pakistan. (Vanaik 1998: 52) It is also seen that the BJP-led government has periodically sought to play down this factor and declare its interest in improving India-China relations claiming that the tests were not carried out with China in mind. Vanaik further says that "the primary factor behind this dramatic shift in India's nuclear policy is the determination of the 'Sangh Combine' to impose its particular vision of not only what constitutes the cultural essence of India and Indian nationalism, but to reshape the total agenda of Indian nationalism and its discourse—of what constitutes the Indian nation, national security, national interests, national (and therefore) international "greatness", etc. (Vanaik 1998: 53)

As discussed earlier, in the *Suo Motu Statement* on May 27, 1998 Prime Minister Atal Bihari Vajpayee claimed that the tests are in response to the "deteriorating regional security situation." (*Suo Motu Statement* by Prime Minister Atal Bihari Vajpayee in the Indian Parliament; *Paper laid on the table of the House on Evolution of India's Nuclear Policy* on May 27, 1998) After conducting comprehensive diplomatic manoeuvres aftermath the nuclear tests, the NDA government promised that the "National Security Council will advise the government in this regard and also in the establishment of a credible nuclear deterrence. These are the minimum requirements in this recently inaugurated era of global inequality and increased vulnerability". (*NDA Manifesto* 1999)

After conducting the tests and declaring India as a Nuclear Weapons State what left for BJP was to put in place a credible deterrent capability with appropriate command and control structure. The NSAB on August 1999 released a Draft Nuclear Doctrine, which has been operationalised since 2003, that calls for "a doctrine of credible minimum nuclear deterrence" under which nuclear weapons would be used for "retaliation only." (*Draft Report of NSAB on*

Indian Nuclear Doctrine, 17 August, 1999) However, the important aspect of BJP's approach is that, it kept its promise by conducting the nuclear tests in 1998 and proclaims to have provided India, at least in principle, a credible nuclear force which other political parties unfortunately could not. In its 16th Lok Sabha Election Manifesto, the BJP views India's neighbourhood "sensitive" and aims to "modernise armed forces" including a *revision and update* of India's current nuclear doctrine to make it relevant to challenges of current times. (BJP *Election Manifesto 2014*: 37-39) After assuming power, if BJP deliver this pledge a new chapter would be opened in India's nuclear history and regional security discourse.

Note

1. The CPI began to function with Marxist totalitarian outlook, keeping itself in constant touch with Moscow and Peking and other subversive and revolutionary movements in the different parts of the world. In 1930, the CPI was formally affiliated to the *Communist International*. It is based on principles and philosophy of Marx, Engels, Lenin and Stalin.

6

Extra-regional Powers and National Security: Views of the Three Parties

It is argued that the threats to India's security arose not merely from Pakistan and China but from the policies pursued by the big powers over the years and Pakistan's attitudes "were only symptoms of a more fundamental security challenge posed by two big powers" (Subrahmanyam 1999: 12). Also, India's nuclear doctrine proposing a "credible minimum nuclear deterrence" for "retaliation only" defines the "fundamental purpose of Indian nuclear weapons" is "to deter the use and threat of they use of nuclear weapons by any State or entity against *India and its forces*"; and it also assures that India will not use nuclear weapons against non-nuclear weapon states or states not aligned to nuclear weapon states. This underlines the fact that nuclear threat from any nuclear weapon state or threat from states aligned with them would be dealt with nuclear retaliation. This raises the question, beside Pakistan and China, which countries might pose such kind of threats to India? The previous chapters analysed perceptions of three parties regarding nuclear threats to India from nuclear weapon states in the region. This chapter, therefore, looks into these parties' perspectives on other nuclear weapons countries outside the region and if they are a factor in India's nuclear weapon strategy.

If "Indian strategic policy has largely been responsive to major external events" (Cohen 2005: 154), its nuclear strategy must also be linked with the policies and involvement of outside powers in South Asia. As commonly viewed, India's missile programme, especially the *Prithvi* missile is Pakistan–specific and the

Agni missile is China specific. (Dixit 1997) Also India's nuclear disarmament initiatives were linked to Chinese nuclear weapons programme. However, certain aspects of Super Power involvement in and around South Asia seem exacerbated India's nuclear weapon programme. Here, an attempt is made specifically to examine in what way and if the nuclear weapons programme of India is linked with the policies of nations outside the region, especially from the point of view of the three parties. More specifically, the chapter examines the perceptions of the three political parties on the policies of nations like USA, Russia (former USSR), UK, etc., in relation to India's national security conception and nuclear weapons strategy. But, before going into the details of the postures of specific countries, it is pertinent to identify the links between nuclear postures of extra-regional powers and India's threat perceptions.

South Asian Security Architecture and Outside Powers

A major portion of the region that constitutes South Asia today was mainly British India before 1947. More often, British India's security policy is identified with British Viceroy Lord Curzon's ideas of three-front frontier he formulated to insulate India from the expansionist move of Czarist Russia known as "Great Game."[1] Curzon's security architecture highlighted thereby India's centrality in the Indian Ocean littoral, Asia and the world as a whole. Laying out the essence of his arguments, Curzon wrote in his essay *The Place of India in the Empire* (1909):

> The central position of India, its magnificent resources, its teeming multitude of men, its great trading harbours, its reserve of military strength, supplying an army always in a high state of efficiency and capable of being hurled at a moment's notice upon any point either of Asia or Africa—all these are assets of precious value. On the West, India must exercise predominant influence over the destinies of Persia and Afghanistan; on the North, it can veto any rival in Tibet; on the north-east and east it can exert great pressure upon China, and it is one of the guardians of the autonomous existence of Siam. On the high seas, it commands the routes to Australia and to the China Seas. (Curzon 1909: 12)

In Curzon's "forward policy" formulation, India's frontier was consisted of three levels: (1) Administrative frontier which was directly under British control; (2) Extended zones or frontiers that British had influence over; (3) Buffer states which are special arrangements like Afghanistan, Tibet and Burma. (Sarela 2005: 18) Curzon postulated a role for India within the matrix of the British imperial interests and his ideas constituted an Indo-centric vision of South Asia and the Indian Ocean littoral. This notion of regional supremacy has left a legacy that the post-British India followed in dealing with the region, with the demise of British rule in India and the partition that followed culminated in an "Indo-centric" region owing to many inherent factors. First, the asymmetry between India and rest of South Asian countries is substantial. In respect of economic prowess, military might, territorial expanse, no other country in the region matches India. Around eleven times, since its independence, India has been involved militarily or otherwise in the internal affairs of its small neighbours. (Muni 1993: 11–12) At the root of this attitude of India, according to S.D. Muni, "is the gradually growing autonomous capitalist state of India, highly sensitive to its security concerns and to its ideological preferences in the region". (Muni 1993: 11–12)

Subsequent policies and actions by India seem to have generated a negative security perception among the South Asian neighbours vis-à-vis India which persist till today. From Indira Gandhi's tenure, India has followed towards its small neighbours a policy called India's Monroe Doctrine.[2] Attempts have always been made by India to insulate the region from outside powers, claiming the region as India's natural and exclusive *sphere of influence*. (Raja Mohan 2003) Special treaty arrangements were made in this regard in order to restrict the neighbours to look towards outside powers. The Indo-Bhutan treaty of 1949 (revised in 2007) and Indo-Nepal treaty of 1950 are such examples, where these countries were made obliged to consult India in the sphere of their defence and foreign policy. India also played crucial role in establishing multi-party constitutional democracy in Nepal during 1950s. India's relation with Pakistan has its root in the partition of British India and subsequently the Kashmir issue remained a perpetual source of tension. Apprehensions were expressed when Sikkim merged with India in 1975.

As a result of the assertive postures, small countries in South Asia seem to have developed a "fear psychosis vis-à-vis India" (Upreti 2003: 258). However, in response, counter-balancing India's influence, these small countries have often invited outside powers like China and United States through alliances or otherwise. The intention here is to highlight India's security environment versus its neighbours to identify the role, if any, of the extra-regional powers in India's nuclear weapons decision making. Also the attitude and policies of these external powers, especially China at times seem to have exacerbated India's security concerns. For example, China follows a strategy the "string of pearls" to encircle India by building of bases at strategic locations.[3] (Pehrson 2006)

Another aspect in identifying the role of extra-regional powers in influencing India's nuclear weapons decision-making is to locate the link between South Asian regional security architecture. In other words, it is to identify the spillover effect of regional security environment influenced by the external powers on India's nuclear weapons decision making process. The security environment in South Asia to which Barry Buzan described as "security complex" (Buzan 1991: 190) is a classical example of rivalry among the global powers, where the complex in "conflict formation mode" draw in outside intervention along the lines of its own internal split.[4]

Same is the case with other South Asian neighbours, who try to balance India at times by aligning with the extra-regional powers. To that extent, the extra-regional powers have also tried to become stakeholders, thus perpetuating the conflict to a deeper level. Also, some countries in the region have tried to form ties with countries of the neighbouring region. For example, though South Asian and Middle Eastern security dynamics generally are geographically separated, there are many interlinking issues that fused the concerns of both the regions together. Pakistan's attempt to balance India by seeking ties first with Iran and later with Saudi Arabia and India's attempt to build friendly relations with Iran and developing its Chabahar port infrastructure can be viewed in this perspective. (*The Hindu*, July 10, 2004) Gwadar port built by China in Pakistan has evoked concerns in India and Iran and has sparked a tacit competition for *strategic access* among these countries. Another example was the Israeli concern over Pakistan's rhetoric about an 'Islamic' nuclear bomb (Pant 2004), and the rumours mooted during the 1970s that Israel and India might, therefore, find a pressing common cause. Many such intersections can be found that have been proved to be the fault lines along which the arms trade takes place.

Especially in the nuclear environment, security issues attract wider attention as nuclear weapons have global ramifications. It is generally seen how the overlapping regional security is characterised by intense security dilemma: "a situation in which no community can provide for its own security without threatening the security of others". (Herz 1950) For example, the clandestine nuclear network managed by A.Q. Khan spanned over the whole Asia had raised India's concerns and consequent policy decisions. With this background here, it is discussed how the three political parties have viewed nuclear developments in the neighbouring regions or policies of outside nuclear powers influenced India's thinking.

Perception and Views of the Congress Party

As is discussed before, Nehru's statesmanship was never opposed, at least until the Sino-Indian border clash in 1962. Nehru's role-perception of India led him to propound ideas and visions of a wider federation of Asian states, mainly to contain the forces of imperialism, domination and control at the global level. Long before becoming Prime Minister, Nehru said:

> If there are to be federations, India will not fit into a European Federation, where it can only be a hanger-on of semi-colonial status. It is obvious that under these circumstances there should be an Eastern Federation not hostile to the West, but nevertheless standing on its own feet, self-reliant and joining with all others to work for world peace and world federation.
>
> Such an Eastern Federation must inevitably consist of China and India, Burma and Ceylon and Nepal and Afghanistan should be included. So should Malaya. There is no reason why Siam and Iran should also not join, as well as some other nations. That would be a powerful combination of free nations joined together for their own good as well as for the world good. (Quoted in Muni and Raja Mohan 2005: 54)

As India's independence drew close, the AICC in a resolution on Asian cooperation in 1945 said: "A free India will inevitably seek the close and friendly association with her neighbouring countries and would specially seek to develop common policies for defence, trade and economic and cultural development with China, Burma, Malaya, Indonesia and Ceylon as well as other countries of the Middle East". (Quoted in Muni 1993: 14) After India's independence, the Congress Party refined this idea of a broader role of India preparing for a South Asian Federation of India, Iran, Iraq, Afghanistan and Burma. Therefore, it would be erroneous to think the India-led proposal for a federation and closer relations was motivated by independent India's desire to recreate the British Empire. Rather India seems to have erred to realise that her neighbours were also thinking along these lines. (Muni 1993: 14-15) But most of Nehru's enthusiasm faded with the partition of the Indian subcontinent and also with the emergence of Communist China. Subsequent decades saw India's security perception hooked into the geo-strategic make-up of the Indian subcontinent.

However, independent India's concerns to insulate the region from extra-regional powers' influence have often expressed both in the Congress Party's and also in other political groups' deliberations. There was open resistance to the Cold War, particularly the policies of 'containment' pursued by the Western powers during Nehru's leadership. There were repeated denunciation of the US-led military pacts as SEATO, CENTO and the Baghdad Pact that facilitated the great power military presence in or around South Asia in the Congress Party's and Nehru's expressions. (Nehru 1961: 87-98, 182-236) Nehru himself reacted very strongly to the USA efforts to establish a strategic relationship with Pakistan. As early as May 1950, Nehru wrote to Mrs Vijaya Laxmi Pandit, his sister and India's Ambassador to the US, that:

> . . . There is a concerted attempt to build up Pakistan and build down, if I may say so, India. It surprises me how immature in their political thinking the Americans are! They do not even learn from their own or other people's mistakes; more especially in their dealings with Asia, they show a lack of understanding which is surprising. (Quoted in Gopal 1983: 63)

Nehru's disappointment grew as the US-Pakistan military alliance became imminent. He wrote a letter to Prime Minister Mohamed Ali Jinnah in late 1953 saying:

> If such an alliance takes place, Pakistan enters definitely into the region of Cold War. That means to us that the Cold War has come to the very frontiers of India. This is a matter of serious consequence to us, who have been trying to build up an area of peace . . . . It must also be a matter of grave consequence to us, you will appreciate, if vast armies are built up in Pakistan with the aid of American money . . . . (Gopal 1983: 185)

Similarly, when India learnt the possibility of Western support to Nepal to the autocratic Rana regime during the anti-Rana revolution of 1950-51, Nehru expressed concerns saying "we do not like and shall not brook any foreign interference in Nepal". On the other hand, he reiterated Nepal's independence as a sovereign country and urged "every other country to appreciate the intimate geographical and cultural relationship that exists between India and Nepal." (*Parliamentary Debate*, Lok Sabha, December 6, 1950)

India's concerns regarding the strategic consequences of conflicting interests between New Delhi on the one hand and the extra-regional powers on the other have been, in many ways, reflected not only in the pronouncements of leaders of Congress Party but also more prominently reflected in the general meetings of the Party. During the Jaipur session (December 18–19, 1948), the Congress Party expressed its solidarity and stood for ending of all imperialist domination and colonial exploitation of any country or people, and opposed Fascism and all other tendencies which suppress human spirit. (*INC Resolutions on Foreign Policy 1947–66* 1966: 3–5) In the same resolution, it also warned about the consequences of military "entanglement" or alliances that "divide the world into rival groups thus endanger world peace".[5] The party expressed how India is concerned about the freedom and progress its Asian neighbours'. More specifically, the Party expressed grave concern in its Nasik session (September 20–21 1950) over the war in Korea that "brought the prospect of a devastating world war nearer". (*AICC Resolution*, September 1950) It earnestly hoped that "the great nations of the world will not permit fear and passion to endanger the cause of peace for which they all stand". With the same vigour, the Party in its Calcutta session (March 22–23, 1952) also referred to the accelerating drift of Cold War rivalry towards "a terrible catastrophe of another World War". On the other hand, the Party also expressed "its full approval of the Foreign Policy pursued by the Government of India, which while avoiding alignment with any nation or group against another, seeks the friendship of all countries". (*Resolution of the AICC*, Calcutta Session, March 1952) In its Hyderabad session, the Party expressed with "deep concern and grave anxiety the ever-growing tension and deepening crisis in the relations between the Great Powers, who have aligned themselves in rival power blocs, engaged in a "cold war" and poised to strike with their unprecedented armed might, ever mounting to greater dimensions and intensity". (*Resolution AICC*, January 1953)

All these pronouncements by the Party underline the fact that it had left no occasion to highlight the big power threats, both singularly and their alliance with the South Asian states, to India's national security. However, the perceived threat of the Party never translated or advanced in justification of India developing nuclear weapons. Rather, the Party, till Nehru's last years as Prime Minister, was supporting for eventual elimination of nuclear weapons and foreclosing India's chances of producing them. Though in subsequent sessions of the Party discussions involved, India's options for nuclear weapons, the final resolutions had always denounced India's interest in nuclear weapons. Undoubtedly, the party equivocally has protested "the extension of extra-regional great power rivalry and conflict into the subcontinent" which actually "gave India a sense of weakness and vulnerability". (Muni 1993: 19)

The Congress Party had every time promptly raised voice for any interference of major powers directly or indirectly. The US proposal for military aid to Pakistan for its alliance with USA was viewed by the party as an "intervention of great and powerful country" in this region. The party, in its Kalyani session (January 20-29, 1954) expressed that it would "lead to grave and far-reaching consequences which affect the whole of South Asia, and, more particularly, India". (*AICC Resolution*, January 20–29, 1954) Surprisingly, the Party, instead of suggesting the government to devise appropriate security measures, gave a clarion call for "national solidarity". The Kalyani Resolution of the party said:

> The Congress trusts therefore that in this crisis the people of India, whatever their internal differences might be, will present a united front and devote themselves to the development and strengthening of the nation through peaceful processes. It is not by a competition in armaments that India will basically strengthen herself, but by unity self-reliance and the social, economic and industrial development of the nation. (*AICC Resolution*, January 20–29, 1954)

Another instance of the Party's protest was on the discussion of Kashmir issue in the meetings of SEATO and the Baghdad Pact organisations. The AICC expressed regrets in its Bombay session saying, such event "directly concerns the integrity and the sovereign rights of India". (*AICC Resolution*, Bombay, June 2–3, 1956)

Nehru's ideas and efforts were to see India not sucked into the Cold War politics. But, the fear that India might just become a spectator in the East-West conflict and since there was Western presence in some pockets of Indian territory, like the Portuguese-controlled

Goa, Daman and Diu and the French colony of Pondicherry. Therefore, it was feared that in case of the outbreak of war on grounds of strategy and military necessity, the 'Great Powers' would use these enclaves as springboards for offence and this would negative India's efforts to keep out of a world conflict. Therefore, Nehru's decision to take on Goa (and Pondicherry) that angered the US and other NATO allies of Portugal may have the super power threat induced. (Karnad 2002: 86; Cohen 2004: 131)

On the issue of development of nuclear weapons by major powers, the Congress Party voiced grave disappointment over their nuclear test explosions and termed these tests as "a crime against the human race" (*AICC Resolution*, October 24–26 1958: Para 1). In the Avadi session of the AICC, the Congress Party earnestly requested "all concerned to bring about a cessation of the experiments and the immediate consideration of this matter by the Disarmament Commission of the United Nations". (*AICC Resolution*, January 21–23, 1955) When USSR resumed nuclear testing in 1955, Nehru, then at the Belgrade conference, protesting the Soviet act warned that the danger of war "has been enhanced . . . by the recent decision of the Soviet government to start nuclear tests". (*AICC Resolution*, January 21–23, 1955) He sent telegram to A Dutt, India's ambassador in Moscow, "asking him to protest to the Soviet government on the Soviet nuclear tests". (*CIA Released Documents*, 4 November, 1961) But later when erstwhile Soviet Union declared suspension of tests, the Congress Party welcomed the move but *expressed regrets* for other nuclear powers who have not suspended these tests that are taking place "with increasing frequency, regardless of all human considerations". (*AICC Resolution*, October 24–26, 1958) Therefore, in its Bangalore session the AICC urged that the "testing, production and use of nuclear and like weapons" should be "totally banned". (*AICC Resolution*, January 16–17, 1960) This tone of concern for the danger of stockpile of nuclear weapons by major power got repeated reflection in subsequent AICC meetings.[6]

Till up to 1962, the Congress Party followed four "extricably linked basic principles" (formulated in its 1928 Calcutta session) in matters of India's security vis-à-vis extra-regional powers and nuclear weapons. They are: (1) opposition to Imperialism and colonial rule; (b) active sympathy and support to people fighting for independence; (c) opposition to war and devotion to peace; and (d) avoiding foreign entanglements for India.

These four principles that the Congress Party devised and adhered to subsequently, however, clearly mark in them the components of Nehruvian ideology. Though Nehru never influenced, in literal sense, the Congress Party's debate and discussions in AICC meetings, his ideas and thoughts were adequately reflected in each resolution of the Party. But Nehru, as the leader of the Party and the head of the government, was more vocal and assertive on these matters in the Parliament. He had gone to the extent of naming the major powers repeatedly and the way they pose global threat with the destructive weapons. In a statement in Lok Sabha on April 2nd, 1954, Nehru told:

> The United States of America and the Union of Soviet Socialist Republics, we are told, possess this weapon and each of these countries has, during the last two years, effected test explosions unleashing impacts which in every respect were far beyond those of any weapons of destruction know to man. (Nehru, *Selected Speeches*, Sept. 1946-Apr 1961: 187)

On this issue, as Nehru expressed, the considered position of the government of India is to demand for (1) a "standstill agreement" in respect, at least, of these actual explosions; (2) full publicity by those principally concerned in the production of these weapons; (3) private meetings of the sub-committees of the CD; and (4) active steps by States and peoples of the world, who though not directly concerned with the production of these weapons. (Nehru, *Selected Speeches*, September 1946-April 1961: 190) In a subsequent speech in Lok Sabha on the Defence Minister's resolution on *suspension of nuclear tests*, Nehru endorsing one member's view of sending the resolution to the three great powers which possess these hydrogen and atomic bombs, told that "the passage of this resolution in this House should be something rather for the world than for being sent to some other House. We passed the resolution and it is for the world to read it" (*Speech in Rajya Sabha*, 24 May, 1957; *Selected Speeches*, September 1946-April 1961: 197–98) and for the threat that these nuclear weapon powers pose to India and the world at large can only be contained, as Nehru hoped, through a move "towards comprehensive disarmament" programme. On November 27, 1957, Nehru appealed to the USA and the USSR that "it is in the power of America and Russia to solve this crisis and save humanity from the ultimate disaster which faces it". He appealed to them "to stop all nuclear test explosions and thus to show to the world that they are determined to end this menace and to proceed also to bring about effective disarmament".

In his December 17 1957 speech, Nehru directly naming the nuclear powers ambition highlighted the shaking fate of the world if a false step is taken. He said:

Today, the United States of America and the Soviet Union are the powers with the biggest and the most dangerous weapons. The United Kingdom, though presumably weaker, has also joined the Hydrogen Bomb Club. I have no doubt that within a relatively short time, France will also be having its test hydrogen bomb explosions, and other countries will do so before long. When this process goes on, it will become impossible to control this deterioration.

Therefore, we are today at a critical moment in history. If we fail to take advantage of this moment, the results may be very bad. (*Speech in Lok Sabha*, December 17, 1957, *Selected Speeches* 1961: 204)

India not only was skeptic on America's attitude and intentions during the post-Independence period but policies of both UK and USSR were also not friendly at that point of time. In the post-independence period, UK needed India to remain centrally within the British sphere of influence to enable her to retain a semblance of her previous standing as an imperial State still able to project power and safeguard its interests 'east of Suez'. (Darby 1973: 10–12) Soviet Union under Stalin's leadership was also no too friendly towards the Congress Party regime and apprehended by many that he might instigate the Moscow-controlled Indian Communist Party to stir up trouble at home. (Venkatramani 1999: 63-66)

However, all these deliberations of the Congress Party and the clarion calls by Nehru against the threat emanating from nuclear weapons acquired by major powers were never based specifically on India's national security considerations. Rather, nuclear threats from major powers to India were viewed as coterminous with the global security situation. Probably, therefore, Nehru's and Congress Party's policy orientation was mostly idealistic or moralistic instead of a realistic assessment for which India could chuck out a selfish strategy of nuclear weapons programme. The best national security guarantee for India was viewed in disarmament of the nuclear powers. In a sense, Nehru's and Congress Party's policy was prudent as India was never directly threatened by nuclear weapon powers during those years. It is known that in 1958, Bhabha made the public but muted claim of Indian ability to construct nuclear explosive devices within eighteen months of sanction. This was two years before the French nuclear explosion, and six years before the Chinese. (Mirchandani 1968: 229–33) Informal knowledge suggests that Indian government consciously suppressed the demand by scientific-bureaucratic groups for a focused drive to produce nuclear explosive elements during the years 1958–71. (Marwah 1976: 165)

Post-Nehru Era

The Nehruvian apprehension and critic of the major power rivalry and intervention in the regional security context was continuously debated in Congress Party's deliberations in subsequent years. However, different actions by the major powers in the region subsequently strengthened India's apprehension on Super Power intentions of the Indian political leader. (Mishra 986) Subsequent debates in the Party sessions saw the protest on the issue of presence of super powers (military bases) in the Indian Ocean, arms supply to small states in the region and stockpiling of nuclear weapons by the major powers. The presence of US military base in the Indian Ocean (Diago Garcia) and presence of *USS Enterprise* in Bay of Bengal during the East Pakistan crisis (1971) continued to be referred in most of the debates of the Party in subsequent years. The fact that, the *Enterprise* had in 1962 sailed into the Bay of Bengal on a mission in support of India against China has not been emphasised, whereas the later mission has been interpreted as harbinger of an American strategy of encircling India. This event also brought home the impression that how quickly US could change its policies, one year supporting India against China and only a few years later supporting both China and Pakistan against India. This apprehension probably had stimulated Indian interest in both strengthening seaward defence and acquiring a nuclear deterrent. (Cohen 2004: 136)

The *Congress Bulletin* (December 1969) said that "the Congress is opposed to setting up, or continuance, of military, naval or air bases by any outside Power in these regions. It likewise opposes stationing of naval fleets of outside Great Powers in the oceans around us". (*Congress Bulletin 12* 1969: 10) It also outrightly expressed that the Party "rejects the hegemonical claims of Super Powers, their endeavours to stake out spheres of influence and firmly repudiates the doctrine of 'limited sovereignty' for any country". Congress leader Moraji Desai, was very critical of Soviet arms supply to Pakistan as Moscow knew that Pakistan had no other enemy except India. The Congress Party followed with concerned anxiety the change in the attitude of the USSR towards its relations with Pakistan.

The super power threat to India's sovereignty was more visible during Indira Gandhi's leadership. First, during the East Pakistan crisis, the USA, China and USSR were all anxiously watching the unfolding of events and in many ways indicated their seriousness to interfere if required. In fact, non-aligned India probably had faced the gravest threat to her sovereignty during the crisis. After his secret visit to China in July 1971, Kissinger told the Indian Ambassador to Washington L.K. Jha that in case of an Indo-Pakistan War over the Bangladesh issue, if the Chinese were to intervene on behalf of Pakistan, then the US would not be in a position to support India. (Subrahamyam 1998: 30) K. Subrahmayam views the event was "clearly an attempt at intimidation, to prevent India from acting to defend its own national interests and security and conveying a veiled threat about the possible intervention by a nuclear China in support of Pakistan". (Subrahamyam 1998: 30) In fact, later it came to the light how Kissinger pressed the Chinese to intervene against India and the Chinese refused to do so fearing Soviet reaction. (Kissinger 1999)

Subsequently, when India intervened in the crisis that resulted in emergence of Bangladesh as a sovereign nation, USA sent in its Task Force 74 headed by the nuclear aircraft carrier *USS Enterprise* on board of which nuclear weapons were then standard equipment. But, later it was revealed that there were no specific operational directions to the *Enterprise* mission. (Subrahamanyam 1998: 31) President Nixon disclosed later that he did contemplate the use of nuclear weapons at that stage. But the event was sufficient for the Indian government "to assume the worst and treat it as an act of nuclear intimidation". It is assumed that this experience of nuclear intimidation must have influenced Mrs Gandhi in giving the green signal to the Atomic Energy Department to go ahead with the nuclear tests in 1972. (Subrahamyam 1998: 30) It is reported how Mrs Gandhi apprehended US as a direct threat to her political career. The accounts by Inder Malhotra and Pupul Jayakar reveals that Indira Gandhi feared a covert Western attempt (through the CIA) to oust her from power in the mid-1970s, particularly in the aftermath of the violent coup that eliminated Sheikh Mujibur Rahman of Bangladesh. (Jayakar 1992; Malhotra 1990) Owing to all these factors, perhaps Mrs Gandhi was clear about whom primarily to deter with a nuclear arsenal—China and, after 1971, more remotely, the US. (Karnad 2002: 306)

In subsequent deliberations of the Congress Party, though the debate on the nuclear threat to India's national security was not focused on any particular nation, pronouncements of Party members' in public forums often vindicated that one of the motives behind India acquiring of nuclear weapons was the perceived threat from super power activities. For example, the Congress leader and defence minister C. Subramaniam, while delivering at the National Defence College in 1979, spelled out seven factors that might provoke India into exercising the weapons-option. Out of the seven reasons he spelt out, six involved major powers. (Subramaniam 1979: 12) They include:

1. Pakistan's acquiring nuclear weapons;
2. No halt to the growth of 'warheads' in the American and Soviet nuclear arsenals;
3. The UK, France and China continuing with their nuclear weapons programmes;
4. The attitude to clandestine nuclear weapons development projects in Israel, South Africa and Taiwan;
5. The type of access afforded non-nuclear US allies and Warsaw Pact partners to the American and Soviet nuclear arsenals;
6. The interventionist tendencies' of the nuclear powers; and
7. The process of legitimation or de-legitimation of nuclear weapons.

Another Congress leader who later became President of India, Shankar Dayal Sharma, raising concerns over the military bases in Indian Ocean, moved a resolution in the AICC meeting in December 1980 saying:

As you are aware we have the worry about Indian Ocean. We had passed a resolution in the last Session that Indian Ocean should be made a zone of peace but we find that not only a military base in Diego Garcia is being established but also it is being expanded. In 1971, India succeeded in getting a resolution passed in, UND that it should be a zone of peace but inspite of that we find they are going merrily about it. (*Minutes of the AICC*, December 6-7, 1980)

And the fear of a possible alliance among Pakistan, China and US in black-mailing India was always existent in Indian leaders mind. There were many such emerged situations, where India felt the heat of such an alliance. For example in 1990, Nawaz Sharif came out with the proposal of bringing in the five nuclear weapons powers into the Indo-Pakistan nuclear issue. (Subrahmaniam 1998: 46-47) It was also known by that time that both the US and China were behind Pakistani's nuclear programme.

The Congress Party during Rajiv Gandhi's leadership was equally apprehensive of the major powers' probable threat to India's security and sovereignty. In his address to the Joint Meeting of US Congress on June 13, 1985, he said: "India is apprehensive about the establishment of military bases in various parts of the world. We are directly affected by the militarisation of the Indian Ocean and the inflow of the increasingly sophisticated arms into our neighbourhood." (*Prime Minister Rajiv Gandhi: Statement on Foreign Policy*, 1985: 82) Same tone of concern for the external power involvement in the region was visible in his address to the National Press Club on June 14, 1985. On the arms supply by US to Pakistan, Prime Minister Rajiv Gandhi expressed that "we are against any escalation in the arms race . . . . We are in favour of a zone of peace in the whole area, including the Indian Ocean, and we like to include that no nuclear weapons are in that area". (*Prime Minister Rajiv Gandhi: Statement on Foreign Policy*, 1985: 109–10)

With the end of the Cold War and withdrawal of Soviet forces from Afghanistan, the geo-politics of South Asia has undergone tremendous changes. Also India's stature and relations with the major powers especially its relation with US has seen drastic altercation. The Party no more sees any direct threat from the major global powers to India's national security. In most of the AICC resolutions, only the disarmament and non-proliferation issues have been featured, but not the threat the major powers pose to India. However, some strategic thinkers view US still poses a "latent threat" and China will continue to remain as "principal threat" to India. (Karnad 2002: xvii) Dmitry Rogozin, Chairman of the Foreign Affairs Committee of the Duma, once said: The current warmth in Indo-US relations cannot hide the fact that the growth of the Indian deterrent is seen as threatening by the United States". He recalls that not too long ago the US Department of Defence justified the hypersonic bomber programme in terms of its being able specifically to hit targets in India, among other countries. (*Vayu* 2000) This suggests that India is safe only as long as it toes the American line.

Stephen Cohen argues that "outside powers continue to play an important role in Indian strategic calculations, especially when they are perceived to have links to troublesome neighbours. In this, the US and various Islamic states, and China are singled out". (Cohen 1998: 155) He highlights the supportive American response to Indian policies in the 1999 Kargil crisis that has moderated India's suspicion of US, nevertheless remains very deep despite recently evolving friendly relations between them. Not only that, the 'maximalist hawks' and 'moderate pragmatists' see the US as a "distant threat". But, the Indo-US relations today has developed to such an height (and it is assumed to improve more intensively in decades ahead), neither the Congress Party nor any other political group can foresee a tussle between both the democracies.

BJP's Perceptions on External Threat to India

As discussed in previous chapters, the strategic vision of the BJP, that manifested in making India an overt nuclear weapons state in 1998, is rooted in its early organisational and leaders' aspiration of a 'strong' vibrant India. The Sangh Parivar (of which the BJP is a part) embodying Hindutva ideology has often pronounced the vision of overcoming Indian 'weakness' by strengthening the defence forces of India.[7] However, BJP claims itself as *not an ordinary party in pursuit of power for the sake of power alone,* rather it is *part of a wider movement,* which is guided by the ideology of nationalism and whose goal is to bring about India's all-round national resurgence. (BJP *Tasks Ahead,* E/4/2005: 2)

Unlike the Congress which was non-aligned with a tilt towards the Soviet Union, the BJS was for non-alignment with a clear sympathy for the United States. But, the Party was critical about US involvement in South Asia, especially its military alliance with Pakistan. It was of the view that in case of future conflict, US will use the small pockets of territory in possession of foreign powers. In a resolution in December 1953, the party expressed that "sandwiched between the two wings of Pakistan and studded with these foreign-pocket bases on the sea-cost, India might virtually be turned a prisoner in her own home"; therefore, the party urged the government "to take energetic action to liquidate these pockets". (*CWC Resolution,* Dec 20, 1953, *BJS Party Documents Vol 3,* 1973: 29)

When US resumed arms aid to Pakistan in 1954, the BJS put the blame squarely on the Indian government for its mishandling of the situation which led the US to befriend Pakistan. (*CWC Resolution*, 20 Dec., 1953, *BJS Party Documents Vol. 3*, 1973: 21, 30) The party *Resolution on Defence and External Affairs* (1973) says: ". . . the responsibility for this lies mainly on our own foreign office, which has grossly mishandled our international policies . . . . Our government has unnecessarily indulged in international involvements, which have brought about this grave situation". The party's willingness to come close to the US was more pronounced after the Chinese aggression. Party General Secretary Deendayal Upadhyaya once stated "we shall definitely be aligned with the Western world, because they have indicated their willingness to help us". (Quoted in Das 1978: 792) Also another prominent BJS leader, M.L Sondhi, wrote in his book that "Non-alignment has prevented India from exposing the incompatibility of the long term interests of Pakistan and those of United States of America and Soviet Union." (Sondhi 1968: 7)

However, it is unclear what exactly BJS strategic doctrine was. (Ghosh 1999: 327) What followed, it seems, was an unspoken, yet discernible, pro-West tilt as opposed to the Congress's pro-Soviet tilt, without conceptually integrating it into the Party's strategic doctrine. This ambiguity in the Party's posture seems to have developed owing to the difference of opinion between its two stalwarts Balraj Madhok and Deen Dayal Upadhyaya. Both leaders' stand on Indo-US relations had always been different from each other. While Madhok was all for aligning India with the USA, Upadhyaya was a bit cautious. (Kishore 1969: 78) But, subsequent leaders of the Party seem to be more pragmatic. For example, when erstwhile Soviet Union changed its attitude towards India, and the intensity of public opinion in America grew against US involvement in Vietnam and Cambodia, the Party leader Atal Bihari Vajpayee warned that these factors should make Indian leaders realise that if India's freedom, integrity and sovereignty are at any time endangered, we can depend only on our own Jawans, our own arms and our own resources, and on none else. (*Presidential Address*, Bharatiya Pratinidhi Sabha Session, July 18-19, 1979: 18) From this point of view, the party suggested to give top priority to development of nuclear technology, as it is necessary for national defence and economic growth.

Another BJS leader, L.K. Advani, in his presidential Address at the 18th All India Session on Febrary 9-11 1973 warned also about the situation in the Indian Ocean, where the super-powers muscle for domination. He suggested for expansion of India's naval strength and to explore the possibility of naval understanding with littoral countries. (*Presidential Address*, 18 All India Session, Feb 9-11 1973: 17) The BJS position on issues of other regions like West Asia and Israel was based on the Nehruvian ideology of peaceful existence: insistence on continuing "full-fledged diplomatic relations with Israel and India playing an effective role in striving for peaceful coexistence between the Arabs and the Israelis". (*BJS Central Working Committee Resolution*, June 30, 1967: 137–38)

The BJS was generally hostile to the Soviet Union, particularly during the Internal Emergency. From the beginning, it was anti-Communist in its political leanings and therefore, its stand regarding Indo-Soviet relation. (Kishore 1969: 84) It was unpleasant for the Party when former Soviet leaders placed India in the 'imperialist camp' and considered its independence to be fake and spurious. But Indo-Soviet relations improved later mainly owing to Nehru's ideological inclination towards USSR and Communism. (Kishore 1969: 84) Later, the Party was convinced of a Soviet hand in Indian politics to the detriment of India's democratic culture. (Ghosh 1999: 331) Also, the Janata Party-led coalition government (in which BJS was a constituent), emphasised on "genuine non-alignment" had a clear anti-Soviet slant. But, this attitude did not reflect itself in the Jana Sangh's outlook to the Soviet after forming government in coalition with the Janata Party. After a year in power, Vajpayee who was foreign minister in Morarji Desai's cabinet, was gratified to report on the continued friendship and trust between the two countries.

Same kind of shift was also marked in its stance on India acquiring nuclear weapons. After joining Janata Party coalition, the Jana Sangh seemed to have compromised on its advocacy for nuclear weapons for India, may be out of the coalition compulsions. It didn't object to Janata Party-led government's advocacy not only for total renunciation of nuclear weapons but also against all PNE in the future. Speaking at a seminar organised by the School of International Studies of Jawaharlal Nehru University, New Delhi in May 1978, the then External Affairs Minister and Jana Sangh leader Atal Bihari Vajpayee said:

> The only way to prevent proliferation of nuclear weapons is to bring about complete cessation of the production of nuclear weapons and simultaneously cut off the manufacture of all weapon-grade fissionable material . . . . There can be no doubt

> about India's policy. We can set an example abjuring the manufacture or acquisition of nuclear weapons. We have pledged the manufacture or acquisition of nuclear weapons. We have pledged ourselves to developing nuclear technology exclusively for peaceful purposes. (Vajpayee 1978: 380)

In the same seminar, while answering a comment on his Party's pledge for nuclear weapons, Vajpayee in his characteristic humour retorted that after coming to power "I have dropped the bomb". (Quoted in Ghosh 1999: 330) This contradictory policy of the Party was criticised as "a fretful tokenism". (Ray 1978)

With the backdrop of an intense regional and global geo-political activity, the BJP started its journey in 1980. Undoubtedly, clear trends can be marked in BJP's pronouncements on India's national security in the early stage of its evolution as a national party and its views on the same during its rise to the centres of power at the national level. It seems, at the early stage of its emergence as a national party, the BJP perceived threats to India both from the Super Power rivalry in the Indian sub-continent and neighbouring Pakistan as well. After forming government at the national level, the sources of its threat perception seem to have widened—overall posture of the Super Powers and their interventionist activities anywhere in the world including South Asia. During the initial phase, the BJP disapproved the continued presence of Soviet armed forces in Afghanistan and called for India's determination to pursue an independent foreign policy. (Zaid 1980:650) It was equally critical about US policy in arming Pakistan to fight the proxy war. In his Presidential Address at the National Council Session April 1981, Atal Bihari Vajpayee told:

> India and Pakistan, in fact the entire region, needs peace. Russian troops on the Khyber Pass and American warships in the Indian Ocean, both imperil this peace. The real clash of interests is between this region and the super powers and not among nations of this region. (*Presidential Address*, BJP National Council Session, Apr 25 1981)

The resolution adopted at the National Executive meeting of the BJP in April 1981 summarised the danger out of the super power rivalry as "overlapping arcs of crisis encircle the Indian subcontinent". (*BJP Foreign Policy Resolutions and Statements 1980-99*: 5) It further said that the Party does not recognise the right of nations to intervene or interfere in the affairs of another on the basis of imperial concept of 'spheres of influence'. In its views, the international scene in early 1980s vitiated India's security environment and strategically India faced an unprecedented triangular bind with China in Aksai-Chin, USSR in Afghanistan and the USA in Diego-Garcia. (*BJP National Executive Meeting Resolution*, Apr 23, 1981)

These lines of argument have often been expressed in subsequent years. Highlighting the "alarming" situation in the sub-continent, Vajpayee, in his Presidential Address in January 1984 at the Fifth National Council Session said, "the mounting superpower rivalry in the Indian Ocean region is a matter of concern to all the littoral nations". He criticised Mrs Gandhi for not being able to obtain universal endorsement for the proposal of holding an International Conference on declaring Indian Ocean as a Zone of Peace. (*Presidential* Address, 5th National Council Session of BJP, January 6-8, 1984: 9) Same tone of resentment could also be seen in the April 1984 Ahmadabad Resolution of the Party. The resolution said:

> . . . it is necessary to treat the developments in Afghanistan, since Soviet occupation of that country, as being part of a heightened super-power involvement in South, Southwest and West Asia. We would, therefore, treat developments in Afghanistan along with heightened super power presence in the Indian Ocean and include in our security concerns the tragedy of the continuing Iran-Iraq War in the Gulf. . . . An important factor contributing to deterioration in India's security environment is the US supply of armaments to Pakistan. This is a matter of grave concern to us, yet it needs to be understood that it reflects more the effect than the cause. The cause is the importation into our peripheries of super power interests and involvements. (*Resolutions*, BJP National Executive, March 31–April 2, 1984: 16)

In response to the perceived threat emanating from the presence of external powers in the region, the Party advocated for (1) "a regional call for the super powers to withdraw from the Indian Ocean and a dismantling of all naval bases like Diego Garcia; and (2) an early end of Iraq-Iran war and an end to all super power involvement in the Gulf. (*Resolutions*, BJP National Executive, March 31–April 2, 1984: 17) In its Election Manifesto 1984, the Party promised to "initiate fresh endeavours for a withdrawal of foreign forces from Afghanistan, a political solution of the Afghan problem, free from outside intervention . . . ." (*BJP Lok Sabha*

Election Manifesto, 1984: 21) The Party's perception regarding external threats to India was essentially based on its views on regional developments only where Super Powers were involved. This is amply clear from the resolution adopted by the Party in June 1989 where it said:

> The BJP makes it abundantly clear that the principal challenge that the country faces in the field of external relations is regional; it lies in a proper ordering of our relations with all our neighbours. India's national and security interest will be served only through a larger awareness of the regional demands, regional needs, regional fears and regional sentiments of South, South-West, and South-East Asia. (*Resolution*, National Executive Meeting, June 9-11, 1989: 10)

But during the end of the Cold War and aftermath, BJP's formulation on India's national security seem to have expanded beyond the region. The Party viewed that owing to the erosion of its non-aligned position in the post-Cold War period, its strategic flexibility has been severely curtailed and it rendered its alternative policy options uni-dimensional. (*Resolution*, National Executive Meeting, June 9-11, 1989: 10) Even the security environment emerged after the end of the Cold War is "challenging" as "international relations continue to be governed by the law of the jungle". (*BJP Election Manifesto 1991*) The occupation of Kuwait by Iraq and consequent US retaliation in defiance of the UN resolution is viewed by the Party as a warning for India not to neglect its defence. The Party, therefore, decided to equip India with Blue Water Navy, which will be the first Navy in the Indian Ocean from Singapore to Aden. And it will also encourage research and further development on Arjun battle tank, Light Combat Aircraft, Army Radio Engineering Network and Prithvi and other missiles. (*BJP Election Manifesto 1991*)

It is often viewed that the BJP is West-oriented and in the later stage, is also seen how eagerly the BJP-led NDA government initiated a strategic partnership with the USA. But behind its West-oriented image, the Party has always remained critical of the Euro-American alliance (that includes Soviet Union among its partners) which, it viewed, is all pervasive in its influence on international economy, polity, defence and culture. (*National Executive Meeting Resolution*, Sep 30, 1991) This conception of the Party got strengthened further in the post-Cold War environment, which it characterised as fluid and turbulent. The Party raised alarm for arming of

Pakistan by this Alliance and particularly the "pro-Pakistan tilt" of the USA. When the news of US willingness to supply dozens of F-16 aircraft was aired in 1994, the BJP firmly expressed that "India should continue to develop and deploy an indigenous missiles system ... in order to provide absolute security against aggression, urgently commence the process to manufacture and arm defence forces with nuclear weapons". (*Resolution*, BJP National Executive Meeting, September 15–17, 1994: 12–13) Also the Gulf War, where the US was involved raised the issue of "who will control oil", was considered by the BJP as a "global tragedy of immeasurable dimensions". (*BJP Resolution*, Plenary Session, February 1 1991: 6) The Party viewed that the United Nations in its present form cannot bring the just order in the world as four of the five permanent members of the UNSC are allies. (*Resolution*, National Council on International Situation, May 1–3, 1992: 11)

Unlike the BJS phase, BJP's stand against Israel was manifestly stronger. The Party unequivocally condemned Israel's brutal action against the PLO in Lebanon and rejected its all attempts at regional hegemonism. (*BJP Resolution*, National Executive Meeting Aug 1982) This was probably in tune with BJP's overall anti-US stand particularly in the context of US-Pak strategic tie-up. This changed attitude was clearly discernible in the party resolutions compared to those of the BJS. In the earlier phase, the BJS was more critical of the Indian government for letting the US come closer to Pakistan, but BJP was critical of the US itself for endangering South Asian security. (Ghosh 1999: 342–43) Neither was the Soviet Union spared for complicating the situation by intervening in the non-aligned Afghanistan.

Therefore, the Party saw no peace even after the end of Cold War as there are attempts to impose a new world order based on the military and economic strength that has "vitiated the international atmosphere". (*National Executive Meeting Resolution*, June 9 1994) Perhaps, owing to its inherent skepticism of the emerging world order dominated by the Euro-American alliance, which it viewed derogatory to India's national security, BJP in both of its two *Election Manifesto* (1996 and 1998) proposed following defence preparedness measures.

1. Expedite the serial production of *Prithvi* and make *Agni* I operational for the deployment of these missiles. In addition, hasten the development of *Agni* series of ballistic missiles with a view to increasing their range and accuracy;

2. Strengthen the Air Force fleet with new generation aircraft;
3. Make qualitative and quantitative improvement in our naval capabilities;
4. Invest in R&D in areas of defence and missile technology so that India become increasingly self-reliant
5. Peg defence-related expenditure to real requirements;
6. Enhance the traditional and technical capabilities of our external intelligence agencies.

However, the Party, for securing India's frontiers against any future aggression, strongly suggested for a pro-active diplomacy, especially defence diplomacy, coupled with adequate preparedness of armed forces. (*BJP Election Manifesto 1996*: 37) "Mindful of the existing global disequilibrium" the Party also advocated directing India's foreign policy to fight for "sovereign equality amongst nations". (*BJP Election Manifesto 1996*: 31) In its election manifesto 1998, where the party expressed to "re-evaluate the country's nuclear policy and exercise the option to induct nuclear weapons", described India facing "grave challenges to its integrity and security" as the "internal and external security environment has deteriorated sharply in the last decade". (*BJP Election Manifesto 1998*)

But remarkable difference in its description of security challenges for India from the major powers like USA can be viewed subsequently. In most of its earlier resolutions, the USA and its involvement in regional affairs is vehemently criticised but once the Party saw prospects of formation of government at the centre, its critical posture towards the USA seems to have moderated. Only the Party highlights the global (and regional security) order without naming any country as threat. First, in an interview, answering the question "what was the compulsion to carry out the tests now?", Vajpayee repeatedly emphasised both regional and *global security realities* as the reasons. He said:

> Important measures that are guided by national security considerations don't follow immediate compulsions. Rather, they are guided by long-term imperatives based on a sound appraisal of regional and *global security realities*. It is important for us and the world to know that by conducting the latest tests, India has responded to a stark regional and *global reality* that has evolved over the past 50 years. (*India Today*, May 25 1998: 38)

Second, in its *Election Manifesto 1999* the Party said, "in today's unipolar world, it is of paramount importance that India constantly maintains and strengthens the state of preparedness, morale and combat effectiveness of our Armed Forces". (*BJP Election Manifesto 1999*: 8) It is clearly evident from these two pronouncements that the Party followed a realist approach towards India's national security, instead of accusing particular states as it used to during the Jana Sangh days. BJP's pronouncements subsequently seem to have focused on the challenges and opportunity for India becoming a world power. And the party viewed that power can be achieved through strengthening India's national security. Hence, security consideration was the top priority in the foreign policy calculation of the BJP. In pursuit of this, the Party, while proposing to acquire both nuclear and conventional weapons with latest technology, expected to cooperate, to the fullest extent, with France, Germany, Britain, Israel, etc., while continuing close cooperation with Russia. (Chiriyankandath 2004: 202) In the aftermath of the nuclear tests in 1998, the BJP-led NDA government initiated the Indo-US strategic partnership. A sense of idealism and ambition can be seen in its vision when it vigorously campaigned for securing a permanent seat for India in the UNSC by emphasising the age-old dictum *Basudhaiva Kutumbakam* (whole world a family). (Swain 2001: 149)

Views of the CPI(M) on Extra-Regional Threat to India

At the outset, the Communist Party of India (Marxist) thinks that India's security is threatened not so much by China or Pakistan as by the United States. (Banerjee 1966) In almost every pronouncement of the Party, the USA has been termed as an "imperialist power" and the penetration of American imperialism is the biggest threat to India's "national independence and sovereignty". (*Political-Organisational Report of the Central Committee 1968*) The Political-Organisational report of 1968 also said that "The necessity and urgency of mobilising the widest anti-imperialist democratic forces and building a powerful and broad-based anti-imperialist movement to defeat the chief aggressor and world gendarme, U.S. imperialism and its imperialist allies". The other power from the socialist world—Soviet Union—was also in the scanner of the CPI(M) for destabilising India's security environment. Despite perceiving such threats to India, the Party interestingly opposes India acquiring nuclear weapons (*People's Democracy*, May 26, 1974: 2) and suggested drastic reduction in the defence expenditure (*Report of the Central Committee 1968*). On the other hand, it suggested

India to quit the Commonwealth and develop new relations with the neighbours and Afro-Asian countries with the aim to isolate USA as the chief enemy of world peace from its allies, especially Britain (the immediate enemy) and the Commonwealth. (Nizami 1971: 50–51)

At the organisational level, the CPI(M) stands for nuclear disarmament and views India's security lies in a nuclear weapons-free world; nevertheless, it congratulated the scientists for successfully conducting the nuclear tests both in 1974 and in 1998. But at the individual level, some members of the Party support India acquiring nuclear weapons under certain circumstances. For example, P. Ramamurthi is reported to have said that it is open to any country to manufacture its own nuclear weapons if it felt threatened, "Particularly when the nuclear powers had not refrained from making nuclear bombs and stockpiling all such weapons. If feel threatened, India certainly has the right to manufacture atom bombs if it so desired." (*The Statesman*, May 12, 1966) Contrarily, the Party has never been supportive of India's nuclear weapons programme even though, according to its pronouncements, India has come under "the frenzied attacks of neo-colonialism led by U.S. imperialism—in the form of economic aggrandisement, political blackmailing and enmeshing . . . in military alliances". (*Political Resolution Adopted by the 8th Congress*, December 23–29, 1968)

USA as a Security Concern: The CPI(M) senses threats to India from USA in different ways. First, it sees America as an imperialist power, which has already penetrated into India in the form of both military and non-military ways. During the Cold War period, through forming military alliances and building military bases across Asia and Indian Ocean, it had encircled the region, thereby encircled India for its larger design to fight ideological war with the Soviet Bloc. (*CPI(M) Election Manifesto 2009*) In the post-Cold War phase, the penetration of American capital and India's growing reliance on American aid is viewed by the Party as just "a bulwark of neo-colonialism" and will create dangerous situation for the country. (Karat 2000) Also the Party thinks that American imperialism has tremendously sharpened and it is directly facing the people of India in the shape of frontal attacks on their standard of living and jobs and of direct imposition of starvation and destitution on millions. On the other hand, monstrous military blocs like NATO, SEATO, CENTO and ANZUS built with the leadership of USA have complicated the geo-political scenario of this region.

The Party is of the view that the American intelligence agency CIA is involved in India for long, mainly active in the North-Eastern region, to destabilise it. (*Political Resolution*, December 23-29, 1968) Its agents were directed to study social tension and how to use them for the purpose of destabilising the situation under the code name "Project Brahmaputra". According to the Marxist doyen P. Ramamurti, the US State Department launched its covert operation 'Project Brahmaputra' with the agreement of the Special Operation Research Office of the George Washington University taking help from the US outfits in India. (*Documents of the Communist Movement in India*, XIX: 501)

While the Party is not bothered about the Chinese direct threat to India (rather demand the government to have friendly relations with it), it is very critical about the USA's alliance with and supply of arms to, Pakistan. The US military pact with Pakistan and supply of arms is claimed to be a cause of concern for the Party. But, it criticised the Government of India for downplaying this threat for the loans and credits secured from Washington and screening the inimical role of the US imperialists from the Indian people. A Party resolution says, "the enemy of India (US) was presented as a helpful friend" by the government itself. (*CPI(M) Political Resolution*, June 27-July 2, 1972: 17) It accused USA for constantly opposing all liberation struggles and always taking hostile attitude towards India at every crucial turn in politics. Ever since the East Pakistan crisis of 1971, the CPI(M) at every occasion raises "the treacherous character of the American imperialism". It criticises the US for accusing India being "the aggressor" and threatening India by sending the Seventh Fleet to the Bay of Bengal. (*CPI(M) Political Resolution*, June 27-July 2, 1972: 17–18)

US presence in the Indian Ocean has been one of the main argument in CPI(M)'s views of challenges to India's security. The Party resolution on Asian Security Pact adopted by the Polit Bureau on March 10, 1974 said:

> The recent agreement between the USA and Britain to develop Diego Garcia Island, just a thousand miles from India, in the midst of the Indian Ocean, half-way between Africa and Australia, into a full-fledged major naval and air base of American imperialists with their nuclear missiles, poses a grave threat to the security of Afro-Asian nations and other littoral countries of the Indian Ocean, especially to India . . . . (*CPI(M) Resolution* adopted by Polit Bureau, March 10, 1974)

Therefore, the CPI(M) gave a clarion call for an Asian Security Pact to pinpoint the real nature and source of threat to the freedom and security of Asian nations. (*CPI(M) Resolution* adopted by Polit Bureau, March 10, 1974) According to the Party, the real enemy to Asian nations is American Imperialism and the threat arises from its aggressive designs in Asia. Therefore, the proposed Asian Security Pact, it suggested, was mainly to direct Asian unity against American and other imperialists' designs in Asia and to warn them to abolish immediately all war bases in Asia and withdraw forces from these bases including in the Indian Ocean. In this pursuit, the Party felt it urgent to forge unity amongst the Asian countries and people to defend their security and sovereignty and rebuff the American imperialists' threat. In this effort, the Party urged effective participation of Socialist China, Democratic Republic of Korea and Democratic Republic of Vietnam along with other Asian countries that stand against the imperialist America and its Asian allies. The party also suggested two approaches in this endeavour: (1) pursuance of a policy of non-alignment as a struggle against imperialism (*CPI(M) Political Resolution*, April 1978); and (2) implementation of the 1971 UN Declaration aimed at establishing a "Zone of Peace" in the Indian Ocean area.

When a nuclear-fuelled power pack (spy device) was installed by USA on the heights of Nanda Devi with the knowledge of the Janata government (April 1978), the CPI(M) vociferously condemned the act. (*Statement of the Polit Bureau*, 18 April, 1978) The Party statement said that "this collaboration was with U.S. imperialism, which ever since the early fifties, has stood against India at all crucial moments, while building different military alliances like SEATO and CENTO to bully India". But when the Diego Garcia issue did not appear in the statement of the NAM Foreign Ministers' Conference, the Party accused Indira Gandhi government for its "vacillation in its foreign policy" approach. (*Documents of the Eleventh Congress* of the CPI(M), January 1982: 29)

In most of its subsequent pronouncements, the Party highlighted two important developments which have sufficient bearings on India's security perception. First, the arming of Pakistan by US and second is expansion and increasing activities of US in Diego Garcia. Arming of Pakistan is considered by CPI(M) as an "imperialist conspiracy", which is a gravest danger both to the democratic forces of Pakistan and the people of India. (*Documents of the Eleventh Congress* of the CPI(M), January 1982: 294) The

Pakistani military clique is acting as a tool of US imperialism which has received military aid and F-16 planes and therefore, poses a serious threat to India and the entire region. This act of US and Pakistan infact "brought the danger of war to India's doorstep". (*Documents of the Eleventh Congress* of the CPI(M), January 1982: 381) The Party also criticised US for refusing to supply nuclear fuel for Tarapore nuclear plant on the plea that the newly enacted US law does not permit the supply of such fuel supply while supplied Pakistan modern arms even though it is known that Pakistan is working on a nuclear bomb. This made the Party to suspect US which it viewed was bent on feverishly arming Pakistan's military rulers to create a constant threat of war between the two countries. (*CPI(M) Central Committee's Press Communiqué,* October 27, 1980) In this way, as the Communiqué says, USA is playing the Pakistan card to create the danger of war and danger to the security of India and to pressurise India to shift her foreign policy, especially her stand on Afghanistan. On the other side, the Pakistani dictator, unable to seize any issue to mobilise the people, was using the Afghanistan-card by acting as the anti-Soviet spearhead of the USA to stockpile arms to be used against India. (*CPI(M) Central Committee's Press Communiqué,* October 27, 1980)

The second important issue that the Party frequently raises is the "standing danger of India and all littoral States" emanates from the Diego Garcia military base of US in the Indian Ocean. The base, known to harbour nuclear arsenals, makes possible to conduct military operations against littoral States and in successive intervals has been expanded with additional personnel and resources. Therefore, the *Election Manifesto 1980* of the Party demanded "bold action against the latest aggressive moves of the US imperialists in Diego Garcia and in Indian Ocean region and for making it a *zone of peace*". The 12th Congress of the Party adopted a resolution expressing grave concern on USA activities in the following words:

> In the Indian sub-continent, the USA conspires to surround India with a ring of reactionary governments subservient to it, supplies sophisticated arms to Pakistan for purposes of aggression, tries to rouse chauvinist feelings against India taking advantage of the ethnic conflict in Sri Lanka, and openly supports internal disruptive and secessionist forces in pursuance of its policy of dismemberment of India. The U.S. imperialists are trying to ring India with hostile bases in Pakistan, Sri

> Lanka, Bangladesh and the Indian Ocean. Through its agents and reactionary elements in India, it directs attacks on the Indo-Soviet Treaty of Friendship and India's friendship with Socialist countries.
>
> ... Regardless of the wishes of the littoral States, the U.S. is militarising the Indian Ocean, its nuclear arms-ships are swarming all over it. It has established a nuclear naval base at Diego Garcia which constitutes a serous threat to the security of many nations, including India. [*CPI(M) Political Resolution,* Dec 25–30 1985]

But the strategy the Party suggested and the approach it adopted in reaction to all these developments gives an impression that except raising the awareness on certain issues, it has no such concrete policy prescription. The dangerous scenario narrated by the Party out of the USA engagement in Indian Ocean and Asia required "a realistic strategy" if India wish to counter. (*CPI(M) Political Organisational Report,* May 1986: 3) But the Party, as usual, called for mass mobilisation of anti-imperialist people to unmask imperialist plans. This is clear from the Vijayawada Party Congress Resolution which said:

> The Eleventh Congress . . . expresses its grave concern over the growing danger which threatens to plunge the world into a nuclear holocaust. It regards this development as a danger to the existence of mankind and calls upon all people of goodwill in India to be aware of the danger and resist it. . . . It is the urgent task of the working class and all progressive sections to combat this danger, expose and unmask imperialist plans before the people and mobilise all peace-loving anti-imperialist forces to save the world from nuclear devastation. (*CPI(M) Political Organisational Report,* May 1986: 3–4)

In pursuit of this lofty goal, the Party also observed a week-long programme on a mass scale in West Bengal, where people were mobilised in defence of world peace and in opposition to the US imperialist drive towards militarisation of space and the drive to atomic war. In Kerala, Tamil Nadu, Andhra Pradesh, Tripura and several other states, a week-long congregation was arranged to campaign in defence of world peace. The Party also vowed during the 12th Congress "to redouble its activities on the peace front and carry the message of world peace, while exposing the war-mongering U.S. imperialism and their henchmen". [*CPI(M) Political Organisational Report,* 12th Congress, May 1986: 6]

In 1995, when India decided to sign the Indo-US military cooperation agreement, CPI(M) expressed grave concern. The Polit Bureau of the Party expressed its strong opposition to the decision taken by the first Indo-US Army Executive Steering Committee to exchange officers on courses and military exercise and developing Army-to-Army cooperation. It expressed that the US strategy towards India is clear. "After the dismantling of the Soviet Union, it wants to ensure that no major third world country emerges with an independent economic military power". The Party said the military cooperation would "spell a grave threat to India's independence and sovereignty as this cooperation seeks to integrate India the strategic military cooperation of the United States". [*CPI(M) Polit Bureau Statement,* Jan 15, 1992] And the growing Indo-US defence collaboration may have harmful implications for India's sovereignty and foreign policy and will compromise India's security interests. (*Central Committee Report on Political Developments,* Oct 18–20, 1995)

Therefore, the Politbureau called for scrapping of the Indo-US military cooperation pact signed in January 1995 and immediate cancellation of the joint naval exercises in March that year. The Pact, the Party said, "provides the Americans ample opportunities to penetrate the Indian defence establishment". [*CPI(M) General Elections* 1996: 5] It criticised vehemently the Narasimha Rao government for "jeopardising India's vital security interests by continuing with the totally uncalled for collaboration with the Pentagon and the U.S. armed forces". (*Politbureau Statement,* Feb 3 1996)

The Party advanced two-fold justification for its opposition to the India-USA military cooperation. First, the US administration exerted tremendous pressure on India not to deploy *Prithvi* missiles and stall further testing of the *Agni* missiles. Also it barred India from following an independent nuclear policy. These anti-India policies coupled with the adoption of the Brown amendment to resume arms supplies to Pakistan, the Party expressed, constituted "an inimical factor to India's security interests". Though US did not provide F-16 fighters then, the Congress sanctioned the arms deal which included *Orion Reconnaissance planes* and *Harpoon missiles.* This situation was viewed by the Party as a "trap" for the Rao Government "to yoke India and Pakistan together under military hegemony in the subcontinent". (*Central Committee on Political Developments,* October 18–20, 1995)

Second, the Party suspected that the joint naval exercise will be on a longer scale and duration than one conducted in May 1996.

And "some of the U.S. naval vessels like the nuclear submarine, to be deployed for the exercise, may carry nuclear weapons" which is not in interest of India's security. (*Polit Bureau Statement*, February 3rd, 1996) It therefore, demanded cancellation of the Indo-US military cooperation agreement which links up India with the US global strategy and also demanded removal of nuclear weapons from the US military base in Diego Garcia. [*CPI(M) Election Manifesto 1999*: 7] It accused Prime Minister Vajpayee "for mounting an aggressive anti-China campaign in his letter to the US President" and deliberately ignoring "the long-standing threat perception of India concerning the US nuclear base in Diego Garcia". [*CPI(M) Polit Bureau Statement*, May 15, 1998] In its Manifesto for the *16th Lok Sabha Elections 2014*, the Party wish to stop further steps to enter into military collaboration agreements with the US, desires not to renew the Defence Framework Agreement, and promote the policy of no foreign military bases in South Asia. (p. 19)

Stand on Soviet Policies: The CPI(M) not only slammed the policies of USA impacting India's security but also equally pointed its fingers towards the other Super Power for its attempt to escalate India's security vulnerabilities. Particularly, the Party was very critical about Soviet arms aid to Pakistan in 1968. First, the Party criticised the Indira Gandhi government to cover its diplomatic failure, when Mrs Gandhi said, "any country was free to give aid to any other country—though we are not happy about it". (Basu 1998: 377) This Soviet decision, as the party viewed, highlighted the "crisis of the foreign policy of the Government of India". [*CPI(M) Central Committee Resolution*, August 1968: 3] Second, the party also highlighted the changed Soviet stand towards India and the end of India's exclusive friendship with Soviet Union. (*People's Democracy*, July 14, 1968) Third, the Party viewed that arms aid has much to do with Pakistan's friendship with China and it is, no doubt, an attempt to wean her away from People's China. And India's shift does not seem to be the only reason for the change in Soviet attitude. As India is given arms to fight China, Pakistan is also given arms to wean her away from China. Lastly, huge aid is offered at a time of military dictatorship in Pakistan. This helped bringing legitimacy to the military government.

The Party expressed worries for Soviet aid to Pakistan which created fresh problems in India in the form of incessant demands for (1) increased defence expenditure; (2) for greater reliance on US; and (3) for more chauvinist stand on Kashmir. The Party hoped

India to realise that all this is due to her bankrupt anti-China policy and not settling the Kashmir issue to the satisfaction of the people in the Valley. Therefore, the Central Committee of the Party warned "against reactionaries who, utilising the Soviet government's arms supply to Pakistan are campaigning to force the India government give up her friendly relations with socialist countries and totally align with U.S. imperialism". (*Central Committee Resolution*, August 1968: 4) To save India's economy and independence, the central committee demanded the government to:

1. Give up its hostility to China and create conducive climate to negotiation;
2. Initiate talks with the leaders of the people of Kashmir;
3. Take steps to settle all outstanding problems with Pakistan;
4. Stop all aid forthwith from imperialist countries. (*Central Committee Resolution*, August 1968: 5)

However, unlike the perceived threats from USA, threats from Soviet Union did not feature frequently in CPI(M) subsequent pronouncements. Even the issue of Soviet arms aid to Pakistan was criticised by the Party rather moderately. While explaining rationale of Soviet aid to Pakistan, the Party criticised the Government of India for mismanaging the situation. May be the socialist brethrenhood was the motive while considering Soviet actions.

Notes

1. The term *Great Game* is used for the strategic rivalry and conflict between the British Empire and the Russian Empire for supremacy in Central Asia. The classic *Great Game* period is generally regarded as running from the *Russo-Persian Treaty* of 1813 to the *Anglo-Russian Convention* of 1907.
2. The "Monroe Doctrine" was introduced on December 2, 1823 by the US stating that further efforts by European countries to colonise land or interfere with states in the Americas would be viewed by it as acts of aggression requiring US intervention. The Doctrine asserted that the Western Hemisphere was not to be further colonised by European countries, and that the United States would neither interfere with existing European colonies, nor in the internal concerns of European countries.
3. China's growing interest and influence from the South China Sea through the Indian Ocean and on to the Arabian Gulf has been

described as a "String of Pearls" approach. Each "pearl" in the "String of Pearls" is a nexus of Chinese geopolitical influence or military presence. Hainan Island, with recently upgraded military facilities, is a "pearl." An upgraded airstrip on Woody Island, located in the Paracel archipelago 300 nautical miles east of Vietnam, is a "pearl." A container shipping facility in Chittagong, Bangladesh, is a "pearl." Construction of a deep water port in Sittwe, Myanmar, is a "pearl," as is the construction of a navy base in Gwadar, Pakistan. Port and airfield construction projects, diplomatic ties, and force modernisation form the essence of China's "String of Pearls." The "pearls" extend from the coast of mainland China through the littorals of the South China Sea, the Strait of Malacca, across the Indian Ocean, and on to the littorals of the Arabian Sea and Persian Gulf. China is building strategic relationships and developing a capability to establish a forward presence along the sea lines of communication (SLOCs) that connect China to the Middle East.

4. A "Security Complex" is defined as a group of states whose primary security concerns link together sufficiently closely that their national securities cannot realistically be considered apart from one another.
5. The perceived danger out of the military entanglements was also sounded in the Delhi Session of AICC in October 1951.
6. Raipur session (Oct 29-30, 1960), Madurai Session (Oct 4-5 1961), Durgapur Session (May 28-29 1961), Bhavanagar Session (Jan 6-7 1961), Patna Session (Jan 5-6, 1962), Durgapur Session (Jan 9-10 1965)
7. It is often described that the Sangh Parivar comprises numerous front organ isations of which the most prominent are the Vishwa Hndu Parishad (VHP) or World Hindu Council; the Bajrang Dal or Lord Hanuman's Troops and the Rashtriya Swayamsevak Sangh which is the parent organisation of the family whose electoral wing is the BJP. Its ideology is based on V. D. Savarkar famous injunction 'Unite Hindus and Militarise Hinduism'.

Section-C
Regime Obligation

For obvious reasons, the nuclear non-proliferation regime has influenced greatly India's nuclear weapons decision making. In the first two decades since Independence India focused on global nuclear disarmament and building up of nation-wide nuclear infrastructure. During subsequent decades one can mark India's vociferous advocacy for a non-discriminatory non-proliferation regime. It does not mean that India abandoned her advocacy for eventual elimination of nuclear weapons in her quest for non-discriminatory non-proliferation regime. In the post-Indo-US nuclear deal years, Indian diplomacy seems to "focus on nuclear arms control and confidence-building, as opposed to the traditional emphasis on total elimination of nuclear weapons." The changing diplomatic postures, and consequent domestic debate, as usual, seem to have conditioned by various political party perspectives and leadership dispositions. This section enquirers India's approach towards non-proliferation issues from party perspectives, temperament of the political leadership and various dimensions of the national debate on nuclear non-proliferation issues.

7

Non-proliferation and Disarmament: Stands of the Three Parties

For more than one reason, the nuclear non-proliferation regime has sufficient bearing on India's nuclear weapons decision making. If India's nuclear policy in the first two decades since independence was focused on global nuclear disarmament and building up of national atomic infrastructure, subsequent decades mark her concern for the non-discriminatory non-proliferation regime. It does not mean that India subsequently abandoned her advocacy for eventual elimination of nuclear weapons in her quest for non-discriminatory non-proliferation regime. But, the domestic debate involving India's nuclear disarmament and non-proliferation policies, as usual, seem to have conditioned by various political party perspectives and leadership dispositions. This chapter enquires into India's approach towards non-proliferation issues from party perspectives, temperament of the political leadership and various dimensions of the national debate on nuclear non-proliferation issues.

Prior to her independence, India had laid considerable stress on nuclear disarmament and prohibition of the use of atomic weapons. The Indian leaders, Mahatma Gandhi, Jawaharlal Nehru, had a built-in revulsion for the atom bomb which they considered as an evil and "awesome development". (Jain 1974: 7) As early as September 1945, the All India Congress Committee resolution (Patna) deplored the appearances of the atom bomb (Jain 1974: 7). Jawaharlal Nehru had proposed banning of "all tests of nuclear and thermonuclear weapons and experimental nuclear weapons by mutual agreement" as far back as 1955. (*The Hindu*, August 6, 2001) Addressing a public meeting in 1946, he stated that it was "a grave responsibility for any country to use atom bombs". (Norman 1965: 264) Speaking in the Constituent Assembly on January 2nd, 1947, he observed that the conflict in the contemporary world was between the atom bomb and the spirit of humanity. He expressed the hope that India would always lay stress on the "spirit of humanity" and that the human spirit would ultimately prevail over the atom bomb. (Quoted in Ghatate 1966: 296) On December 6, 1950, Nehru disapproved "the idea of using the atom bomb anywhere at any time and much less in the particular context of war in the Far East", i.e., the Korean War. (Quoted in Berkes and Bedi 1958: 64–65)

Various surveys indicate that the resentment in the political circles on non-proliferation regime, as it evolved is overwhelming. One such survey conducted by Ashis Nandy during early years of the regime (1972) reveals that about 82 per cent of the respondents (various political party members) were against the NPT. (Nandy 1972: 1537) Table No. 1 shows, while the 'extreme' right was slightly more favourable to the NPT (mainly the contribution of the pro-American Swatantra Party), the dominant centrist party, the Congress, remained blatantly hostile to the treaty.

Later when the Communist bloc got split, the China-tilted faction (CPIM) also joined the Centrists in rejecting the Treaty but linked it to their policy of "non-weaponisation". The BJP later

Table. 7.1 Attitudes of Different Types of Elites to the NPT (1972)

	Attitudes to the NPT				
Party Type	*Yes*	*Qualified Yes*	*Qualified No*	*No*	*Total*
Congress	0.0	5.9	29.4	64.7	100.0
Rightists	22.2	22.2	22.2	33.3	99.9
Communists	10.0	10.0	0.0	80.0	100.0
Socialists	0.0	8.3	8.3	83.3	99.9
Regional Parties	0.0	20.0	0.0	80.0	100.0
Independents	12.2	4.1	13.5	70.3	100.0

Source: Ashis Nandy, "The Bomb, the NPT and Indian Elites", *EPW*, August 1972, p.1539.

joined this group for its disavowal of the Treaty. However, when Prime Minister Vajpayee went for the nuclear tests in 1998, BJP was reportedly "considering to sign the CTBT" (Chakravartty 1998: 35) as New Delhi became a nuclear weapons state. Irrespective of these minor differences among the political groups, there exists a broad consensus among different strands of political opinions in the country not to accede to the treaty in its 'present form'.

The Congress Approach

Nehru Era

The Congress Party, being the mainstream political organisation, was privileged to articulate India's nuclear policy decisions in the post-Independence period. In order to understand the party's role in formulating India's non-proliferation policies, one needs to keep in mind that the monolithic Party was a happy blend of many contradictory ideologies and was also led by an overarching leader like Nehru though many other influential leaders surrounding him had differential convictions.

As has been highlighted in the earlier chapters, Jawaharlal Nehru, since pre-Independence period till his death in 1964, remained the Congress "party's principal authority and spokesperson" (Bhatia 1979: 2). Though Nehru, in the post-Independence period, remained President of the AICC only for four years (1951-54), his leadership and grip over the party was unchallenged. His articulation on Indian foreign and security policy matters had always the approval of the AICC.[1] Nehru's preponderant role in matters of statecraft can be judged from Neelam Sanjiva Reddy's presidential address in the sixty-seventh session of the INC at Patna on January 4th, 1962 where he said:

> . . . It is our good fortune that our Prime Minister, who is a great world Statesman and to whom many nations of the world look up for guidance and inspiration, is still at the helm of our affairs. . . . We all pray to God that he should be spared for a long number of years more to continue to guide us on the right path. We have to draw inspiration from him and constantly work hard for the service of the nation. (*Presidential Address* of Shri Neelam Sanjiva Reddy, INC Sixty-seventh Session, Srikrishnapuri, Patna, January 4, 1962: 12)

Nehru's articulation on nuclear and foreign policy issues can clearly be observed from his reply to a criticism—"why should we get entangled in disarmament and other matters?"—in the Lok Sabha, where he said, he was "surprised and a little pained to hear those remarks reflecting". He observed that the question of disarmament was more important than any other problem, internal and external, national or international, because it was a national problem, apart from being an international one. The whole future survival of India and every Indian "depends upon it". It equally affected the great powers. He further said, "If we can help in any way in that, obviously we should do so because it is our concern and it is our problem". (Quoted in Sethi 1999)

The Congress Party's and moreover, Nehru's policy on nuclear issues in the immediate post-Independence period had mainly two anchors. First, the Congress government had to define its policies in relation to the arms control and disarmament talks from 1945 onwards in an environment, where the Western block and Communist nations were ranged on opposite sides. Second, ideas for the peaceful use of nuclear energy, such as those contained in President Eisenhower's "Atoms for Peace" plan of 1953, demanded a suitable response from New Delhi. By that time, policy response in all these matters seem to be firm from India with Nehru's direction owing to the fact that the ruling "Congress party was well entrenched in power" and enjoyed six years of uninterrupted power since Independence. (Bhatia 1979: 54) India's interest and strategy in joining the disarmament negotiations and Disarmament Commission was partly based on Nehru's own understanding of the world politics. As early as 1953, Nehru's desire was not to see any important international organisation dominated by the great powers. The Congress Party, as a whole, emphasised general agreement by major powers to expedite the process of disarmament. At the Agra meeting (July 6-7, 1953), the AICC welcomed the "lessening of tension between great powers". The Committee expressed hope for a conference of representatives of the great powers to "meet at an early date to discuss informally to consider the question of disarmament . . . ."

Nehru's own understanding and conviction was well reflected in his expression during a Lok Sabha debate in May 1954 on the merits of Eisenhower's "Atoms for Peace" speech. He expressed doubts about participating in an organisation which was controlled by the great powers. (*The Hindu*, May 11, 1954) Therefore, in December 1955, Indian delegation at General Assembly proposed enlarging the Disarmament Commission (CD) and its subcommittees. (Rajan 1964: 94–95)

India's interest and consequent policy regarding arms control and disarmament was undoubtedly based on Nehru's idea of world politics. Although, the Cabinet was composed of powerful stalwarts, foreign policy, including nuclear policy-making, was left to Nehru. In the Congress Party, there was virtually no one to question him in these fronts. It was Nehru personally who defined the broad framework of India's nuclear policy and there was no "formal mechanisms" to decide on these matters. (Ganguly 1994: 142) It was in his direction Indian representatives at the international level were deliberating. For example, Mrs Vijayalaxmi Pandit was instructed by the government to withhold wholehearted approval of the Baruch Plan because India may lose its sovereign right to explore and use its abundant natural resources like thorium. (Ganguly 1994: 142) India's reaction to the Baruch proposals was delayed until other countries' views were available for being considered by all member states. (Chakma 2004: Chapter V)

This attitude of India was viewed based on Nehru's conception of sovereign equality by which national interest of weaker countries like India from being trampled upon in the event of an agreement between the great powers (Bhatia 1979: 42). Krishna Menon, Nehru's Left-wing adviser who succeeded Mrs Pandit, told the CD in the same Nehruvian strategy on the role of the smaller powers to act as catalytic agents to bring the great powers together instead of supporting either Cold War camp (*General Assembly Official Records*, March 21, 1953). The Congress government's policy towards arms control and disarmament was primarily based on Nehru's perception of India's importance—"meant that Indian views had to be represented at conferences of international significance". (Bhatia 1979: 42) Speaking in the General Assembly Debate on September 28, 1953, Krishna Menon pleaded for a declaration by General Assembly on the non-use of the weapons of mass destruction. (Jain 1974: 38)

After 1953, India's nuclear policy was characterised by two dominant trends: (1) the demand for wider representation at international disarmament negotiations; and (2) proposals for a ban on nuclear tests. By that time, the Congress Party was well entrenched in domestic politics and externally too; the prospect of better relations with the Communist countries, particularly China, seemed to augur well for Nehru's policies. After the American Hydrogen bomb tests in 1954, there was an outcry in the Parliament owing to the reported contamination of a Japanese fishing boat (*The Statesman*, April 10 1954). Nehru called for a standstill of nuclear bomb testing and had his views forwarded to the UN Secretary General in April 1954, and in October 1954, his proposal was repeated by Krishna Menon in the General Assembly (*UN Document D.C. 44*). India was elected to the CD. But, the biggest value of Congress government's policy under Nehru was that it could resist the imposition of safeguards and sought to keep its nuclear options open for the future. Second, as a consequence of its diplomatic support for general disarmament and a nuclear test ban, the Indian government created for itself the image of a country which would never allow its atomic scientists to develop atomic bombs for any reason at any time. (Bhatia 1979: 69)

At the domestic front, both Nehru and the Congress Party expressed their deep concern for the development of hydrogen bomb. In a statement in Lok Sabha on April 2, 1954, Nehru told: "I welcome this opportunity to state the position of the Government and, I feel sure, of the country on the latest of all the dread weapons of war, the hydrogen bomb, and its known and unknown consequences and horrors". On India's position, he said: "We have maintained that nuclear (including thermonuclear) ... knowledge and power should not be used to forge these weapons of mass destruction. We have advocated the prohibition of such weapons, by common consent, and immediately by agreement amongst those concerned, which latter is at present the only effective way to bring about their abandonment." (*Lok Sabha Debates*, April 2nd, 1954) In regard to the elimination and prohibition of atomic weapons, during the debate Nehru told: "The Government proposes to continue to give the closest and continuous consideration to such steps as they can take in appropriate places and contexts in pursuit of our approach and the common objective". With an aim to expedite the pending progress towards "the prohibition and elimination of these weapons of mass destruction", the Government of India (GOI) would consider for putting forward a "standstill agreement" and in pursuit of these objective "GOI will use its best efforts". (*Statement in Lok Sabha*, April 2nd, 1954)

The Congress party fully endorsed Nehru's all these pronouncements. In the Avadi Session of the AICC, the issue was discussed in length. The AICC Resolution unanimously recognised the hydrogen bombs are a menace not only to world peace but to civil isation itself. Through this resolution the Party earnestly requested all concerned to bring about a cessation of the experiments and the immediate consideration of this matter by the CD. (*INC Resolutions on Foreign Policy 1947-66*, 1966: 33-34) Also Nehru sent the message to the First International Conference on the Peaceful Use of Atomic Energy held in August 1955 saying:

> . . . Now this conference will, I hope, turn people's minds still more from the evil aspect of the misuse of this great force which has come into man's hands and show the way to peaceful progress and co-operation.
>
> This Conference is of a new type and very different from normal conferences because it leads us to the threshold of the atomic age. We have to adjust ourselves to this new age, to act accordingly, and to think in terms of peace and not of destruction. (Jain, vol. II 1974: 12)

Not only in the United Nations Nehru did raise the menace of nuclear weapons at every international fora. At the Third Meeting of the Commonwealth Prime Ministers' Conference, London, (January 1955) he said, "we should seek to ban the use of such weapons, and even experimental explosions; and, secondly, that we must seek to ban the occasion for their use in war—we must, in fact, try to outlaw war altogether". (*Selected Works of J Nehru*, vol. 28, 2001: 198) By saying this he did not mean for unilateral disarmament. But in his views, many unwarranted "developments had made the need for disarmament so great that despite all its difficulties it must be tackled". At the same time, the Congress Party at its Amritsar session (February 11-12 1956) expressed discontent for the "continuing rivalry among major powers in producing the most destructive weapons of war" which is a "setback" in the disarmament process. Therefore, as expressed by Nehru himself at the Asian-African Conference, Bandung (April 18, 1955), the main "question before Congress and Nehru was how to convince the countries concerned" (*Selected Works of Jawaharlal Nehru* 2001: 210).

In its endeavour to propagate India's own disarmament conviction, on June 27, 1956, the Indian Permanent Representative, in a *Note Verbale* to the Secretary-General of the UN, asked for an opportunity to present the views of the Government of India orally before the Disarmament Commission. India's request was acceded and Krishna Menon appeared before the Commission on July 12, 1956. On the basis of his statement, the Government of

India presented a *Note Verbale* dated July 25, 1956 which listed the following proposals:

1. Cessation of all explosions of nuclear and other weapons of mass destruction;
2. Prohibition of the further use of fissionable material for military purposes;
3. Prohibition of the transfer of fissionable material from civilian to military stocks;
4. An agreement by those powers most advanced in the production of weapons of mass destruction to dismantle in public, as a token of their will towards disarmament, a limited number of atomic or hydrogen bombs and to make available for peaceful purposes the fissionable material contained in these weapons; and
5. Prohibition of export or conveying of nuclear weapons to other countries by those countries at present manufacturing such weapons. (*Disarmament Commission Document DC/98*, 31 July 1956)

Also, in subsequent deliberations by Nehru and resolutions of the Congress Party, unanimous approach towards nuclear weapon issues is clearly evident. In a speech in Rajya Sabha on a private member's resolution on nuclear explosions on May 24, 1957, Nehru said, "we suggest that the nuclear tests should be suspended and ultimately banned. Even if the countries concerned agree to the proposal, I do not mean that it will put an end to all dangers. But it will stop the progressive rot that is going on, and spread a certain feeling all over the world against these weapons being produced or misused." (*Selected Speeches* 2001: 195) In another speech on disarmament in the Lok Sabha on September 2nd, 1957, Nehru said, "we have been greatly interested in disarmament and in the efforts made towards disarmament. . . ." In another statement, Nehru while appealing to the USA and USSR said:

> I speak for myself, but I believe that I echo the thoughts of vast numbers of people in my country as well as in other countries of the world. I venture, therefore, to make this appeal to the great leaders, more especially of America and Russia, in whose hands fate and destiny have placed such tremendous power today to mould this world and either to raise it to undreamt heights or to hurl it to the pit of disaster. I appeal to them to stop all nuclear test explosions and thus to show to the world that they are determined to end this menace and to proceed

> also to bring about effective disarmament. The moment this is done, a great weight will be lifted from the mind of man. (*Selected Speeches* 2001: 202)

Fully endorsing Nehru's ideas and views the AICC resolution at Guahati on January 18-19 1958 said that:

> . . . the most sinister of all the threats that face the world, is that of atomic destruction. The stoppage of the manufacture and use of atomic weapons of mass destruction is essential, if the way to peace is to be ensured. Explosion for test purposes of these weapons are gravely harmful to the peoples of the world, irrespective of their nationality of their geographical position or their policies. . . . These tests are part of the preparation for a nuclear war and therefore, of possible annihilation. The Congress calls for immediate suspension of these tests by all concerned. (*INC Resolutions* 1966: 54–55)

In the same resolution the Party said, "the most urgent and imperative tasks of the time" is disarmament and "a halt in the armaments race". And the Congress appealed "to the governments of the world, particularly to the atomic powers, to respond to the call of world opinion to pursue negotiations towards agreements on disarmament, which at present appear to be deadlocked." (*INC Resolutions* 1966: 54–55) Raising the apprehension on the progress made in disarmament process, the AICC resolution at Hyderabad (October 24–26 1958) viewed the continued nuclear test explosion as "crime against the human race and adds to the risks of the annihilation of civilisation". Noticing no substantial advance made in respect of world disarmament, the Congress Party in its Nagpur session viewed "cooperation between all nations . . . is essential" to achieve the goal. (*Congress Session*, Nagpur, Jan 9–11 1959)

Regarding the procedural aspect of nuclear disarmament, both Nehru and the Congress Party were of the view that disarmament and arms control should go hand in hand but in a phased manner. While the Congress resolution at the Bangalore session hoped that "the testing, production and use of nuclear and like weapons will be totally banned" ("International Affairs", *Congress Session*, Bangalore, Jan 16–17, 1960), the Raipur session of the AICC advocated for "progressive disarmament . . . accompanied by progressive controls and inspection and the two processes must go together." Further the Raipur resolution says that:

. . . In order to avoid the fear of one group of countries becoming relatively more powerful in arms than the other group, a balance will have to be maintained in the process of disarmament. . . . In view of nuclear weapons spreading to other countries and their manufacture becoming simpler and less expensive, it may become exceedingly difficult, if not impossible, for any effective control to be exercised at a later stage. Therefore, the testing, manufacture, stocking, and use of nuclear weapons must be ended and thus the overwhelming fear of a nuclear war removed. ("International Situation", *Resolution, AICC Raipur,* Oct 29–30, 1960)

Not only did there exist a consensus in the Congress Party on Nehru's ideas and policies on nuclear disarmament and arms control but also there was absolute agreement among the members of parliament as a whole. It is evident from the assertion of the Praja Socialist Party member Surendranath Dwivedy who said, "I am not going to refer in my speech to larger problems such as disarmament, control of nuclear weapons, colonialism, etc., with which probably there is not much disagreement." (*Lok Sabha Debate,* Nov 22, 1960: 1641) Another non-Congress member, Mohammed Imam, recognising Prime Minister Nehru's endeavour said, "so far as disarmament is concerned, I do not think any country or any nation is opposed to it. . . . we want disarmament because we know that unless there is disarmament there would be no peace. Now the question is: how to achieve disarmament? We have come to the conclusion that disarmament cannot be achieved now on account of the mutual distrust existing between the nations. That distrust must be removed. So I say that our Prime Minister should have concentrated himself on how to remove the distrust." (*Lok Sabha Debates,* Nov 22., 1960: 1694) During the same debate, the Congress member Dr Deorao Yeshwantrao Gohokar elaborated India's efforts in respect of the Eleven Nation Disarmament Plan. (*Lok Sabha Debates,* Nov 22, 1960: 1660)

From the above deliberations one can deduce that throughout the first-half of the 1960s, Nehru and the Congress party in all their deliberations had emphasised nuclear disarmament which would, in their views, solve the proliferation problem. Speaking in the Parliament on November 22, 1960, Nehru said: "If nothing effective is done in regard to disarmament in the course of the next three or four years it may perhaps become too late to deal with it. . . . Once this spreads to many countries, it will become exceedingly difficult to have any effective disarmament or any effective machinery of control". (*Selected Speeches* 2001: 193) These attitudes reflected in India's objections to the creation of IAEA, but once the agency was formed, India fought from within it against the development of an extensive safeguards system. In the Bhavanagar session of the Congress (January 6–7, 1961), the Congress Party highlighted the imperative of abolition of all weapons of war. And, "the only realistic approach to effective disarmament" in its view, "is one which would ensure general and complete disarmament and a world without war." The Party considers other approaches for 'limitation' and 'balanced' reduction of weapons may appear practical but are incapable to bring about genuine disarmament; rather"in the event of an outbreak of a conflict, the weapons agreed to be abandoned would soon return to service". (*AICC Resolutions on Foreign Policy 1947–1966*, 1966: 70) In this regard, the Party approved the declaration and the general plan of directives made in the Ten-Power draft resolution and urged the General Assembly to approve and implement them in the next session. In the same way, at the Durgapur session (May 28–29 1961), the party expressed concern for delay in reaching a global agreement for disarmament and suspension of nuclear test explosions. The AICC, in the Madurai session (October 4–5 1961), deeply regretted and deplored the resumption of nuclear tests by countries saying the tests are "not only harmful to the present and future generations of mankind, but also increase the possibility of war". (*AICC Resolutions on Foreign Policy 1947-1966*, 1966: 66)

The Congress Party was always advocating for talks on the substantive issues of nuclear disarmament and control. At the Patna session of the Congress (January 5–6, 1962), the Party, welcoming the resumption of talks in the disarmament negations, reiterated its stand for "global disarmament, with effective steps for control and inspection, leading to the outlawry of war, can alone solve and end these crises."

However, India's attitude towards nuclear disarmament was viewed to be altered during the 1960s, mainly after the Chinese aggression and subsequent nuclear tests explosions by it. According to Shrikant Paranjpe, the Chinese nuclear test of 1964 brought in a major shift in the Indian stand. India dropped the terminology "non-dissemination" in the context of the spread of nuclear weapons and started to use the term "nonproliferation" (Paranjpe 1997: 35). India viewed the Chinese tests aggravated the problem of non-proliferation. The shift in Indian position is clearly marked in the statement by the Indian Ambassador B.N. Chakravarty on May 4th, 1965 at the UNGA. He demanded for "tangible progress towards disarmament, including a comprehensive test ban treaty, a complete freeze on the production of nuclear weapons and means of delivery as well as a substantial reduction in the existing stocks". (*UNGA, Documents on Disarmament* 1965: 148)

A cursory look on the Congress party's deliberations, Nehru's views and consequent debate in the Parliament during this phase would reveal that India's early nuclear policy was expressed in the language of 'disarmament' "rather than security". (Beaton 1972: 167) India's traditional disarmament diplomacy, as articulated by Nehru and Krishna Menon in the 1950s, regarded disarmament as a realistic rather than a utopian possibility. (Kapur 1976) But the Chinese aggression and its nuclear tests demanded a fresh look for its nuclear policy towards the end of Nehru era. Nehru and his aides, at every possible fora raised the nuclear proliferation threat. Largely owing to India's repeated emphasis, as early as 1958, attempts were made at the global level to negotiate a treaty to halt nuclear testing. In 1963, Soviet Union, USA, and UK negotiated the Partial Test Ban Treaty (PTBT) which prohibited nuclear testing in the atmosphere, under water and in outer space. France and China did not join the treaty. India outrightly subscribed to the treaty with the belief that it was the first step towards a comprehensive test ban treaty. Nehru viewed the agreement as an important landmark in the history of international cooperation and understanding and hope that it would lead to wider agreements in other collateral tension-reducing measures and to speedy conclusion of a treaty on general and complete disarmament. (*Foreign Affairs Record*, MEA, July 1963: 154)

Overall, *three nuances* underlay Nehru's disarmament diplomacy: first, Nehru was against international control of atomic energy; second, he focused essentially on the political nature of disarmament; third, his interest in nuclear disarmament was closely guided by his appreciation of technological changes in the atomic field. (Kapur 1976: 107–8) According to Shyam Bhatia, as a consequence of India's diplomatic support both for general disarmament and a nuclear test ban, New Delhi created for itself the image of a country which would never allow its atomic scientists to develop atomic bombs for any reason at any time. (Quoted in Kapur 1976: 69) But Bharat Karnad is of the opinion that on nuclear policy matters, Nehru relied exclusively on the illustrious scientist. Other diplomats being relegated by Nehru only to make an impression on the disarmament issue. But the nuclear disarmament rhetoric Nehru swaddled it in, in the hands of lesser leaders and an overcautious foreign policy establishment, "ended up choking the country's progress towards a nuclear weapons capability for some thirty odd years, which Nehru primarily strove for". (Karnad 2002: 279)

Shastri and Gandhi Era

Between October 1964 and mid-1966, India's nuclear policy underwent important, halting shifts that reflected domestic and international pressures and interests. Perkovich is of the opinion that "the ambitions and personal outlooks of a handful of key people also determined these shifts. Two scientists—Bhabha and Sarabhai—and two Prime Ministers –Shastri and Gandhi–played the leading roles, but their preferences were filtered through the screen of Congress Party politics." (Perkovich 1999: 123)

At the Durgapur session of the Congress (January 9–10, 1965), the Party deplored the nuclear explosion conducted by the People's Republic of China "in defiance of world opinion and the sustained efforts being made by the vast majority of the nations of the world towards cessation of nuclear tests". It further said that "proliferation of atom bomb has increased the menace to the peoples of the world". Also the Congress recognised that "the Moscow Test Ban Treaty helped to achieve a measure of success and hopes that the countries who have not already done so should subscribe to the treaty which should also be extended to cover underground tests." (*INC Resolutions on Foreign Policy 1947-66*, 1966: 81–82)

During 1966 to 1968, concerns regarding nuclear non-proliferation were raised in the Parliament several times. The Congress leaders each time reiterated the Party's stand by saying that though India has the capacity to produce nuclear bomb it is in the larger interest that proliferation of the same technology should be curbed and New Delhi is "in the front row" in such initiative. On March 8, 1966, during the Question Hour in the Rajya Sabha, replying to U.S. Dugal's question "whether Government's attention has been drawn to press reports about Pakistan's plans to test its first atom bomb", Mrs Gandhi said: "The Government of India deplore the conducting of nuclear tests, despite the Partial Test Ban Treaty, as an act of injurious to the welfare of mankind, and contrary to the efforts of all peace-loving nations to achieve a Comprehensive Test Ban". (*Documents: Rajya Sabha Debate*, Patil 1969: 53) On behalf of the Government, Minister of External Affairs, M.C. Chagla made a statement regarding non-proliferation of nuclear weapons on March 27, 1967 in the Lok Sabha, where he said:

> The Government of India shares with the international community the anxiety arising from the proliferation of nuclear weapons. They favour an early agreement on such a treaty and will be willing to sign one which fulfils the basic principles laid down by the United Nations.
>
> . . . A satisfactory agreement on nonproliferation of nuclear weapons will have to take into account the peculiar circumstances in which certain countries are placed. So far as India is concerned, aside from its anxiety to see the conclusion of a non-proliferation treaty as a step towards achievement of general and complete disarmament and more particularly nuclear disarmament, India has a special problem of security against nuclear attack or nuclear blackmail. This aspect, which hardly needs elaboration, must necessarily be taken into full account before our final attitude to a nonproliferation treaty is determined. (*The Lok Sabha Debate*, March 27, 1967; Patil 1969: 59)

After the Chinese Hydrogen bomb test on June 17, 1967, the then Minister of Defence Swaran Singh, deploring the event, said: "when the Partial Test Ban Treaty was signed in 1963, it was recognised that further conduct of nuclear tests in the atmosphere would pose grave danger to the health of human beings through increased radioactive fall-out. China did not sign this treaty. This repeated violation by China of the collective will of international community has naturally evoked strong criticism and great concern . . . . The Government of India views this development with grave concern." (*Lok Sabha Debate*, Vol. V, Second Series, 1967/1889 (Saka): 6655) In the mean time, USA and Soviet Union developed common interests against horizontal nuclear proliferation but presented separate draft of the nuclear non-proliferation treaty. During a discussion on call-attention motion, on India's reaction to this agreement between both the super powers, in the Lok Sabha on March 14, 1968 Smt. Tarakeshwari Sinha asked about the exact position of India on this matter. Mrs Gandhi replied that "the Government of India's position is not rigid. If the treaty were to be changed and we feel that it was in our interest, we shall sign it and we have made it clear in no uncertain terms that the present draft treaty does not give us any satisfaction. And Mrs Gandhi also made it clear that "the guarantee of security could not be a *quid pro quo* for signing the nonproliferation treaty in its present form". (*Lok Sabha Debates*, Phalguna 24, 1889 (Saka), March 14 1968: 739)

So, during 1967–68, the nuclear question in India "shifted from whether India should actually produce nuclear weapons to whether India should sign a treaty relinquishing *the right* to produce weapons". (Perkovich 1999: 134) The non-proliferation issue came up in the Parliament during the voting on the Demands for Grants under the control of the Ministry of External Affairs on April 3–5, 1968. Members like M.R. Masani and M.L. Sondhi from CPI and Jan Sangh, respectively, raised the non-proliferation issue and India's policy thereof. The main contention of both these parties were that the "Government seems to be altogether without a policy on this subject". (Their views are discussed in detail in subsequent sections.) On April 5th , 1968, replying to this debate in the Lok Sabha, Prime Minister Gandhi gave a passionate long speech saying:

> . . . we shall be guided entirely by our enlightened self-interest and the considerations of national security and of course, adherence to our values . . . . We have already made it clear that the draft treaty in its present from does not fully conform to the principles enunciated in the General Assembly Resolution No. 2028 of the 20th Session.
>
> ... It is very important, therefore, for the nuclear weapon powers to undertake as soon as possible meaningful negotiations on a series of measures leading to nuclear disarmament. The present draft treaty acknowledges the need for such negotiations, but unfortunately, the non-participation by some nuclear weapon powers will make it only partially effective and what is more, the other nuclear weapon powers insist on their right to continue to manufacture more nuclear weapons. (*Documents: Lok Sabha Debates*, Patil 1969: 55–57)

In the same speech, Mrs Gandhi stated that "the Government of India does not propose to manufacture nuclear weapons. This is a unilateral decision taken many years ago and is unrelated to the treaty on nonproliferation of nuclear weapons." Rather she promised to make efforts for nuclear disarmament because, in her view, "it is only through nuclear disarmament that discrimination would be eliminated and equally between nations re-established" and this is "the best interests of the country". At the same time, she also warned the House that "not signing the treaty may bring the nation many difficulties. It may mean the stoppage of aid and the stoppage of help. . . . I personally think that although it will involve sacrifice and hardship". (*Documents: Lok Sabha Debates*, Patil 1969: 55–57)

However, Mrs Gandhi's concerns on the consequences of not signing the treaty received sufficient support from the Congress Party members. Vijaya Lakshmi Pandit was of the opinion that "the Government would not be high-pressurised into signing any treaty which is not in India's interest. There is no need to do that through fear. . . . America cannot afford to deny aid to this country. If she wants to preserve democracy in India, she will give you aid whether you sign or you do not sign. It is for our government to take a strong stand on the matter." (*Lok Sabha Debates*, 5th April, 1968, Chaitra 16, 1890 (Saka): 2640) Another Congress member Smt. Sushila Rohtagi, disagreeing on the question of Jana Sangh's assertion on nuclear armaments, said:

India has always been a signatory to the banning of the nuclear weapons and nuclear tests. India has always stood for total and complete disarmament, that there should be total non-proliferation, that there should be no stockpiling of armaments. Why should India suddenly change its attitude today? Why should India change the stand for which Buddha, Gandhiji and Nehru lived and preached? There must be some reason for it. By changing this attitude what do we gain? We lose prestige and we cease to be peaceful nation. Even if we produce a few bombs that will not be able to help us or to protect us since it will be incompatible to meet the demands of the race of the nuclear nations, and we would only deviate from our stand, and at the same time we mortgage the future of our country. (*Lok Sabha Debates*, April 5th, 1968, Chaitra 16, 1890 (saka): 2648)

But the discussions in the Parliament did not exhibit the subtle shift that the Congress government was in the process of embarking on in its stand on the Non-proliferation Treaty. On 27 March, 1967, Lok Sabha debate on nuclear policy Minister of External Affairs, Mr Chagla unequivocally expressed that India should not sign the NPT as it stands because, in addition to failing to provide security for non-aligned states such as India, it would impede future development of peaceful uses of nuclear energy. The

Secretaries Committee expressed its hope that the treaty would be improved and that the issue of protection of non-nuclear states would be clarified. In consonance with his apprehensions, Chagla, in a press interview on May 3rd, 1967 characterised the draft treaty as discriminatory and a "step away from disarmament". He said that India could not give up the right to experiment with nuclear technology for peaceful purposes. (*Foreign Affairs Record 1967*, MEA Library 1995: 101)

At that juncture, the Congress Government was buffeted between two opposite currents: (1) for the first time, the proposed non-proliferation treaty signified the emergence of a new, yet undefined bond between the two super powers who had heather to been rivals; (2) in opposing their initiative on the non-proliferation front, New Delhi was completely going against the entire trend of foreign policy in the past. (Mirchandani 1968: 146-47) Despite the risk, the Congress government expressed its dismay over the treaty. Deputy Prime Minister Moraji Desai, during his foreign tour, conveyed to Robert McNamara India's strong objection to the treaty both on the grounds of security and discrimination. Defence Minister Swaran Singh formally pronounced in the UN General Assembly that nuclear disarmament could not be achieved by the preservation of exclusive rights, privileges and options "sought to be retained by certain armed and powerful countries, while measures are to be taken to limit the actions of the threatened and unarmed countries". (Mirchandani 1968: 148) Speaking at Warsaw during a state visit, Prime Minister Indira Gandhi said: "We see danger both in horizontal and in vertical proliferation. While seeking agreement on the non-proliferation treaty, we should like to emphasise the balance of obligations which must prevail for nuclear disarmament. The stockpiling of armaments is a cause for fear and distrust". (Quoted in Mirchandani 1968: 149)

The nuclear non-proliferation treaty and India's response remained a major political issue at home. Almost every political party and its member participated in the debate on what should be India's policy on the matter. But interestingly Shyam Bhatia points out a different perspective when he depicts that it was a decisive time as Congress Government was actually preparing its justification for carrying out future nuclear test then. (Bhatia 1979: 141–42) According to him, "it was only in 1968, after four years of running the plutonium plant and after sufficient stocks of plutonium had accumulated to begin basic theoretical work on explosions, that Sarabhai approached Mrs Gandhi and told her preparations could now begin for a nuclear test, if the government so wished". (Bhatia 1979: 141) Bhatia further says: "by the time the *Poornima* project had been sanctioned in 1968, the government had a wide range of reasons to justify a nuclear test. They included domestic pressures, security problems emanating from the Chinese nuclear programme, an unsatisfactory Nuclear Non-Proliferation Treaty and economic benefits associated with the development of nuclear explosive technology. In consultation with Atomic Energy Commission, Mrs Gandhi decided to base her strategy on the last reason, just as Shastri had done for reasons of cost effectiveness". (Bhatia 1979: 141–42)

But complete contrast views can be found in Mrs Gandhi's nuclear policy decisions subsequently. According to Ashok Kapur, "the internal setting was such that Indira Gandhi was in the process of gaining her ascendancy in Indian politics in the late 1960s and she neither understood nor cared for nuclear affairs." (Kapur 1976: 52) Kapur suggests that one needs to see Indira Gandhi, indeed the Nehru family, as actors, and Indian politics as theatre where the aim is to create an illusion of reality and to achieve a rapport with the audience to achieve an effect of the moment. He cites the example of her January 1966 decision to cancel the nuclear test project which he attributes to Mrs Gandhi's inexperience, to the pressure of other priorities (i.e. staying in power), and to the nature of bureaucratic advice. The reason behind her decision in February 1968-not to sign the NPT may be her fear of Cabinet disapproval, the nature of bureaucratic advice and the impression that the Treaty was not popular in India. Kapur considers that Mrs Gandhi made the case against the NPT on grounds of "principle and national interest" which are vital part of her and India's nuclear posture on the treaty but had nothing to do with the "motivation" behind his decision. Rather consideration of her own, and her party's prestige, and pressure of bureaucratic politics from below and not a carefully considered assessment of the national interest governed her decision regarding NPT. (Kapur 1976: 49) Kapur advances the hypothesis that during 1966-69, Indira Gandhi's priority was to establish her ascendancy in Indian politics. In other words, domestic politics was paramount in her all policy pronouncements including on nuclear matters.

Though Indira Gandhi, soon after becoming Prime Minister in 1966, launched a dynamic programme for nuclear research development, *consciously* "qualified it by restricting it exclusively for peaceful purposes". (Kaul 1988: 157) Though, domestic political considerations were paramount in Mrs Gandhi's thinking, overall Congress Party's stand on NPT reveals that she had full confidence of her Party members. Mrs Gandhi's final decision to reject the NPT was taken after the issue was extensively debated in her cabinet.

Interestingly, Ashok Kapur in his earlier writing (*India's Nuclear Option*, 1976) says that "in light of Mrs Gandhi's preoccupation with domestic concerns, India came very close to signing the NPT, given the foregoing array of bureaucratic maneuvers." Many senior bureaucrats from MEA, except V.C. Trivedi and T.N. Kaul, like Rajeshwar Dayal, Jagat Mehta and Rikye Jaipal favoured signing the treaty. Morarji Desai and Y.B. Chavan were the principal cabinet members who argued against the treaty. Kapur says the original draft of Mrs Gandhi's speech in late November 1967 favoured India's adherence to the NPT. But her cabinet was unanimously against the treaty. (Kapur 1976: 196) Therefore, her decision not to sign might not have based on any deep conviction in principle against NPT; rather on the basis of a careful reading of Indian public opinion polls which showed that "a majority rejected the NPT and favoured an Indian decision towards nuclear weapons". (Kapur 1976: 196) It shows that there was considerable ambivalence within the Congress Party regarding the decision on NPT.

It is possible that nuclear issues were among the least of Indira Gandhi's worries as her government was more concerned toward the general elections of April 1967. It can be evident how much important the nuclear issues were for her if one analyses her speech in the Lok Sabha on April 5 1968. One can get the impression that Mrs Gandhi and the Congress Party's policy on non-proliferation was nothing different from India's traditional vocal aversion to nuclear weapons. However, if the assumption 'political status of the decision-maker is paramount in shaping nuclear policy' is any guide, "foreign policy issues have a domestic use" especially in the hands of the Prime Minister who does not trust, and is unwilling to give credit to, his or her colleagues. (Kapur 1976: 197) Then, it is not merely on the basis of the merits of the issue (NPT) that the decision was settled in India. But, once the threat from the domestic politics front (adversaries) passes, public opinion does not become a key variable. This aspect is clearly perceptible if one sees how Mrs Gandhi, after gaining a majority in the Parliament, went for the nuclear test in 1974 without taking confidence of other fellow party members. But Mrs Gandhi, during her speech in Lok Sabha on November 2nd, 1966, mentioned that "all parties, with the exception of Hon. Member Shri M.R. Masani, have generally supported the stand taken by the Government of India in not signing the Treaty in its present form". (*Statement* by Indira Gandhi, Srivastava 1985: 34) This indicates that all other parties were of the same view that the Congress Party had on NPT. It also suggests that Mrs Gandhi must have extensive consultations with other party members before arriving at the decision to withhold India's support for the treaty.

Whatever may be the nuances of Mrs Gandhi's decisions on NPT, it is quite clear that the Congress Government led by her was firm to "protect India's national interest by not unilaterally surrendering its sovereign right to manufacture nuclear weapons even though she has of her own free choice decided to exploit nuclear energy for peaceful purposes only" (Khilnani 1984: 42). In his statement before Parliament on March 17 1967, the Foreign Minister Chagla made it clear that "the non-proliferation treaty should be such as not to impede the growth of nuclear science and technology in the developing countries where the need of such development is great". Again on March 27, 1967 he said in a statement to both houses of the Parliament that India should examine the text of any draft treaty submitted to the Committee in the light of the principles enunciated in the *UN General Assembly Resolution No. 2028 (XX)*.[2] Shri Chagla underlined that "a satisfactory agreement on non-proliferation of nuclear weapon would have to take into account the peculiar circumstances in which certain countries are placed" and "India had a special problem of security against nuclear attack or nuclear blackmail". He emphasised that this aspect must be taken into consideration before India's final attitude to the non-proliferation treaty was determined. India's vulnerable position on her northern frontier and her susceptibility to nuclear blackmail from China, and the USA are important factors governing the firm stand taken by India on the question of non-proliferation. (Khilnani 1984: 44)

From outside, one may get the impression that Mrs Gandhi's decision for nuclear test (May 1974) was deliberately timed before the 1975 NPT Review Conference probably to remind the promoters of the NPT that India has apparently lost interest in arms control and the test was a commitment against the NPT. The test may be viewed as a "climax of India's opposition to the NPT" and is just exercising of the verbal position it had taken during the treaty negotiation. The Congress Party stood by Mrs Gandhi's all nuclear decisions. In the AICC Resolution December 6-7, 1980, the Party expressed that "in safeguarding India's sovereign right to develop and use nuclear technology for peaceful purposes, India has continued to oppose discriminatory arrangements such as the Nuclear Non-proliferation Treaty while urging the conclusion of a general convention of the total prohibition of the use or threat of use of nuclear weapons". (*INC Resolution*, December 6-7, 1980: 13) The party unequivocally urged that "India shall continue its quest for self-reliance in the peaceful uses of nuclear energy".

Post-Indira Phase

Except for occasional queries on the Indian position and some issues relating to disarmament negotiations, the Parliament or the AICC sessions did not witness a serious debate on the implications of the Indian stand on the NPT. However, owing to the debate over Indian stand on the NPT and the consequent non-participation in the review conferences, the issue remained on the domestic public domain. The May 1974 nuclear test continued to raise questions about India's non-proliferation position. At the same time, India continued to view the Treaty discriminatory, but reiterated her intention not to produce nuclear weapons and right to develop nuclear energy for peaceful purposes. (Noorani 1988: 415) However, the issue of pressure from Canada, US and Soviet Russia on India to accept NPT was raised many a times in the Parliament.[3]

During Rajiv Gandhi's period (1984-89), Congress party's policy towards the NPT continued as it was during Indira Gandhi and Morarji Desai. The policy of nuclear ambivalence, criticism of the non-proliferation regime on almost the same lines continued as it was during Indira Gandhi's Prime Ministership. His initiative for the Six Nations Appeal for Disarmament made first in 1984 and followed up on an almost annual basis constituted a counter to the discriminatory nature of the NPT. Rajiv Gandhi once stated that the role of the Six Nation Initiative was to help governments by arousing awareness amongst the people about dangers to human from nuclear weapons. His Minister of State for External

Affairs, Natwar Singh, told Parliament on 7th December, 1987 that India was not prepared to sign the NPT. (*Lok Sabha* Debates, November 7th, 1987) Rajiv Gandhi in the beginning wanted India to join the NPT, but eventually accepted scientific and military advice to promote Indian missile development. (Kapur 1976: 42)

More importantly, Rajiv Gandhi was increasingly concerned about the clandestine nuclear weapons activities of Pakistan and the Chinese programme as well. He was critical about US role in bolstering Pakistan's nuclear appetite by providing sophisticated arms. Rajiv Gandhi was quoted, in December 1987, as saying; "we coexisted with the Chinese bomb for 20 years, but a Pakistani bomb? I don't know and I cannot be sure that we will be able to co-exist with it". (Noorani 1988) Rajiv told DPA, the German news agency, that, "Pakistan having a nuclear weapon is not quite the same as some other country having a nuclear weapon. We have lived with the Chinese nuclear bomb and not developed our own weapons for many years now. So it is not that we can't live with a nuclear neighbour". (*Hindustan Times*, June 6th, 1988) In a speech before the United Nations, Rajiv Gandhi argued that:

> We cannot accept the logic that a few nations have the right to pursue their security by threatening the survival of mankind ... nor is it acceptable that those who possess nuclear weapons are freed of all controls while those without nuclear weapons are policed against their production. History is full of such prejudices paraded as iron laws: That men are superior to women; that white races are superior to the coloured; that colonialism is a civilising mission; (and) that those who possess nuclear weapons are responsible powers and those who do not are not. (Address by Rajiv Gandhi, General Assembly, A/S-15/PV.14, 9 June 1988)

In subsequent decades, Rajiv Gandhi's approach and policies towards the nuclear issues have constantly been refereeing point in almost every resolution of the Congress Party. At the Tirupati session of the AICC (79th Session, April 14-16 1992), the Party members recalled Rajiv Gandhi Action Plan for Nuclear Disarmament and extensively discussed India's commitment towards a non-violent world order. At the Surajkund session (March 27-28 1993) the Party emphasised that: India should be prepared to consider any proposal on nuclear non-proliferation which is non-discriminatory, universal and in the security interest of all nations. (*AICC Resolution*, Surajkund Session, March 26-27, 1993: 25) Likewise, in the Delhi session of AICC (June 10-11 1994), the Party, reiterating Rajiv Gandhi's proposal, said that nuclear non-proliferation would be successful only when the nuclear weapon states will be determined towards the treaty. Unless any effort made at the regional and sub-continental level India cannot agree to this ever. (*AICC Resolution*, New Delhi Session, June 10-11, 1994: 32)

The Congress Party fully endorsed Prime Minister Narasimha Rao's policy towards the non-proliferation regime. Prime Minister Rao refused to sign the NPT and kept the nuclear weapons option open in a declaratory way. Recognising Rao's efforts for a nuclear weapons free world, in its New Delhi session, the AICC expressed satisfaction over the support of the Prime Minister Shri Rao and President Clinton for the efforts for non-proliferation of weapons of mass destruction and their eventual abolition. (*AICC Resolution*, New Delhi Session, June 10-11, 1994: 34) But, as Natwar Singh revealed in the Parliament, "when CTBT was under discussion or the NPT was under discussion" Narsimha Rao "was thinking of exploding the nuclear device" (*Parliament Debate*, May 27 1998; Jai 1998: Appendix). However, with the emergence of BJP as an influential political force in the country and its rhetoric for making India a "strong nation armed with nuclear weapons", the Congress Party has never sidelined its stand for nuclear disarmament. In its 1998 Election Manifesto the Party said that it "will continue its efforts for total and complete disarmament" and India's "nuclear policy will continue to be for peaceful, developmental purposes". However, it warned that India "will not be found wanting in case of any threat by hostile forces". (INC, *Election Manifesto 1998*)

In its 1999 Election Manifesto, the Congress Party also reiterated its stand by saying that its "approach to the CTBT, the FMCT and other global regimes of nuclear non-proliferation must be integrally linked to the over-arching goal of the time-bound elimination of nuclear weapons". Criticising the BJP's adventurism, the Congress Party said in the manifesto that the "BJP has wilfully destroyed the national consensus on nuclear matters. That consensus will now be meticulously rebuilt. India will reiterate at every opportunity its steadfast commitment to time-bound universal nuclear disarmament, leading to general and complete disarmament." (INC, *Election Manifesto 1999*) When the NDA government led by BJP consulted for a national consensus on India's approach towards CTBT, the national party was not averse to the signing of the CTBT. (*The Indian Express*, December 18, 1999) But the Party advocated for concrete steps to ensure that the nuclear weapons available with Indian and Pakistan are never used. In its view, India cannot afford to relax its vigil since it is surrounded by nuclear weapons states. At the same time, India must never allow a nuclear arms race to develop in the region. The Party said that the proposed ideas like the no-first-use pact, non-targeting population centers, advance-warning, etc., need to be studied carefully. And "India, Pakistan and China have a joint responsibility for nuclear non-proliferation in this region". (*The Indian Express*, December 18, 1999) But the 81st Session of the AICC clarified the reason for India's non-adherence to the nonproliferation treaty. The Resolution said:

> The decision not to sign the non-proliferation treaty was taken with a basic aim in mind and this basic aim was in national interest: maintain the independence of decision making and discard discriminatory treaties. (*AICC Resolution*, Bangalore Session, March 17-18, 2001: 107)

However, the Congress Party was critical about the BJP-led coalition government's policy on the issue of CTBT. It criticised the BJP in its Bangalore session by saying that India's leadership role in the movement for eliminating nuclear weapons has been lost, especially "under the leadership of the BJP". This suggest that either the party discounted the political mileage the BJP accrued out, of the tests or it was in favour of maintaining the ambiguous nuclear posture which provided space for India to propagate her moral position at the global level. The party while emphasising Rajiv Gandhi Action Plan, therefore, reiterated its stand that a nuclear weapons-free world would not only enhance India's security but also ascertains the safety of the entire world. At the same time, the Party opposed the unjust divide of the world where nuclear weapons in the hands of a few nations are considered safe and the same is unsafe with others. (*AICC Resolution*, Bangalore Session 2001: 107-08) In the minutes of the AIICC meeting in Delhi (May 24, 2002), the Congress Party gave a clarion call for India to take the lead in a global campaign for nuclear free world. The minutes of the meeting said:

> We are living in difficult and dangerous times. Shri Rajiv Gandhi's dream of a nuclear free world remains our constant commitment. The up-dated Rajiv Gandhi Action plan for

> Nuclear Weapons Free and Non-violent World Order remains the sheet anchor of the Congress party's disarmament policy. . . . People who speak of wars in a world with nuclear weapons overlook the unthinkable potential of damage and disaster. (*Minitues of AICC Meeting*, New Delhi, May 24, 2002: 45)

Realistically, in the *AICC Resolution* (August 21 2004), the Party also pointed out that "Nuclear non-proliferation remains a pressing concern but the threat of international terrorism has become very urgent." Therefore, the Congress Party pressed for renewed efforts to speed up the negotiations under U.N. auspices on the draft Comprehensive Convention on International Terrorism and the Convention for the suppression of acts of Nuclear Terrorism. But a marked difference can be seen in the Party's 2004 Election Manifesto where for the first time it advocates for "maintaining a credible nuclear weapons programme" while assuming the traditional "leadership role in promoting universal nuclear disarmament and working for a nuclear weapons free world order." (INC, *Manifesto 2004*) in its earlier pronouncement the Party had always remained ambivalent about the weapons status. Probably the Party was assured about the inevitability of a nuclear India and acceptability in the international community.

In its 82nd Plenary Session in Hyderabad in January 2006, the Congress Party emphasised that though India is not a member of the NPT, it *suo moto* fulfills the majority of conditions including a unilateral moratorium on further nuclear tests. And India's record in the matter of non-proliferation of sensitive technologies is irreproachable. (*82nd Plenary Session of INC*, Hyderabad, January 23, 2006: 96-97)

The last and current phase of the debate over the Congress Party approach towards the non-proliferation issue sparked off with the momentum in Indo-US civil nuclear cooperation. The Manmohan Singh government's determination to go for the deal and subsequent withdrawal of support of the Left parties from the UPA coalition government generated a nation-wide debate. In response to the allegation by the Left and BJP (inclding other independent thinkers who oppose the deal) that Congress government has compromised India's sovereignty by accepting the terms of the deal with US, the Congress Party said:

> The 123 Agreement is signed between two countries as equal partners. . . . The Congress Party reaffirms its abiding com-

> mitment to nuclear non-proliferation and total nuclear disarmament which is universal and verifiable as was proposed by Rajiv Gandhi at the Special UN Session on Disarmament in 1988. . . . The 123 Agreement entails no obligations for India to sign CTBT/FMCT. We, however, remain committed to a voluntary, unilateral moratorium on nuclear testing. We are also committed to negotiate on FMCT in the Conference on Disarmament. (*India's Nuclear Energy Programme and The 123 Agreement with the United States*, 2008, INC)

An introspection on the Congress Party policy in the post-Pokhran II period would reveal that the party has "endorsed BJP's overtures . . . embracing its decision to develop nuclear weapons." (Swamy 2004) This is discernible from the AICC political resolution in 2007 where it says "our credible minimum nuclear deterrent is maintained purely from the point of view of securing the country's defences". But the Congress Party has always emphasised its commitment to comprehensive, universal nuclear disarmament. In this regard the 2007 resolution says, "We have never compromised in this belief even as strategic compulsions have forced us into nuclear weaponisation. . . . The AICC also calls upon the Congress-led UPA government to actively build upon the Rajiv Gandhi Action Plan for a Nuclear Weapon-Free and Nonviolent World Order ...." (*AICC Political (Omnibus) Resolution*, November 17 2007, New Delhi) On the issue of joining NPT, the Congress Party made its views clear especially when the Indo-US nuclear deal raised uproar. On July 29, 2009, Prime Minister Manmohan Singh stated in the Parliament that *India cannot accept calls for universalisation of the NPT* and there is no question of India joining the NPT as a non-nuclear weapon state. (*The Indian Express*, 24 September, 2009)

This view was also conveyed to UN Security Council when it passed a resolution calling for universal adherence to the NPT in September 2009 which President Obama presided over. India's Permanent Representative to the UN Hardeep Puri wrote to the US Ambassador to the UN Susan Rice on India's position. He said, India could not "accept any obligations arising from treaties that India has not signed or ratified" and "this position is consistent with the fundamental principles of international law and the law of treaties". (*The Indiannews*, September 24, 2009) He added that "Nuclear weapons are an integral part of India's national security and will remain so, pending non-discriminatory and global nuclear disarmament". India will remain out of the NPT and continue to have nuclear weapons, unless the treaty was made more equitable but at the same time, he noted, India had an "unwavering commitment" towards non-proliferation and eventual disarmament. The Congress Party new member and the then Minister of State for External Affairs Shashi Tharoor also said India will not adhere to any treaty such as the NPT, and will not sign it as long as it is discriminatory. (*The Indiannews*, September 26, 2009) This is how the Congress Party evolved and maintained its stand on the nuclear non-proliferation issues. In its latest election manifesto (2014) the Party, without going into detail unlike before, only says "India will contribute to world-wide efforts in creating and managing institutions to deal with challenges like . . . non-proliferation . . . ." ("Your Voice Our Pledge", *Lok Sabha Elections 2014 Manifesto*, p. 47)

Views of the Right Wing

During the 1970s, when the issue "should India sign the NPT" was dominating politico-strategic spectrum, the only political party that urged India to sign the NPT and to accept a US-Soviet umbrella was the pro-West, business-oriented, Swatantra Party. While the Moscow wing of India's Communist Party argued against the US nuclear umbrella proposal, only Jan Sangh urged India to acquire nuclear arms. The party's views were described as rooted in a nationalist reaction against the behaviour of the superpowers and China. (Patil 1969: 79) Within these viewpoints the Jan Sangh, the ancestor of the BJP constructed its viewpoints which the BJP subsequently carried forward.

Bharatiya Jana Sangh

As a precursor of the BJP, Jana Sangh viewed the NPT as an attempt to sanctify the existence of Five Nuclear Powers by placing permanent technological barriers on Indian research, thereby preventing India from taking a meaningful part in disarmament discussions. (*Jana-Deep* 1968: 53) The party criticised the government approach to this Treaty as "one-sided" and a callous disregard of our strategic and security problems". According to M.L. Sondhi, the Jana Sangh was totally opposed to any arrangement by which India is asked to sign away its right to produce nuclear weapons. (*Jana-Deep* 1968: 53) Criticising Congress Government's failure to manufacture a nuclear device for India, Jana Sangh viewed that "every passing day confirms the impression that the country is drifting". (*Organ-*

iser, October 26, 1964: 3) Jana Sangh had always of the view that "the nation's determination to build up military strength adequate enough to frustrate the gravest challenge to its independence and integrity should not be limited by any pseudo-pacifist inhibitions." (*BJS Resolution No. 3*, Bharatiya Kary Samiti, December 4-6, 1964)

In its Bhopal meeting in March 1968, the Party blamed the Soviet Russia and USA for mounting pressure on India to sign the non-proliferation treaty. It felt that Government of India is "somewhat weakening in its resolve not sign the treaty in its present form." Mainly Jana Sangh's objection to the Treaty was based on four points:

1. While on one hand, the non-atomic nations bind themselves down not to head for marking atomic weapons, on the other hand, nuclear-haves are allowed to continue in their efforts to increase their stock-piles, devastating powers and delivery system, which is incomprehensible;
2. If the Super Powers expected non-nuclear powers to deny themselves voluntarily nuclear weapons, they must undertake certain responsibilities to halt and reverse the arms-race. It is a painful fact that nuclear powers have failed to shoulder this responsibility;
3. The non-nuclear nations cannot accept a treaty which at one hand would allow the nuclear powers to stock-pile nuclear weapons and on the other make the non-nuclear nations dependent upon other for their security;
4. The guarantee which was offered to non-nuclear-nations against atomic attack is altogether insufficient, unsatisfactory and unacceptable. This guarantee is being made a subject of veto by bringing in the Security Council. It would not only amount to further strengthening the dominance of big powers over the world but would also entirely leave the non-nuclear countries at their mercy.

Therefore, the Party warned the government to "beware of non-proliferation treaty" and not "to commit the folly of allowing itself to be pressurised into signing the proposed treaty". It suggested that "if the government today is not in a position to take courage in both hands and decide to produce the atom bomb, the option for India going nuclear must not be given up. The Indian people will not forgive any weakness or vacillation in this respect." (*BJS CWC Resolution*, March 22, 1968) Till 1970s, the BJS continued its objection for the discriminatory non-proliferation regime and advocated the necessity of nuclear deterrence for India.

Views of Bharatiya Janata Party

The BJP, since its inception, stood for nuclear weapons for India's and voiced against the discriminatory non-proliferation regime. In all its deliberations, the party vouched for a strong India equipped with atomic weapons. During the years, before coming to power, it supported Congress governments' decision not to sign the NPT. In its National Council "Resolution on International Situation", May 1992, the Party said:

> While government's decision not to sign the N.P.T. is welcome, the country must guard against the insistence of the U.S. and others that India and Pakistan agree to freeze their nuclear programmes and to implement the I.A.E.A. full-scope safeguards on their nuclear programmes. In today's situation this implies that after such a freeze, Pakistan would remain a nuclear weapons state and India a non-nuclear-weapon state. Let no one argue that Pakistan can never be trusted to do any such thing. Secondly, there is no way in which anybody could be certain as to the number of nuclear devices in Pakistan's possession. There is no scientific method fool-proof enough in this regard. Pakistan could easily hide a nuclear device in a basement. (*BJP National Council Resolution*, May 1992: 12)

However, the Party was sceptical about Congress-led coalition's assurance not to sign the NPT and also about its ability to "resist the pressure for arranging a regional arrangement which would amount to giving up the nuclear option". (*BJP National Executive Meeting*, November 7th, 1992: 9) Criticising the NPT for its "double standard" in its 1992 Executive Meeting the BJP expressed it believe in the principle of sovereign equality of nations. It advocated that "as long as nuclear weapons are not outlawed for every country in the world, India must not only retain its nuclear option but must immediately manufacture and deploy such weapons. (*BJP National Executive Meeting*, Nov 7 1992: 10) If one analyses the Party's vision of India which outrightly aspires for a "powerful" nation, one could easily come across its self-proclaimed righteousness: Powerful BJP for Powerful India ("*Shaktishali Bharat ke liye Shaktishali BJP*", *Vision Document 2004*). The party views that, to secure India's interest in the challenging and rapidly changing world, New Delhi needs a "vigorous exercise of diplomacy". In pursuit of this, India should proudly propagate the "principle of sovereign equality of nations". Pressure on India to conform to regimes of non-proliferation is being viewed by BJP as grave concern for India's sovereignty. In the Bhubaneswar session of the National Executive Meeting, the BJP raised its concern about the Narasimha Rao Government's incapability to resist the pressure to conform to "discriminatory" NPT. The Resolution says:

> There are enough signs to give rise to the belief that the pressure is having its effect and the Government of India is embarking on the slippery road of concessions in these two fields as it has already in the economic sphere. The Government keeps on saying that it will not sign the N.P.T. but there are indications that Government cannot resist the pressure to come to some regional arrangement which would amount to giving up the nuclear option. (*Resolution*, National Executive Meeting, Bhubaneswar, 6–8 November, 1992: 9)

The BJP blamed vehemently the Narasimha Rao Government for not successfully safeguarding India's vital interests in the international arena because the Congress government was "dithering and drifting internationally as it is domestically". (*Resolution*, National Executive Meeting, Bhubaneswar, November 6-8, 1992: 13) Therefore, the need of the hour, the party suggested, is to resort to a "pro-active diplomacy" though it stands committed to a nuclear-free world. In its 1996 Election Manifesto, the Party suggested not to agree to the CTBT (and NPT in their present discriminatory form) unless there is a simultaneous agreement for a time-bound global elimination of nuclear weapons in their entirety. (*BJP Election Manifesto 1996*: 37) In the same manner, the Party also told in the *Manifesto* that it will not agree to the Fissile Material Control Regime (FMCR) and the Missile Technology Control Regime (MTCR). In BJP's view, the fact that the NPT has been extended permanently makes immutable a dangerous state of affairs. The treaty permanently legitimised the continued possession by nuclear weapon states of stockpiles that can destroy the world many thousands of times over. It does so without any binding commitment from these nations to strive for the goal in which India and others stand for complete elimination of nuclear weapons.

One distinguishing aspect of BJP and its nuclear decisions is that, being a cadre-based party, hardly any dissent among its members and the party as a whole can be marked. Where as one can find many instances of differences among the leaders of Congress Party over nuclear issues. The indefinite extension of NPT in 1995 generated a fresh wave of debate in the country and all political parties and leaders equally criticised the treaty as derogatory. The BJP president L.K. Advani while addressing the Plenary Session at Bombay on November 10-12, 1995 said:

> We regard the NPT and its recent extension and ratification as an iniquitous arrangement. We believe that a Comprehensive Test Ban Treaty can be arrived at about not through the creation of 'nuclear apartheid'. We cannot recognise that thesis which advocates different treatment for the national interests of one, and a totally different yardstick for others. (*Presidential Address by L.K. Advani*, Plenary Session, Bombay November 10-12, 1995)

However, Advani, reiterating his Party's commitment to a global and total elimination of WMD, said, "India must reserve to itself the right to take all such decisions as are in the interest of the nation". (*Presidential Address by L.K. Advani*, Plenary Session, Bombay November 10-12 1995) He urged the government to join the BJP to express this thought from the sovereign platform of the Parliament. Though there exists considerable differences of opinion on nuclear weapons policy, a consensus among all political parties not to accept the Treaty in its present form is persistent.

During the Sixth NPT Review Conference (2000), the BJP-led NDA coalition was in power at the Centre and decided not to attend the Conference. In the *Suo Motu Statement* in Rajya Sabha (May 9, 2000), the Minister of External Affairs Jaswant Singh said that "the NPT community needs to understand that India cannot join the NPT as a non-nuclear weapon state. Statements by NPT States Parties about India rolling back its nuclear programme are mere diversions to prevent focused attention on the basic goals of the NPT". Reminding India's commitment for a global nuclear weapons free world, Jaswant Singh mentioned that, "though not a party to the NPT, India's policies have been consistent with the key provisions of NPT that apply to nuclear weapon states". On the other hand, Singh pointed fingers towards the nuclear weapon States Parties to the NPT and their allies who have not diminished the role of nuclear weapons in their respective or collective security calculus; instead, new doctrines and justifications have been developed. For example, NATO's new strategic concept (ten years after the end of the Cold War) re-emphasised the need for nuclear weapons. Even after more than three decades, the nuclear weapon States Parties to the NPT remain to be persuaded to begin any kind of collective, meaningful negotiations aimed at global nuclear disarmament. Instead of displaying special responsibility to implement Article VI of NPT, these countries appears to have arrogated a special right to possess nuclear weapons and only for their exclusive security. Therefore, the Review Conferences held so far failed to reach any agreement. As a result, the non-nuclear weapon state parties to the NPT have increasingly felt let down by the lack of progress on disarmament, as well as non-compliance with the basic provisions of the Treaty.

However, India's commitment to global nuclear disarmament and lasting non-proliferation remains undiluted, said Jaswant Singh. Further he said, India had been and would remain a responsible member of the international nuclear non-proliferation regime and will continue to take initiatives and work with likeminded countries to bring about stable, genuine and lasting non-proliferation, thus leading to a nuclear-weapon-free-world. While willing to commence negotiations on Nuclear Weapons Convention, India also remains ready to participate in agreed and irreversible steps to prepare the ground for such negotiations. A global no-first-use agreement and a non-use agreement against non-nuclear weapon states would meet the longstanding requirement for legally binding negative security assurances and assurances to nuclear-weapon-free zones. (*Suo Motu Statement*, 9 May 2000, Rajya Sabha)

It seems the BJP's views on NPT are in no way different from all other political parties. Both the Congress and CPI(M) have expressed their opposition to India's adherence to the "Treaty at its present form" in many occasions. Though nuclear issues are debated in a wide spectrum and across the party lines, a national consensus always exists for India's articulation on the non-proliferation issues.

Similar is the case with the CTBT issue. On CTBT negotiations, BJP has always linked the test ban issue with the global elimination of nuclear weapons. A BJP member, Prakash Mani Tripathi opined in the Lok Sabha that "We, the BJP, have been demanding that CTBT should be linked to the elimination of nuclear weapons globally within a specified time frame". (*XI Lok Sabha Debates Session II, Budget*, 31 July 1996) During the Treaty negotiations, Jaswant Singh also harped for a successful conclusion so that the 'entry into force' does not go beyond the stipulated dead line, September 1999. He advised for a national consensus on the issue and the BJP did consult other political parties on the question. (*The Indian Express*, 18 December 1999)

After BJP-led NDA coalition coming to power at the Centre and the Pokhran-II nuclear tests in 1998, the CTBT issue was widely debated in the country. Prime Minister Vajpayee convened a meeting of all political parties to prepare the ground for a national consensus on India signing the Treaty and thereby joining the global non-proliferation regime. While the Vajpayee coalition government has virtually acknowledged the need for signing the CTBT, the BJP leadership feared that a hasty decision on the subject could be politically risky and therefore disastrous. (Iype 1998) Nearly all the Opposition parties led by the Congress and the Left Front vehemently went against India signing the CTBT. While the majority political opinion in India was that the government cannot agree to the CTBT without any gains for the country in return, Pakistan's willingness to sign the treaty without waiting for India and the Western nations' unwillingness to indulge India on any pre-conditions *vis-à-vis* the CTBT had put the Vajpayee government on the horns of a dilemma. (Iype 1998)

For quite some time it was debated that the discriminatory aspect of CTBT is no longer valid for India as it has conducted its nuclear tests successfully. India has enough data and technology now to conduct sub-critical tests, which are not banned under the CTBT. The US State Department had voiced to lift the sanctions only if New Delhi announces a halt to further testing and signs the CTBT. Subsequently, the Jaswant Singh-Strob Talbott talks brought home the impression for some time that India may consider signing the treaty. Prime Minister Vajpayee also told Parliament that the country did not have any real reason to oppose the CTBT as—after the May nuclear tests—the treaty is no longer discriminatory to India. (Iype 1998) But the BJP-led NDA coalition government desisted from taking any concrete steps fearing adverse political fallout. Since signing the CTBT is an emotive issue for major opposition parties like the Congress and the Left Front, many BJP leaders also feared that the issue is potential to rock the minority Vajpayee government. More importantly, the Congress Party was feared which could publicise the CTBT signature as a sell-out of vital security interests.

In the first ever interview after the 1998 nuclear tests, Prime Minister Vajpayee, replying to the question what is his reaction to the US insistence on India to sign the CTBT, said:

> We have made our stand on the CTBT very clear. We have indicated our readiness to discuss certain provisions of the treaty on a reciprocal basis. But, taken as a whole, the CTBT is discriminatory because it allows nuclear weapons states with advanced technology capabilities to continue their nuclear weapons programme. And so also is the Nuclear Non-Proliferation Treaty (NPT). There is no question of India accepting any treaty that is discriminatory in character. No one should have any illusions on this score. ("India is now a Weapons State", Interview with Prime Minister Atal Bihari Vajpayee, *India Today* May 25 1998)

This shows that the post-Pokhran II nuclear tests, at least for some time, created the dilemma whether to accept CTBT as India has tested nuclear devices and also voluntarily declared moratorium as further tests may not be needed. Perhaps owing to the opposition parties' pressure, Vajpayee government was apprehensive to take another such drastic step again. For example, the Congress Party's Pachmarhi conclave urged the government to refrain from signing the treaty and press for global disarmament. (Iype 1998) Natwar Singh, who headed the foreign affairs cell in the Congress government, in an interview said, "Congress will oppose tooth and nail any move from the Vajpayee government to sign the CTBT because we are not ready to accept a half-baked global non-proliferation regime". (Iype 1998) Further he remarked that, "ever since the nuclear tests in May 1998, the Vajpayee government has been talking and behaving in a partisan manner on vital security issues like the CTBT. The government cannot keep the Opposition parties in the dark as to what is happening in the crucial Singh-Talbott talks. He warned that "if the Vajpayee government is eager to sign the CTBT just because that will bring US President Bill Clinton to India this year, then it will be a disastrous decision". (Iype 1998) Finally, the NDA government refrained from going ahead of accepting the CTBT in its present form.

Though, it may look from outside that the BJP was in favour of CTBT after Pokhran II, but certainly not to become a non-nuclear weapons state party. It has always been in favour of India not to adhere to NPT, CTBT and FMCT as a non-nuclear weapon state. Rather it has always demanded the government not to accede to

Comprehensive Test Ban Treaty nor agree to fissile materials cut-off for weapon purposes nor accept the provisions of discriminatory Missile Technology Control Regime (MTCR) and unless a treaty is established for the total elimination of nuclear weapons universally within a stipulated time frame". (*Resolution,* BJP National Executive Meeting, December, 23–24 1995: 17) During the debate in parliament on nuclear tests in 1998, Prime Minister Vajpayee said, "our decision not to sign the NPT was in keeping with our basic objectives. . . . Successive Governments thereafter have taken all necessary steps in keeping with that resolve and national will, to safeguard India's nuclear option. This was the primary reason behind the 1996 decision for not signing the CTBT, a decision that also enjoyed consensus of this House". (*XII Lok Sabha Debates,* Session II, (Budget), "Statement by Prime Minister", May 27, 1998) It may be the overwhelming domestic public euphoria after the tests and the BJP's over confidence to be recognised as a nuclear weapons state prompted its leadership to look the CTBT issue afresh. Also it may mainly to convince and motivate the US leadership to soften their criticism over Indian tests in 1998.

The BJP on Indo-US Nuclear Deal and Non-proliferation Issues

The BJP viewed "the Indo-US nuclear deal as "a three-in-one document comprising a civilian energy cooperation agreement with the US, de facto NPT and de facto CTBT". (Mitra 2008: 131) The purpose of the Hyde Act passed by the US legislature, the Party said, "is to impose on India, bilaterally, conditionalities which are worse than those incorporated in the NPT and the CTBT, in perpetuity and without an exit clause". (BJP, *Unfair Deal,* 2006: Foreword)

Reminding Prime Minister Manmohan Singh's promise in the Parliament that "nuclear agreement will not be allowed to be used as a backdoor method of introducing NPT type restrictions on India", L.K. Advani expressed in Lok Sabha that even if we make nuclear weapons an integral part of our national security as Dr Singh mentioned, it will not restrict the "NPT to come our country from the backdoor". (Advani 2006: 8) BJP president Rajnath Singh remarked during his Presidential address at the National Council Meeting (Decmber 23–24, 2006) that the Party "do not agree at all with the present agreement because India is not being accepted as a nuclear state. Rather, restrictions akin to the CTBT and NPT have been imposed on any kind of nuclear tests in the future". (Singh 2006: 21)

In an interview to *The Organiser* Rajnath Singh said, "India has always been against signing CTBT and NPT, but by this deal we are becoming an indirect signatory to this". Further he mentioned that:

> The BJP cannot accept this deal in this form at any cost. This will make India accept all the conditionalities of CTBT and NPT. We cannot test a nuclear device without the permission of America and this will captivate our nuclear weapons programme and this is discriminatory. . . . It is okay if the developed countries including America had recognised India as a full nuclear power. This has not happened. India has always been against signing CTBT and NPT, but by this deal we are becoming an indirect signatory to this. We will oppose this. (BJP, *Press Interviews*, Shri Rajnath Singh, 2007: 41, 44)

Same kind of disapproval of the deal is also evident by another BJP leader Jaswant Sinha when he elaborated the reason why the deal is not acceptable to BJP. He said, "The declared objective of the US in entering into this deal with India is to bring India within the global non-proliferation regime. We have always regarded this regime as discriminatory and therefore we have not signed either the NPT or the CTBT. . . .It (the deal) has now trapped the UPA Government into signing an agreement bilaterally whose provisions are more stringent than the provisions of the NPT and the CTBT". (Sinha, August 2008)

The Party also opined that the waiver granted by the NSG has actually "worsens India's strategic interest". (*Political Resolution*, September 12-14, 2008) Reason is that India is still treated as a Non-Nuclear Weapon State by the NSG, therefore, will have to live up to all the non-proliferation commitments prescribed for Non-Nuclear Weapon States including testing. Further, under the relevant NSG guidelines any nuclear fuel state before making any transfer to India would have to consider whether, the governmental actions are supporting of nuclear non-proliferation. Therefore, any future test done in national interest would seriously impact nuclear commerce with any NSG member. (*Political Resolution*, September 12–14, 2008: 22–23) Most of the BJP leaders have the impression that the civil nuclear deal with US has a hidden agenda to bring India into the non-proliferation fold. Arun Shourie, Member of the Rajya Sabha, told in a speech that "in regard to nuclear weapons, especially in regard to India, the USA has had four objectives. The first one is that one way or the other to get India to abide by the NPT even if you cannot make it sign." (*Speech in Rajya Sabha*, 17 August, 2006) Mr Shourie, citing Condoleezza Rice's statement—"India is not, and is not going to become a Member of the NPT as a nuclear weapon state . . . we are simply seeking to address an untenable situation",—questioned the "untenable situation" she mentioned. Asserting his observation, Mr Shourie said, US' declared objective is to strengthen the NPT regime by making India a party to it through this Agreement. (*Political Resolution*, September 12-14, 2008)

The debate over the nuclear deal also raised the issue of CTBT and FMCT and India's policy thereof. The BJP viewed the Indo-US nuclear deal as a ban in perpetuity on India's future nuclear testing, therefore, the deal goes beyond the CTBT. The Party viewed that the US aim is to impose CTBT-plus obligation on India while refusing to accede to the CTBT itself. (*The Times of India*, January 8, 2007) To the allegation that BJP also wanted to conclude a similar deal with the US and Vajpayee had agreed to sign the CTBT when BJP was in power, BJP leader Yashwant Sinha said, "The Government (Congress) is spreading two lies about us. . . . The truth is . . . that we wanted to strategic partnership with the US". (Sinha 2008) And as far as signing the CTBT is concerned, Vajpayee addressing the UN General Assembly on September 24, 1998 said that India is willing to move towards a legal formalisation of the obligations contained in the CTBT but he expects that other countries will adhere to this treaty without condition. This imply that if the five nuclear weapon states and other states like Pakistan were willing to adhere to this treaty without condition, India will do so too. But the Indo-US nuclear deal signed by Congress government goes beyond even the CTBT by specifying the technical terms what is prohibited for India. On the other hand, Mr Sinha accused Manmohan Singh for agreeing with Bush to "work with the US for the conclusion of a multilateral FMCT." (Sinha 2008) Surprisingly, in its latest election manifesto (2014) the Party has uttered absolutely nothing on nuclear disarmament and nuclear non-proliferation. Rather the Party has promised to "follow a two-pronged independent nuclear programme, unencumbered by foreign pressure and influence, for civilian and military purposes. . . ." (BJP Election Manifesto 2014: 39)

Standing of the Left

Since the fourth general election in 1964, the opposition parties seemed to have acquired considerable influence in the formulation of foreign policy of the country. Among the most persistent, vocal, and influential critics against Indian support for the nuclear non-proliferation treaty was the Praja Socialist Party (PSP) and Samyukta Socialist Party (SSP) who received powerful support from the Jan Sangh. (Rusch 1969: 755) Both parties were united by the same arguments in opposition to India signing the treaty. Speaking for the SSP, Madhu Limaye, stressed that the treaty perpetuates a monopoly of nuclear power among a small group of nations and that India should not barter away its "nuclear option" for concessions but keep alive the threat of India becoming a nuclear weapons power. (*Indian Recorder and Digest*, June 1967: 9) Ram Manohar Lohia viewed the treaty to have created an "international nuclear caste system". Whereas Nath Pai, PSP deputy Lok Sabha leader and Prem Bhasin, the General Secretary, warned that if India signed the treaty it would become a "nuclear vassal" or "satellite" of the super powers. The only acceptable conditions to the PSP are if all the existing nuclear weapons powers sign, including France and China, all agree not to produce or test nuclear devices and all plan for the destruction of existing stockpiles. (*Janata*, 7 May, 1967: 3)

The series of persuasive arguments that the socialists developed against the Treaty received widespread support. Appealing to a nationalistic egalitarianism, they pointed to the treaty's "discrimination" between nuclear weapon and non-nuclear weapons states in favour of the former. In their views:

1. The treaty does not stop the nuclear arms race, but merely limits the number of nuclear weapons, since the non-nuclear powers must refrain from acquiring or making nuclear weapons, while the nuclear powers can keep and increase their stockpiles;
2. Underground explosions, even for peaceful research and development purposes, are forbidden to the non-nuclear states but the nuclear states may continue even for military purposes;
3. Control and supervision applies only to non-nuclear signatories.

These arguments presented by them caused a nation-wide debate which posed a new challenge for the Congress Party; if they consider for accepting the treaty they would be accused of sacrificing India's national interests.

Views of CPI(M)

The CPI(M) claims to have an "independent line" and "consistent" position on the non-proliferation regime. Firstly, "it does not accept the demand of the five nuclear weapon states, including China, that India becomes a signatory to the NPT and the CTBT." (Karat 2008: 166) Secondly, the Party strongly views India as a sovereign, independent country which safeguards its security interests in a world still dominated by imperialism. It envisages for India an active and progressive role in working for universal nuclear disarmament which is in the interest of all peoples and world peace. Therefore, it opposed BJP's attempt to weaponise and strongly advocates that India's interest will be better served by cherishing the policy of universal nuclear disarmament. Thirdly, while refuse to sign discriminatory treaties like the NPT and the CTBT, India should campaign internationally for a review of these regimes so that a genuine basis is created for advancing towards universal nuclear disarmament. (Karat 2008: 113) Till this is achieved, India will continue to update its technological capability and keep the nuclear option open. According to the Party, "the only correct nuclear policy which will meet India's requirements as a country with an independent foreign policy which is committed to peace and non-alignment is to desist from going in for nuclear weaponisation".

The catchy phrases—"independent line" and "consistent position"—that the Party claims to have maintained in regard to what should be India's nuclear non-proliferation policy, need careful examination. First, the "independent line" indicates that its policy is completely different from the policies of other political parties. While other parties, especially the Congress and the BJP, are equally critical about the NPT and CTBT, they favoured at certain point nuclear weaponisation by India. In that respect, the CPI(M), beside being critical about the treaties, links them with the other parties' attempt for weaponisation. It does not consider nuclear weaponisation is in the best interest of India, therefore advocates for halting of the same. The Party vehemently criticised the BJP-led government's determination to make the bomb which it viewed simply "an extension of the chauvinist foreign policy which is integral to the RSS outlook" or the "mascot of the RSS." (Karat 2008: 108–9) According to Prakash Karat, the CPI(M) General Secretary, the Congress and the BJP in their pursuit to achieve the nuclear weapons state (NWS) status either advocate an unprincipled understanding with the US or bargain to join CTBT in return for some intangible concessions from the US. In contrast, for the CPI(M), "the only correct nuclear policy which will meet India's requirements as a country with an independent foreign policy which is committed to peace and no-alignment is to desist from going in for nuclear weaponisation". (Karat 2008: 113)

However, other political parties point their fingers towards the CPI(M) for its affiliation with the communist China and its support for the Chinese nuclear weapons programme. To recall, in 1964 when China explored its first nuclear device, the Party did not condemned it, rather expressed solidarity. On the other hand, the CPI(M) opposed the Pokhran-II tests conducted in May 1998. What could be the reasons behind two different stances? Prakash Karat gives an elaborate explanation in this regard. First of all, he says, the CPI(M) is against nuclear weapons as a means of war as they are weapons of mass destruction which will annihilate the conditions for life on the Earth. That is why the CPI(M) stands for the elimination of all nuclear weapons and for universal nuclear disarmament. Secondly, he says, one need to see the historical context in which nuclear arsenal was developed by nations.

The US first made nuclear weapons in 1945; it targeted and threatened the Soviet Union and the socialist countries with these weapons. The Soviet Union, in response, developed and tested its hydrogen bomb in 1953. When the Chinese revolution succeeded in 1949, the US intensified its strategic offensive against the rising tide of socialism by a policy of encirclement and "containment of China". The US made no secret of its tactics of nuclear blackmail to try and intimidate China. In the face of direct military threats by the US, including the deployment of nuclear weapons, China compelled to go nuclear. When China requested for Soviet assistance to upgrade its nuclear capabilities, it was denied. In the background of the deteriorating relations between the two socialist countries, this denial of cooperation in the nuclear field became one of the factors which precipitated the Sino-Soviet rift in 1962–63. When China exploded a nuclear device in 1964 and subsequently went ahead with making nuclear weapons, the CPI(M) did not oppose this move just as the Communists in India did not oppose the Soviet Union acquiring nuclear weapons in the fifties. The CPI(M) considered it appropriate for Socialist China to take all necessary measures to defend itself against the aggressive American strategy of "containing China" and rolling back communism there.

It is true that the international situation now is completely different from the earlier years. But Karat views India did not face any direct nuclear threat in all these years as China did from the USA and its allies. Unlike China, India did not face at any time a direct nuclear threat after independence. Its relations with the US had many ups and downs but at no time did the US ruling circles see India as an adversary. On the contrary, the US viewed India as a potential power against China during the Indo-China conflict in 1962 and extended military aid and an "air umbrella" at India's request. After the collapse of Soviet Union, in the post-1991 period, there has been no change in the strategic situation adversely affecting India as far as the nuclear issue concerned. The nuclear policy India pursued, till 1998, is all the more relevant in the new world situation. In its pursuit of making the world free of nuclear weapons, the international forums for disarmament and non-proliferation could have been used by India for mobilising world opinion that the five nuclear weapon states should commit to a time-table for dismantling nuclear weapons. The CPI(M), therefore, blames the BJP-led government for disrupting the potential role India could have played in this process. That is why the party argues against weaponisation and thinks that India's interests will be better served by the earlier policy of maintaining our independent capability without going in for weaponisation and adhering to the position of not signing the existing discriminatory and unequal treaties like the NPT and the CTBT.

Secondly, to examine the party's claim that its stand on non-proliferation issue as "consistent", one needs to look into the CPI(M)'s resolutions consistently. As is discussed earlier, this party, like any other party, believes in universal disarmament, therefore, its views are linked both to the non-proliferation and test-ban. Subsequent sections look into the CPI(M)'s views on these three aspects—disarmament, non-proliferation and test-ban—by locating them in various party deliberations since its inception, thereby evaluate how consistent the Party is.

Similar to the Socialists views, the CPI(M) links its arguments on non-proliferation and test-ban treaty with the issue of global nuclear disarmament. But the distinguishing factor in CPI(M)'s views is that it sees the nuclear discourse through the prism of "imperialism" and capitalism. It says, the global nuclear divide (nuclear haves and nuclear have-nots) is simply a part of the capitalist imperial design against which the Third World must unite. But, interestingly, it justifies Soviet Russia's cooperation with other nuclear weapon powers in mobilising support for the nuclear non-proliferation regime. The "Ideological Resolution of the CPI(M)" April 1968 says:

> ... The attitude of the Soviet leaders on the entire issue is based on the unwarranted premise that their collaboration with the Anglo-American imperialists is a greater guarantee for the preservation of peace, for the outlawing of the use of atomic weapons and for averting a thermo-nuclear war, than the unity of the entire socialist camp, its economic, political, military might and its all-round development and its unrelenting struggle against imperialism on every front. (*Ideological Resolution of the CPI(M)*, April 5-12, 1968)

So, "the Soviet leaders risked a rift and even split in the socialist camp over the non-proliferation issue". (Basu 1998: 67) Probably this was the path Indian leftist leaders followed when India's long-term national interest and nuclear weapons status was in question. The CPI(M) seem to have maintained consistency in its position on India's nuclear discourse, particularly on three important aspects: (A) Global nuclear disarmament is in India's best interest and India should play a lead role in it (not different from any other party's view); (B) no nuclear weaponisation, rather need to keep the option open; and (C) non-signatory to the "discriminatory" NPT as it perpetuates imperialist nuclear design of the capitalist countries.

While all other parties rejected the NPT mainly owing to its discriminatory nature, the CPI(M) rejects it for two reasons: (1) it is discriminatory; and (2) it imbibes 'imperialist' capitalist design. The second reason is unique as no other party thinks in that way. The CPI(M), in its every deliberation, has been raising the "imperial design" of the major powers to which India is gradually succumbing to. In its 1977 Lok Sabha Election Manifesto, the Party condemned "U.S. imperialists", for praising the new Indian Government and offering more economic aid, and to "enmesh India in an anti-national derogatory agreement on nuclear progress and use of nuclear power for peaceful purposes". (*CPI(M)'s Manifesto of Lok Sabha Election—1977*) However, the Party's Central Committee supported the stand of the Government on NPT and justified its refusal to sign it. First, the Central Committee of the

Party was of the opinion that the unilateral declaration by the Congress government for giving up explosion, even "for peaceful purposes was not only uncalled for but detrimental and derogatory to national interests and prestige". (*CPI(M)'s Manifesto of Lok Sabha Election—1977*) Therefore, it advised the government "to set the record straight during President Carter's visit" to India because renewed pressure would be exercised by the US, especially "economic blackmail", "to coerce India to accept dictated conditions on nuclear development". (*Documents of Communist Movement in India, 1975-77*: 457-58) Second, when Morarji Desai visited USA and reiterated India's unilateral moratorium on further atomic explosions the Party expressed that Shri Desai "has only made an anti-national concession and compromised the nation's honour". (*Statement on Current Situation*, June 1978) This suggest that the Party was in favour of keeping the test option open, signifying India's weapons option should be ambiguous and more importantly when India deals with the United States only. This stand of the Party gives an impression that its perception and advocacy for India's nuclear policy should strictly correlate US actions. This attitude is fully evident in its successive arguments.

The CPI(M) opines that the US pressure was intensified, especially during the Carter Administration. The Indo-US Agreement for Fuel for the Tarapur Plant (1963) got the first burnt. The Party was of the opinion that the agreement worked without any hitch till 1976. But from 1977, the Carter Administration began putting pressure on India to accept the NPT. For this purpose, the USA even went on delaying necessary supplies to India. Owing to the blackmailing attitude of the US, the Central Committee of the Party urged all parties to demand the "abrogation of the 1963 India-US agreement" and substitute France as the supplier. (*Statement*, Central Committee of CPI(M), Sept 1982) The same tone of criticism on US pressure to accept NPT was also advanced in CPI(M)'s Lok Sabha Election Manifesto 1980. It "called up the people to lend their full support" to the nuclear programme. However, the Party stood by the government's decision "to refuse to sign" the NPT as it involved "one-sided application of restrictions". (Ranadive, *CPI(M) Main Speeches*, Eleventh Congress, January 1982: 17)

Inspite of its opposition to unjust divide of the global nuclear order, the party was never away from its clarion call for global elimination of nuclear weapons. In the Thirteenth Congress (January 1989, Trivandrum), the Party welcomed the INF Treaty and extended support to the various peace initiatives like the nuclear weapons free zones concept advanced by the Berlin Conference, the nuclear corridor in Europe, a nuclear free Europe, de-nuclearisation of the Asia-Pacific region, and proposals for complete disarmament. (*Resolutions*, Thirteenth Congress of the CPI(M), January 1989) Also in the same resolution, the Party called upon the peace movement and world public opinion to be vigilant against imperialist designs of the US.

The Polit Bureau of the CPI(M) expressed its concern for mounting pressure of the USA on the Indian Government to sign the NPT during Reginald Bartholomew, US Under-Secretary of State for International Affairs, visit to India during November 1991. The Party released a Press statement (November 22, 1991) "warning the Government of India not to resile from its past stand". It expressed that "the arguments for India not being a party to the NPT are still sound and valid in the present international situation". The Party also suggested the government that if it is contemplating any new step in this regard, it "must place before the Parliament and the Indian people for a full debate". (*Polit Bureau Press Statement,* November 22, 1991) In this regard, the Central Committee of CPI(M) issued a Communiqué after its meeting held in New Delhi on March 19-22, 1992 where it says:

> The pressure to conform by signing the NPT or to participate in the five-nation meeting on non-proliferation is being sustained at a high pitch by the Bush administration.... Above all, U.S. imperialism has exposed its crude hegemonistic designs by the Pentagon paper which identifies India as a threat and proposes curving its potential strength and influence on South Asia. (*Central Committee Communiqué,* March 19-22, 1992)

In the same Communiqué the party highlighted how the US utilised the disclosure that Pakistan possesses the nuclear bomb to pressurise India into signing the NPT. And also it criticised Indian government to succumb to US pressures by collaborating in the military sphere. Political Resolution of the Party Congress had noted the dangerous move of establishing long-term military collaboration with the USA. It can be noted that CPI(M) has been more critical about not any other nuclear weapon states but the US policy and thereby evaluates the non-proliferation regime vis-à-vis India. In 1995, the Party raised the issue of "sustained pressure" from US "to sign the NPT or regional multi-lateral treaty on proliferation" and also pressurising Russia to cancel the agreement to sell cryogenic rocket engines to India. (*Political Resolution Adopted by the 15th Congress of CPI(M)*, 3-8 April 1995) Same kind of criticism can be marked in its 11th Lok Sabha Election Manifesto (1996) where it viewed to "rebuff imperialist efforts to subvert our independent development and resistance to its attempts to impose its NPT and CTBT and cancellation of the military cooperation pact with USA". (*CPI(M) Manifesto*, Eleventh Lok Sabha Elections 1996: 16) In almost all its resolutions, the Party highlights both the double standard of the US in matters of nuclear disarmament and India's gradual slide into the imperialist trap.

In the post-Pokhran II period, the Party apprehended that "using sanctions, greater pressures will be mounted on India by imperialism to sign the unequal and discriminatory treaties like the NPT and the CTBT". Therefore, it warned that "the BJP-led Government will not be allowed to capitulate on India's long-standing consensual decision of not signing these treaties". (*Statement*, Polit Bureau of the CPI(M), 15 May, 1998) The Polit Bureau called upon "all peace-loving patriots to rally together in carrying forward India's long-cherished desire to rid this planet of all nuclear weapons and force the government to adopt positions which will help preserve peace and security in the region".

The CPI(M)'s views on India's nuclear policy discourse, including on the NPT, in the post-1998 period are based on broadly four issues:

(1) As usual the Party suggested that India must not go in for making or deploying nuclear weapons;
(2) India must refuse to sign the discriminatory treaties like the NPT and CTBT;
(3) India must declared no-first-use of nuclear weapons; and
(4) India must campaign for non-discriminatory agreements to check nuclear weapons proliferation and for achieving universal nuclear disarmament.

Though commended the Indian scientists for conducting successful nuclear tests, the CPI(M) criticised BJP's nuclear policy for several reasons. First, the Party in its October 1998 *Political Resolution* said the BJP's nuclear policy has made India more vulnerable to imperialist pressures. Second, the tests bound to generate instability in the region. A situation of instability in the region will only help imperialist strategic designs. Third, India has been made more vulnerable to pressures to sign discriminatory treaties like the NPT and the CTBT. Even in its Lok Sabha election *Manifesto 1998*, the Party reiterated its stand saying "India does not sign any discriminatory treaty on nuclear weapons like the NPT and or the CTBT". (*CPI(M) Manifesto*, Lok Sabha Elections 1998) Rather it advocated for universal nuclear disarmament through "a non-aligned foreign policy with anti-imperialist orientation". (CPI(M) *Political Resolution*, March 2002)

Undoubtedly, the CPI(M) has consistently been opposing what it calls the "US-led hegemony" of an unequal order and treaties like the NPT which perpetuate the monopoly of nuclear weapons in the hands of a few, without advancing towards universal nuclear disarmament. This stand of the Party has also been more vigorously pronounced during the Indo-US civil nuclear deal negotiations.

CPI(M) Stand on CTBT

The CPI(M)'s views on CTBT is no way different from its stand on the NPT. It considers the test ban treaty "discriminatory" and "India should not be a party" to it owing to several reasons. (*The Hindu*, 25 September, 2009) Firstly, CTBT did not have a time frame for the elimination of nuclear weapons by the NWS. Secondly, the treaty permits the maintenance of nuclear stockpiles and to continue refining and developing the nuclear arsenals of the NWS through sub-critical experiments. Thirdly, CTBT do not prohibit the making and deployment of nuclear weapons; it only bars resting of nuclear devices by exploding them. (Karat 2008: 347) More importantly, the Party says "none of these objections to the treaty have been invalidated after 1998 nuclear tests". (Karat 2008: 347) Therefore, it vehemently criticised the nuclear weapon states, especially the US, that since they have acquired the know-how of sub-critical tests and computer simulation and do not need underground tests, they now trying to restrict others for the same. It criticises the US for imposing on India the discriminatory treaty. It also warned the BJP and Vajpayee government when (after 1998 tests) it voluntarily offered to consider signing the CTBT. The BJP's argument that "having declared India to be a nuclear weapon state, the CTBT should be signed so that we can weaponise and maintain a stockpile just as the NWS" was rejected by the CPI(M) for the reason that the US and the Security Council is not going to give India that recognition.

In retrospect, the Party viewed BJP's willingness to consider CTBT as "capitulation to US pressures". (*Political* Resolution, 16th Congress of the CPI(M), October 1998) Totally opposing India signing CTBT, the CPI(M) General Secretary Harkishan Singh Surjeet said in a press conference that:

> The Government was enacting a drama with periodic statements that it would not sign the CTBT and at the same time conducting secret talks with the US on signing it. Given the BJP-led Government's determination to continue whole hog with the liberalisation of the economy, it could not withstand US pressure on the CTBT issue. (Singh 1998)

The CPI(M) apprehended that an agreement with the US leading to the "signing of the CTBT and development of nuclear weapons will be a real setback" for the struggle against nuclear weapons. (Karat 2008: 350) As a credible and only alternative to signing the CTBT, the Party viewed, is "to declare that India has weapons capability after the Pokhran II tests but it is committed to not go for weaponisation. And "joining the CTBT and similar other agreements can always be considered in the future when the international climate produces worthwhile steps for nuclear disarmament". (Singh, Address in Press Conference, 21 September, 1998: 350–51)

Subsequently, the Party welcomed the United Front government's refusal to sign the test ban treaty. (*Report on Political Developments*, CC of CPI(M), Oct 29-31, 1996 and July 1998) But the Party seems to put forward its opinions on nuclear issues almost in similar language in a repetitive manner. For example, the *Political Organisational Report 1998*, the CPI(M) called for India "to continue to oppose discriminatory treaties and not sign the CTBT". Similarly, in its 1999 Election Manifesto, the Party also stood for "not signing CTBT" and criticised the BJP government for succumbing to US pressures for agreeing to sign the treaty. It viewed that the US is banking on the BJP to complete the act of betrayal of India's interests by signing the CTBT and making undisclosed the commitments on the FMCT.

Regarding FMCT, the CPI(M) does not think it as a genuine arms control measure; therefore, advised government to take a consistent position from NPT to CTBT to the proposed FMCT, whereby the nuclear hegemony of the NWS is challenged. In its 1999 Election Manifesto as usual expressed its commitment to work for universal nuclear disarmament and demanded "a commitment by the nuclear weapon states for denuclearisation within a time frame." (*Election Manifesto of the CPI(M)*, 13th Lok Sabha, 1999: 5, 11)

It is an open ended question as to what extent the Party has influenced the non-proliferation policy of India. But party leader Prakash Karat proclaims that the CPI(M) can legitimately claim to have played a major role in building up popular opposition to the BJP's nuclear policy along with other opposition forces. According to him, BJP was isolated in the Lok Sabha debate on the issue in May 1998 owing to the firm opposition by the CPI(M). (Karat 2008: 351-52)

CPI(M) Views on Indo-US Nuclear Deal and Non-Proliferation

In the wake of the domestic political row over the Indo-US nuclear deal, the major Left Parties of India—CPI(M), CPI, Revolutionary Socialist Party and All India Forward Bloc—brought out a document titled "Left Stand on the Nuclear Deal" (July 2008) explaining why they oppose the deal. Especially regarding the non-proliferation regime vis-à-vis the deal, the document draws a link between the US obligation as NPT signatory and its obligations under the 123 Agreement. In the process they highlight the wordings of the Hyde Act which states to unravel the intension of the US for coming forward for such a deal. The Party quoting the Act says: "such cooperation with a non-NPT signatory like India" can occur if:

> . . . the country has a functioning and uninterrupted democratic system of government, has a foreign policy that is *congruent* to that of the United States, and is working with the United States on key foreign policy initiatives related to non-proliferation. (Section 102 (6) B, *Henry J. Hyde U.S.----India Peaceful Atomic Energy Cooperation Act of 2006*)

The particular "congruence" with US foreign policy which the left parties view "amounts to a subversion of India's independent foreign policy". In their views, the UPA's claim that the reference in Art. 2.1 of the 123 Agreement is *innocuous* simply marks its ignorance of the sharp differences between the international obligations of India and US. Since India is a non-signatory and the US is a nuclear weapons state signatory to NPT, it is therefore *necessary to consider the possible conflict between the obligations of the US under the NPT and its obligations under the 123 Agreement* (emphasis added). It is relevant to note that the Hyde Act explicitly insists on the US maintaining its obligations under the NPT. In this way, the Left view the Deal as a trap to bring India closer to the discriminatory NPT.

The Left Parties, therefore, requested for providing a list of international treaties relevant to the 123 Agreement. When the UPA government finally went ahead with the deal, the CPI(M) expressed that "the Manmohan Singh-led government has negated the country's earlier position on NPT and CTBT to develop a strategic alliance with US imperialism by reducing India as its subordinate ally". In its Central Committee Report, the party expressed that the United States situates the India-US deal within the nuclear non-proliferation architecture and it has become an instrument for the US to pressurise India on various counts especially foreign policy. With the stance adopted by the Obama administration pressure would likely to be mounted on India to sign the discriminatory NPT and the CTBT. (*CPI(M) Report on Political Developments*, October 2009: 17) These perspective of the CPI(M) seem to be identical with the views of the BJP on the Indo-US civil-nuclear deal vis-à-vis the NPT. In its latest election manifesto (2014), the Party has pledged to pursue universal nuclear disarmament through the UN, provide parliamentary sanction for moratorium on testing; seek removal of nuclear weapons from the US military base in Diego Garcia in the Indian Ocean. (p. 19) Comparatively, it has pledged more than the other two parties in its manifesto.

Notes

1. This aspect is clearly evident in consecutive AICC Resolutions. The Nasik Resolution of Congress (20-21 September 1950) said, "The Congress approves of the policy pursued by the Government of India"; the Calcutta session (March 22-23 1952) reaffirming the resolution of the Nasik Congress in regard to foreign policy said: "The Committee expresses its full approval of the Foreign Policy pursued by the Government of India". The Indore session of the Committee (13-14 September 1952) also said, "while approving of the foreign policy pursued by the Government of India, this Committee trusts that India will continue to work for peace and international cooperation and will be ready to serve this cause, whatever the changing circumstances might be". In the Avadi session (January 21-23 1955)

"the Congress records its full appreciation of the policy of the Government of India in the realm of international affairs".

2 The Resolution (Nov 19, 1965) laid down certain principles on the basis of which ENDC was to negotiate an international treaty to prevent proliferation of nuclear weapons. The treaty to prevent proliferation of any loopholes which might permit nuclear or non-nuclear weapons in any form; it was to embody an acceptable balance of mutual responsibilities and obligations of the nuclear and non-nuclear powers; it was to be treated as a step towards achievement of general and complete disarmament and more particularly nuclear disarmament; and the treaty should have acceptable and workable provisions to ensure its effectiveness. Nothing in the treaty, it was recognised, should adversely affect the right of any group of States to conclude regional treaties in order to ensure the total absence of nuclear weapons in their respective territories.

3 Lok Sabha Debates, Vol. XLII (11), August 29 1974, Col. 101; Vol. XLV (12), November 20 1974, Cols. 114; Vol. XLV(12), November 21 1974, Cols. 40-63; Vol.X (4), March 1 1978, Cols. 189-90; Vol. X (4), February 23 1978, Cols. 213-214; Vol. XII (4), March 23 1978, Cols. 213-214; Vol. 1(1), January 30 1980, Cols. 71-72.

Conclusion

All Party to the Gate Crash

The original sin of any writer, says Robert D. Kaplan, "to see the world only from his or her point of view." Therefore, objectivity is illusory, this study is no exception.

In the preceding chapters, it is endeavoured to investigate different *dynamics of India's nuclear weapons policy-making* from the point of view of the three political parties—INC, CPI(M) and BJP. The intention was to identify only the nuances in the relationship between India's nuclear weapons policy and her domestic politics discourse focusing on the nature, problems and style of policy-making on different aspects by these three parties. In the process, two underlying assumptions have been tested. While the first assumption—*national political leadership is a more determining factor than political parties in India's nuclear weapons policy-making*—found to be partially true, the second assumption—*India's nuclear policy does not change with the change of government and changes despite the same party forming the government*—fully confirms. However, during the course of study, many intriguing templates of nuclear weapons policy vis-à-vis political parties have emerged, which are discussed in subsequent sections along with comparative narrative on the role of three parties.

Before summing up, it is pertinent to keep in mind the baseline political templates within which India's nuclear discourse has evolved. First, among the three political parties, the Indian National Congress has remained in power for more years than any other party. The BJP was only once in power, now for the second time for almost one term, but with a rainbow coalition earlier, of 13 political parties. The CPI(M) has never formed government at the centre, but at times it was partner in coalition governments. The motive is to highlight the relative position of the three parties in the domestic politics and assess thereby their comparative role and influence on nuclear policy matters. It is obvious that the Congress Party views have acquired more space in the study than the BJP and further lesser space in case of the CPI(M). Second, India has a Westminster system of government, where the Prime Minister, and his cabinet, becomes *primus inter pares*. The leader of the party that has the support of majority in the Parliament becomes the Prime Minister and his views are more or less considered as the views of the party he belongs to. There is no instance where a decision of the Prime Minister is rejected by the party he belongs to or there is no instance where he takes decisions without the consent of the party as a whole. Third, no Prime Minister has ever foreclosed or could foreclose the weapon-option outright. Even there was tacit consensus among all the mainstream political parties on India's sovereign right to nuclear weapons for national defence; in other words, for long, the consensus among all political parties was to keep the weapons option "open" (to be exercised at exigency). Therefore, the BJP-led NDA's decision to conduct the tests and declare India as a nuclear weapon state is nothing but the exercise of reserved-weapon-option. However, the claim that the emerging 'exigency' (deteriorated national and regional security situation) for which it decided to test has been a contentious debate. Fourth, India's nuclear weapons discourse was not only about acquiring of nuclear weapons; but also includes its policy towards the non-proliferation regime, national security, nuclear weapons programme of neighbouring countries, etc. Therefore, each of these aspects was examined in separate chapters, primarily from the perspectives of the three parties' perspectives.

One spontaneous anxiety is, *which political party should be given credit, and how much* in shaping India's nuclear weapons policy? In the same way, which leader(s) should be given how much credit? However, the main emphasis in the study is to compare political party which played what role in shaping India's nuclear weapons policy that has evolved through many topsy-turvy atmosphere during the last six-decades. So, the sections that follow compare the three political parties played the role in the evolution of India's nuclear weapons policy by analysing different facets of nuclear policy-making. The comparative analysis that this section is attempting to furnish, in fact, is an endeavour to reveal the systematic structure and perception variance leading to differential policy-orientations among the three parties towards nuclear weapons. The goal is to find why some of their views are similar and why some are not.

This is to know the general underlying structure which generates or allows such similarity or variation.

The first assumption that Indian political leaders play more determining role than her political parties in shaping nuclear weapons policy denotes two aspects: (1) in nuclear matters, view of the leadership of the party concerned is paramount than the aggregate views of other party members; and (2) if interpreted positively, it suggest that there is absence of any gulf between the opinion of the party members and its leader on nuclear matters. These two aspects can only be examined by an in-depth analysis of the organisational process and structure of the party. If the status of the leaders of Indian political parties is analysed, certainly the party leader is endowed with enormous vitality. Generally, the leader of the party that has the support of majority of members becomes the Prime Minister. The strict discipline and hierarchy maintained in the party structure reinforces the preeminence of the party leader. Above all, the most experienced and senior member generally becomes the party leader, therefore always gets unconditional backing of the whole party. Of course, the personality and stature of the leader matters most to garner wholehearted support of the members of the party. However, parties and party leadership is subject to rivalries and therefore, equation and weight of the leader in the party organisation determines the policy-making ability of the leader.

First, the case of leadership of Congress Party during Jawaharlal Nehru and Lal Bahadul Shastri and their pattern of nuclear policy-making is a case in point. Nehru's leadership of the Congress Party and the nation as a whole was unquestioned and unchallenged. In foreign policy and defence matters, Nehru's ideas and policies were considered eventual and there was great support from the Party for all his decisions. Towards the end of his tenure, there was some dissent among the party members on his defence policies, mainly after the Sino-Indian border debacle. But, the Congress Party in every resolution expressed unanimous support to his policies. At the Durgapur Congress of the Party, K.C. Pant, a young party member then, vociferously argued for India acquiring nuclear bombs. But the same resolution came out with a "no-bomb" policy supporting Nehru's vision of nuclear disarmament and peaceful use of nuclear technology.

Undoubtedly, Nehru's personality as a Congress leader and his acumen on foreign and defence affairs was accepted across board. His credential as leader of the Congress Party was never questioned or subject to rivalry. His own scientific temper and orientation towards nuclear technology was reflected in his vision of India endowed with cutting-age scientific technology. Therefore, he kept the nuclear energy portfolio with him. His patronage of Bhabha's research and settling of a country-wide scientific-technical infrastructure was purely manifestation of his own vision and responsibility for leading India towards excellence. Though the Congress Party, since inception has aspired and strived to build modern independent nation, Nehru's ideas and decisions were the guiding force for the Party, especially in foreign policy and nuclear issues. But subsequent leaders of the Party seem not to have such grip over the Party unlike Nehru, therefore, decisions on nuclear issues in subsequent years by other leaders have faced mêlée.

For example, Lal Bahadur Shastri, who succeeded Nehru as leader of the Congress Party and Prime Minister, was a staunch Gandhian and completely against nuclear weapons. Though a disciplined Congress man, he was known to have faced strong competition as the favoured leader of the Party from Indira Gandhi. The leadership vacuum that emerged within the Congress and India at large after Nehru could not be filled up by any such stalwart and of course not by Shastri. So, the equation between Shastri as head of Congress and other members of the Party became unstable. The kind of respect and position Nehru was conferred by the Party members was not the same in case of Shastri for obvious reasons. However, both the Congress leaders have taken important decisions on nuclear matters though in different contexts, where the Congress Party as a variable seems to have played differential role. Nehru's policies on nuclear issue were endorsed by the party and members without any visible dissent.

In case of Lal Bahadur Shastri, his policy not to foreclose India's nuclear weapons option and authorisation of the SNEP was result of intensive pressure from the members of the Congress and opposition parties in the wake of the Chinese nuclear tests. Though important decisions were taken by both the leaders, Nehru's policies were manifestation of his personal motivation, while Shastri's policy was mostly outcome of his compelled responses to the resentment of Party members. In other words, while Nehru's policies were symbolic of his leadership style, Shastri's policies were manifestation of his weak position in the Party and his consequent strategy to manage Party members' resentment. Two distinct factors seem to differentiate the policy-making styles of the two leaders. First, the distinctive leadership styles based on interests and experiences of the leader in a particular issue area. On foreign policy and security (nuclear) matters, Nehru was the unchallenged leader having international repute while Shastri was relatively inward looking. Second is the "setting" that determines differential policies. While Nehru started the journey in the post-Independence period with anxieties of an emerging Asian nation in the Cold War setting, Shastri took over in a more turbulent regional atmosphere—two hostile neighbours with nuclear weapons.

Moreover, the parliamentary system in India started to entrench towards the end of Nehru era and the *orientation towards conflict* of opinions in Prime Ministerial context also started to emerge. It was subject to the ability and power of the Prime Minister, who generally is an influential leader of the party in power, to allow or suppress the conflict. Since parliamentary system is more collective ability of the Prime Minister-to influence disagreement or conflict expressed depends on his own *personality, motivation to lead* and *task orientation*. Therefore, political leaders are more a determining factor than the political parties when the relative position of the leader is strong and influential. Party becomes paramount, when the leader is comparatively less assertive. This generalisation can be tested also in case of other Congress Prime Ministers and their nuclear policy-making.

Other Congress Prime Ministers like Indira Gandhi, Rajiv Gandhi, Narasimha Rao and Manmohan Singh have equally taken *specific nuclear weapon-related decisions, but in specific political contexts*. By the time Indira Gandhi became Prime Minister, the split between "pro-bomb" and "no-bomb" in the Party was wide. Indira Gandhi's rival for the Prime Ministership Morarji Desai, Deputy Prime Minister then, was a staunch supporter of no-bomb policy. Whereas K.C. Pant, as usual, was arguing in favour of bomb. But Mrs Gandhi was more into stabilisation of her leadership in the Congress Party and her government. Therefore, like Shastri, Indira Gandhi also avoided the liabilities of either embracing nuclear weapons or rejecting the option completely, mainly because of her unstable position in the Party. But during her second-term as Prime Minister, Mrs Gandhi had absolute faith and control over her Party. Her equation with Party Presidents like Jagjivan Ram, Shankar Dayal Sharma, and Dev Kanta Borooah was cordial. Moreover, the East Pakistan crisis and her decisive action won her the identity of a 'strong' leader. It is believed that during this time she gave order for the nuclear explosion.

Therefore, the equation between the Prime Minister as a national leader and his stature and position in the party s(he) belongs to is the determining factor in nuclear weapons policy-making in India. This is amply clear in case of Rajiv Gandhi. The Congress Party under the leadership of Rajiv Gandhi won 415 out of total 542 Lok Sabha seats in the 1984 Lok Sabha election. From 1983 to 1985 Rajiv Gandhi was also the President of the Congress Party. His image as a young dynamic leader with the backing of 49 per cent of electorate, Rajiv Gandhi advocated his proposal for eventual and phased elimination of nuclear weapons by the year 2010 in the UN General Assembly. Had his proposal been seriously taken by others, Rajiv Gandhi would have given a different tilt to India's nuclear weapons programme. Realising the difficulty in nuclear disarmament initiative, he constituted a committee (with the suggestion of Admiral R.H. Tahiliani, the then Chiefs of Staff) consisting of APJ Abdul Kalam, R Chidambaram, General K Sunderji, Admiral K.K. Nayyar and Air Marshal Green. The committee produced the report saying a minimum credible deterrent of about 100 warheads can be developed in about seven years and it will cost about Rs 7,000 crore. (Subrahmanyam 2008)

Prime Minister Narasimha Rao and Manmohan Singh are two distinguished Congress leaders, whose policy decisions were equally important. After a long spell of Gandhi-family leadership, Narasimha Rao took over the leadership of the Congress Party (1992-97) and the government. His ability to manage the coalition for full five-years and steer the economic reform is praiseworthy. The strong will among various centrist parties to unite together not to allow the 'fundamentalist' party like BJP to come to power seem to have helped Rao to manage his coalition government. However, by that time the internal divide between pro-bomb and no-bomb had waned, rather the matter was, if any government can test and manage the wrath of the world community. From where Rao got the confidence to dare order for nuclear test in 1995, which was caught by US satellite, is a matter of speculation. In the same way, Manmohan Singh's policies on nuclear matters reveal one important dimension: the equation between the ruling party President and the Prime Minister. The synergy between Sonia Gandhi as Congress Party President and Manmohan Singh as Prime Minister seems to be cordial, especially on nuclear issues, although Sanjay Baru in his book *The Accidental Prime Minister* (2014) says Singh was 'defanged' by the Congress in his second term with Sonia Gandhi deciding on key appointments as he seemed to "surrender" to her and to the allies. Undoubtedly, under the leadership of Sonia Gandhi, the Congress Party seems to have become more cohesive and hierarchical where consent of the "High Command" is the determining factor behind actions of the leader of the government. The decision for Indo-US nuclear deal that tested the strength of Indian parliamentary system and coalition politics actually had the strong backing of cohesive, strictly hierarchical Congress Party, where one find complete absence of dissent on nuclear issues. One can easily mark the *disappearance of internal dissent on nuclear matters in Congress Party* unlike during Nehru and Indira Gandhi-Prime Ministership which had influenced their nuclear policies in more than one way.

In the same manner, the internal dynamics of other political parties, their leaders and policy-making pattern can be examined. From the beginning, the CPI(M) has a no-bomb policy and at no circumstances, there was any duality of opinion among its members and leaders. At no point of time, one could find any dissent among the leaders of the Party like Prakash Singh Badal, D. Raja, Jyoti Basu, Sitaram Yechury, Prakash Karat and Brinda Karat, especially on nuclear weapons issue. On the other side, one could find the same tradition in the BJP where exists no dissent in internal debate for nuclear bomb. Unanimity can be observed among the BJP cadres and at no point of time there was found any dissent. Atal Bihari Bajpayee, L.K Advani, Jaswant Singh, Jaswant Sinha, Sushma Swaraj, Arun Jaitly and Venkaiah Naidu, etc., have one view without doubt. Though Vajpayee took the decision to conduct the nuclear tests in 1998 without taking members into confidence, his policy was not in contrast to any other BJP leaders' or members' views. Therefore, comparing the internal debate on nuclear weapons policy of the three parties, one may find the CPI(M) and BJP are situated at the extreme ends with extreme stance—"no-bomb" and "pro-bomb"—and the Congress Party is situated somewhere in between imbibing both views, though this trend has been changed during later years.

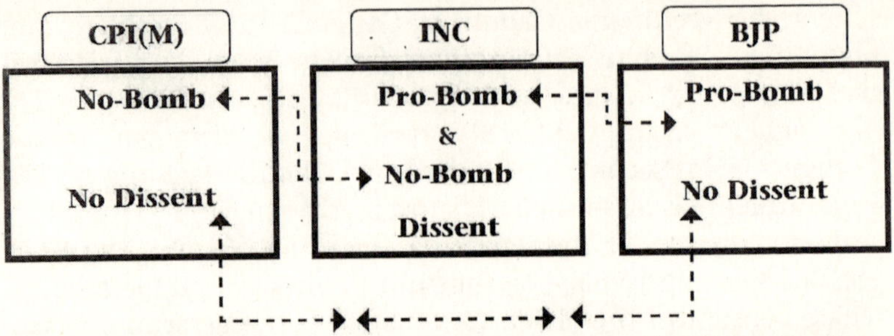

Fig. 1: Earlier Postures of and Equation among the Three Parties

In the subsequent years, this equation among the three parties seems to have changed. While the Congress Party has been settled with "option open" policy and one find the dissolve of no-bomb faction within it, most probably starting from the 1970s, the BJP has maintained its usual unanimous "pro-bomb" policy. So, at the extreme end BJP stood for nuclear bomb posture whereas the CPI(M) stands for the unanimous no-bomb policy. But one common feature of their postures is the respective internal unanimity on the stand—there is no internal dissent on the stand by any of their members. Therefore, the configuration or equation among the three parties on nuclear weapons policy after Pokhran-I look like the figure designed below.

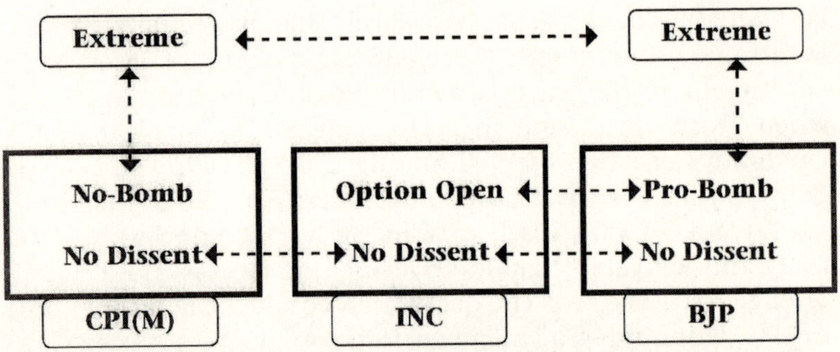

Fig. 2: Post-1974 Postures of and Equation among the Three Parties

In the post-Pokhran II period, the debate over India "should-might-will-can go nuclear" has been stopped and replaced by another debate on what should be the nuclear posture and its policy regarding their use, quantity, command and control structure. In this new debate, the Congress Party position is almost similar to that of the BJP's, whereas the CPI(M) maintains its no-bomb policy as usual. The difference between BJP and Congress Party's nuclear weapons policy is now more of degree, not of kind. The BJP wants to retain India's sovereign right to conduct nuclear tests in future, therefore, criticised the Manmohan Singh Government's for blindly accepting the Indo-US civil nuclear deal that claimed to have the hidden agenda for capping India's strategic programme.

As different Indian political parties have different attitudes towards nuclear weapons, their policy orientation supposed to be different from each other. At various stages of the national politics, the three parties have become part of the government according to their electoral performance. As mentioned earlier, at the national level, while the Congress party has formed government more than any other party, the BJP has formed government only once. The CPI(M) has remained part of different coalition governments only. Beside the three parties, the Janata Party with coalition partners, prominently the Bharatiya Jana Sangh which was vocal about India going nuclear, had formed the government at the centre from 1977 to 1979. Change of governments, mid-term elections, factions, coalition formations, hung-parliaments, etc., are part of parliamentary system which reflect on the changes if any in policies of the incumbent by another successor.

The second assumption that *India's nuclear policy does not change with the change in government and changes despite the same party forms the government* seems valid. It is expected that having different attitude towards nuclear issues, the three political parties must take different policy courses on the same issue. An observation on the evolution of India's nuclear weapon policy reveals that replace of one government by another political party do not necessarily bring changes in nuclear weapon policy. Rather, on many occasions, it is found that India's nuclear policy has changed when the same party came to power again. For example, after Nehru, though Shastri was reluctant to pursue nuclear weapons programme nevertheless kept the option open by saying that "India should not embark on nuclear weapons programme *now.*" The Indira Gandhi government in the initial years did not follow any substantial policy decision on nuclear matters as her main focus was her political consolidation. But during later years of her leadership, she re-looked the nuclear policy and ordered for the Pokhran-I test in 1974.

In 1977, India experienced the first non-Congress government at the centre. Janata Party and its leader Moraji Desai were averse to nuclear weapons and put on hold India's programme but could not completely roll it back. After 1979, when Indira Gandhi returned to power, the nuclear weapon programme was resumed. The same Congress Government under Rajiv Gandhi was prepared to abandon and phased elimination of nuclear weapons provided other nuclear powers were ready to do so. But his successor Narasimha Rao, leading a multi-party coalition, gave order for test preparations. When the BJP came to power, it robustly pursued and carried forward the policy of Narsimha Rao. The CPI(M), known for its nuclear weapons aversion, was a major partner of the Congress-led coalition government headed by Manmohan Singh. However, for quite sometime, it continued threatening to withdraw support till it withdrew support finally on July 9, 2008. However, the CPI(M) never demanded or pursued nuclear weapons aversion policy partnering with the Congress-led UPA government. Rather, it withdrew support accusing Congress Party of acting at the behest of US agenda for India to the detriment of an independent foreign policy and strategic autonomy.

By using an analogy, one may describe India's nuclear weapons endeavour as *a stream, sometimes over-flown and some other time submerged*, but never been dried. Whenever political attention is away or apathetic, the scientific-bureaucratic community (the strategic enclave) had kept the flow alive. There, in fact, no particular date when India's nuclear weapons policy decisions were taken, unlike Pakistan which decided to develop nuclear weapons during the secret meeting in Multan on January 20, 1972 where Zulfikar Ali Bhutto vowed to build nuclear bomb no matter if Pakistan "eat grass or leaves, even go hungry". Therefore, to Ashok Kapur, India's nuclear weapon policy decisions were "ad hoc" in nature which he views as "scientific and political czarism" in India's nuclear policy-making. In the hind side, there thrives an intimate scientific-political interaction. The relationship between the Indian Prime Ministers after Nehru and the leaders of India's atomic energy and space programme has remained intimate and mutually supportive. By and large, this provides the political leaders to exercise their will when they think fit and in turn the scientific community also satisfies its interest by convincing and keeping the political leadership on its side.

Convergence and Divergence

In the preceding chapters, specific issues on India's nuclear weapons policy have been examined on the basis of views of three parties. It is possible that some policy decisions arrived at various stages were ad hoc in nature, but the views expressed or stands taken by different political parties on these specific aspects, more or less, based on respective ideological leanings, principled opinion or on the basis of merit of the occasion. While on the non-proliferation and disarmament aspect, the three parties have almost similar views, on national security vis-à-vis nuclear weapons, the three parties seem to have differential opinions. The evolution process of India's nuclear weapons discourse, therefore, marks intense and prolonged debate over certain issues. The following section intends to compare and analyse the views and policies of the three parties on the issues that have already been discussed in the preceding chapters.

Domestic Politics and Nuclear Weapons Policy-Making: In the second chapter of the study, it is highlighted that nuclear weapon has an "awesome appearance on the political scene". It is also raised that the *political-nuclear interface* is not forthright in a multi-party democracy like India. Sometimes, it is seen how nuclear policy decisions have created ripples in domestic politics and this interface has complicated the political atmosphere as supremacy of parliament and the prerogative of the executive to take initiative are integrated into the system. And the executive remains in power as long as he enjoys the confidence of the members of the parliament. It is to enquire which party has used the nuclear weapons issue how much and in what way.

Though many nuclear policy decisions are taken at different stages, mainly the leaders of Congress and the BJP known to have taken major decisions by virtue of their capacity to form the government. As the CPI(M) has never formed the government at the centre, except remaining as coalition partner, it has never find chance to exercise the prerogative of taking nuclear policy decisions like other parties. Moreover, first, by examining the parties' election manifestos, one would find how these parties have made nuclear issue as a plank in their electoral strategy. Second, by analysing the timing and context of their decisions, one can understand the utility of nuclear issues for their political strategy. In its various deliberations in the initial period after Independence, the Congress Party has mentioned the nuclear issues only in the context of global nuclear disarmament with a global perspective, not specifically for domestic consumption. It seems, nuclear issues have never been factors in domestic political scene aftermath Independence, unlike in the later years, especially after 1962 and more intensively in the post-1964 period when China tested its nuclear devices.

In the post-1962 period, the Congress Party election manifestos mentioned nuclear issues and its opinions under the heading of "International Situation" and no mention of India's own nuclear weapon programme can be found, rather it showed ambivalent posture. It is true that among other parties, the Congress Party held nuclear weapons for India as important, but had always shown ambiguous attitude towards full-fledged nuclear weapons programme. Rather what the Congress Party emphasising implicitly was that, instead of becoming nuclear weapon power, it is necessary to become a technological and economic power first. There were occasional debates in the Parliament on nuclear weapons option, but most of the time it was sidelined on the pretext that the cost of developing them would be enormous and the urgent need for the nation is economic development. Probably, this ambivalent position of Congress gave a sense to the outside world that India finally or at least in the near future would not overtly go nuclear. However, this ambivalent policy of Congress may have served some purpose.

On the other hand, for BJP, nuclear weapons are vital for national power and status. In its strategic thinking, it is not necessary for a country to wait for developing economic and technological power before developing military power, rather the reverse is true: national power comes primarily from military strength. Therefore, BJP followed the policy of "security first, and the rest will follow" policy. In this sense, the BJP follows an "offensive" attitude towards India's nuclear weapons programme and more importantly, it places this argument before the electorate. In its every election manifesto, the BJP has highlighted the necessity of nuclear weapons and its resolve to develop them by appealing the electorate to elect the Party to build India strong.

However, the CPI(M), similar to Congress Party's ambivalence, links the nuclear weapons issue more with global trends and remained critical about India going nuclear. Surprisingly, it remained defensive on China's nuclear weapons programme, therefore, it is often accused of having "double standard" attitude in the domestic political debate. But similar to the Congress Party's economy-first policy, the CPI(M) holds a "security abstinence" and "uplift of working class-first" policy.

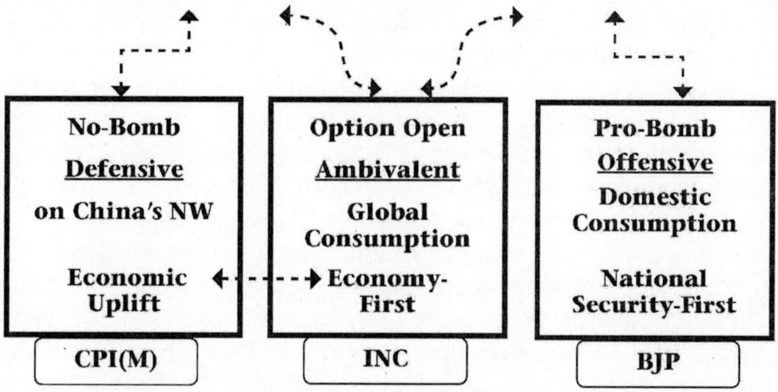

Fig. 3: Position of Three Parties on N Weapons in Domestic Politics.

Then in what way, if any, domestic politics played its part? The four instances where nuclear weapons policy decisions were taken by these three parties can be examined to highlight a trend though not consistent. Lal Bahadur Shastri gave go ahead for the SNEP when his position within the Congress Party was vulnerable but there was relative political stability in the country with Congress Party having largest majority in the Parliament. Indira Gandhi went for Pokhran-I test when her position within the Congress was dominant; though her popularity after the East Pakistan crisis heightened at the national level, the political scene at the centre was not smooth. In 1998, when Vajpayee went for Pokhran-II tests, his position within the BJP was unchallenged and full of admiration. However, during that time, national political situation was severely unstable owing to the absence of clear majority in the legislature. Lastly, when Manmohan Singh went daringly to separate India's strategic nuclear programme from the civilian, mainly for pushing through the civil nuclear cooperation with US, his position within the Congress Party was devoid of dispute and from outside the chemistry between the Party President Sonia Gandhi and him was cordial on nuclear issue. But the national political situation was no better as he was heading the UPA coalition where the CPI(M) was hesitant to go along. So, one may conclude that *when the situation of the leader within the party is stable, but not national politics, nuclear weapons policy decisions are taken* mainly at the initiative of the Prime Minister. In a way, this may have served the purpose to divert national attention from the factional political situation towards a catchy event. Another aspect is the glue attached to nuclear issues that attracts wider audience, therefore, every political faction want to secure a foothold.

The National Security Factor: The issue of national security vis-à-vis nuclear weapons also marks differential opinion among the three parties. In the immediate post-Independence period, national security conception was mainly concentrated on national development, both in economic and technology terms and not purely in defence terms. But 1960s onwards, the Congress Party, though felt the security threats in terms of attack from neighbouring countries, was ambivalent to resort to full-fledged nuclear weapons programme. In 1968, when there was wide-spread apprehension about Pakistan's nuclear programme, Mrs Gandhi discarded the view saying Pakistan is not in a position to make a nuclear bomb. On the China front, the Congress Party was divided into three camps—the "no-bomb posture", "a crash-programme with small nuclear arsenal", and a "steadier, less provocative long-term programme". Though, it is not clear if China was the sole factor in Mrs Gandhi's decision to test in 1974, undoubtedly China's repeated nuclear tests raised anxieties among the Congress Party members. The Congress Party also does not see nuclear threat to India from any nuclear powers outside the region, rather it linked national nuclear security with the larger global nuclear security, thereby emphasising eventual global elimination of nuclear weapons.

Therefore, one may conclude that the Congress Party did not link clearly the imperative of India acquiring nuclear weapons for national security. Rather, the secretive nature of Congress nuclear policy seems to have continued from Indira Gandhi's tenure. For that matter, the Congress maintained a no-bomb posture publicly while inching towards weapons capability covertly. In the aftermath of East Pakistan crisis, though Mrs Gandhi known to have given go ahead for feasibility study of a test, the Congress Party deliberations and public pronouncements maintained a no-bomb posture. So, the Party has never publicly established or drawn the link between national security scenario and the imperative of India acquiring nuclear weapons. Finally, when the BJP declared India as a nuclear weapon state after conducting tests in 1998, the Congress Party has accepted the nuclear weapon status on the pretext that global nuclear disarmament process has failed. This is amply clear from Congress Party President Sonia Gandhi's statement in January 2007 when she said nuclear weapons becoming a "strategic compulsion" for India, "born out of the failure to persuade the world to abolish".

The BJP, on the other hand, links India's nuclear weapons programme directly to security environment and its status as a strong and developed nation. The Party considers threats from Pakistan and China as "real" for which India must develop nuclear arsenal and be ready with optimum defence preparedness. In this respect, the BJP is complete in comparison to the Congress and CPI(M) views. While the Congress and CPI(M) were never considered, nuclear weapons with India would heighten its status as a great nation, the BJP has always vouched with the notion that strong security preparedness is first and all other would follow. Therefore, in BJP's construct, security can be bargained from a platform of strength only and when justice is denied, peace is threatened and security of a nation is at stake, there should be no morality.

For the CPI(M), India's national security is threatened not so much by China or Pakistan as much by the US. The party instead suggests a peaceful settlement of all disputes with China and Pakistan. But the gravest danger to India as seen by CPI(M) is the "imperialist USA" which has military bases all over. Therefore, it demands closer of the Diago Garcia base in the Indian Ocean which harbours nuclear arsenals of USA. Despite this threat perception, the Party does not prescribe India for nuclear weapons. On the other hand, the CPI(M) views the 1998 nuclear tests and the period that followed as "a dangerous new phase in India's external and nuclear policies" for the reason that India will be "more vulnerable to imperialist pressure". Furthermore, it does not subscribe to those who advocate nuclear weapons as a path for India's "great power" status. But, the Party's Polit Bureau press statement brings a new dimension to their stand. The statement says that "India should have an independent nuclear policy" thereby suggest the nuclear cooperation with US is a matter of joining the "empire" as a junior partner.

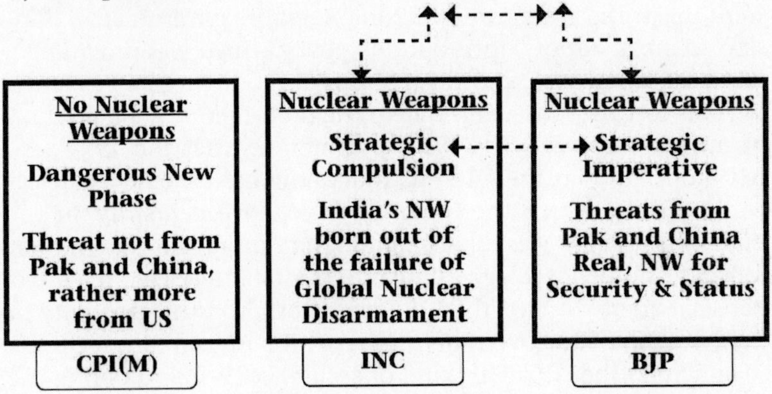

Fig. 4: Three Party Positions on India's Nuclear Weapons Post-1998

In the post-Pokhran II period, the nuclear weapons policy of both the Congress Party and the BJP seem to proximate in the sense that they have acknowledged the necessity of nuclear weapons for India though in different perspectives. While the Congress Party views India's nuclear weapons as "strategic compulsion" and they were born out of the failure of global nuclear disarmament, the BJP finds them as "strategic imperative" to neutralise threats from both Pakistan and China. On the other hand, the CPI(M) continues to adhere to the no-bomb policy and do not consider nuclear weapons as any symbol of great power the way BJP does.

India and the Non-Proliferation Regime: There exists a consensus among the political parties all along not to adhere to the "discriminatory" non-proliferation regime in present form. Each party supports to see India maintaining independence in nuclear policy-making and discard discriminatory treaties. Each party also is in favour of advancing for eventual elimination nuclear weapons through the disarmament process. Rajiv Gandhi's proposal for phased elimination of nuclear weapons leading towards a nuclear weapons-free world at the UN in 1988 has been a referring point for all parties. They are in favour of linking India's approach towards non-proliferation regime to the over-arching goal of the time-bound global elimination of nuclear weapons.

However, inter-party criticism on each other's non-proliferation policy is there. When the BJP-led NDA government expressed "readiness to discuss certain provision" of CTBT after conducting tests in 1998 and declared India as nuclear weapon state, the Congress Party criticised the BJP for "willfully destroying the national consensus on nuclear matters". Even the Congress party went up to the extent of criticising Bajpayee government's decision to break out of "open option" policy which was providing a "recessed deterrence" posture. For this, the Congress Party viewed as India lost the leadership role in the movement for elimination of nuclear weapons. The BJP, for sometime after the 1998 test, felt proper to join the CTBT as India now has become a nuclear weapon state, which the Congress criticised vehemently. In the same way, the BJP was criticising the Narasimha Rao government for successfully not safeguarding India's vital interests in the international arena. In fact, the BJP was doubtful on the capability of the Narsimha Rao government to resist the pressure from the US to adhere to the NPT. This kind of accusation is found during the Indo-US civil nuclear deal negotiations when both the BJP and the

Left parties were accusing the Congress for falling into the trap of the NPT and CTBT through the deal. The civil nuclear deal, in the views of the BJP and Left, is the non-proliferation regime in disguise which actually carries the NPT conditionality of all and CTBT. Therefore, as they view, the deal would impose CTBT-plus obligations on India.

The Congress Party views, though not expressed verbally, the Indo-US civil nuclear deal as a flyover to bypass the NPT and avail benefits of a nuclear weapon state. This stand of Congress is in complete contrast to the other two parties, who consider the deal as non-proliferation trap in disguise.

The CPI(M) links arguments on non-proliferation and test-ban with global nuclear disarmament. However, the difference among the three parties is that, while the BJP and the Congress see the regime discriminatory, the CPI(M) describe it as a tool of "imperialism" and "capitalism" and target the US as the major culprit. Therefore, the Indo-US civil nuclear deal viewed by the party as "real setback" as it would lead to overt possession of nuclear weapons by India but with the mercy of the US which will bargain for signing the CTBT. Among other convergence and divergence between the CPI(M) and other political parties, one distinguishing feature of the Party is that it has maintained a straightforward position all along on India's nuclear discourse: "no nuclear weapons", "no signing of CTBT" and "global nuclear disarmament". Comparatively, other two parties, at certain point of time, some way or the other, have divulged from their original stand which is not the case with CPI(M).

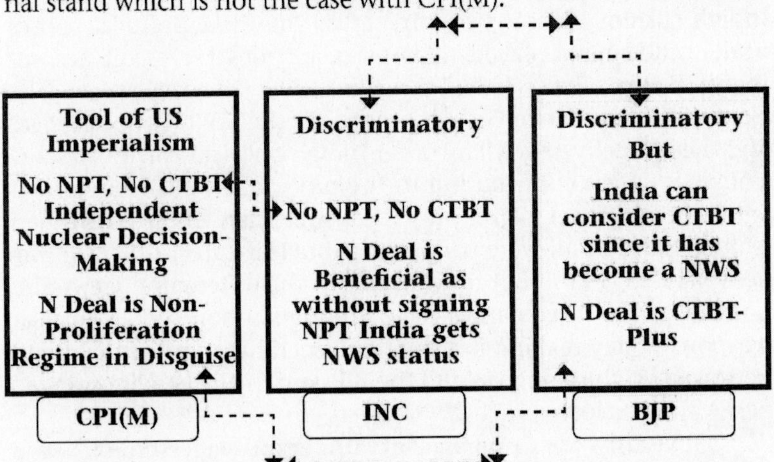

Fig. 5: Views of Three Parties on Nuclear Non-Proliferation Regime

In comparison, the attitudes of parties towards three non-proliferation regime differ only in degree, not of kind. All agree that the regime is discriminatory and India should not accept it in its present form. But one major difference with the CPI(M)'s stand in comparison with other two parties on the role of USA. While it vehemently accuses USA as imperialist power that uses non-proliferation regime as a tool, interestingly, it justified [Soviet] Russia's cooperation with other nuclear weapon powers in mobilising support for the nuclear non-proliferation regime.

Who should be Given Credit, How Much?

India now is a self-proclaimed nuclear weapon state with "second strike" capability based on a "minimum credible deterrence". Undoubtedly, this capability is culmination of series of advertent decisions and relentless scientific efforts that helped *India doing it when it could.* However, for some, it is a political decision; for more knowledgeable persons, it is a technological decision. For a few others, it is an economic precipitation, not a decision! Whatever be the nature of the trigger, this accomplishment has various anchors. The role of political parties and their leaders, especially the three parties taken up in this study, is most determining than others. But as soon as one start counting their steps, one may tend to confront with one difficult question *who should be given credit, and how much?*

It would be fallacious, and extremely difficult, to assign full credit to any single variable that involved in the culmination of India's current nuclear weapon status. The three political parties under study have played their parts and deserve credit accordingly. To Surya Prakash, *India's nuclear bomb has many fathers.* The Congress Party conceived and nurtured the CPI(M) questioned, and the BJP delivered. Many other Indian political parties and factions have their contribution in the process as well. Therefore, it would be irrational to give only the obstetrician whole credit than is due. Rightly, "all were party to the nuclear gatecrash" (*The Pioneer,* May 25, 1998). But to what extent the differential views and policies of the three parties have impinged upon India's nuclear weapons policy-making is a puzzle. Generally, most of the credit bestowed on the Congress and the BJP, and the CPI(M) is criticised being anti-nuclear.

Obviously, the Congress Party under the leadership of Nehru conceived the nuclear policy of India and successive Congress leaders nurtured it though conditioned by the turns and twists of the situation. Sometimes, the adverse circumstances did not allow the Congress government and its leaders to cross the Rubicon; other time, its own inhibitions did not permit. Prior to the 1998 nuclear tests, successive Prime Ministers had kept their feet on the brake pedal, even as the strategic enclave pressed the accelerator. Conflicting interests and considerations, many of them domestic, were responsible for the self-restraint. This process got settled in an ambiguous posture for quite some time, that seemed appropriate. So long as the Congress Party had control of the national polity, its traditional preference for nuclear ambiguity automatically became India's national policy. It is now well known that the Congress government came close to changing that posture several times after 1992, at least as far as testing was concerned. (Tellis 2001: 101)

The BJP, remaining outside the government, promised to exercise nuclear weapons option and kept the promise after forming government by daringly testing in 1998, which previous leaders could not succeed. However, India's decision to acquire nuclear weapons is not a function that may be only associated and specifically with the BJP. The BJP's decision to pursue nuclear capability is, in a way, a continuation of similar nuclear options considered by previous Indian governments. It is true, as long as the nuclear issue was hanging fire, each new Prime Minister felt compelled to reconsider the subject *de novo*. (Karnad 2002: 268)

On the other side, the CPI(M), if positively interpreted, while giving different taste to the nuclear debate, wished a "no-nuclear weapons" posture for India. By providing the critic on the policies of other parties' and leaders', it made the domestic nuclear weapons debate more democratic.

Political leaders have played leading roles but their preferences were filtered through the screen of the party they belonged to. However, India's nuclear policy cannot be explained without recognising the central role of many individuals. (Perkovich 2002: 20) Since Nehru's time, Indian policy-making has relied on personality and other unpredictable factors. Though considerable strategic thinking behind all nuclear policy decisions were always made, all Indian political leaders, especially those who have tried to lay their hand on the nuclear option seem to be aware of the Napoleonic strategic policy-making philosophy: every policy decision is "two-thirds analysis, and one-third leap in the dark", but they tried their best to ensure that any leap on them should not land in the dark. Probably that is the reason why India's nuclear weapons trajectory took a longer road and wider spectrum.

The Way Forward

Understanding the articulation process of India's nuclear weapons policy-making in the past by the mainstream political parties is the goal of this study. Many would claim the past has little to tell about the future nuclear policy and the probable trends. How these parties would articulate the stand on nuclear issues in future is an intriguing subject. By observing the past pattern, one can extrapolate the leadership style, equation of the leader in the party he belongs to, pattern of their decision-making today to envisage how they would formulate their views in the future.

By the time the manuscript was getting ready, the 16th Lok Sabha election was in full swing. The three parties brought out their election manifestos and BJP's manifesto caught the media attention for pledging for an "Independent Strategic Nuclear Programme", specifically by studying in detail the nuclear doctrine, and "revise and update it, to make it relevant to challenges of current times." (*BJP Election Manifesto 2014*: 39) While the Congress Party without touching the nuclear weapons issue directly promised for "a comprehensive security doctrine that combines conventional and strategic measures" ("Your Voice Our Pledge", *Lok Sabha Elections 2014 Manifesto*: 46), the CPI(M) has promised to provide"parliamentary sanction for moratorium on testing and strive for a denuclearised environment in South Asia" and removal of nuclear weapons from the US military base in Diego Garcia in the Indian Ocean." [*CPI-M Manifesto for the 16th Lok Sabha Elections, 2014*: 19]

Comparatively, the BJP and the CPI(M) have promised more than the Congress Party in regard to India's nuclear weapons policy and strategy. However, what would constitute the Congress Party's idea of "a comprehensive security doctrine" for India once it comes to power is subject to anybody's guess. In retrospect, how the Congress-led UPA government nurtured India's nuclear deterrent and strategy for the last one decade? Have the successive Congress Party government really *frittered away* the strategic gains acquired by India during Vajpayee regime on nuclear programme, as the BJP accused in its manifesto? Will BJP revise India's

NFU policy? Will CPI(M) be able to de-nuclearise South Asia and remove nuclear weapons from Diego Garcia?

Two weeks before the poll, Prime Minister Manmohan Singh in an international seminar organised by IDSA and Indian Pugwash Society in New Delhi said that "more and more voices are speaking out today that the sole function of nuclear weapons, while they exist, should be to deter a nuclear attack. If all states possessing nuclear weapons recognise that this is so and are prepared to declare it, we can quickly move to the establishment of a global no-first-use norm." (Inaugural Address by Dr Manmohan Singh, April 2, 2014) In clarification to the hype of BJP revising India's nuclear doctrine, party president, Rajnath Singh has reportedly said that "no review of NFU was planned". The BJP's Prime Ministerial candidate Narendra Modi in a TV interview has also clarified that if he comes to power he would not alter the doctrine that Vajpayee had laid down, especially the 'no first use' posture. If this is to be believed, BJP's promise of revising and updating India's nuclear doctrine can be equated with Congress promise for a new "comprehensive security doctrine". For that matter, the BJP and Congress views on India's nuclear strategy till date is a matter of degree, not of kind. And, CPI(M) stand on these issues today mark no difference from earlier stand.

However, BJP's allegation on Congress for frittering away the strategic gains India accrued during Vajpayee regime is debatable. The crowning achievement during the one decade Congress rule was the Indo-US nuclear deal that saw India break free from nuclear apartheid state to nuclear multi-aligned country. This was achieved without compromising India's strategic nuclear capability. It passed a stringent nuclear liability Bill in Parliament. On the strategic front, during this period India's nuclear delivery capability being extended to China with the range of Agni missile crossing 5,000 km. The third leg of India's nuclear deterrent is getting ready with Arihant as India's first indigenously-built nuclear-powered submarine with Submarine Launched Ballistic Missile (SLBMs). The BMD and MIRV programme has been advanced. Considering all these, the report card of UPA on strategic matters seems fairly strong and India's current missile modernisation, viewed by Western scholars, going beyond the minimum credible deterrence. (Krepon 2014; Kristensen 2013) Therefore, the BJP's remark about the Congress' lack of performance on the nuclear weapons issue is rather shortsighted, says Chengappa. In fact, Vajpayee would not have been able to order the 1998 nuclear tests just months after his second tenure had the previous Congress-led government not kept India's nuclear option in a state of readiness. In retrospect, BJP's main allegation against the Indo-US nuclear deal was that it circumscribed India's sovereign right to conduct further nuclear tests if situation warrants. It is the BJP-led NDA government who went for a self-imposed moratorium. But the nuclear deal, in BJP's view, has curtailed India's sovereign right to test perpetually coming under US pressure and this is probably what BJP indicates when its 2014 Manifesto said Congress has "frittered away" India's strategic gain during Vajpayee regime.

Nevertheless, with the rhetoric of revising India's nuclear doctrine in its 2014 Election Manifesto, the BJP had raised an unwarranted debate with national, regional and international repercussions. There is certainly scope to fine-tune India's nuclear deterrent to keep it "credible" given the fast changing regional security environment. Especially, with the introduction of TNWs by Pakistan, the nuclear threshold in South Asian has been lowered drastically. India has to take a stock of the new security environment and readjust, if required, its nuclear strategy in the foreseeable future. That is a valid exercise for any new government, but political parties should avoid chest-thumping on this critical issue before really doing anything substantial on the ground. (Chengappa 2014)

Looking the way forward, one may argue that a revision of India's nuclear doctrine is overdue. So far, the debate over the expediency of the doctrine in its current shape has been confided to the academic circles in Delhi. Even Western scholars view India's doctrine in vogue is similar to the US doctrine of massive retaliation during 1950s. Since the debate has surfaced in the political circles now with the BJP's manifesto advocating for a second thought on it, one can expect that the doctrine will go through an official scrutiny sooner or later. The NSAB that formulated the draft in 1999 is the appropriate forum to initiate such a scrutiny after obtaining a political authorisation. This would initiate a nation-wide political as well as strategic debate regarding the contours of India's new nuclear doctrine.

Three plausible outcome can be envisaged at this juncture. First, there may not be any visible altercation in the provisions of the doctrine keeping in mind its wide acceptability today and India's aspiration for NSG membership in the future. Second, as a logical evolution, India would look for a doctrine which can provide"flexible response" options "allowing policy makers every possibility in a crisis---pre-emptive strike, counter-force and counter---value targeting, even assured destruction through massive retaliation." (Shukla 2014) This option is easy said than done. Equating BJP's nuclear test decision in 1998 with its urge to revise the doctrine today would be misleading. Most probably, BJP after coming to power may authorise the NSAB to debate on alternative doctrinal options and do nothing thereafter. Third, by going extra mile in the Indo-US strategic partnership and the civil nuclear deal, the BJP may bargain for reserving India's right to further test with assurance of not exercising the right. This would be equally difficult an option to retain. Last but not the least, the future contours of India's nuclear deterrent would rest on the stature and position/equation of the future Prime Minister with the leader of the party and party members he belongs to.

APPENDIX—1

Draft Report of National Security Advisory Board on Indian Nuclear Doctrine

August 17, 1999

1. Preamble

1. The use of nuclear weapons in particular as well as other weapons of mass destruction constitutes the gravest threat to humanity and to peace and stability in the international system. Unlike the other two categories of weapons of mass destruction, biological and chemical weapons which have been outlawed by international treaties, nuclear weapons remain instruments for national and collective security, the possession of which on a selective basis has been sought to be legitimised through permanent extension of the Nuclear Non-proliferation Treaty (NPT) in May 1995. Nuclear weapon states have asserted that they will continue to rely on nuclear weapons with some of them adopting policies to use them even in a non-nuclear context. These developments amount to virtual abandonment of nuclear disarmament. This is a serious setback to the struggle of the international community to abolish weapons of mass destruction.

2. India's primary objective is to achieve economic, political, social, scientific and technological development within a peaceful and democratic framework. This requires an environment of durable peace and insurance against potential risks to peace and stability. It will be India's endeavour to proceed towards this overall objective in cooperation with the global democratic trends and to play a constructive role in advancing the international system toward a just, peaceful and equitable order.
3. Autonomy of decision making in the developmental process and in strategic matters is an inalienable democratic right of the Indian people. India will strenuously guard this right in a world where nuclear weapons for a select few are sought to be legitimised for an indefinite future, and where there is growing complexity and frequency in the use of force for political purposes.
4. India's security is an integral component of its development process. India continuously aims at promoting an ever-expanding area of peace and stability around it so that developmental priorities can be pursued without disruption.
5. However, the very existence of offensive doctrine pertaining to the first use of nuclear weapons and the insistence of some nuclear weapons states on the legitimacy of their use even against non-nuclear weapon countries constitute a threat to peace, stability and sovereignty of states.
6. This document outlines the broad principles for the development, deployment and employment of India's nuclear forces. Details of policy and strategy concerning force structures, deployment and employment of nuclear forces will flow from this framework and will be laid down separately and kept under constant review.

2. Objectives

1. In the absence of global nuclear disarmament India's strategic interests require effective, credible nuclear deterrence and adequate retaliatory capability should deterrence fail. This is consistent with the UN Charter, which sanctions the right of self-defence.
2. The requirements of deterrence should be carefully weighed in the design of Indian nuclear forces and in the

strategy to provide for a level of capability consistent with maximum credibility, survivability, effectiveness, safety and security.

3. India shall pursue a doctrine of credible minimum nuclear deterrence. In this policy of "retaliation only", the survivability of our arsenal is critical. This is a dynamic concept related to the strategic environment, technological imperatives and the needs of national security. The actual size components, deployment and employment of nuclear forces will be decided in the light of these factors. India's peace time posture aims at convincing any potential aggressor that: (a) any threat of use of nuclear weapons against India shall invoke measures to counter the threat: and (b) any nuclear attack on India and its forces shall result in punitive retaliation with nuclear weapons to inflict damage unacceptable to the aggressor.
4. The fundamental purpose of Indian nuclear weapons is to deter the use and threat of use of nuclear weapons by any State or entity against India and its forces. India will not be the first to initiate a nuclear strike, but will respond with punitive retaliation should deterrence fail.
5. India will not resort to the use or threat of use of nuclear weapons against States which do not possess nuclear weapons, or are not aligned with nuclear weapon powers.
6. Deterrence requires that India maintain:
   (a) Sufficient, survivable and operationally prepared nuclear forces,
   (b) a robust command and control system,
   (c) effective intelligence and early warning capabilities, and
   (d) comprehensive planning and training for operations in line with the strategy, and
   (e) the will to employ nuclear forces and weapons

7. Highly effective conventional military capabilities shall be maintained to raise the threshold of outbreak both of conventional military conflict as well as that of threat or use of nuclear weapons.

3. Nuclear Forces

1. India's nuclear forces will be effective, enduring, diverse, flexible, and responsive to the requirements in accordance with the concept of credible minimum deterrence. These

forces will be based on a triad of aircraft, mobile land-based missiles and sea-based assets in keeping with the objectives outlined above. Survivability of the forces will be enhanced by a combination of multiple redundant systems, mobility, dispersion and deception.

2. The doctrine envisages assured capability to shift from peacetime deployment to fully employable forces in the shortest possible time, and the ability to retaliate effectively even in a case of significant degradation by hostile strikes.

4. Credibility and Survivability

The following principles are central to India's nuclear deterrent:

1. Credibility: Any adversary must know that India can and will retaliate with sufficient nuclear weapons to inflict destruction and punishment that the aggressor will find unacceptable if nuclear weapons are used against India and its forces.
2. Effectiveness: The efficacy of India's nuclear deterrent be maximised through synergy among all elements involving reliability, timeliness, accuracy and weight of the attack.
3. Survivability:

   I. India's nuclear forces and their command and control shall be organised for very high survivability against surprise attacks and for rapid punitive response. They shall be designed and deployed to ensure survival against a first strike and to endure repetitive attrition attempts with adequate retaliatory capabilities for a punishing strike which would be unacceptable to the aggressor.

   II. Procedures for the continuity of nuclear command and control shall ensure a continuing capability to effectively employ nuclear weapons.

5. Command and Control

1. Nuclear weapons shall be tightly controlled and released for use at the highest political level. The authority to release nuclear weapons for use resides in the person of the Prime Minister of India, or the designated successor(s).
2. An effective and survivable command and control system with requisite flexibility and responsiveness shall be in place. An integrated operational plan, or a series of sequen-

tial plans, predicated on strategic objectives and a targetting policy shall form part of the system.

3. For effective employment the unity of command and control of nuclear forces including dual capable delivery systems shall be ensured.
4. The survivability of the nuclear arsenal and effective command, control, communications, computing, intelligence and information (C412) systems shall be assured.
5. The Indian defence forces shall be in a position to, execute operations in an NBC environment with minimal degradation.
6. Space based and other assets shall be created to provide early warning, communications, damage/detonation assessment.

6. Security and Safety

1. Security: Extraordinary precautions shall be taken to ensure that nuclear weapons, their manufacture, transportation and storage are fully guarded against possible theft, loss, sabotage, damage or unauthorised access or use.
2. Safety is an absolute requirement and tamper proof procedures and systems shall be instituted to ensure that unauthorised or inadvertent activation/use of nuclear weapons does not take place and risks of accident are avoided.
3. Disaster control: India shall develop an appropriate disaster control system capable of handling the unique requirements of potential incidents involving nuclear weapons and materials.

7. Research and Development

1. India should step up efforts in research and development to keep up with technological advances in this field.
2. While India is committed to maintain the deployment of a deterrent which is both minimum and credible, it will not accept any restraints on building its R&D capability.

8. Disarmament and Arms Control

1. Global, verifiable and non-discriminatory nuclear disarmament is a national security objective. India shall continue its efforts to achieve the goal of a nuclear weapon-free world at an early date.

2. Since no-first use of nuclear weapons is India's basic commitment, every effort shall be made to persuade other States possessing nuclear weapons to join an international treaty banning first use.
3. Having provided unqualified negative security assurances, India shall work for internationally binding unconditional negative security assurances by nuclear weapon states to non-nuclear weapon states.
4. Nuclear arms control measures shall be sought as part of national security policy to reduce potential threats and to protect our own capability and its effectiveness.
5. In view of the very high destructive potential of nuclear weapons, appropriate nuclear risk reduction and confidence building measures shall be sought, negotiated and instituted.

Source: *Ministry of External Affairs, India.*

APPENDIX—2

Cabinet Committee on Security Reviews Progress in Operationalizing India's Nuclear Doctrine

The Cabinet Committee on Security (CCS) met today to review the progress in operationalizing of India's nuclear doctrine. The Committee decided that the following information, regarding the nuclear doctrine and operational arrangements governing India's nuclear assets, should be shared with the public.

2. India's nuclear doctrine can be summarized as follows:

(i) Building and maintaining a credible minimum deterrent;

(ii) A posture of "No First Use": nuclear weapons will only be used in retaliation against a nuclear attack on Indian territory or on Indian forces anywhere;

(iii) Nuclear retaliation to a first strike will be massive and designed to inflict unacceptable damage.

(iv) Nuclear retaliatory attacks can only be authorised by the civilian political leadership through the Nuclear Command Authority.

(v) Non-use of nuclear weapons against non-nuclear weapon states;

(vi) However, in the event of a major attack against India, or Indian forces anywhere, by biological or chemical weapons, India will retain the option of retaliating with nuclear weapons;

(vii) A continuance of strict controls on export of nuclear and missile related materials and technologies, participation in the Fissile Material Cut-off Treaty negotiations, and continued observance of the moratorium on nuclear tests.

(viii) Continued commitment to the goal of a nuclear weapon free world, through global, verifiable and non-discriminatory nuclear disarmament.

3. The Nuclear Command Authority comprises a Political Council and an Executive Council. The Political Council is chaired by the Prime Minister. It is the sole body which can authorize the use of nuclear weapons.

4. The Executive Council is chaired by the National Security Advisor. It provides inputs for decision making by the Nuclear Command Authority and executes the directives given to it by the Political Council.

5. The CCS reviewed the existing command and control structures, the state of readiness, the targetting strategy for a retaliatory attack, and operating procedures for various stages of alert and launch. The Committee expressed satisfaction with the overall preparedness. The CCS approved the appointment of a Commander-in-Chief, Strategic Forces Command, to manage and administer all Strategic Forces.

6. The CCS also reviewed and approved the arrangements for alternate chains of command for retaliatory nuclear strikes in all eventualities.

Source:*http://pib.nic.in/archieve/lreleng/lyr2003/rjan2003/04012003/r040120033.html*

Bibliography

Abraham, Itty., *"Towards a Reflective South Asian Security Studies"*, in South Asia Approaches the Millennium, ed. Marvin G. Weinbaum and Chetan Kumar Boulder, Colo.: Westview Press. 1998

___________ (1998) *The Making of the Indian Bomb: Science Secrecy and the Postcolonial State*, London: Zed Books.

Acharya, Alka, *"India-China Relations: Beyond the Bilateral"*, Economic and Political Weekly, Vol. 40, No. 14 (April 2–8, 2005), pp. 1421–1424.

Adeney, Katharine, Lawrence Sáez, *Coalition politics and Hindu nationalism*, Routledge, 2005

Advani, L.K., "Nuclear Swaraj is in Jeopardy", *Unfair Deal*, BJP Publication No. E/16/2006.

Ahmar, Moonis. ed. (2001) *The CTBT debate in Pakistan*, Har-Anand Publications Pvt. Ltd. New Delhi, 2001.

AICC Political (Omnibus) Resolution, Nov 17, 2007, New Delhi.

AICC Resolution, "Disarmament and Discontinuance of Nuclear and Thermo-Nuclear Weapons Tests, Hyderabad, Oct 24–26, 1958.

AICC Resolution, "International Affairs", Bangalore, January 16–17, 1960.

AICC Resolution, "International Affairs", Bombay June 2–3, 1956.

AICC Resolution, "United States Military Aid To Pakistan", Kalyani, Jan 20–29, 1954.

AICC Resolution, 79th session, Tirupati, April 14–16, 1992.

AICC Resolution, Bangalore Session, March 17–18, 2001.

AICC Resolution, New Delhi Session, June 10–11, 1994.

AICC Resolution, Surajkund Session, March 26–27, 1993.

Alberts, David S. and Daniel S. Papp, (ed.) *Information Age Anthology: The Information Age Military*, Vol. III, C4ISR Cooperative Research Programme (CCRP) Publication Series, March 2001.

Albright, David. (1994) "South Africa and the Affordable Bomb", *The Bulletin of the Atomic Scientists*, July/August 1994, Vol. 50, No. 4, pp. 37–47.

Albright, David and Mark Hibbs, "India's Silent Bomb", *The Bulletin of Atomic Scientists*, September 1992, pp. 27–30.

Alexander, Kristian P., "The Impact of Think Tanks on US Foreign Policy: Examining the Case of Iran and Nuclear Proliferation", paper presented at the annual meeting of the International Studies Association, Town and Country Resort and Convention Center, San Diego, California, USA, available at: http://www.allacademic.com/meta/p98633_index.html

Ali, Tariq, *The Nehru and the Gandhis: An Indian Dynasty*, London: Picador, 1985.

All India Congress Committee "Resolution on Political Situation", *Congress Marches Ahead*-May *10*, 1974.

All Parties Conference 1928. Report of the Committee appointed by the conference to determine the principles of the Constitution for India, All India Congress Committee, 12–13, Allahabad, 1928.

All Set for Tashkent", *People's Democracy*, January 2, 1966.

Allingham, Michael. (2002) *Choice Theory: A Very Short Introduction*, Oxford University Press.

Allison, Graham and Philip Zelikov (2004) "Essence of Decision: Explaining the Cuban Missile Crisis", in Robert K. Yin edited *The Case Study: An Anthology*, UK: Sage.

Allison, Graham T., "Nuclear Weapons Congress", in Graham T Allison et al, eds. *A Primer for the Nuclear Age,* CSIA Occasional Paper Series, University Press of America Inc. 1990.

Allison, Graham T., Albert Carnesale, Joseph S. Nye, Jr., (1985) *Hawks, Doves, and Owls: An Agenda for Avoiding Nuclear War*, New York: W.W. Norton & Company.

____________ (1971) *Essence of Decision: Explaining the Cuban Missile Crisis*, Little, Brown, Boston.

Almond, *Comparative Politics Today: A World View*, Pearson Education India, 2003.

Anand, Vinod, "Management of Defence: Towards an Integrated and Joint Vision", *Strategic Analysis*, February 2001, Vol. XXIV No. 11, pp. 1973–1987.

Anderson, Robert S., *Nucleus and Nation: Scientists, International Networks, and Power in India*, Chicago: University of Chicago Press, 2010.

Appadorai, A. and M.S. Rajan (1985) *India's Foreign Policy and Relations*, New Delhi: South Asian Publishers Private), 1985.

Arnett, Eric. (1998) 'Norms and Nuclear Proliferation: Sweden's Lessons for Assessing Iran', *The Non-proliferation Review*, Winter, pp. 32–43, http://cns.miis.edu/pubs/npr/vol05/52/arnett52.pdf

__________, *Nuclear Weapons and Arms Control in South Asia after the Test Ban*, Oxford University Press, 1998.

Art, Robert J., Bureaucratic Politics and American foreign policy: A Critique, *Political Science*, Vol. 4, pp. 467–90.

Asaro, Peter M., "Transforming society by transforming technology: the science and politics of participatory design", *Accounting Management and Information Technology*, 10 (2000), pp. 257–290. http://www.peterasaro.org/writing/Asaro%20PD.pdf

Bajpai, Kanti P., "The BJP and the Bomb", in Scott Douglas Sagan edited *Inside Nuclear South Asia*, Stanford University Press, pp. 25–55, 2009.

____________ (2006), "The BJP, Domestic Politics in India, and the Bomb", paper presented at the seminar organised by School of International Studies, Jawaharlal Nehru University on Asian Politics: Implications on Security and Foreign Policy, on March 6–7.

Bandhu, Deep Chand, *History of Indian National Congress, 1885-2002*, Gyan Publishing House, 2003

Banerjee, Sivadas (1967), "The Communist Split", in M. Pattabhiram (ed.) *General Elections in India*, New Delhi, pp. 83–88.

____________ (1966) "Unleashing New Forces is Main Hope of Left CPI", *The Statesman* (Calcutta), 2 December.

UNESCO (2004) Basic Texts, Constitution of the United Nations Educational, Scientific and Cultural Organisation, Paris, [Online: web] Accessed on 10 October 2007, URL: http://unesdoc.unesco.org/images/0013/001337/133729e.pdf#page=7

Basrur, Rajesh M. "*Minimum Deterrence and India Pakistan Nuclear Dialogue: Case Study on India*", LNCV Publications, 2006.

____________ (2001) "Nuclear Weapons and Indian Strategic Culture", *Journal of Peace Research*, Vol. 38, No. 2, March, pp. 181–98.

____________ "India's Nuclear Security: Strategic Culture and Doctrine", http://www.pircenter.org/data/news/basrur.pdf, accessed on June 13, 2011.

Basu, Jyoti., "Challenges of the 21st Century", Nehru Memorial Lecture 1998, *The Peoples' Democracy*, Issue No. 45 and 46, 1998.

________, *Documents of the communist movement in India*, Volume 6, National Book Agency, 1997.

Baxter, Craig, *Government and politics in South Asia*, Westview Press, 1993.

Beaton, Leonard. and John Madox, *The Spread of Nuclear Weapons*, Chatto and Windus, 1962.

____________ (1972) *The Reform of Power*, New York: Viking Press.

Beaufre, Andre. (1965) *Deterrence and Strategy*, trans. by R.H. Barry, London: Faber and Faber.

Bell, Chad E. (2000) "India: The Party System from 1963 to 2000", August, [Online: web] Accessed on Feb 22, 2009, URL: http://janda.org/ICPP/ICPP2000/Countries/0-AngloAmerica/08-India/India%201963-2000.htm

Berkes, Ross N. and Mohinder S. Bedi, *The Diplomacy of India*, Stanford, 1958.

Bharatiya Jana Sangh Party Documents, Vol. 5, Bharatiya Jana Sangh Central Office, New Delhi, 1973.

"Bharatiya Janata Stand", *Times of India*, January 20, 1987.

Bhatia, Shyam (1979) *India's Nuclear Bomb*, Ghaziabad: Vikas Publishing House Pvt. Ltd.

Bhatt, Sheela, "Why Advani backed the N-deal", http://www.rediff.com/news/2007/aug/27sheela.htm, August 27, 2007.

Bhushan, K., and G. Katyal, *A.P.J. Abdul Kalam: The Visionary of India*, APH Publishing, 2002.

Bidwai, Praful and Achin Vanaik, "A very political bomb", *The Bulletin of the Atomic Scientists*, 1998.

Bidwai, Praful and Achin Vanaik, *"After the CTB... India's Intentions"*, *The Bulletin of Atomic Scientists*, March-April 1997, pp. 49–50.

Birla Institute for Scientific Research (1982) *India and the Atom*, New Delhi: Allied Publishers Private Ltd.

Biswas, Palash, "Alliance Adultery" in *Troubled Galaxy Destroyed Dreams*, July 12, 2008, URL: http://www.merinews.com/article/indo-us-nuclear-deal-and-coalition-politics/136422.shtml

BJP Election Manifesto 1991

BJP Election Manifesto, 1996.

BJP Resolution, National Executive Meeting, April 23,1981.

BJP Resolutions, National Executive Meeting, Ahmedabad, March 31–1–2 April 1984.

BJP, "Integral Humanism", [Online: web] Accessed on Jan 26, 2008, URL: http://www.bjp.org/content/view/444/396/

BJP, Debate in Parliament (2006) *Indo-US Nuke Deal: Unfair Deal,* Publication No. E/16/2006, New Delhi.

BJP, *Indo-US nuclear deal: Why does BJP Oppose It?,* Bharatiya Janata Party, 2008

BJP, *Vision Document 2004,* [Online: web] Accessed on Jan 26, 2008, URL: http://www.bjp.org/content/view/448/425/

BJP *Election Manifesto 2014, Ek Bharat Shreshtha Bharat,* New Delhi

BJS CWC Resolution, March 22, 1968, Bhopal

BJS Party Documents, *Resolution on Defence and External Affairs,* Vol. 3, 1973.

BJS Party Documents, Vol. 3, Resolutions on Defence and External Affairs, BJS Central Office, New Delhi, 1973.

BJS Resolution No. 3, Bharatiya Kary Samiti, Dec. 4–6, 1964.

Bobb, Dilip. (1994) "A Quiet Triumph", *India Today,* June 15, 1994.

Borgohain, Rooplekha. (1982) *The Indian National Congress: A Study of its Decision-Making Process (1947-55),* New Delhi: Intellectual Publishing House.

Born, Hans. (2007) National Governance of Nuclear Weapons: Opportunities and Constrants, Policy Paper – No. 15, Geneva Centre for the Democratic Control of Armed Forces (DCAF).

Bose, Deb Kumar. (1985) "India's Options in Nuclear World", *Economic and Political Weekly,* September 21.

Bracken, Paul. (1999) *Fire in the East: The Rise of Asian Military Power and the Second Nuclear Age,* New York: Harper Collins.

Brass, Paul. (1990) *Politics of India Since Independence,* Cambridge, UK: Cambridge University Press.

Brown, Michael E., *America's strategic choices,* MIT Press, 2000.

Butler, Nicola and Mark Bromley, *Secrecy and Dependence: The UK Trident System.*

Buzan, Barry., Charles Jones, and Richard Little, eds., *The Logic of Anarchy: Neo-realism to Structural Realism,* New York: Columbia University Press, 1993.

_____________ (1991) *People, States and Fear: An Agenda for International Security Studies in the Post-Cold War Era,* 2nd edition, Harvester Wheatsheaf.

Buzzard, Anthony, "On Limiting Atomic War", *Bulletin of Atomic Scientists*, pp. 216-22, 1957.

Calogero, Francesco. (1999) "Some Remarks on the Indian Draft Nuclear Doctrine", UNESCO, LNCV and USPID-Nuclearisation of South Asia, 20–22 May, City Hall, Como, Physics Department, University of Rome "La Sapienza" and Pugwash Office, ROMA (Italy), [Online: web] Accessed on June 12, 2010, URL: http://www.mi.infn.it/~landnet/NSA/calogero.pdf

Campbell, Kurt M., Robert J. Einhorn, Mitchell Reiss, "*The Nuclear Tipping Point: Why States Reconsider Their Nuclear Choices*", Brookings Institution Press, 2004.

Caul, Miki L and Mark M. Gray, "*From Platform Declarations to Policy Outcome: Changing Party Profiles and Partisan Influence over Policy*", in Russell J. Dalton and Martin P. Wattenberg edited *Parties without Partisans: Political Change in Advanced Industrial Democracies*, Comparative Politics, March 14, 2002, pp. 208–37.

Chakma, Bhumitra, "*Toward Pokhran II: Explaining India's Nuclearisation Process*" Modern Asian Studies, CUP 39:1:189–236, 2005.

Chakravartty, N., *Mainstream*, Volume 37, Issues 1–26, 1998.

Chamberlain, Nigel. Nicola Butler, Dave Andrews (2004) 'US-UK Nuclear Weapons Collaboration under the Mutual Defence Agreement: Shining a Torch on the Darker Recesses of the 'Special Relationship', British American Security Information Council (BASIC), June.

Chand, Attar, *Nuclear policy and national security*, Mittal Publications, 1993.

Chand, Manish (2008) 'Brajesh Mishra, Pakistan prime drivers behind 1998 n-tests', *The Indian News*, May 7, http://www.thaindian.com/newsportal/uncategorised/brajesh-mishra-pakistan-prime-drivers-behind-1998-n-tests_10046146.html, accessed on Aug 20, 2008.

Chari, P.R. (2000) "India's Nuclear Doctrine: The Confused Ambitions", *The Non-proliferation Review*, Fall/Winter, pp. 123–35.

Chaube, S.K., "*Ideology and Politics in India*", in S.K. Chaube and Susheela Kaushik (eds.) Indian Democracy at the Turn of the

Century, New Delhi: Kanishka Publishers and Distributors, 1999.

Chaulia, S.S., "*BJP, India's Foreign Policy and the "Realist Alternative"* to the Nehruvian Tradition", *International Politics*, Vol. 39, Number 2, June, pp. 215–234, 2002.

Chawla, Anil. (2004) "The Crisis of Ideology in Indian Politics", 26 July, http://www.samarthbharat.com/ideologycrisis.htm, accessed on Aug 20, 2008

Chawla, Prabhu, "India is Now A Weapons State", Interview with Atal Bihari Vajpayee, *India Today*, 1998, available at: URL: http://www.fas.org/news/india/1998/05/980518-interview.htm

Chellaney, Brahma. (2007) "Don't Nuke The Facts", *The Times of India*, January 9 2007.

__________, "Nuclear Tests Boost Indians' National Pride", *The Washington Times*, May 16, 1998.

Chengappa, Raj. (2000) *Weapons of Peace: The Secret Story of India's Quest to be a Nuclear Power*, New Delhi: HarperCollins.

__________, "Nuclear Doctrine not Matter for Fiddling", http://www.tribuneindia.com/2014/20140420/ground.htm, April 20, 2014

Cherian, John., "*The BJP and the Bomb*", Frontline, Vol. 15, No. 8, 1998.

"Chinese nuclear test and CTBT", *XI LOK SABHA DEBATES Session II*, Budget Wednesday, July 31, 1996.

Chiriyankandath, James. (2004) "*The Commonwealth Journal of International Affairs*" *The Round Table*, Vol. 93, Issue 374, pp. 199–211.

Cho, Sung-Ju, "Giving Up to Survive: Domestic Conditions Under Which States Renounce Nuclear Weapons", prepared for delivery at the 2005 Annual Meeting of the American Political Science Association Washington, D.C., September 1–4, 2005.

Cho, Sung-Ju, "Giving Up to Survive: Domestic Conditions Under Which States Renounce Nuclear Weapons", lecture delivered at the 2005 Annual Meeting of the American Political Science Association Washington, D.C., Sept 1–4, 2005, [Online: web] Accessed on Mar 20, 2010, URL: http://www.virginia.edu/politics/grad_program/print/wwdop-2006-paper-cho.pdf

Chopra, A.K. (1984) *India's Policy on Disarmament*, New Delhi: ABC.

Cimbala, Stephen J., *Nuclear weapons and strategy: U.S. nuclear policy for the twenty-first century*, Taylor and Francis, 2005.

Cirincione, Joseph, Jon Wolfsthal, Miriam Rajkumar, *Deadly Arsenals: Nuclear, Biological, and Chemical Threats*, Washington, DC: Carnegie Endowment for International Peace, 2005.

Cohen, Avner. (1998) *"Before the Beginning: The Early History of Israel's Nuclear Project"*, Israel Studies, Vol. 3, No. 1, Spring, pp. 112–139.

____________ (1998) *Israel and the Bomb*, Columbia University Press

____________ "Secrecy: Nuclear Weapons and Liberal Democracy: Some Preliminary Thoughts", Center for International and Security Studies and the Program on Global Security and Disarmament, University of Maryland, USA.

Cohen, Avner, Steven Lee, *Nuclear Weapons and the Future of Humanity: The Fundamental Questions*, Rowman and Littlefield, 1986.

Cohen, Stephen P., *"Image and Perception in India-Pakistan Relations"*, in MS Rajan and Shivaji Gganguly, eds., *Great Power Relations, World Order and the Third World*, New Delhi: Vikas Publishing House, 1981.

____________ (1998) "Nuclear Weapons and Conflict in South Asia", [Online: web] Accessed on 29 Feb 2008, URL: http://www.brookings.edu/articles/1998/1123india_cohen.aspx?p=1

____________ (2005) *India Emerging Power*, Oxford University Press, New Delhi.

Communist Party of India (Marxist) Report on Political Situation Manifesto of the Congress Party General Elections, 1989.

CPI(M) *Manifesto for the 16th Lok Sabha Elections, 2014.*

Congress Bulletin no December *12*, 1969.

Congress Sessions at a Glance, "54th Session – Meerut", INC, December 23, 1946.

Congress Manifesto *Lok Sabha Elections 2014, Your Voice Our Pledge*, New Delhi.

Connor-Linton, Jeff, "Author's style and world-view in nuclear discourse: A quantitative analysis", *Journal of Cross-Cultural and Interlanguage Communication*, Volume 7 (1–2) Jan 1, 1988

Constituent Assembly of India (Legislative Debates), 2nd sess., Vol. 5, April 6, 1948.

Constitution & Rules of Indian National Congress, [Online: web] Accessed on June 25, 2008, URL: http://www.aicc.org.in/Constitution%20FINAL%2012.6.08.pdf

Couper, Frank E., "*Indian Party Conflict on the Issue of Atomic Weapons*," Journal of Development Areas, Vol. 3, No. 2, 1969.

Corcoran, Edward A., "Strategic Nuclear Weapons and Deterrence", [Online: web] Accessed on November 23, 2007, URL: http://www.globalsecurity.org/wmd/library/report/2005/sndeterrence.htm.

CPI(M), *Against Nuclear Jingoism*, New Delhi: National Book Centre, 1998.

CPI(M) Central Committee Communique issued after its Meeting Held in New Delhi on March 19–22, 1992.

CPI(M) Politbureau Statement on "Indo-US Army Executive Steering Committee: Grave Threat to India's Sovereignty", *People's Democracy*, New Delhi Feb 2 1992.

CPI(M) *Political Resolution* adopted at the 17th Congress, Hyderabad, March 19–24, 2002.

CPI(M) Report on Political Developments, Central Committee, October 23–25, 2009.

CPI(M)'s Manifesto of Lok Sabha Election – 1977", *People's Democracy*, February 6, 1977.

CPI(M), Central Committee, "Review of the 15th Lok Sabha Elections" (Adopted by the Central Committee at Its Meeting Held On June 20 and 21, 2009) URL: http://www.cpim.org/documents/2009-15%20ls%20election%20review.pdf

Croft, Stuart and Phil Williams. (1991) "*The United Kingdom*" in Regina Cowen Karp edited *Security with Nuclear Weapons?: Different Perspectives on National Security*, SIPRI, May 9, pp. 145–48.

Curzon, Lord (of Kedleston) (1909) *The Place of India in the Empire*, London: John Murray.

Dahl, Robert (1985) *Controlling Nuclear Weapons: Democracy Versus Guardianship*, Syracuse University Press, New York.

Dalton, Russell J. and Martin P. Wattenberg, "Introduction", *Parties without Partisans: Political Change in Advanced Industrial Democracies*, Comparative Politics, March 14, 2002.

Darby, Phillip. (1973) *British defence policy east of Suez, 1947-68*, London: Oxford University Press for the Royal Institute of International Affairs.

Das, Parimal Kumar (1978) "The Myth of Consensus", *International Studies* (New Delhi), 17.

Davis, Zachary S. and Benjamin Frankel, (1993) eds., *The Proliferation Puzzle: Why Nuclear Weapons Spread and What Results* (London: Frank Cass).

DeGroot, Gerard J. (2005) *The Bomb: A History of Hell on Earth*, London: Pimlico

Delhi Domestic News Service, April 27, 1987 in FBIS-Near East and South Asia (NESA), April 28, 1987, p. Er.

Delhi Domestic News Service, May 13, 1982, in FBIS-SA, May 14, 1982, p.

Denver, David and Gordon Hands (1990) "Issues, Principles or Ideology? How young Voters Decide", *Electoral Studies*, Vol. 9, Issue 1, March, pp. 19–36.

Deshmukh, B.G. (1994) *"The Inside Story"*, *India Today*, February 28, 1994.

_________ (2004) *A Cabinet Secretary Looks Back*, New Delhi: Harper Collins.

Deshmukh, Chintamani, *Homi Jehangir Bhabha*, National Book Trust, 2003.

Diaz, Tom, "Gandhi Warns U.S. Is 'Soft' on 'Islamic Bomb' Threat", *Washington Times*, 1987.

"Disputed Legacy", *India Today*, May 15, 1988.

Dixit, Aabha, "Missile Race in South Asia: Linear Progression Required to Cap Race?", *Strategic Analysis*, IDSA, September, 1997.

Dixit, J.N., *India Pakistan in War and Peace*, New Delhi: Books Today, 2002.

_________ (2003) *India's Foreign Policy 1947-2003*, New Delhi: Picus.

Don Ward, Michael and A.K. Mahajan, *"Defense Expenditures, Security Threats, and Governmental Deficits: A Case Study of India, 1952-79"* Journal of Conflict Resolution, Vol. 28 No. 3, September, 382–419, 1984.

Draft Report of National Security Advisory Board on Indian Nuclear Doctrine, Embassy of India, Washington, DC, August 17, 1999.

Draft Report of National Security Advisory Board on Indian Nuclear Doctrine, August 17, 1999, [Online: web] Accessed on

March 11, 2009, URL: http://www.indianembassy.org/policy/CTBT/nuclear_doctrine_aug_17_1999.html.

Draft Report of NSAB on Indian Nuclear Doctrine, August 17, 1999, [Online: web] Accessed on 10 May 2009, URL: http://www.indianembassy.org/policy/CTBT/nuclear_doctrine_aug_17_1999.html

Eisenhower, Dwight, "*Atom for Peace*", given to the 470th Plenary Meeting of the United Nations General Assembly on Tuesday, December 8, 1953.

Eiser, J. Richard, Joop Pligt, Russell Spears, *Nuclear Neighbourhoods: Community Responses to Reactor Siting*, University of Exeter Press, 1995.

e-journal, U.S. Department of State / February 2010, Vol. 15 / No. 2, pp. 13–15, [Online: web] Accessed on 10 May 2010, http://www.america.gov/media/pdf/ejs/0210.pdf

Election Commission of India, (1955) *Report on the First General Election in India*, 1951–52, Vol. 1, (General), Delhi: Manager of Publications.

Election Manifesto 1998, Indian National Congress.

Election Manifesto of CPI(M) for 1980 Lok Sabha Elections.

"Election Watch", *Journal of Democracy*, Volume 2 (1991), http://muse.jhu.edu/journals/journal_of_democracy/election_watch/v002/index.html accessed on March 12, 2009.

Election Commission of India, *Statistical Report on General Elections, 1996 to the Eleventh Lok Sabha, Volume I* (National and State Abstracts and Detailed Results), New Delhi. http://eci.nic.in/eci_main/statisticalreports/LS_1996/Vol_I_LS_96.pdf

Elkin, Jerrold F and W. Andrew Ritezel, "*The Indo-Pakistani Military Balance*", Asian Survey, Vol. 26, No. 5, pp. 518–538.

Epstein, William (1977) "Why States Go—And Don't Go—Nuclear", *Annals*, AAPSS, 430, 1997.

Farnham, Barbara, "Political Cognition and Decision-Making", *Political Psychology*, Vol. 11, No. 1, pp. 83–111, 1999

Farr, Warner D., '*The Third Temple's Holy Of Holies: Israel's Nuclear Weapons*', The Counter-proliferation Papers, Future Warfare Series No. 2, USAF Counterproliferation Center, Air War College, Air University, Maxwell Air Force Base, Alabama, September, 1999.

'Fears of Nuclear War', [Online: web] Accessed on Oct 10, 2010, URL: http://www.nhk.or.jp/bunken/english/pdf/070601-08.pdf

Fisher, Cathleen S., "Reformation and Resistance: Nongovernmental Organ isations and the Future of Nuclear Weapons", *Report No. 29*, The Henry L. Stimson Center, May 1999. Available at http://www.stimson.org/images/uploads/research-pdfs/ReformationandResistance.pdf, accessed on June 15, 2010.

Fitzpatrick, Mark T., A. I. Nikitin, Serge Oznobishchev, *Nuclear doctrines and strategies: national policies and international security*, OS Press, 2008.

Ford, Harold P., Francis X. Winters, *Ethics and nuclear strategy?*, Woodstock Theological Center, 1977.

Foreign Affairs Reports (New Delhi), Vol. 19, Nos. 9-10-11, Sep-Oct 1970.

Foreign Policy Resolutions and Statements 1980-99, Publication No.: E/17/99, BJP: The Study Committee on Foreign Affairs, 1999.

Forsberg, Randall et al., *Nonproliferation Primer*, Cambridge: MIT Press, 1995.

Foster, Jr., John S. and Keith B. Payne (2007) "What Are Nuclear Weapons For?", Forum on Physics and Society of The American Physical Society, October, Vol. 36, No. 4, [Online: web] Accessed on Sep 6, 2010, URL: http://units.aps.org/units/fps/newsletters/2007/october/foster-payne.cfm

Frank, Jerome D., "*Psychological aspects of the nuclear arms race*", Bulletin of the Atomic Scientists, Apr 1976, pp. 22–24.

Frankel, Francine R., *Indias Political Economy 1947-2004*, New Delhi: Oxford University Press, 2005.

_______________ (1978) *India's Political Economy, 1947-77: The Gradual Revolution*, Princeton, N.J.: Princeton University Press.

Freedman, Lawrence, *The Evolution of Nuclear Strategy*, Palgrave Macmillan, 1989.

Frey, Karsten., '*Of Nuclear Myths and Nuclear Taboos*', Peace Review, Vol. 18, NO. 3, July-September, pp. 341–347, 2006a.

Frey, Karsten, "*Nuclear Weapons as Symbols: The Role of Norms in Nuclear Policy Making*", Barcelona: IBEI Working Papers. 2006b.

Ganguly, Sumit "India's Pathway to Pokhran II", *International Security*, Vol 23, No. 4, Spring, pp. 148–77., 1999.

_____________ (1994) "*The Prime Minister and Foreign and Defence Policies*", in James Manor (ed.), *Nehru To the Nineties: The Changing Office of Prime Minister in India*, New Delhi: Viking.

______________(1983) *"Why India Joined the Nuclear Club"*, Bulletin of the Atomic Scientists, 39: 4 April.

Garfield, Susan (1994) *"Atomic Priesthood"* is Not Nuclear Guardianship: A Critique of Thomas Sebeok's Vision of the Future, Nuclear Guardianship Forum, On The Responsible Care of Radioactive Materials, Issue # 3, Spring.

General Assembly Official Records, First Committee, 581st meeting, March 21, 1953.

Gerston, Larry N., *Public Policy Making: Process and Principles*, New York: M.E. Sharpe Inc., 2010.

Ghatate, Narayan M., "Disarmament in India's Foreign Policy 1947-65", Ph.D. Thesis of the American University Washington D.C., 1966.

Ghose, Arundhati, "Disarmament and India's Nuclear Diplomacy: Evolution of a Reluctuant Nuclear Weapon State", in Atish Sinha, Madhup Mohta, ed. *Indian foreign policy: challenges and opportunities*, Academic Foundation, 2007.

Ghose, Shankar. *Mahatma Gandhi*, New Delhi: Allied Publishers Limited, 1991.

Ghosh, Ajoy. (1962) *Articles and Speeches*, Moscow.

Ghosh, Deva Prasad., *Presidential Address* at the Bharatiya Jana Sangh Pratinidhi Sabha, Jaipur Session, 1956.

Ghosh, Partha S., *BJP and the Evolution of Hindu Nationalism: From Periphery to Centre*, New Delhi: Manohar Publications, 1999.

Ghosh, Partha S. and Rajaram Panda, *"Domestic Support for Mrs. Gandhi's Afghan Policy: The Soviet Factor in Indian Politics"*, *Asian Survey*, Vol. 23, No. 3 (Mar 1983), pp. 261–279.

Gompert, David C. (1998) 'Rethinking the Role of Nuclear Weapons', National Defence University, Washington D.C., Number 141, May. http://www.ndu.edu/inss/strforum/SF141/forum141.html

Gopal, S., (ed.) (1980) *Jawaharlal Nehru: An Anthology*, OUP.

Gopal, Sarvepalli (1979) *Jawaharlal Nehru, A Biography*, Vol. 2, London: Jonathan Cape.

GoI (1960) White Paper III; Notes, etc., Nov. 1959, March 1960, New Delhi.

Graham, B.D., *"The Jana Sangh and Bloc Politics, 1967-80"*, *Commonwealth and Comparative Politics*, Vol. 25, Issue 3, November, pp. 248–66, 1987.

Gregory, Shaun R. (1996), *Nuclear Command and Control in NATO*, London: Macmillan Press Ltd.

Griffin, M.A., "*Specifying Organisational Contexts: Systematic Links between Processes in Organisational Behaviour*", *Journal of Organisational Behavior*, 28/7, 859–863, 2007

Gupta, Nandlal. (1964) "*Real Face of Hindu Communalism*", *Mainstream* 2, (21 & 22), January 25, pp. 39–41.

Gupta, Shekhar. (1994) "*Nawaz Sharif' Bombshell*", *India Today*, September 15.

Halperin, Morton H. (1961) Nuclear Weapons and Limited War, *The Journal of Conflict Resolution*, Vol. 5, No. 2, June, pp. 146–166.

Harvey, John R. 'Seeking A Responsive Nuclear Weapons Infrastructure and Stockpile Transformation', paper presented to the National Academy of Sciences Symposium on: *Post-Cold War U.S. Nuclear Strategy: A Search for Technical and Policy Common Ground* on August 11, 2004.

Harvey, John R. (2004) "Seeking A Responsive Nuclear Weapons Infrastructure and Stockpile Transformation", presented to the National Academy of Sciences Symposium on "Post-Cold War U. S. Nuclear Strategy: A Search for Technical and Policy Common Ground", 11 August, http://www7.nationalacademies.org/cisac/Harvey_Presentation.pdf

Hasan, Joya, (ed.) (2002) *Parties and Party Politics in India*, New Delhi: OUP

_________ 2010, in Jayal, Niraja Gopal and Pratap Bhanu Mehta, eds. *Politics in India*, Oxford University Press: New Delhi, pp. 241–253.

Haass, Richard and Gideon Rose, *A new U.S. policy toward India and Pakistan: report of an independent task force*, Council on Foreign Relations, USA,1997.

Hazelhurst, Peter. (1970) "Atom Bomb Urged for India", *Times of London*, May 11, 1970.

Heginbotham, Stanley J., "The 1971 Revolution in Indian Voting Behavior", *Asian Survey*, Vol. 11, No. 12, The 1971 Indian Parliamentary Elections: A Symposium (Dec., 1971), pp. 1133–52

Henry J. Hyde U.S.-India Peaceful Atomic Energy Cooperation Act of 2006.

Herz, John H. (1950) "Idealist Internationalism and Security Dilemma", *World Politics*, Vol. 2.

Hilali, A. Z. (2001) "India's Strategic Thinking and Its National Security Policy", *Asian Survey*, September/October, Vol. 41, No. 737–764.

_________ (2001) *"India's Strategic Thinking and Its National Security Policy"*, *Asian Survey*, Vol. 41, No. 5 (Sep.-Oct.), pp. 737–764.

Hiren Mukerjee, *"Manufacture of Nuclear Weapons"*, Lok Sabha Debates (10th Session), Third Series, Vol. xxxv (10, November 27, 1964, columns 2279–82

Hirose, Takako, *Two Asian democracies: a comparative study of the single predominant party systems of India and Japan*, Konark Publishers, 1994

Hoffmann, Steven A. (1989) *India and China Crisis*, University of California Press

Horton III, Roy E. (1999) "Out Of (South) Africa: Pretoria's Nuclear Weapons Experience", Occasional Paper #27, USAF Institute for National Security Studies, August, [Online: web] Accessed on Dec 30, 2010, URL: http://www.fas.org/nuke/guide/rsa/nuke/ocp27.htm; http://www.tni.org/detail_page.phtml?page=archives_vanaik_avery.

Hoyt, Timothy D. (2003), *"Shades of Realism: The Impact of Personality, Ideology, and Systemic Pressures on Indian Foreign Policy"*, in UK Heo and Shale A. Horowitz (eds.) *Conflict in Asia: Korea, China-Taiwan and India-Pakistan*, London: Praeger, pp. 139–59.

Hu, Weixing, *"New Delhi's Nuclear Bomb: A Systemic Analysis"*, *World Affairs*, 163(1) (Summer 2000), pp. 28–38.

Hymans, Jacques E.C. (2006) *The Psychology of Nuclear Proliferation: Identity, Emotions, and Foreign Policy*, Cambridge University Press

_______________ (2006a) *"Theories of Nuclear Proliferation: The State of the Field"*, *Non-proliferation Review*, Vol. 13, No. 3, November, pp. 455–65.

_______________ (2006) *The Psychology of Nuclear Proliferation: Identity, Emotions, and Foreign Policy*, Cambridge University Press.

Inaugural Address by Dr Manmohan Singh, Prime Minister of India on A Nuclear Weapon-Free World: From Conception to Reality, April 2, 2014, http://idsa.in/keyspeeches/InauguralAddressShriManmohanSingh

IBN Live, 'No first use' nuke policy to continue: Krishna, http://ibnlive.in.com/news/no-first-use-nuke-policy-to-continue-krishna/146129-3.html, 16 March 2011.

Ideological Resolution of the CPI(M), adopted at Burdwan, April 5–12, 1968.

in the 21st Century, British American Security Information Council, Research Report 2001. 3 November 2001.

"India should not sign NPT: CPI(M)", *The Hindu*, September 25, 2009, http://www.thehindu.com/news/national/article24984.ece

INC History, Congress Sessions At A Glance, 54th Session – Meerut, 1946, [Online: web] Accessed on Dec 12, 2010, URL: http://www.indianyouthcongress.in/history054.htm

INC Resolutions on Foreign Policy 1947-1966, AICC: 1966, New Delhi.

INC Sixtyseventh Session, Presidential Address of Shri Neelam Sanjiva Reddy, Srikrishnapuri, Patna, Jan 4th, 1962.

"India Announces Review of Nuclear Policy", *Reuters*, March 27, 1987.

"India is now a Weapons State", Interview with Prime Minister Atal Bihari Vajpayee, by *India Today*'s Executive Editor Prabhu Chawla, http//www.indianembassy.org/pic/pm-interview.htm, accessed on July 15, 2007.

"India Debates the Nuclear Bomb (1991)", URL: http://filtercoffee.nationalinterest.in/2011/03/15/india-debates-the-nuclear-bomb-1991/, 15 March 2011, accessed on June 19, 2011.

"India Must Make N-Bomb: BJP", *Times of India*, July 22, 1985.

"India says won't sign NPT", *The Indian Express*, Sep 24, 2009.

"India Should Go Nuke – Vajpayee", *News India*, December 11, 1987.

"India will not sign 'discriminatory' NPT: Tharoor", *The Indiannews*, September 26, 2009, [Online: web] Accessed on Dec 12, 2010, URL: http://www.thaindian.com/newsportal/india-news/india-will-not-sign-discriminatory-npt-tharoor_100252484.html, accessed on Oct 22, 2009.

"India's Defence Strategy in the Next Decade" – Address by C Subramaniam, Defence Minister to the Officer Students of the National Defence College, New Delhi, October 29, 1979.

India's Nuclear Energy Programme and The 123 Agreement with the United States, 2008, INC, [Online: web] Accessed on 22 Aug

2010, URL: http://www.aicc.org.in/new/document-layout.php?id=51

Indian Express, "Revise 'no-first-use' n-policy: Jaswant", http://www.indianexpress.com/news/revise-nofirstuse-npolicy-jaswant/763040/, March 16, 2011

Indian National Congress Resolutions on Foreign Policy 1947-66, AICC, New Delhi, 1966.

Indian Nuclear Doctrine, A Draft Paper proposed by the NSAB. (Publicly released by the Ministry of External Affairs in New Delhi on August 17, 1999)

Indian Recorder and Digest, Vol. 13, No. (June 6, 1967).

Indira Gandhi, interview with Steve Patton, US News and Service World Report, January 23, 1982, in Prime Minister Indira Gandhi, *Statements on Foreign Policy*, January-March 1982 (New Delhi: Government of India, 1982).

Indira Gandhi, *Statement to Lok Sabha*, March 28, 1984, quoted by Foreign Minister Narasimha Rao, *Lok Sabha* Debates, 7th ser., Vol. 46, No 27, March 30, 1984, Col. 398.

Indrajit Gupta: Speeches in Parliament, edited by Anil Rajimwale, New Delhi: People's Pub. House, 2002.

Interview with Prime Minister Atal Bihari Vajpayee, *"India is now a Weapons State"*, *India Today* [Online: web] Accessed on August 23, 2008, URL: http://www.indianembassy.org/pic/pm-interview.htm

"Interview, Atal Bihari Vajpayee", interviewed by Prabhu Chawla, *India Today*, May 25, 1998.

Iype, George (1998) "PM to call all-party meet over CTBT", 9 Sep 1998 [Online: web] Accessed on August 23, 2008, http://www.rediff.com/news/1998/sep/09ctbt.htm

Jabeen, Mussarat, Muhammad Saleem Mazhar and Naheed S. Goraya, *"SAARC and Indo-Pak Relationship"*, *Journal of Political Studies*, Vol. 1, Issue 2, 2010, pp. 127–145.

"J.S. Asks Government to Make A-bomb", *The Hindustan Times*, November 11, 1964.

Jaffrelot, Christophe. (1998) "The Bahujan Samaj Party in North India: No Longer Just a Dalit Party?", *Comparative Studies of South Asia, Africa and The Middle East*, Vol. XVIII No. 1, pp. 35–52.

Jai, Janak Raj, *Pokhran II: The Explosion that Rocked the World*, New Delhi: Regency Publications, 1998.

Jain, B.M. (1994) *Nuclear Politics in South Asia*, New Delhi: Rawat Publications.

Jain, J.P. (1974) *India and Disarmament Vol. 1, Nehru Era: An Analytical Study*, New Delhi: Radiant Publisher.

Jain, Sumitra Kumar, *Party politics and centre-state relations in India*, Abhinav Publications, 1994

Jain, U.C., and Jeevan Nair, *Encyclopaedia of Indian Government and Politics: Political Parties*, Pointer, 2000.

Jones, Mark P., *"The Role of Parties and Party System in the Policy Making Process"*, prepared for the workshop on State Reform, Public Policies, and Policymaking Processes, Inter-American Development Bank, Washington D.C. February 28-March 2, 2005.

Chandra, Bipin. (1998) *"Jan Sangh: The BJP's Predecessor"*, *The Hindu Online*, May 11, 1998 http://www.proxsa.org/politics/hindutva/bipanchandra.html, accessed on May 12, 2008.

"Jana Sangh Drive for N-arms", The Hindustan Times, October 20, 1964.

Jana Sangh Wants an Indian Bomb", The Statesman, Delhi, December 7, 1964.

Janata, Vol. XXII, No. 16 (May 7, 1967).

Jawaharlal Nehru Memorial Fund (1986) *Jawaharlal Nehru: Letters to Chief Ministers*, Vol. 3, New Delhi.

Jayakar, Pupul *Indira Gandhi*, Viking, Penguin India: New Delhi, 1992.

Jayal, Niraja Gopal, *Democracy in India*, Oxford University Press, 2001.

Jayapalan, N., *Indian society and social institutions*, Atlantic Publishers and Distri, 2001.

Jayasekera, Deepal. (2008) "Why India's Stalinists oppose the US nuclear deal", *World Socialist* Website, July 15, 2008. [Online: web] Accessed on Sept 2, 2009, URL: http://www.wsws.org/articles/2008/jul2008/indi-j15.shtml

"JD(S) extends unconditional support to UPA", *Hindustan Times*, May 19, 2009.

Jhangiani, Motilal A. *Jana Sangh and Swatantra: A Profile of the Rightist Parties in India*, Bombay: Manaktalas, 1967.

Joeck, Neil. (1990) *"Tacit Bargaining and Stable Proliferation in South Asia"*, *Journal of Strategic Studies*, Vol. 13, No. 3 (September).

Johari, Jagdish Chandra, *Comparative Politics*, Sterling Publishers Pvt. Ltd., 1982.

Joo, Han Sung. (2007) "*North Korea: A Deal is better than Nothing*", February 15, http://www.time.com/time/magazine/article/0,9171,1590173,00.html

Joshi, Manoj. (1998) "*Deadly Option*", *India Today*, May 4, http://www.india-today.com/itoday/04051998/defence.html, accessed on March 12, 2009.

Kamath, P.M. (1999) "*Indian Nuclear Tests, Then and Now: An Analysis of US and Canadian Responses*", Strategic Analysis, August (Vol. XXIII No. 5).

Kangas, Jack L., *Nuclear weapons decision-making: An application of organisation theory to the "mini-nuke" case*, Stanford University, 1984.

Kanwal, Gurmeet, *Nuclear defence: Shaping the Arsenal*, Knowledge World in association with Institute for Defence Studies and Analysis, 2001.

Kapoor, Priya, "*Of Moral Positions and Nuclear War: Novelist Arundhati Roy as Peace Activist*", *Global Media Journal*, Vol. 8, Issue 15, Fall 2009, pp. 1–14.

Kapur, Ashok., "*India's Security and Defence Policies Under Indira Gandhi*" in Yogendra K. Malik and Dhirendra K. Vajpeyi edited *India: The Years of Indira Gandhi*, Brill Academic Pub, 1988.

Kapur, Ashok. (1988) "*Indian Security and Defence Policies under Indira Gandhi*", in Yogendra K. Malik and Dhirendra K. Vajpeyi, ed. *India: The Years of Indira Gandhi*, Brill, pp. 42–59.

__________ (1976) *India's Nuclear Option: Atomic Diplomacy and Decision Making*, New York: Praeger Publishers.

__________(2003) *Regional Security Structure in Asia*, London: Routledge.

Kapur, S. Paula, *Dangerous deterrent: nuclear weapons proliferation and conflict in South Asia*, NUS Press, 2009.

__________, "The Indian Nuclear Programme: Motivation, Effects, and Future Trajectories", in Olav Njolstad, ed., *Nuclear Proliferation and International Order: Challenges to the Non-Proliferation Treaty*, Taylor and Francis, 2010, pp. 13–23.

Karanjia, R.K., *The Philosophy of Mr. Nehru*, London: George Allen and Unwin, 1966.

Karat, Prakash, *Politics and Policies: A Marxist Perspective*, Hyderabad: Prajasakti Book House, 2008.

____________ (2000) "CPI(M) Programme: Basic Strategy Reiterated", *The Marxist*, Vol. 16, No. 03, July-December. [Online: web] Accessed on March 4, 2010, URL: http://www.cpim.org/marxist/200003_marxist_progrm_pk.htm,.

____________ (2004) "Implications Of BJP Rule: The Election Battle Ahead", 20 April, [Online: web] Accessed on December 21, 2009, URL: http://www.cpim.org/marxist/200401_marxist_bjp%20rule.doc,.

Karnad, Bharat, *Nuclear Weapons and Indian Security: The Realist Foundations of Strategy*, New Delhi: Macmillan India Limited, 2002.

Kashyap, Subhas C., (1995) *Our Constitution*, New Delhi: NBT.

____________, *Parliament in the Indian polity*, Govt. of India Press, 1987.

Katzenstein, Peter J. (1996) *Cultural Norms and National Security: Norms and Identity in World Politics*, Columbia University Press, New York.

Kaul, T.N. *Ambassadors Need Not Lie: Some Aspects of India's Foreign Policy*, Vol. 1, New Delhi: Lancer, 1988.

Kelleher, Catherine M., The Issue of German Nuclear Armament, *Proceedings of the Academy of Political Science*, Vol. 29, No. 2, The "Atlantic Community" Reappraised, November, pp. 95–107, 1968.

Kellerman, Barbara Allision Redux: Three More Decision-Making Models, *Polity*, Vol. 15, No. 3, Spring, pp. 351–367, 1983.

Key Highlights of General Election 1967 to the Fourth Lok Sabha, Election Commission of India, [Online: web] Accessed on November 25, 2008, URL: http://www.eci.gov.in/SR_KeyHighLights/LS_1967/Vol_I_LS_67.pdf

Khan, Rasheeduddin, *Rethinking Indian Federalism*, Inter University Center for Humanities and Social Sciences, Simla, 1997.

Khilnani, Niranjan M., *Relations of Indian Foreign Policy*, New Delhi: ABC Publishing House, 1984.

Kiernan, Kevin. "*Why Do States Give Up Nuclear Arsenals? Proliferation as Economic Bargaining*", *Bolonga Centre Journal of International Affairs*, Volume 13 / Spring, 2010.

Kissinger, Henry, *The White House Years*, New York: Little Brown & Co, 1979.

Kishore, Mohammed Ali. (1969) *Jana Sangh and India's Foreign Policy*, New Delhi: Associated Publishing House, 1969.

Kohli, Atul. ed. (2001) *The Success of India's Democracy*, UK: Cambridge University Press.

Koopmans, Ruud and Jan Willem Duyvendak (1995) "The Political Construction of the Nuclear Energy Issue and Its Impact on the Mobil-isation of Anti-Nuclear Movements in Western Europe", *Social Problems*, Vol. 42, No. 2, May, Berkeley: University of California Press.

Kothari, Rajni., *Politics in India*, New Delhi: Orient Longman, 1970.

___________, "The Congress 'System' in India", *Asian Survey*, Vol. 4, No. 12 (Dec., 1964), pp. 1161–1173.

Krepon, Michael., "Whatever Happened to Minimum, Credible Deterrence?", *Arms Control Wonk*, 6 January, 2014.

Krepon, Michael, Ziad Haider, and Charles Thornton. (2004) "Are Tactical Nuclear Weapons Needed in South Asia?", [Online: web] Accessed on November 23, 2007, URL: http://www.stimson.org/southasia/pdf/ESCCONTROLCHAPTER6.pdf,.

Krepon, Michael and Julia Thompson, *Deterrence Stability and Escalation Control in South Asia*, Washinton DC: Stimson, 2013.

Kristensen, Hans M., *"India's Missile Modernisation Beyond Minimum Deterrence"*, *FAS Strategic Security Blog*, Federation of American Scientists, October 4, 2013.

Kronstadt, K. Alan. (2004) *"India's 2004 National Elections"*, *CRS Report for Congress*, July 12.

Kumar, G. Gopal, *Regional political parties and state politics*, Deep and Deep Publications, 1986.

Kumara, Kranti and Keith Jones, *"Indo-US nuclear deal could be casualty of India's fractured domestic politics"*, World Socialist Website, accessed on June 26, 2011, URL: http://www.wsws.org/articles/2007/nov2007/indo-n13.shtml, November 13, 2007.

Kumar, Shivaji, "National Security of India: A Social Constructivist Approach", [Online: web] Accessed on Sep 23, 2010, URL: http://www.allacademic.com//meta/p_mla_apa_research_citation/0/7/0/9/1/pages70915/p70915-1.php

Kumara, Kranti and Keith Jones. (2007) "Indo-US nuclear deal could be casualty of India's fractured domestic politics",

13 November, [Online: web] Accessed on Dec 28, 2009, URL: http://www.wsws.org/articles/2007/nov2007/indo-n13.shtml,.

Kurien, C.T. (2008) "*Coalition Time*", Frontline, Vol. 25, Issue 3, Feb. 2–15, 2008.

Kux, Dennis. (1992) *India and the United States: Estranged Democracies 1941-1991*, Washington DC: National Defence University Press.

Lague, David. (1998) "*Beijing blames New Delhi for tension*", *Sunday Age*, May 31, 1998

Lavoy, Peter R. (2006) "*Nuclear Proliferation over the Next Decade: Causes, Warning Signs, and Policy Responses*", Nonproliferation Review, Vol. 13, No 3, November, pp. 433–54.

Left Stand on the Nuclear Deal, July 2008, published by Hari Singh Kang from 27–29 Bhai Veer Singh Marg, Gole Market, New Delhi.

Let Pak Make Bomb: India Won't, *Hindustan Times*, November 29, 1985.

Lather, Rajiv, "Re-Organisation of Indian Defence Setup", *Indian Defence Review*, Oct-Dec. 1999.

Levi, Adrian and Catherine Scott-Clark, *Deception: Pakistan, the United States and the Global Nuclear Weapons Conspiracy* (2007) New Delhi: Penguin Books.

Levy, Jack S. (1997) '*Prospect Theory, Rational Choice, and International Relations*', International Studies Quarterly, Vol. 41, No. 1, March, pp. 87–112.

"Leyland arm to develop port, rail link in Iran", *The Hindu*, Jul 10, 2004.

"*Left Withdraws Support from Manmohan Singh Govt*", *People's Democracy*, XXXII (27), July 13, 2009.

Liebl, Vernie. (2009) "*India and Pakistan: Competing Nuclear Strategies and Doctrines*", *Comparative Strategy*, Volume 28, Issue 2 April, pp. 154 – 163.

Lijphart, Arend. (1996) "*The Puzzle of Indian Democracy: A Consociational Interpretation*", American Political Science Review, Vol. 90, No. 2.

Lindsay, James M., 'Congress and Nuclear Weapons', *Political Science Quarterly*, Vol. 107, No. 2, Summer, pp. 353–354,1992.

Locke, John, *Two treatises on government*, London: R. Butler, Bruton-Street, Berkeley Squire, 1821.

Lodal, Jan. (2001) The Price of Dominance: The New Weapons of Mass Destruction and Their Challenge to American Leadership. Jan Lodal Council on Foreign Relations Press.

Lok Sabha Debate, 5th Ser., Vol. II, no.5, March 17, 1972, cols. 130–31.

Lok Sabha Debates, Nov 23, 1964, col. 1280.

Lok Sabha Debates, November 7, 1987.

Lok Sabha Debates, Series 2, Vol. 13, no. 23, March 13, 1958.

Lok Sabha Election Manifesto 1984, BJP.

Malcolmson, Robert W. (1985) *Nuclear Fallacies: How We Have Been Misguided Since Hiroshima*, McGill-Queen's Press – MQUP, 1985.

Malcolmson, Robert W. *Nuclear Fallacies: How We Have Been Misguided Since Hiroshima*, McGill-Queen's Press, 1985.

Malhotra, Inder, *"The making of the Bomb: Let us clear up the nuclear confusion"*, *The Tribune*, (Chandigarh), December 29, available at http://www.tribuneindia.com/2004/20041229/edit.htm#4 , 2004.

____________(1990) *Indira Gandhi: A Personal and Political Biography*, London: Hodder and Stoughton.

Mallik, Mohan J. (1998) *"India Goes Nuclear: Rationale, Benefits, Costs and Implications"*, *Contemporary Southeast Asia*, Vol. 20, No. 2, August, pp. 191–215.

Malik, Yogendra K. and Ashok Kapur, *India: fifty years of democracy and development*, APH Pub. Corp., 1998

Manning, Robert A., Ronald Montaperto, Brad Roberts Cochairs (2000) *'China, Nuclear Weapons, and Arms Control: A Preliminary Assessment'*, Council on Foreign Relations.

Manoff, Robert Karl, *"The Media: Nuclear Secrecy vs. Democracy"*, Bulletin of Atomic Scientists, January 1984, pp. 26–29.

Marwah, Onkar, *"India's Nuclear Program: Decisions, Intent, Policy"*, in William Overholt, ed. *Asia's Nuclear Future*, Westview Press, 1976.

Markandan, K. C., *Aspects of Indian polity*, Volume 2, ABS Publications, 1990.

Masani, Zareer, *Indira Gandhi: A Biography*, Hamilton, 1975.

Masselos, Jim, *Indian Nationalism: A history*, New Dawn Press, 2005.

Mathur, K.D. and P.M. Kamath, *Conduct of India's Foreign Policy*, New Delhi: South Asian Publishers, 1996.

Mattoo, Amitabh (1999) *"India's Nuclear Policy in an Anarchic World"*, in Amitabh Mattoo (ed.), India's Nuclear Deterrent: *Pokhran II and Beyond*, New Delhi: Har-Anand Publications.

Maxwell, Neville (1974) *"Reconsiderations: Jawaharlal Nehru"*, Foreign Affairs, 52 April.

McLean, Scilla, (ed.) (1986) *How Nuclear Weapons Decisions are Made*, London: Macmillan Press.

MEA Library, *Foreign Affairs Record 1967*, Vol. XIII, January No. 1, 1995.

Mearsheimer, John (1998) *"Here We Go Again"*, New York Times, May 17, 1998.

Medvedev, Zhores A. (1979) *"Stalin and the Atomic Bomb"*, [Online: web] accessed on February 26, 2007, URL: http://www.spokesmanbooks.com/Spokesman/PDF/medvedev.pdf, 21 December.

Mehra, Ajay K., D.D. Khanna, Gert W. Kueck, eds., *Political Parties and Party Systems*, Sage Publications: New Delhi, 2003.

Menon, Raja. *'Nuclear Doctrine in South Asia'*, in P.R. Chari, Sonika Gupta and Arpit Rajain, eds., *Nuclear Stability in South Asia*, New Delhi: Konrad Adenauer Foundation/Institute of Peace and Conflict Studies/Manohar, 2003

Menon, Raja. (2000) *A Nuclear Strategy for India*, New Delhi: Sage.

Menon, Rajan, "A Nuclear South Asia: What to Do, What Not to Do", http://cas.lehigh.edu/casweb/content/default.aspx?pageid=271, accessed on April 6, 2007.

Meyer, Stephen M., *The Dynamics of Nuclear Proliferation, Chicago*, IL: University of Chicago Press, 1984.

Mukherjee, Rohan and David M. Malone, *"Indian Foreign Policy and Contemporary Security Challenges"*, International Affairs, 87:1 (2011) 87–104.

Quirk, Michael J. (2008) "Consequences, Moral Rules, and Nuclear Deterrence", Bellerose, N.Y.: *Journal of Social Philosophy*, Vol. 19 Issue 1, April 30, pp. 26–29.

Miller, George H. *"How a Nuclear War would be Fought"*, *Bulletin of Atomic Scientists*, May 1979, pp. 25–33.

Ministry of External Affairs, GoI (1959) White Paper I: Notes, Memoranda and Letters exchanged and Agreements signed between the Governments of India and China 1954-September.

Minitues of AICC Meeting, New Delhi May 24, 2002.

Minutes of the AICC Meeting, December 6–7, 1980.

Mirchandani, G.G. (1968) *India's Nuclear Dilemma*, New Delhi: Popular Book Service

Mishra, Brajesh, *"Mao's Smile Revisited: Sino-Indian Relations During an Important Period"*, *Indian Foreign Affairs Journal*, Vol. 1, No. 4, October-December, 2006.

Mishra, Dina Nath., *"Towards Making India Invincible"*, *The Observer*, May 21, available at URL: http://www.hvk.org/articles/0598/0095.html, 1998

Mishra, R.N., *Indian Ocean and India's Security*, Mittal Publications, 1986.

Mitra, Chandan Arguments in Favour of Indo-US nuclear deal are dubious", *Indo-US Nuclear Deal: Why does BJP opposes it?*, BJP, August, pp. 129–32, 2008.

Mitra, S. (2003), *"Democracy from Above: The Post-Colonial State and the Electoral System in India"*, Paper presented at the annual meeting of the American Political Science Association, Philadelphia, August 27, http://www.allacademic.com/meta/p63475_index.html

Raja Mohan, C. (2004) *"Portrait of Rao as N-rchitect"*, *Indian Express*, December 28, 2004, http://www.indianexpress.com/oldstory.php?storyid=61667.

__________, *"No First Use and India's Nuclear Transition"*, Pugwash Meeting no. 279 on "No First Use of Nuclear Weapons", London, UK, November 15–17, 2002.

Morris-Jones, W. H. (1967) "The Indian elections: How much has changed?", *The Round Table*, Vol 57, Issue 227, July, pp. 284–290.

"Motion Re: International Situation", *Lok Sabha Deabates*, Nov 22 1960.

Moynihan, Daniel Patrick. (1998) *Secrecy: The American Experience*, Yale University Press, New Haven.

"Mrs Gandhi Reiterates India's Policy of Using Nuclear Power for Peaceful Purposes Only", *India News*, August 1, 1983, p.1.

Mueller, John (1998) *"The Escalating Irrelevance of Nuclear Weapons"*, in T.V. Paul, Richard J. Harknett, and James J. Wirtz, (eds.) *The Absolute Weapons Revisited: Nuclear Arms and the Emerging International Order*, Ann Arbor: University of Michigan Press, pp. 73–98.

Muralidharan, Sukumar and John Cherian, *"The BJP's Bombs"*, *Frontline*, Vol. 15, No. 11, May 23 - Jun 5, 1998, URL: http://www.flonnet.com/fl1511/15110040.htm, accessed on 19 June 2011.

Muni, S.D. and C Raja Mohan (2005) *"India's Options in a Changing Asia"*, in R.R. Sharma edited *India and emerging Asia*, New Delhi: Sage, 52–79.

Muni, S.D. *Pangs of Proximity: India and Sri Lanka's Ethnic Crisis*, New Delhi: Sage Publication, 1993.

Namboodiri, P.K.S. (1985) "Pak Nuclear Capability", *Times of India*, May 11, 1985.

Nanda, B.R. (ed.) (1972) *Socialism in India*, New Delhi: Vikas Publishing House Pvt. Ltd.

Nanda, Krish. (1971) *"Will India Go Nuclear?"*, Bulletin of the Atomic Scientists, December, pp. 39–41.

Nandy, Ashis. (1972) *"The Bomb, the NPT and Indian Elites"*, *EPW*, August, 1533–39.

Narain, Iqbal. (1990) "Nehru's Scientific Temper and Concept of Modernity", in BN Pande edited *A Centenary History of the Indian National Congress 1885-1985*, Vol. V, AICC and Vikas.

Narayanan, K.R., *"Nehru's Vision of India and the World – Then and Now,"* Nehru Memorial Lecture, New Delhi, November 13, 1997.

Ministry of Information and Broadcasting (1995) *Narasimha Rao, Selected Speeches*, Vol. 3, July 1993-June 1994, New Delhi.

"Nath Pai Wants to Produce the Bomb", *Indian Express*, October 19, 1964.

Naval Studies Board, National Research Council, *Post-Cold War Conflict Deterrence*, Washington, D.C.: National Academy Press, 1997.

Nayar, Kuldip. (1972) *India after Nehru*, New Delhi: Vikas Publishing House Pvt. Ltd.

"Nehru Protest To Moscow On Nuclear Tests", CIA Released Documents, Created: 11/4/1961, [Online: web] accessed on 11 May 2011, URL: http://www.faqs.org/cia/docs/91/0000782341/NEHRU-PROTEST-TO-MOSCOW-ON-NUCLEAR-TESTS.html#ixzz0g4E62PFx

Publication Division, Government of India (1961) *India's Foreign Policy, Selected Speeches,* September 1946-April 1961, New Delhi.

Nehru's Speech in Lok Sabha, India, *Parliamentary Debates,* Part II, vol. VIII, Dec 6, 1950.

Nikolenyi (2009) *"The Indian National Congress Party after the dynasty",* CSABA, March 4, https://circle.ubc.ca/bitstream/handle/2429/5483/ubc_1994-0577.pdf?, accessed on October 8, 2009.

"No hardline Hindu agenda this time", Pioneer June 27, 2004

Nolan, Janne E. (1999) *An Elusive Consensus: Nuclear Weapons and American Security after the Cold War,* Washington: Brookings Institution Press.

Non-official Resolutions Received for the AICC Session Bombay, May 21–23 1966.

Noorani, A.G. (1991) *"History of the BJP (1980-1990)",* Mainstream, March 30, 1991.

__________ (1967) *"India's Quest for a Nuclear Guarantee", Asian Survey,* Vol. 7 No. 7, July, pp. 490–02.

__________ (1988) *"Indo-US Nuclear Relations", Asian Survey,* Vol. XX(4), April.

__________ (2006) *"Nehru's legacy in foreign affairs",* Frontline, Volume 23, Issue 15, July 29-August 11, 2006.

__________(1988) "Rajiv Gandhi's Nuclear Policy", *Indian Express* (New Delhi), April 11, 1988.

Noorani, Abdul Gafoor and Abdul Majeed, *The RSS and the BJP: a division of Labour,* LeftWord Books, 2000.

Norman, Dorothy. (ed.) *Nehru: The First 60 Years,* Vol. 2, New York: John Day, 1965

NTI, "Nuclear Chronology", http://www.nti.org/e_research/profiles/India/Nuclear/2296_2803.html, accessed on 15 Dec 2009.

"NUCLEAR ANXIETY: Indian's Letter to Clinton on the Nuclear Testing", *The New York Times,* May 13, 1998 [Online: web]

accessed on May 10, 2011, URL: http://www.nytimes.com/1998/05/13/world/nuclear-anxiety-indians-letter-to-clinton-on-the-nuclear-testing.html

Nuclear India (Bombay), Vol. 5, No. 5, January 1967.

Nye Jr., Joseph S. (1986) *Nuclear Ethics*, New York: Free Press.

Oberdorfer, Don (1984) "Pakistan Concerned about Attack on Atomic Plants", Washington Post, October 12.

Odom, William E. (1983) The Soviet Approach to Nuclear Weapons: A Historical Review, *Annals of the American Academy of Political and Social Science*, Vol. 469, *Nuclear Armament and Disarmament*, September, pp. 117–135.

Ogilvie-White, Tanya. (1999) *"Is There A Theory of Nuclear Proliferation? An Analysis of the Contemporary Debate"*, The Nonproliferation Review, Fall, pp. 43–60.

Opening Remarks by the Congress President at the meeting of the All India Congress Committee at Sirifort Auditorium, New Delhi, April 6, 1998. http://www.congresssandesh.com/AICC/president/speech/meeting_aicc_siri_fort.htm

Oppenheimer, Robert J. (1953) *'Atomic Weapons and American Policy'*, Foreign Affairs July.

Osgood, Robert E., *Nuclear Control in NATO*, Washington DC: Washington Centre for Foreign Policy Research.

Palmer, Norman Dunbar, *The Indian political system*, Houghton Mifflin, 1971.

Pahwa, Pran, *Command and Control of Indian Nuclear Forces*, United Service Institution of India, Knowledge World, 2002.

Pandey, Saroj, *"About BJP"*, http://www.sarojpandey.org/About_BJP.html

Pande, Savita. (1995) *The Future of NPT*, New Delhi: Lancers.

Pant, Harsh V. (2004), *"India-Israel Partnership: Convergence and Constraints"*, *The Middle East Review of International Affairs*, Vol. 8, No. 4, Article 6 - December, http://meria.idc.ac.il/JOURNAL/2004/issue4/jv8no4a6.html, accessed on March 3 2010.

Parasnis, R.V. (2002), *"Remembering a War, the 1962 India-China Conflict"*, The Rediff Special, http://www.rediff.com/news/2002/dec/18chin.htm, December 5, 2002.

Parliamentary Debates (Rajya Sabha), written answers to questions, 86th sess., Vol. 86, no.4, November 15,x 1973, cols. 138–39.

Pathak, K.K. *Nuclear Policy of India: A Third World Perspective*, New Delhi: Gitanajali Prakashan, 1980.

Patnaik, Tandra., *Nehru's Concept of Scientific Humanism: An Alternative Model for Future Society*, 1990.

Paulose, T.T. (1978) *Perspectives of India's Nuclear Policy*, New Delhi: Young Asia Publications, 1978.

Paul, T. V., *The tradition of non-use of nuclear weapons*, Stanford University Press, 2009.

Pehrson, Christopher J., "*String of Pearls: Meeting the Challenge of China's Rising Power across the Asian Littoral*", URL: http://www.strategicstudiesinstitute.army.mil/pdffiles/pub721.pdf, July 2006.

Perkovich, George. (2002) *India's Nuclear Bomb: The Impact on Global Proliferation*, New Delhi: Oxford University Press.

Perkovich, George and Deepti Choubey (2007) "*Nonproliferation's Contribution*".

Peters, Anne and Stefan Griller, 'Democracy and New Modes of Governance', Project No. 4, September, http://www.eu-newgov.org/database/PUBLIC/P21410-01-P0401_Project4_Outline.PDF

Persson, Torsten and Guido Tabellini, *The Economic Effects of Constitutions*, Cambridge: MIT Press, 2003

Pillai, S. Devadas. (ed.) (1977) *The Incredible Elections: 1977*, Bombay: Popular Prakashan.

Politbureau Press Statement (Nov 22, 1991) CPI(M), "U.S. Pressure on India to Sign NPT", *People's Democracy*, New Delhi, December 1, 1991.

Political Organisational Report, 12th Congress of the CPI(M), Calcutta December 25–30 1985, published by Hari Singh Kang on behalf of CPI(M), New Delhi May 1986

Political Organisational Report, 16th Congress of CPI(M), 5–11 October 1998, Culcutta.

Political Resolution Adopted by the 15th Congress of the CPI(M) held at Chandigarh on April 3–8, 1995.

Political Resolution Adopted by the 16th Congress of the CPI(M) held in Calcutta on October 5–11, 1998.

Political Resolution Adopted by the 8th Congress, 23–29 December 1968, Cochin, Kerala.

Poplai, S.L. (ed.) (1962) *General Elections in India*, Bombay: Allied Publishers.

Potter, William C. (2003) *"The Diffusion of Nuclear Weapons"*, in Emily O. Goldman and Leslie C. Eliason (eds.), *The Diffusion of Military Technology and Ideas*, Stanford, CA: Stanford University Press, pp. 146–78.

Powell, Ralph L. (1965) *"Great Powers and Atomic Bombs Are "Paper Tigers"*, *The China Quarterly*, No. 23, July.-Sep., pp. 55–63.

Power, Paul F. (1964) *"Indian Foreign Policy: The Age of Nehru"*, The Review of Politics, Vol. 26, No. 2, April, pp. 257–286.

Prakash, Ved and Kulwant Rai Gupta, *Indo-U.S. Civil Nuclear Deal, Volume 1*, Atlantic Publishers & Dist, 2007.

Presidential Address by Atal Bihari Vajpayee, 5th National Council Session of BJP, Jan 6–8, 1984.

Presidential Address by L.K. Advani, Plenary Session, Bombay November 10–12, 1995. *Foreign Policy Resolutions and Statements 1980-99*, BJP, Publication No.: E/17/99

Presidential Address by Shri Rajnath Singh and Adopted Resoulutions, National Executive Meetings 12–14 Sep 2008 (Bengaluru), BJP Publication/2008, New Delhi.

Presidential Address, A.B. Vajpayee, Bharatiya Pratinidhi Sabha Session of BJS, Chandigarh, 18–19 July 2010.

Presidential Address, L.K Advani, 18th All India Session of BJS, Deendayal Nagar, Kanpur, 9–11 February 1973.

Press Interviews Shri Rajnath Singh, BJP Publication No. H/1/2007, New Delhi, 2007

Press Statement, The Polit Bureau of the Communist Party of India (Marxist), July 21, 2005, www.cpim.org

Preamble of the UNESCO Constitution, http://unesdoc.unesco.org/images/0013/001337/133729e.pdf#page=7, accessed on October 10, 2007.

Price, Thomas J. (1975) Behaviour Modes: Towards a Theory of Decision-Making, *The Journal of Politics*, Vol. 37, pp. 417–35.

Prime Minister Indira Gandhi, *Lok Sabha Debate* on foreign affairs, April 5, 1968, http://www.indianembassy.org/policy/Disarmament/disarm10.htm, accessed on June 11, 2009

Prime Minister Rajiv Gandhi: Statement on Foreign Policy, New Delhi: External Publicity Division, MEA, May-Aug 1985.

Puri, Rajinder (2008) "Bull's Eye", *Outlook*, July 28, 2008, http://119.82.71.51/article.aspx?238034

Pye, Lucian W., "*Why One-Party Dominant Systems Decline*", in Myron Weiner, Ashutosh Varshney, Gabriel Abraham Almond, eds. *India and the politics of developing countries: essays in memory of Myron Weiner*, Sage, 2004.

Ragheb, M. (2007) Chapter 3, 'Japanese Nuclear Weapons Program', https://netfiles.uiuc.edu/mragheb/www/NPRE%20402%20ME%20405%20Nuclear%20Power%20Engineering/Japanese%20Nuclear%20Weapons%20Program.pdf, 9 February, accessed on 10 January 2010.

Raja Mohan, C. (2003) "*Beyond India's Monroe Doctrine*", *The Hindu*, January 2, 2003.

Rajagopalan, Rajesh. (2005) *Second Strike: Arguments about Nuclear War in South Asia*, New Delhi: Penguin/Viking.

Rajan, M.S. (1964) *India in World Affairs, 1954-56*, London: Asia.

Rajen, Gaurav. (2006) "*The Problematic of a Nuclear Force-in-Being, a Stable Deterrence, and the Issue of Non-deployment*", *SASSU Research Report No. 5*, South Asian Strategic Stability Unit, February.

Rajiv Gandhi: Selected Speeches and Writings, Vol. I, October 1984-Demember 1985, (New Delhi: Ministry of Information and Broadcasting, 1987).

Rajkumar, N.V. (1952) *The Background of India's Foreign Policy*, New Delhi: All-India Congress Committee.

Ralhan, Om Prakash (1998) *Post-independence India: Indian National Congress*, New Delhi: Anmol Publication.

Rahm, Julie M., "*Russia, China, India: A New Strategic Triangle for a New Cold War?*", *Parameters* (U.S. Army War College Quarterly) 31, No. 4 (Winter 2001) pp. 87–96.

Ram, N. (1999), *Riding the Nuclear Tiger*, New Delhi: Left Word Books.

Ramachandran, R. (1999) "*Unclear nuclear identity*", Frontline, Volume 16, Issue 18, Aug 28-Sep 10, 1999.

Ramanna, Raja. (1991) *Years of Pilgrimage: An Autobiography*, New Delhi: Viking.

Rana, Mahendra Singh, *India Votes: Lok Sabha and Vidhan Sabha Elections 2001-05*, Sarup & Sons, 2006.

Ranadive, B.T. (1982) "*Speech Introducing Draft Political Resolution*", Main Speeches at the Eleventh Congress of the CPI(M), Vijaywada, Jan 26–31.

Rangaswamy, K. (1964) *"Leaders Reject Demand for Atom Bomb"*, Hindu, Nov. 9, 1964, p.1.

Rao, C.N.R., *"Science and technology policies: The case of India"*, Technology in Society, Vol. 30, Issues 3–4, August-November 2008, pp. 242–247.

"Record of Compromising India's Security", *CPI(M) General Election*, 1996.

Reddy, G.K. (1985) *"Nuclear Option Open if Pak. Gets the Bomb"*, The Hindu, May 5, 1985

Reiss, M. (1995) *Bridled Ambition: Why Countries Constrain Their Nuclear Capabilities*, Woodrow Wilson Center Press, Washington DC.

'Reliable Replacement Warhead another Unneeded Nuclear Weapon', Friends Committee on National Legislation, http://www.fcnl.org/pdfs/nuclear/RRW_Fact_Sheet.pdf, accessed on 10 Jan 2010

Report on Political Developments adopted by the Central Committee of the CPI(M) in its Meeting Held on October 18–20, 1995 published in November 1995.

Report on Political Developments since the Last Central Committee Meeting of the CPI(M), adopted by the Central Committee of the CPI(M) in its meeting held in New Delhi on July 16–18, 1998.

Report on Political Developments, adopted by the Central Committee of the CPI(M) in its meeting held in New Delhi on October 29–31, 1996.

Resolution 82nd Plenary Session of INC, Hyderabad, January 23, 2006.

Resolution adopted at National Council meeting on Political Resolution and International Situation on May 1–3, 1992, Gandhi Nagar, Gujarat, BJP Publication, New Delhi.

Resolution adopted at Plenary Session, Jaipur on February 1, 1991, BJP Publication New Delhi.

Resolution adopted at the National Executive Meeting held at Vadodra on June 9, 1994.

Resolution Adopted at the National Executive meeting of the BJP held at Cochin on April 23, 1981.

Resolution adopted at the National Executive meeting of the BJP held at Thiruvanthapuram on September 30, 1991.

Resolution adopted by CPI(M) Central Committee Session at Jaipur August 7–11, 1968.

Resolution of the AICC, Calcutta Session, March 22–23, 1952.

Resolution of the AICC, Hyderabad-Dn Session, January 17–18, 1953.

Resolution of the Central Committee, CPI, Delhi, April 1954.

"Resolution on International Situation", Indian National Congress Resolution, 6–7 December 1980, AICC, 24 Akbar Road, New Delhi, pp. 11–17.

Resolution, BJP National Executive Meeting, New Delhi, December 23–24, 1995.

Resolution, BJP National Executive Meeting, Patna, September 15–17, 1994.

Resolution, National Executive Meeting, Bhubaneswar, November 6–8, 1992.

Resolution, National Executive Meeting, Palampur, June 9–11, 1989, BJP Publication, New Delhi.

Resolutions Adopted by the Thirteenth Congress of the CPI(M) held at Trivandrum from December 27, 1988 to January 1, 1989.

Resolutions of the 11th Annual Session of the BJS, Ahmedabad, December 28–30, 1965.

Robinson, Bill *"Canada's connections to nuclear weapons"*, The Ploughshares Monitor, Vol. 23, No. 3, Autumn. http://www.ploughshares.ca/libraries/monitor/mons02b.html, 2002

Rochlin, Robert *"US Arms Control and Disarmament Agency, memorandum, Comments on Non-Proliferation Background Papers of December 12, 1964"*, December 31, 1964

Rosen, George, *"The Internal Debate on the Indian Nuclear Weapons Programme: Some Preliminary Observations"*, Memorandum RM-5313-ISA May 1967, http://www.dod.gov/pubs/foi/reading_room/771.pdf, accessed on Jan 10, 2010.

Rudolph, Susanne Hoeber and Lloyd I. Rudolph, *"Congress learns to lose: From a one-party dominant to a multi-party system in India"* in Edward Friedman, Joseph Wong edited *Political transitions in dominant party systems: learning to lose*, Taylor and Francis, 2008

Rusch, Thomas A. (1969) *"Indian Socialists and the Nuclear Non-Proliferation Treaty"*, The Journal of Asian Studies, Vol. 28, No. 4, Aug, pp. 755–770.

Sabato, George A. and Jairam Ramesh, "*Atoms for the Third World*", Bulletin of the Atomic Scientists, March 1980, pp. 36–43.

Sadasivan, S.N. (1977) *Party and Democracy in India*, New Delhi: Tata McGraw-Hill.

Sagan, Scott D. (1996-97) "*Why Do States Build Nuclear Weapons? Three Models in Search of Bomb*", International Security, Vol. 21, No. 3, Winter.

Saha, Santosh C., *Religious fundamentalism in the contemporary world: critical social and political issues*, Lexington Books, 2004.

"*Sangh Leaders Want India to Make Bomb*", The Indian Express, Delhi, October 21, 1964.

Sanghvi, Vijay, *The Congress, Indira to Sonia Gandhi*, Gyan Publishing House, 2006.

Saran, Shyam, "India's Nuclear Weapons Not for National Pride", http://ris.org.in/images/RIS_images/pdf/tribune-9may%20 2013.pdf, May 9, 2013.

Sarela, Narendra Singh. (2005) *The Shadow of the Great Game: The Untold Story of India's Partition*, New Delhi: HarperCollins.

Sarkar, Sumit. (1998) "*The BJP Bomb and Aspects of Nationalism*", Economic Political Weekly, Vol. 33, No. 27, July 4–10, pp. 1725–30.

Sartori, Giovanni. (1976) *Parties and Party Systems: A Framework for Analysis*, Vol. 1 Cambridge: CUP, pp. 192–200.

Sauer, T. (2007) "Coercive Diplomacy Revisited: The Iranian Nuclear Weapons Crisis", Paper presented at the annual meeting of the International Studies Association 48th Annual Convention, Hilton Chicago, Chicago, on February 28, available at http://www.allacademic.com/meta/p178706_index.html

Schaper, Annette, *Looking for a Demarcation between Nuclear Transparency and Nuclear Secrecy*, PRIF Report No. 68, Peace Research Institute Frankfurt, Germany.

Scheinman, Lawrence, *Atomic Energy Policy Under the Fourth Republic*, Princeton, NJ: Princeton University Press, 1995.

Schelling, Thomas, "*The Legacy of Hiroshima: A Half-Century Without Nuclear War*", http://www.puaf.umd.edu/IPPP/Summer00/legacy_of_hiroshima.htm, accessed on June 13, 2009.

Schwartz, William A., and Charles Derber. (1990) *The Nuclear Seduction: Why the Arms Race Doesn't Matter – And What Does*, Berkeley: University of California Press.

"Scramble by Rivals to Support Victorious UPA", May 19, 2009, http://www.thaindian.com/newsportal/politics/scramble-by-rivals-to-support-victorious-upa-lead_100194657.html#ixzz0bFGOE4Hf

Sen, Gautam, *Conceptualising security for India in the 21st Century*, University of Poona. Department of Defence and Strategic Studies, National Centre of International Security and Defence Analysis, Atlantic Publishers and Dist., 2007.

Sen Gupta, Bhabani. (1985) "Ambivalent Stand", *India Today*, May 31, 1985.

Sen, Amartya, *"India and the Bomb"*, Journal of Peace Economics, Peace Science and Public Policy, 6, October, pp. 16–34, 2000.

Sheth, D.L. (ed.) (1975) *Citizens and Parties*, New Delhi: Allied.

Shukla, Ajai, *"Come Out of the Nuclear Closet"*, Business Standard, April 15, 2004

Sethi, Manpreet. (1999) *"India's Pursuit of Nuclear Disarmament: Efforts Must Continue"*, *Strategic Analysis*, June, Vol. XXIII No. 3.

Sharma, Dhirendra. (2005) "India's Nuclear Estate", Philosophy and Social Action, Vol. 31(4).

Simon, Herbert. (1955) *"A Behavioural Model of Rational Choice"*, Quarterly Journal of Economics, February.

Singh, Harjeet, *South Asia Defence and Strategic Year Book*, 2007, Panchsheel, 2007.

Singer, J. David. (1961) 'The Level-of-Analysis Problem in International Relations', *World Politics*, Vol. 14, No. 1, Oct., pp. 77–92.

Singh Sidhu, Waheguru Pal and Jing-Dong Yuan. (1999) *"Cooperative Monitoring for Confidence Building: A Case Study of the Sine-Indian Border"*, Cooperative Monitoring Centre Occasional Paper 13, Sandia National Laboratories, Albuquerque, August.

Singh, Mahendra Prasad, *Split in a Predominant Party: The Indian National Congress in 1969*, Publications, 1981.

Singh, M.P. and Rekha Sexena, *Indian Politics: Contemporary Issues and Concerns*, PHI Learning Pvt. Ltd. 2008.

Singh, Manvendra. (2008) *"The nuclear deal's essence is politics"*, July 08 [Online: web] Accessed on Sep 1, 2008, URL: http://www.rediff.com/news/2008/jul/08ms.htm.

Singh, Rajnath, *Presidential Address, National Council Meeting, December 23–24, 2006,* Lucknow, BJP Publication No. E/15/2006, New Delhi.

Singh, Surjeet, Address to the Press Conference, New Delhi, September 21, 1998.

Sinha, Yashwant. (2008) *"ABC of Indo-US Deal"* in *Indo-US Nuclear Deal: Why does BJP oppose it?*, August, pp. 55–75.

Slocombe, Walter B. (2006) *Democratic Civilian Control of Nuclear Weapons*, Policy Paper – No. 12, Geneva Centre for the Democratic Control of Armed Forces, Geneva, April.

Snowman, Daniel. (2006) *"President Truman's Decision to Drop the First Atomic Bomb"*, Political Studies, Vol. 14 Issue 3, Dec. pp. 365–373.

Snyder, Richard C., et al. (1962) *"Decision-Making" in Snyder, Bruck and Sapin eds. Foreign Policy Decision-Making: An Approach to the Study of International Politics,* New York: The Free Press.

Solingen, Etel (1994) *"The Domestic Sources of Nuclear Postures: Influencing Fence-Sitters in the Post-Cold War Era"*, Institute on Global Conflict and Cooperation IGCC Policy Papers, University of California.

Sondhi, M.L. (1968) *Wanted: A National Foreign Policy*, Delhi: Navchetan Press.

Sood, Prashant. (2010) *"In Rahul's Footsteps, Congress Builds a youth base"*, Politics News, 13 Apr 2010.

"Soviet Arms Aid to Pakistan", Editorial, People's Democracy, July 14 1968.

Spector, Leonard S. (1990) *Nuclear Ambitions*, Colorado: Westview Press.

Sreedhar, (ed.) (1987) *"A.Q. Khan Interview with Nawa-e-Waqt, February 10, 1984"*, in *Dr. A.Q. Khan on Pakistan Bomb*, (ed.) New Delhi: ABC.

Srivastava, Govind Narain, ed. (1985) *Non-Alignment and Nuclear Disarmament,* Indian Institute for Non-Aligned Studies, New Delhi, May.

Srivastava, C.P., *Lal Bahadur Shastri: A Life of Truth in Politics,* OUP: New Delhi, 1995.

Publication Division, Ministry of Information and Broadcasting, GOI (1961) *"Statement in Lok Sabha"*, April 2, 1954 in J. Nehru,

India's Foreign Policy: Selected Speeches, Sep. 1946-April 1961, Bombay, August 15.

The Statesman, 'No-first-use: Need for second look', March 15, 2011, http://www.thestatesman.net/index.php?option=com_content&view=article&id=362632&catid=36

Statement on Current Situation, June 1978, *People's Democracy,* New Delhi, June 18, 1978.

Statement, *"CPI(M)'s Stand: India Should Not Induct Nuclear Weapons",* Polit Bureau, May 15, 1998.

Statement, *"On the Agreement for Fuel for the Tarapur Plant",* Central Committee of CPI(M), People's Democracy, New Delhi, Sept 12, 1982.

Statistical Report on General Elections, 1985 to the Eight Lok Sabha", *Election Commission of India,* http://eci.nic.in/SR_KeyHighLights/LS_1985/Vol_I_LS_85.pdf

Subrahmanyam, K. (1999) *"Fostering Newer Panipats: India's Lack of Strategic Planning",* The Times of India (New Delhi), January 5, 1999.

________________ (1998) *"Indian Nuclear Policy – 1964-98: A Personal Recollection",* in Jasjit Singh ed. Nuclear India, Knowledge World, New Delhi.

________________ (2009) *"Narasimha Rao and the Bomb",* Strategic Analysis, Oct-Dec 2004, pp. 593–595, available at: www.idsa.in/publications/strategic-analysis/2004/oct/K%20Sub.pdf, accessed on 10 Mar.

________________ (2004) *"P.V. Narasimha Rao and the Bomb: How he pushed development of N-deterrent",* The Tribune, December 29, 2004.

________________ (1998) India's Nuclear Policy – 1964-98: *"A Personal Recollection",* in Jasjit Singh ed. *Nuclear India,* New Delhi: Knowledge World, pp. 26–53.

________________, *"Rajiv was temperamentally a man of peaceful intent",* July 2008, URL: http://www.rediff.com/news/slide-show/slide-show-1-an-interview-with-k-subrahmanyam/20110210.htm, accessed on July 4, 2011.

Subramaniam, C. *"India's Defense Strategy in the Next Decade",* Transcript of address delivered by Shri C. Subramaniam, Defence Minister, to the Officer Students of the National Defense College, New Delhi, on October 29, 1979.

Sud, Hari, "New delays mar Indo-U.S. nuclear deal", UPI Asia.com, accessed on June 26, 2011, http://www.upiasia.com/Politics/2009/09/18/new_delays_mar_indo-us_nuclear_deal/8114/ September 18, 2009.

Sundarji, K. (1993) *Blind Men of Hindoostan*, New Delhi: USB.

Suo Motu Statement by Minister of External Affairs Shri Jaswant Singh: the N.P.T. Review Conference, Tuesday, May 9, 2000 Rajya Sabha.

Suo Motu Statement by Prime Minister Atal Bihari Vajpayee in the Indian Parliament on May 27, 1998.

Suri, K.C. "Parties Under Pressure", 2005, httpt://www.democracy-asia.org/qa/india/KC%20Suri.pdf

Snyder, Bruck and Sapin, eds. (1962) *Foreign Policy Decision-Making: An Approach to the Study of International Politics*, New York: The Free Press.

Swain, Pratap Chandra (2001) *Bharatiya Janata Party: profile and performance*, New Delhi: APH Publishing Corporation.

Swaminathan, R. (2003) "Pokran II: Five Years Later", South Asia Analysis Group, Paper no. 690, May 19 available at URL: http://www.southasiaanalysis.org/%5Cpapers7%5Cpaper690.html, accessed on 23 Nov 2009.

Swamy, Arun R. (2004), *"Back to the Future: The Congress Party's Upset Victory in India's 14th General Elections"*, Occasional Paper, Asia-Pacific Centre for Security Studies, June.

Tannenwald, Nina. (2005), *"Stigmatising the Bomb: Origins of the Nuclear Taboo"*, International Security, Vol. 29 (4), Spring, pp. 5–49.

Tasks Ahead: Immediate and Long-Term, New Delhi: BJP Publication No. E/4/2005

Tellis, Ashley J. (2001), *India's Emerging Nuclear Posture*, RAND Corporation.

Tertrais, Bruno, *"A Comparison between US, UK and French: Nuclear Policies and Doctrines"*, http://www.ceri-sciencespo.com/archive/mars07/art_bt.pdf

Thakurta, Paranjoy Guha and Shankar Raghuraman. (2007) *Divided We Stand: India in a Time of Coalition*, New Delhi: Sage.

"The Bomb and Us", *Organiser* 18 (39), November 9, 1964.

The CPI(M), *Constitution and the Rules under Constitution*, http://www.cpim.org/

"The Jana Sangh Perspective", in *United Asia*, January 1962.

The Nuclear Weapon Archive, *"India's Nuclear Weapons Program: On to Weapons Development: 1960-1967"*, 2001, URL: http://nuclearweaponarchive.org/India/IndiaWDevelop.html

Thorburn, Ingrid A. (2004) *Governing Nuclear Weapons: Opportunities and Constraints of Democratic Accountability beyond Command and Control,* Geneva Centre for the Democratic Control of Armed Forces (DCAF), Switzerland, October.

Tripathy, Devi Prasad, *Congress and Independent India*, New Delhi: Vani Prakashan, 1986

Twelfth Meeting of Experts on the United Nations Programme in Public Administration and Finance, New York, July 31-Aug 11 1995, "Strengthening Government Capacity for Policy Development", http://unpan1.un.org/intradoc/groups/public/documents/UN/UNPAN000754.pdf

U.S. Arms Control and Disarmament Agency, National Intelligence Estimate paper, *"The Indian Nuclear Problem: Proposed Course of Action,"* October 13, 1964, app. 2.

UNDC/PV 156, 29 August 1963.

UNGA, *Documents on Disarmament*, Washington, 1965.

UN General Assembly (1988) *A World Free of Nuclear Weapons: An Action Plan*, Rajiv Gandhi Address in the Third Special Session on Disarmament of, June 9.

Upadhyaya, D. (1979), *The Integral Approach*, New Delhi: Deendayal Research Institute.

Upreti, B.C. (2003) *"India-Nepal Relations: Dynamics, Issues and Problems"*, *South Asian Survey*, Vol. 10, No. 2, 257–274.

Vajpayee, A.B. (1978) *"India's Foreign Policy Today"*, International Studies, 17, pp. 379–8.

Vanaik, Achin. (2006) "Deterrence - who, how, really?: A Critique of India's Draft Nuclear Doctrine", *India Together*, July 13.

__________(1998) *"The Indian Nuclear Tests: Causes, Consequences and Portents"*, *Contemporary Studies of South Asia, Africa and the Middle East*, Vol. xviii no. 1,.

Venkatesan, R. (2008) "Indo-US nuclear deal and coalition politics", June 26, 2008, http://www.merinews.com/article/indo-us-nuclear-deal-and-coalition-politics/136422.shtml

Venkatramani, MS. (1999) *"The Indian Military Mission"*, *Frontline*, May 7, 1999.

Venkatramani, R. (1984) in *Lok Sabha Debates*, 7th ser., 46(22), 23 March 1984, Col. 402.

Vergino, E.S. and M. May. (2003) *'The Governance of Nuclear Technology'*, UCRL-CONF-154694, Lawrence Livermore National Laboratory, United States, September 22.

Varma, Shanti Prasad, Iqbal Narain, Chandra Prakash Bhambhri, *Fourth general election in India, Volume 1*, Orient Longmans, 1968.

"Wake up India", Editorial, *Organiser*, 18 (11), October 26, 1964.

"Wake up India", Editorial-*Organiser*, 18 (11), October 26, 1964.

Waltz, Kenneth N. (1979), *Theory of International Politics*, New York: Random House

_____________ (1981) *"The Spread of Nuclear Weapons: More May Better," Adelphi Papers*, Number 171, London: International Institute for Strategic Studies.

______________ (1995) *"More May Be Better"*, in Scott D. Sagan and Kenneth Waltz, *The Spread of Nuclear Weapons: A Debat*e, New York: WW Norton.

______________, *The Tragedy of Great Power Politics* (New York: W. W. Norton, 2001)

Wendt, Alexander, *"The Agent-Structure Problem in International Relations Theory"*, International Organisation, Vol. 412, No. 3, 1987, pp. 335–370.

Weinraub (1974) *"Atom Test Buoys Indians'* Morale", *New York Times*, May 20, 1974.

Weissman, Steve and Herbert Krosney (1983) *The Islamic Bomb: The Nuclear Threat to Israel and Middle East*, Times Books.

White Paper II; Notes, etc., Sept.-Nov. 1959; White Paper II also includes a 'Note on the Historical Background of the Himalayan Frontier of India' (with map).

Will not join NPT as non-nuclear weapon state: India", http://sify.com/news/will-not-join-npt-as-non-nuclear-weapon-state-india-news-national-jjyw03dadhg.html, September 24, 2009.

Wilcox, Wayne, *"Nuclear Options and the Strategic Environment in South Asia: Arms Control Implications"*, Southern California Arms Control and Foreign Policy Seminar, 1972.

Woolf, Amy F. (2003) *'Nuclear Weapons in Russia: Safety, Security, and Control Issues'*, Congressional Research Service, The Library of Congress, August 15.

__________(2006) "Specialist in National Defense, Foreign Affairs, Defense, and Trade Division, Nonstrategic Nuclear Weapons", CRS Report for Congress, 13 Jan, http://www.acq.osd.mil/ncbdp/nm/news_2_07/CRS%20Report%20on%20Nonstrategic%20Nuclear%20Weapons.pdf, accessed on July 15, 2009.

XII Lok Sabha Debates, Session II, (Budget), "Statement by Prime Minister", Wednesday, May 27, 1998/Jyaistha 6, 1920 (Saka).

Yechury, Sitaram. (1999) *"One Year of BJP-led Government – Neither Stability Nor Ability Only Unmitigated Disaster"*, A CPI(M) Publication, March.

Zaidi, A.M. (ed.) (1980) *The Annual Register of Indian Political Parties: Proceedings and Fundamental Texts*, New Delhi: S. Chand.

Zaidi, A.M and S.G., eds., The Encyclopaedia of the Indian National Congress, *Vol. 22, 1972-73, At War with Poverty*, New Delhi: S Chand & Company Ltd, 1984.

______________ *The Encyclopaedia of the Indian National Congress, Vol. 23, 1974-75, The Lengthening Shadows*, New Delhi: S. Chand & Company Ltd, 1984.

____________, ed., *The Annztal Register of Indian Political Parties, Proceedings and Fundamcental Texts, 1980*, New Delhi: S. Chand and Co., 1981.

Zohlnhofer, Reimut, *"How Politics Matter When Policies Change: Understanding Policy Change as a Political Problem"*, Journal of Comparative Policy Analysis, Vol. 11, No. 1, 97-115, March 2009.

Index